2023

BARRON'S
THE TRUSTED NAME IN TEST PREP

AP

Spanish Language and Culture

PREMIUM

Daniel Paolicchi, M.A.

Alice G. Springer, Ph.D.

Acknowledgments

For my fellow language teachers and all students of Spanish.

© Copyright 2024, 2023, 2022, 2020, 2018, 2016, 2014, 2012, 2010, 2007, 2004, 2000 by Kaplan North America, LLC d/b/a Barron's Educational Series

Previous editions © Copyright 2003, 1998, 1994 by Kaplan North America, LLC, d/b/a Barron's Educational Series

Published by Kaplan North America, LLC d/b/a Barron's Educational Series
1515 West Cypress Creek Road
Fort Lauderdale, Florida 33309
www.barronseduc.com

ISBN: 978-1-5062-9170-3

10 9 8 7 6 5 4 3 2 1

Kaplan North America, LLC d/b/a Barron's Educational Series print books are available at special quantity discounts to use for sales promotions, employee premiums, or educational purposes. For more information or to purchase books, please call the Simon & Schuster special sales department at 866-506-1949.

Table of Contents

PART 4: WRITING SKILLS

PART 5: SPEAKING SKILLS

PART 6: PRACTICE TESTS

Visit Barron's Online Learning Hub for the audio that accompanies this book plus more full-length practice tests.

How to Use This Book

The purpose of this book is to provide you with the best possible preparation for the AP Spanish Language and Culture exam. Using the tools included in this book will help prepare you for success on exam day.

Exam Overview

Read Chapter 1: Preparing for the AP Spanish Language and Culture Exam first to learn all about the format on the test, the types of questions you are going to be asked, the types of sources you will encounter, and what the different sections of the exam will require you to do. A discussion of how the test is scored is also included to give you an idea of what the scorers will be looking for in your responses.

Review and Practice

Next, move on to the review chapters, where you will find extensive practice and commentary for each part of the exam. The more practice you have with answering these AP-type questions, the better prepared you will be on test day.

The book also includes a section called "Cultural Awareness" that highlights any products, practices, and perspectives that are present in the print and audio texts that accompany the activities in the book. Familiarizing yourself with these and taking time to reflect on these aspects of culture and how they are similar to or different from your own community will help you make cultural comparisons, a key skill needed for success on the test.

We have included a Grammar Review in the Appendix for those of you who might need a refresher. It is recommended that you review this section as it will help you with your written responses in the test.

Practice Tests

At the end of the book we included two full-length practice exams. Keep in mind that taking a practice exam under actual testing conditions (all at once and within the time limit) is always best. Each exam includes an explanation of the correct answers. Be sure to read these especially for those questions you answered incorrectly. Use the practice tests to determine sections for which you might need more practice.

Online Practice

In addition to the two practice tests within this book, there are also three full-length online practice exams. You may take these exams in practice (untimed) mode or in timed mode. All questions include answer explanations. The audio for all listening practice is also included online. All listening practice is spoken by native Spanish speakers and represents a variety of sources.

For Students

The organization of this book is designed to take you through each section of the exam, allowing for ample practice in mastering each type of question. By answering the review questions and by taking the practice tests, you will have an indication of how well you will do on the actual exam.

For Teachers

Suggest to your students that they use this book along with their course materials for added practice. When used in tandem with classroom assignments, this book should offer your students the opportunity to use the material to reinforce classroom learning.

The audioscripts for all listening prompts and a Grammar Review can be found on the Barron's Online Learning Hub.

PART 1
Introduction

1

Preparing for the AP Spanish Language and Culture Exam

General Considerations

The AP Spanish Language and Culture exam is a rigorous test of your ability to interpret and communicate in Spanish. It challenges you in a holistic way to demonstrate a high level of proficiency in your listening, reading, writing, and speaking abilities. The exam is designed around six interrelated themes that will test your capacity to analyze and talk about a variety of issues, including practices, products, and perspectives of Spanish-speaking communities and how these compare to those of your own culture, as well as about topics that relate to other disciplines, such as science, business, art, technology, social issues, and so on.

An AP course is designed to be the equivalent of a third-year college course. At that level you should be able to understand a native speaker who speaks at a normal speed, to comprehend and analyze print materials intended for native speakers, and to be able to communicate with ease, both orally and in writing, on a variety of topics. You should be able to recognize appropriate social customs reflected in the language, in areas such as register, and also be able to notice references to traditions, customs, and values particular to Spanish-speaking societies.

Overall, the exam calls for much more sophisticated control of the language and of culture than previous exams, so it is best to prepare thoroughly. Success on the exam lies not in how much you know *about* the language, but rather in your ability to *use* the language to effectively interpret written and oral texts and to communicate at a high level on a number of different topics. This book is designed to do just that. It will prepare you for the exam by helping you develop strategies to build both your communicative and interpretive abilities. Plenty of practice exercises are included so you can gauge your readiness and prepare accordingly. The materials selected for this book include the types of selections you are likely to find on the exam, but they are, by no means, a definitive listing. You need to learn as much as you can about Spanish-speaking history, art, literature, business practices, music, humor, customs, traditions, folklore, and other social and cultural topics, and you will need to incorporate that knowledge into your responses on all parts of the exam.

Exam Overview

Structure

Below you will find general information regarding the structure of the exam and a brief description of each section. For more detailed information and strategies for success in each section, please refer to the section at the beginning of the chapter dedicated to that particular task.

The examination is divided into the following two sections: Interpretive Communication (Multiple-Choice) and Free Response.

STRUCTURE OF THE EXAM				
	Section	Number of questions	Percentage of total exam	Allotted time
Section I: Interpretive Communication (Multiple-Choice)				Approx. 95 mins.
Part A	Print Texts	30 questions	50%	Approx. 40 mins.
Part B	Print and Audio Texts (combined)	35 questions		Approx. 55 mins.
	Audio Texts			
Section II: Free Response				Approx. 85 mins.
Part A	Task 1: Email Reply	1 prompt	50% (12.5% each)	15 mins.
	Task 2: Argumentative Essay	1 prompt		Approx. 55 mins.
Part B	Task 3: Conversation	5 prompts		20 seconds for each response
	Task 4: Cultural Comparison	1 prompt		2 minutes to respond

Section I—Interpretive Communication

Section I is worth 50% of the total score on the examination, and is divided into three parts: Print Texts, Print and Audio Texts (combined), and Audio Texts. All questions in this section are multiple-choice, with both questions and answers printed in the text booklet. At the beginning of each printed and audio source you will be given information about that source so that you can have a contextual base before you begin your task. Section I of the examination is machine-scored, so be sure to bring several sharpened No. 2 pencils to fill out your answer sheet.

Section II—Free Response

Section II is divided into four communicative tasks: Email Reply, Argumentative Essay, Conversation, and Cultural Comparison. Each task is worth 12.5% of the total score. For the written samples, a test booklet will be provided and you must use a blue or black pen on this portion of the examination. You will be asked to submit your recordings in a digital audio file format.

Part A of Section II is the writing section, which comprises the Email Reply (Task 1) and Argumentative Essay (Task 2). For Task 1, Email Reply, your objective is to respond to a formal email that is printed in your test booklet. You will have 15 minutes to read and respond to the email. For Task 2, Argumentative Essay, you are to write an essay in which you respond to a question printed in your test booklet. In addition to the question you are to answer, you will be provided with two print texts and one audio source that present different points of view on the topic. A key component of this task is to gather information from all three texts and use it to support your own point of view on the topic.

Part B of Section II is the speaking portion of the exam, which comprises the Conversation (Task 3) and Cultural Comparison (Task 4). Task 3, Conversation, is a simulated conversation in which you are to initiate, maintain, and appropriately close a conversation. You will be provided with an outline of the flow of the conversation. You will have 5 opportunities to speak. For Task 4, Cultural Comparison, you are to give a two-minute oral presentation in which you answer a question printed in your test booklet. In your response, you have to compare a Spanish-speaking community with your own community. Unlike the previous tasks, you will not be given any additional print or audio material to use in your oral presentation.

Content of the Exam

Themes

The examination is designed around the following six themes:
- **Families and Communities** (*Las familias y las comunidades*)
- **Personal and Public Identities** (*Las identidades personales y públicas*)
- **Science and Technology** (*La ciencia y la tecnología*)
- **Contemporary Life** (*La vida contemporánea*)
- **Global Challenges** (*Los desafíos mundiales*)
- **Beauty and Aesthetics** (*La belleza y la estética*)

These thematic units are broad by design, allowing for multiple topics and contexts within each theme. Before each task, you will be given the overarching theme as a frame of reference. For example, a reading activity that falls under the Families and Communities thematic unit may deal with family celebrations, family structure, education, traditions and values, and so on. Although there are many topics that can fall under each thematic unit, they all will present examples of practices, products, or perspectives from the Spanish-speaking world.

It is also important to remember that these thematic units are interconnected, and one topic that appears in one thematic unit could relate to several other ones. For example, an article about a project in Bogotá, Colombia, that teaches families living in the capital how to grow their own vegetables in small spaces, such as on an apartment terrace, can help answer questions related to several of the thematic units. For example:

- **SCIENCE AND TECHNOLOGY**—How do technological innovations affect our lives and the way we live?
- **FAMILIES AND COMMUNITIES**—How do people in urban environments define quality of life?
- **GLOBAL CHALLENGES**—How do we solve some of the challenges that face world societies?

As you learn about the Spanish-speaking world through these thematic units, you will also be exposed to vocabulary, idioms, and a variety of grammatical structures that will not only reinforce your own knowledge of the language, but will also help you refine your ability to speak and write at a high level about the topic and those related to it. For example, an article on innovative cooking techniques in modern Spanish haute cuisine may present vocabulary that you can use to talk about food and cooking, aesthetics, and national identity. Remember, the exam tests not only your ability to interpret at a high level, but also your ability to communicate clearly on a variety of topics related to the thematic units.

Culture and Making Cultural Comparisons

A major focus of the examination is to promote a deeper awareness of culture, the interconnectedness of language and culture, and how Hispanic cultures compare to and differ from your own community. When thinking of culture, you should be thinking of the products, practices, and perspectives of that particular culture (these concepts are explained in more detail in the Culture section below). Learning the culture of a community also means learning more about matters that generally relate to other disciplines, such as history, geography, gastronomy, literature, music, religion, science, and so on. Language is also affected by culture, as attested by the variances in the language from country to country or even from region to region in any one country, and language is how cultural practices and perspectives are communicated. In order to effectively be able to talk about culture, you must also have the knowledge of these subject matters as well as the necessary vocabulary to appropriately articulate your ideas.

Culture

A common misconception is that all communities in the Spanish-speaking world are alike. Although many share common traits, such as the general language structure and religion, there are many differences within each culture that make each one unique. For example, in Spain it is common to have a three-course meal for lunch, whereas in Costa Rica you would probably be served a one-plate meal called casado, which includes rice, beans, a small slice of meat (chicken, beef, pork), some fresh vegetables, and a plantain. Likewise, dinner in Spain is generally a smaller meal eaten around 9p.m., whereas in Costa Rica it would be a normal-sized meal served between 6p.m. and 8p.m. There are also regional differences in any given country. You might be surprised to learn that in Bogotá, Colombia, in addition to traditional Colombian fare such as arepas and papa criolla, they have a thriving pub scene, akin to those you would find in England, as well as a number of restaurants serving gourmet hamburgers. This is quite different from the coastal regions of Colombia, where seafood and coconut rice are still staples, and the food tends to be spicier than that of the Andean region of the country.

One of the biggest differences in the Spanish-speaking world is the use of vocabulary. Let's take, for example, the word "cake": in most Spanish-speaking countries, the word used is pastel, but in Spain it is also called tarta. In the Dominican Republic and Puerto Rico it is called bizcocho, in Costa Rica queque, and in Argentina, Chile, Venezuela, and Colombia it is torta, a word that in Mexico means "sandwich." This is not unlike some of the regional differences in the United States, where a "submarine sandwich" (a sandwich typically made with French-style bread) is also called a "hero," "hoagie," "grinder," or "po-boy," depending on what part of the country you are in. You can find more differences between English in the United States and in England, where the rear compartment of a car is either a "trunk" (USA) or a "boot" (UK). Therefore, it is important to recognize that each country, and areas within a particular country, will have its differences. One must avoid stereotypes and learn about each culture as its own entity, identifying how it is similar to and different from other cultures, and also appreciating what makes it unique.

Products, practices, and perspectives

When thinking about culture and the concept of culture in general, there are three main components to consider: products, practices, and perspectives. Here is a brief description of each:

- **PRODUCTS**—the creations of the target culture. They can be tangible (toys, food, crafts, etc.) or intangible (dances, literature, music);
- **PRACTICES**—behaviors and interactions that are common in the target culture. Examples include the number of meals eaten during the day and at what time these meals are eaten and the types of food and quantity eaten at those times; what people do in their free time; what time they wake up and go to bed; socially expected behaviors when it comes to dating and table manners; how to dress and act at certain events; holiday celebrations; and so on;
- **PERSPECTIVES**—beliefs that are valued within a culture. Examples include the importance of family and importance of quality over quantity, youth over old age, sports and education, and so on.

When learning about a particular community or culture, think about the relationship between these three components. The perspectives (beliefs) of a culture affect its practices (behaviors), and the products are created to facilitate these practices. For example, in many Hispanic communities, a common perspective is that it is important to eat a meal as a family, for this is when they have the opportunity to talk as a family, share stories, and enjoy each other's company. Another perspective is that the food should be made from scratch with fresh ingredients, and typically it is prepared by the mother as a way for her to show her love for her family. Therefore, a common practice is for the mother to prepare the food while the family and guests help with other preparations, such as setting the table and prep work. The products are the dishes that are served at the meal and likely are created by following recipes that were passed from generation to generation.

You can build your awareness of culture primarily through authentic print and audio texts. The more you expose yourself to the Spanish-speaking world, the better you will understand its products, practices, and perspectives. In addition, take advantage of every opportunity to interact with Spanish speakers, for that will give you the ability to learn more about their culture and can help you clarify any doubts or questions you may have. Finally, in order to have the most complete understanding of Hispanic culture, it is important to expose yourself to as many different communities in the Spanish-speaking world as you can.

Making Cultural Comparisons

As you further develop your knowledge of Hispanic cultures, it is only natural to think about how they compare to and differ from your own culture. Making cultural comparisons is basically doing just that. Remember that to truly understand culture means to understand the relationship between its products, practices, and perspectives. When comparing cultures, you should think not only about what is similar or different, but also why it is similar or different. For example, our eating habits in the United States can be quite different from those in Spanish-speaking countries. The biggest meal of the day both in Spain and in Mexico is lunch, which is generally eaten between 1:00 p.m. and 3:00 p.m. (or later, in some cases). These meals tend to include three courses: an appetizer, a main course, and dessert. They also often include a sobremesa, or conversation afterward, that also serves as a time to relax and digest the food. In these countries, dinner tends to be considerably smaller and is usually eaten between 8:00 p.m. and 9:00 p.m. This is quite different from meals the United States, where lunches tend to be smaller and rushed and the bigger meal of the day is often dinner. Part of the reason why lunch is the biggest meal in Mexico and Spain is because it revolves around the most active part of the day. Since in the evening things tend to slow down, including one's metabolism, a lighter meal is preferred so that the food can be digested more easily overnight. Therefore, when learning about eating habits in Spain, one can clearly see that a belief, or perspective, is that the amount of food consumed should be in relation to one's activity. The resulting behavior, or practice, is to eat bigger meals during lunchtime and to have a much smaller one during dinner. The resulting product in Spain is that many restaurants serve a menú del día (menu of the day) during lunchtime hours that consists of one entrée, a main course, and dessert for a fixed price. In contrast, in the United States lunchtime specials generally tend to be meals that can be fixed and consumed quickly so that the downtime for a meal does not interfere too much with the most productive part of the day.

Finally, when learning about products, practices, and perspectives, it is important to think in terms of how they are similar to or different from those of your own community rather than in terms of being better or worse. Each community is proud of its culture, and although a product, practice, or perspective may seem strange to an outsider, a key part of developing better awareness and understanding of another culture is to accept the target culture as is without passing judgment.

Testing Culture on the Exam

Throughout the exam there will be a number of questions testing your awareness of the target cultures. In the reading and listening portions of the exam, you will have questions asking you to demonstrate understanding of a particular vocabulary word, expression, or idea presented in the print or audio text. As mentioned earlier, words may have different meanings depending on the region or country in which they are used. Even if you believe that you already know what a word means, pay attention to the context in which it is used to see if it could mean something different. In both writing sections and the conversation portions of the exam, your knowledge of culture will be demonstrated through the content of your submission. This includes your ability to use appropriate vocabulary and idiomatic expressions, your ability to recognize the correct tone to use (formal/informal), and your ability to make correct references when referring to the features of the target community. The Cultural Comparison (Task 4) of the exam is the most comprehensive test of your knowledge of culture. Here you will be asked to give a two-minute presentation on a particular topic in which you are to compare the practices, perspectives, and/or products of a community of the Spanish-speaking world with those of your own community. On this section of the exam you will not be given any external aid, and your ability to answer the question and elaborate relies solely on the knowledge you already have of each culture.

Scoring the Exam

To keep the material fresh, new material appears on the exam every year. No matter how the material changes, however, the way your work is evaluated remains the same. Overall scores range from 1 (poor) to 5 (strong). An overall score of 3 on this exam is a passing score. In Section II, it is possible to also earn a score of zero (0) if the response is completely irrelevant to the prompt, a mere restatement of the prompt and/or language in the booklet, or written in English. A hyphen (-) is given to a non-response, meaning that the page is blank or there is no digital recording although the equipment is functioning. Most colleges and universities will award credit for scores of 4 or 5. There are a few that will also give some credit for a score of 3. To find out more information about the policy of colleges and universities when it comes to awarding credit for AP scores, visit the following site:

https://apstudent.collegeboard.org/creditandplacement/search-credit-policies

Scoring Section I

Section I is machine-scored, and the total score for each part is determined by the total number of questions answered correctly. Predicting the number of questions answered correctly and the corresponding AP score for Section I is not an exact science, as it can vary slightly from year to year. However, the following chart can give you a rough estimate of the number of questions you need to answer correctly in order to achieve a certain score.

Part A—Print Texts (30 questions)

Number of questions answered correctly	Approximate AP Score
24–30	5 (Strong)
21–23	4 (Good)
18–20	3 (Fair)
16–17	2 (Weak)
15–0	1 (Poor)

Part B—Print and Audio Texts (combined) and Audio Texts (35 questions)

Number of questions answered correctly	Approximate AP Score
29–35	5 (Strong)
25–28	4 (Good)
20–24	3 (Fair)
17–19	2 (Weak)
16–0	1 (Poor)

Scoring Section II

The scoring of each task in Section II is holistic. This means that each response is considered as a single entity, and its elements are not analyzed separately. For each of the tasks, the main considerations are what the student was able to do (appropriateness of the response within the context of the task, development of ideas), and how the student was able to complete the task (use of language, organization of ideas, and use of register). In order to score well on the communicative tasks, the response has to be appropriate, developed, organized, and understandable. A response that is fully understandable but off topic or inappropriate within the context of the task will likely earn a low score. The same is true for a response in which the student makes the attempt to complete the task but whose language makes the response very difficult to understand.

Below are the descriptions of the scoring guides for each task in Section II. You will notice that often the difference in the descriptors from one score to another is a single word, such as "clearly appropriate" instead of "generally appropriate."

Scoring Guildelines

Task 1—Email Reply

5 (Strong)

- Maintains the exchange with a response that is clearly appropriate within the context of the task.
- Provides required information (responses to questions, request for details) with frequent elaboration.
- Fully understandable, with ease and clarity of expression; occasional errors do not impede comprehensibility.
- Varied and appropriate vocabulary and idiomatic language.
- Accuracy and variety in grammar, syntax, and usage, with few errors.
- Mostly consistent use of register appropriate for the situation; control of cultural conventions appropriate for formal correspondence (e.g., greeting, closing), despite occasional errors.
- Variety of simple and compound sentences, and some complex sentences.

4 (Good)

- Maintains the exchange with a response that is generally appropriate within the context of the task.
- Provides most required information (responses to questions, request for details) with some elaboration.
- Fully understandable, with some errors that do not impede comprehensibility.
- Varied and generally appropriate vocabulary and idiomatic language.
- General control of grammar, syntax, and usage.
- Generally consistent use of register appropriate for the situation, except for occasional shifts; basic control of cultural conventions appropriate for formal correspondence (e.g., greeting, closing).
- Simple, compound, and a few complex sentences.

3 (Fair)

- Maintains the exchange with a response that is somewhat appropriate but basic within the context of the task.
- Provides most required information (responses to questions, request for details).
- Generally understandable, with errors that may impede comprehensibility.
- Appropriate but basic vocabulary and idiomatic language.
- Some control of grammar, syntax, and usage.
- Use of register may be inappropriate for the situation with several shifts; partial control of conventions for formal correspondence (e.g., greeting, closing), although these may lack cultural appropriateness.
- Simple and a few compound sentences.

2 (Weak)

- Partially maintains the exchange with a response that is minimally appropriate within the context of the task.
- Provides some required information (responses to questions, request for details).
- Partially understandable with errors that force interpretation and cause confusion for the reader.
- Limited vocabulary and idiomatic language.
- Limited control of grammar, syntax, and usage.
- Use of register is generally inappropriate for the situation; includes some conventions for formal correspondence (e.g., greeting, closing) with inaccuracies.
- Simple sentences and phrases.

1 (Poor)

- Unsuccessfully attempts to maintain the exchange by providing a response that is inappropriate within the context of the task.
- Provides little required information (responses to questions, request for details).
- Barely understandable, with frequent or significant errors that impede comprehensibility.
- Very few vocabulary resources.
- Little or no control of grammar, syntax, and usage.
- Minimal or no attention to register; includes significantly inaccurate or no conventions for formal correspondence (e.g., greeting, closing).
- Very simple sentences or fragments.

Task 2—Argumentative Essay

5 (Strong)

- Effective treatment of topic within the context of the task.
- Demonstrates a high degree of comprehension of the sources' viewpoints, with very few minor inaccuracies.
- Integrates content from all three sources in support of the essay.
- Presents and defends the student's own viewpoint on the topic with a high degree of clarity; develops a persuasive argument with coherence and detail.
- Organized essay; effective use of transitional elements or cohesive devices.
- Fully understandable, with ease and clarity of expression; occasional errors do not impede comprehensibility.
- Varied and appropriate vocabulary and idiomatic language.
- Accuracy and variety in grammar, syntax, and usage, with few errors.
- Develops paragraph-length discourse with a variety of simple and compound sentences, and some complex sentences.

4 (Good)

- Generally effective treatment of topic within the context of the task.
- Demonstrates comprehension of the sources' viewpoints; may include a few inaccuracies.
- Summarizes, with limited integration, content from all three sources in support of the essay.
- Presents and defends the student's own viewpoint on the topic with clarity; develops a persuasive argument with coherence.
- Organized essay; some effective use of transitional elements or cohesive devices.
- Fully understandable, with some errors that do not impede comprehensibility.
- Varied and generally appropriate vocabulary and idiomatic language.
- General control of grammar, syntax, and usage.
- Develops mostly paragraph-length discourse with simple, compound, and a few complex sentences.

3 (Fair)

- Suitable treatment of topic within the context of the task.
- Demonstrates a moderate degree of comprehension of the sources' viewpoints; includes some inaccuracies.
- Summarizes content from at least two sources in support of the essay.
- Presents and defends the student's own viewpoint on the topic; develops a somewhat persuasive argument with some coherence.
- Some organization; limited use of transitional elements or cohesive devices.
- Generally understandable, with errors that may impede comprehensibility.
- Appropriate but basic vocabulary and idiomatic language.
- Some control of grammar, syntax, and usage.
- Uses strings of mostly simple sentences, with a few compound sentences.

2 (Weak)

- Unsuitable treatment of topic within the context of the task.
- Demonstrates a low degree of comprehension of the sources' viewpoints; information may be limited or inaccurate.
- Summarizes content from one or two sources; may not support the essay.
- Presents, or at least suggests, the student's own viewpoint on the topic; develops an unpersuasive argument somewhat incoherently.
- Limited organization; ineffective use of transitional elements or cohesive devices.
- Partially understandable, with errors that force interpretation and cause confusion for the reader.
- Limited vocabulary and idiomatic language.
- Limited control of grammar, syntax, and usage.
- Uses strings of simple sentences and phrases.

1 (Poor)

- Almost no treatment of topic within the context of the task.
- Demonstrates poor comprehension of the sources' viewpoints; includes frequent and significant inaccuracies.
- Mostly repeats statements from sources or may not refer to any sources.
- Minimally suggests the student's own viewpoint on the topic; argument is undeveloped or incoherent.
- Little or no organization; absence of transitional elements and cohesive devices.
- Barely understandable, with frequent or significant errors that impede comprehensibility.
- Very few vocabulary resources.
- Little or no control of grammar, syntax, and usage.
- Very simple sentences or fragments.

Task 3—Conversation

5 (Strong)

- Maintains the exchange with a series of responses that is clearly appropriate within the context of the task.
- Provides required information (e.g., responses to questions, statement and support of opinion) with frequent elaboration.
- Fully understandable, with ease and clarity of expression; occasional errors do not impede comprehensibility.
- Varied and appropriate vocabulary and idiomatic language.
- Accuracy and variety in grammar, syntax, and usage, with few errors.
- Mostly consistent use of register appropriate for the conversation.
- Pronunciation, intonation, and pacing make the response comprehensible; errors do not impede comprehensibility.
- Clarification or self-correction (if present) improves comprehensibility.

4 (Good)

- Maintains the exchange with a series of responses that is generally appropriate within the context of the task.
- Provides most required information (e.g., responses to questions, statement and support of opinion) with some elaboration.
- Fully understandable, with some errors that do not impede comprehensibility.
- Varied and generally appropriate vocabulary and idiomatic language.
- General control of grammar, syntax, and usage.
- Generally consistent use of register appropriate for the conversation, except for occasional shifts.
- Pronunciation, intonation, and pacing make the response mostly comprehensible; errors do not impede comprehensibility.
- Clarification or self-correction (if present) usually improves comprehensibility.

3 (Fair)

- Maintains the exchange with a series of responses that is somewhat appropriate within the context of the task.
- Provides most required information (e.g., responses to questions, statement and support of opinion).
- Generally understandable, with errors that may impede comprehensibility.
- Appropriate but basic vocabulary and idiomatic language.
- Some control of grammar, syntax, and usage.
- Use of register may be inappropriate for the conversation with several shifts.
- Pronunciation, intonation, and pacing make the response generally comprehensible; errors occasionally impede comprehensibility.
- Clarification or self-correction (if present) sometimes improves comprehensibility.

2 (Weak)

- Partially maintains the exchange with a series of responses that is minimally appropriate within the context of the task.
- Provides some required information (e.g., responses to questions, statement and support of opinion).
- Partially understandable, with errors that force interpretation and cause confusion for the listener.
- Limited vocabulary and idiomatic language.
- Limited control of grammar, syntax, and usage.
- Use of register is generally inappropriate for the conversation.

- Pronunciation, intonation, and pacing make the response difficult to comprehend at times; errors impede comprehensibility.
- Clarification or self-correction (if present) usually does not improve comprehensibility.

1 (Poor)

- Unsuccessfully attempts to maintain the exchange by providing a series of responses that is inappropriate within the context of the task.
- Provides little required information (e.g., responses to questions, statement and support of opinion).
- Barely understandable, with frequent or significant errors that impede comprehensibility.
- Very few vocabulary resources.
- Little or no control of grammar, syntax, and usage.
- Minimal or no attention to register.
- Pronunciation, intonation, and pacing make the response difficult to comprehend; errors impede comprehensibility.
- Clarification or self-correction (if present) does not improve comprehensibility.

Task 4—Cultural Comparison

5 (Strong)

- Effective treatment of topic within the context of the task.
- Clearly compares the student's own community with the target culture, including supporting details and relevant examples.
- Demonstrates understanding of the target culture, despite a few minor inaccuracies.
- Organized presentation; effective use of transitional elements or cohesive devices.
- Fully understandable, with ease and clarity of expression; occasional errors do not impede comprehensibility.
- Varied and appropriate vocabulary and idiomatic language.
- Accuracy and variety in grammar, syntax, and usage, with few errors.
- Mostly consistent use of register appropriate for the presentation.
- Pronunciation, intonation, and pacing make the response comprehensible; errors do not impede comprehensibility.
- Clarification or self-correction (if present) improves comprehensibility.

4 (Good)

- Generally effective treatment of topic within the context of the task.
- Compares the student's own community with the target culture, including some supporting details and mostly relevant examples.
- Demonstrates some understanding of the target culture, despite minor inaccuracies.
- Organized presentation; some effective use of transitional elements or cohesive devices.
- Fully understandable, with some errors that do not impede comprehensibility.
- Varied and generally appropriate vocabulary and idiomatic language.
- General control of grammar, syntax, and usage.
- Generally consistent use of register appropriate for the presentation, except for occasional shifts.
- Pronunciation, intonation, and pacing make the response mostly comprehensible; errors do not impede comprehensibility.
- Clarification or self-correction (if present) usually improves comprehensibility.

3 (Fair)

- Suitable treatment of topic within the context of the task.
- Compares the student's own community with the target culture, including a few supporting details and examples.
- Demonstrates a basic understanding of the target culture, despite inaccuracies.
- Some organization; limited use of transitional elements or cohesive devices.
- Generally understandable, with errors that may impede comprehensibility.
- Appropriate but basic vocabulary and idiomatic language.
- Some control of grammar, syntax, and usage.
- Use of register may be inappropriate for the presentation with several shifts.
- Pronunciation, intonation, and pacing make the response generally comprehensible; errors occasionally impede comprehensibility.
- Clarification or self-correction (if present) sometimes improves comprehensibility.

2 (Weak)

- Unsuitable treatment of topic within the context of the task.
- Presents information about the student's own community and the target culture, but may not compare them; consists mostly of statements with no development.
- Demonstrates a limited understanding of the target culture; may include several inaccuracies.
- Limited organization; ineffective use of transitional elements or cohesive devices.
- Partially understandable, with errors that force interpretation and cause confusion for the listener.
- Limited vocabulary and idiomatic language.
- Limited control of grammar, syntax, and usage.
- Use of register is generally inappropriate for the presentation.
- Pronunciation, intonation, and pacing make the response difficult to comprehend at times; errors impede comprehensibility.
- Clarification or self-correction (if present) usually does not improve comprehensibility.

1 (Poor)

- Almost no treatment of topic within the context of the task.
- Presents information only about the student's own community or only about the target culture, and may not include examples.
- Demonstrates minimal understanding of the target culture; generally inaccurate.
- Little or no organization; absence of transitional elements and cohesive devices.
- Barely understandable, with frequent or significant errors that impede comprehensibility.
- Very few vocabulary resources.
- Little or no control of grammar, syntax, and usage.
- Minimal or no attention to register.
- Pronunciation, intonation, and pacing make the response difficult to comprehend; errors impede comprehensibility.
- Clarification or self-correction (if present) does not improve comprehensibility.

Preparing for the Exam

This book is divided into the four skill areas addressed on the exam: reading, listening, writing, and speaking. Each chapter is devoted to one single skill area but also contains information that will be useful in other skill areas. Strategies are included before each skill to help you, and some practice activities will include additional exercises not tested on the exam, but that are helpful to improving overall interpretive and communicative abilities. Also, after all reading and listening activities, as well as after communicative tasks 1 (Email Reply) and 2 (Argumentative Essay), you will find a section called "Cultural Awareness" that will highlight any products, practices, and perspectives that are present in the print and audio texts that accompany these activities. This is a good opportunity to reflect on these aspects of culture and how they are similar to or different than your own community. This reflection will certainly help you better prepare for Task 4 (Cultural Comparison).

- In addition to using this book as a guide, here are some suggestions that will help you prepare for this exam:
- Use Spanish as much as possible in all four skill areas (speaking, listening, writing, and reading). There is a strong correlation between different skill areas, and improvement in any one area usually affects and enhances ability in other skill areas.
- Build your vocabulary and your ability to use different grammatical structures by using new vocabulary words and repeating phrases and sentences out loud. Speaking the language out loud will help you better internalize the language. You can easily accomplish this on your own by reading your print texts out loud to yourself and by repeating sentences and phrases that you hear in your audio texts.
- When you encounter an unfamiliar word, use context clues to infer its meaning.
- Use circumlocution as much as possible.
- Identify early the skill areas that are most difficult for you and work often on developing them.
- When speaking and writing, don't be afraid to make mistakes. Look at your mistakes as opportunities to improve. After making a mistake, repeat the correct structure a few times and try again later. Many of the mistakes we routinely make are due to having internalized the language incorrectly. The only way to reverse this is by repeating the correct structure often.
- Practice speaking Spanish as much as possible. Speak with other students and with people in your community, or join a tutoring program in your community to teach English to native speakers of Spanish. Often, volunteering to teach English will put you in contact with native speakers.
- Learn as much as possible about customs, history, and current events of various Spanish-speaking countries. This will help develop better awareness of the products, practices, and perspectives of Spanish-speaking communities, and will help you on the free-response section of the exam.

Useful Websites for Additional Practice

There are many websites available to help build your proficiency in Spanish. Here are but a few that you may find helpful:

www.bbc.com/mundo (Extensive news site in Spanish with both print and audio texts)

www.muyinteresante.es (Contains many short articles on a variety of topics)

https://news.un.org/es/ (Official page of the United Nations, with print and audio texts)

www.rtve.es (Spanish online TV and radio channel with multiple shows and stories)

https://radio.garden/ (Website through which you can access any radio station in the world)

www.wordreference.com (Great reference site that can help with defining words and looking up idioms and verb conjugations)

PART 2
Reading Comprehension

2

Reading Comprehension

General Considerations

Reading comprehension is one of the more important skills that you should develop over the course of your preparation. It is the one proficiency skill that is integrated throughout the examination. You will only be tested on your ability to comprehend print texts in Section I, Part A, and in the Print and Audio Texts (combined) portion of Section I, Part B, but you will also need to demonstrate good reading comprehension abilities to successfully complete Section II, Task 1 (Email Reply), and Task 2 (Argumentative Essay).

Format of the Exam

In Section I, Part A, you will be given four reading passages and have to answer a total of 30 questions. The reading portion of the exam is usually divided in following formats:

- Advertisement, pamphlet, promotional material, or announcement (5 questions)
- Fragment of a literary text (7 questions)
- Article accompanied by a graph, table, or chart (11 questions)
- Correspondence (7 questions)

The number in parentheses indicates the typical number of questions you can expect for each reading.

Types of Questions

Reading comprehension is more than simply understanding a text. You will also be tested on your ability to think critically about the selection, infer meaning, make interdisciplinary and cultural connections, and make predictions. Although questions for each reading passage will vary, you can confidently expect them to fall into one of the following four categories:

- **UNDERSTAND CONTENT.** Identify the main idea and details.
- **THINK CRITICALLY.** Identify the purpose of the text, the target audience, point of view of its author, the tone or attitude, and how the author communicates his/her ideas; be able to separate fact from opinion; and make predictions based on information presented in the text.
- **UNDERSTAND MEANING.** Infer the meaning of unfamiliar words and expressions using context clues, and comprehend a wide variety of vocabulary, idioms, and cultural expressions.
- **UNDERSTAND CULTURE AND CONTENT ACROSS DISCIPLINES.** Identify practices, products, and perspectives of Hispanic cultures and information pertaining to other disciplines, such as science, geography, history, art, and so on.

Each question will have four answer choices to choose from. Out of the four options, there will be three distractors, or incorrect choices. These distractors are often not the complete opposite of the correct answer and are never nonsensical or ungrammatical. Sometimes these distractors are based on words that are false cognates or words that cause misconceptions or errors that teachers know students make. Distractors may also only be partially incorrect or correct. When selecting the correct answer, focus on the answer whose idea is correct, not the one that uses similar vocabulary or language seen in the text. You will not be penalized for incorrect answers, so if you don't know the answer, always make an educated guess.

Reading Strategies

The following section contains suggestions for how to better develop your reading comprehension ability and to answer the types of questions you will be asked. First is a list of strategies that you should apply when reading. This is followed by several examples of how to answer the types of questions you will be asked on the exam. After each example, there is a discussion of which answers are correct or incorrect. The logic of the answer is also explained. Pay close attention to the logic so that you can understand your errors.

Suggestions for Reading

You should follow these steps every time you approach a reading comprehension text.

Before Reading the Text

- **READ THE INTRODUCTION AND TITLE.** All reading selections will have a brief introduction about the text and its source. This information is helpful to get you thinking about what information will be presented, as well as the possible point of view of the author and intended audience.
- **SCAN THE WHOLE PASSAGE.** Scanning will help you get a general idea of the topic. Many articles are divided into subsections, and scanning beforehand will allow you to predict what information might be presented in each section.
- **SCAN THE QUESTIONS.** This will give you an idea of what information you will need to find in the passage.
- **USE VISUALS.** If the passage includes a graphic, make a note of its relation to the printed words. This will help you determine the purpose of the visual insert.

While Reading the Text

- **VISUALIZE AS YOU READ.** Imagine in your mind's eye what is being said. This will help you understand the ideas and tone of the text, and reduce the tendency to translate.
- **UNDERLINE KEY WORDS AND IDEAS.** This will allow you to quickly retrieve information from the text.
- **IDENTIFY THE MAIN IDEA.** Look for repetition of words or phrases, or look for words that are topically related.
- **IDENTIFY SETTING, ACTION, AND MAIN CHARACTERS.** When determining the setting, note the time frame and the place of the action. If there is any action, get a general idea of what happens. For more factual texts, such as a report, note when, where, how, and why it happened. If a character has no name, identify him or her by some other characteristic, such as color of hair, personality, or clothing.
- **MAKE NOTE OF ELEMENTS RELATING TO HISPANIC CULTURE.** Remember that the examination tests both language and culture. It is important to identify and understand any products (food, clothing, art, etc.), the practices (customs and traditions), and perspectives (attitudes, values, and ideas) of Hispanic culture and be able to recognize how they differ from those of your own culture. Even if you are not asked a specific question about this information, it is useful to further develop your awareness of Hispanic culture and societies.
- **FOCUS ON WORDS YOU RECOGNIZE AND USE CONTEXT CLUES TO INFER THE MEANING OF UNFA-MILIAR WORDS.** Unknown words are often restated with other words you do know, especially if they are important to understand the passage. There are a number of strategies that can help you infer meaning from

unfamiliar vocabulary, and these are discussed more in depth in the following section.

After Reading the Text

- **REFLECT ON THE READING.** Think of the reading as a whole and synthesize the information presented. Take the information presented to you at face value, regardless of whether or not you agree with the information presented or with the author's point of view.

Answering Reading Comprehension Questions

Always select the answer whose idea best reflects one presented in the text. Don't be distracted by answers that use the same vocabulary found in the text. The correct answer will often paraphrase the information in the text. Use the process of elimination to help answer any questions that you may have left unanswered.

The following exercises will help you better navigate the different types of questions you will find in the reading comprehension portion of the exam.

Understanding Content

Understanding content encompasses one's ability to identify the main idea of a passage and the details relating to the passage.

Identify the Main Idea

The main idea of a text is what the author wants the reader to understand is important in the entirety of the text. This is different than simply identifying what the text is about. To identify the main idea, you should scan the passage, including the title, and make a mental note of those words that are important and begin to think about what they all have in common. Pay particular attention to nouns and verbs. Do not worry about words that you do not recognize. Later you can determine which of the words are really important from among those that you do not know. Ignore words that are not needed to tell what the passage is about.

Práctica

Read the passage and select the best answer for each question that follows.

> —¡Diles que no me maten, Justino! Anda, vete a decirles eso. Que por caridad. Así diles. Diles que lo hagan por caridad.
>
> —No puedo. Hay allí un sargento que no quiere oír hablar nada de ti.
>
> *Línea (5)* —Haz que te oiga. Date tus mañas y dile que para sustos ya ha estado bueno. Dile que lo haga por caridad de Dios.
>
> —No se trata de sustos. Parece que te van a matar de a de veras. Y yo ya no quiero volver allá.
>
> —Anda otra vez. Solamente otra vez, a ver qué consigues.
>
> —No. No tengo ganas de eso, yo soy tu hijo. Y si voy mucho con ellos, acabarán por saber quién soy y les dará por afusilarme a mí también. Es mejor dejar las cosas de este tamaño.

1. ¿Cuál es la actitud del padre de Justino?

   (A) Resignado
   (B) Impávido
   (C) Desesperado
   (D) Asustado

2. ¿Cómo caracterizaría el tipo de hijo que parece ser Justino?

   (A) Egoísta
   (B) Cruel
   (C) Cariñoso
   (D) Temeroso

Respuestas

Pregunta 1: C

The lines by Justino and his father alternate between commands and refusals. The father's every line is a command for his son to go ask, tell, or beg for his life. Justino's every line communicates his desire to not become involved. Through the repetition of the command "Diles," the father communicates his desperation, not resignation, fear, or intrepid behavior.

Pregunta 2: D

Justino's fear for his own life overwhelms any familial love that he may have felt for his father. His constant denial and proffered "reason" are not convincing; they sound like excuses, except that there is a grain of truth to the gravity of the situation as he sees it. At the end, Justino confesses that he does not want to press too much because the sergeant apparently does not realize that Justino is the man's son, and Justino does not want the sergeant to know. Although Justino may be self-centered and cruel, his primary reaction is fear. This is indicated by the constant repetition of his denial, and after each denial, an explanation of his position in the matter.

Think Critically

In addition to understanding the passage, you must also be able to think critically about the information presented in the reading selection. The types of questions on the exam that deal with critical thinking may ask you to consider the purpose and reason of the selection, determine the tone and attitude of the author, identify the intended reader, separate fact from opinion, and make assumptions. The following steps will help you become a better critical reader:

- Read and Summarize. Read the selection first so that you understand the content. Next, try to summarize the information you just read. The summary should be the main message or central idea of the passage.
- Analyze. Look at the evidence presented, draw inferences where you can, and identify the tone.
- Synthesize. Connect the information you read to your own prior knowledge about the theme and any personal experiences you may have on the topic. Remember that all readings somehow relate to one of the six overarching themes.
- Evaluate. Assess the overall work. This is where you can determine the intended audience, the tone of the author, the validity of the argument, what evidence may be missing, and other predictions and assumptions that go beyond the text.

These steps should be implemented in order, and you should develop the habit of thinking critically with all your readings.

Questions About Purpose and Reason

There are two types of questions you are most likely going to see on the exam that deal with purpose and reason: (1) one that asks about the overall purpose of the reading selection, and (2) one that asks about the purpose, the reason, and/or the motivation of a particular event that takes place within the text. Take a look at the following samples.

Práctica 1
Read the passage and answer the questions that follow.

Para los viajes en todas las rutas TACA se permite una pieza de mano con un peso máximo de 22 libras (10 kilos) cuyas dimensiones exteriores (alto + largo + ancho) no exceda de 115 centímetros (45 pulgadas). En los módulos de los aeropuertos están los medidores de equipaje, allí puedes verificar las

Línea dimensiones de tu equipaje de mano con las normas vigentes.

(5) Nuestros Socios LifeMiles Élite (Gold y Diamond) tienen derecho a 2 piezas de mano con un peso máximo de 22 libras (10 kilos) cada una, cuyas dimensiones exteriores (alto + largo + ancho) no exceda de 115 centímetros (45 pulgadas).*

Los Pasajeros Gold Star Alliance en clase ejecutiva tienen derecho a 2 piezas de mano con un peso máximo de 22 libras (10 kilos) cada una, cuyas dimensiones exteriores (alto + largo + ancho) no exceda

(10) de 115 centímetros (45 pulgadas).*

*Excluye vuelos desde/hacia Estados Unidos; las regulaciones pueden variar por país y pueden ser modificadas por las autoridades de cada país en cualquier momento y sin previo aviso.

—*www.taca.com/esp/syi/bag/bagbagpol.asp?id=14*

---

1. ¿Cuál parece ser la función de este trozo?

   (A) Informarle a la gente de los diferentes tamaños de equipaje
   (B) Presentar la política de equipaje de mano de una compañía aérea
   (C) Mostrar los beneficios de ser socio de un club
   (D) Explicar las diferencias en regulaciones por distintos países

2. ¿Qué función tienen los medidores de equipaje (línea 4)?

   (A) Para medir las dimensiones de las piezas de equipaje
   (B) Para averiguar cuánto puede caber en las maletas
   (C) Para encontrar el peso del equipaje
   (D) Para asegurar que sea una pieza de mano reglamentaria

Respuestas

Pregunta 1: B

This piece informs the general public about what type of carry-on luggage is permissible. It only presents one size—the maximum weight and dimensions allowed, thus eliminating (A). Choice (D) really has nothing to do with the selection, and, although the passage does include information about different membership groups, it never makes an attempt to persuade someone to try to become a member, thus eliminating (C) as an option.

Pregunta 2: D

Be careful not to be tricked by the repetition of a form of the word medir in the question and in the first option. The medidor does not measure luggage, nor does it weigh the bag. It is used to verify that the piece of luggage is small enough to be considered a carry-on according to the established reglamento, or regulations.

Práctica 2

Read the passage and answer the questions that follow.

> Y las manifestaciones callejeras se suceden. Pueden hacerse para la defensa del medio ambiente o contra un alcalde superviviente de la dictadura, a favor de los obreros panaderos o del Polisario, pero a juzgar por las fotografías o telediarios, lo más importante para los participantes es estar allí, ser vistos y
>
> *Línea*
> (5) oídos. Cada vez que una cámara de cine o fotografía les enfoca miran fijos, sonríen, levantan los brazos; en las fotos de periódicos, los de adelante aparecen satisfechos y orgullosos; los de detrás, se asoman por entre las cabezas entre los afortunados para "estar" a su vez común en esas fotografías de grupos infantiles.

1. Según el autor, ¿por qué participa la gente en las manifestaciones callejeras?

   (A) Para ser vista y reconocida
   (B) Para celebrar sus nuevas libertades
   (C) Para protestar la censura del gobierno
   (D) Para efectuar algún cambio social

2. ¿Cómo reaccionan esas personas al ver una cámara?

   (A) Tratan de ocultar los rostros.
   (B) Se enorgullecen de su supuesta importancia.
   (C) Tienen miedo de ser reconocidos.
   (D) Se enfadan porque sacan fotografías de ellos.

Respuestas

Pregunta 1: A

Don't be tricked by the reason the protests take place. The question asks you why the people choose to participate. According to the text, the author believes the people solely want to be seen and heard. No indication is given as to whether they actually support the protest itself.

Pregunta 2: B

This answer is quite straightforward. The other three all convey a similar idea—that of not wanting to be seen.

Determining Tone and Attitude

One of the more difficult aspects of reading is determining the tone of the passage. The tone or attitude of the passage refers to the author's relationship to his or her material or to the readers, or both. By changing voice or manner, a writer can create a particular tone in a work. Sometimes the writer's attitude is revealed in the use of figures of speech, such as hyperbole (exaggeration), various types of images (simile, metaphor, or metonym), humor (puns), or other devices, such as personification. In the following passages, notice the choice of words and how they are used to create a particular tone. This tone or attitude, at times, can indicate what type of writing the passage presents.

Práctica 1

Read the passage and answer the question that follows.

> El primordial objeto de la vida, para muchos millones de norteamericanos, está en "divertirse" o "troncharse de risa." "Divertirse" no es ningún asunto complicado. El cine constituye la mayor de las diversiones. Bailar, jugar a los naipes, patinar, o besar y abrazar en un coche a una muchacha en cualquier momento es
>
> *Línea* divertirse. Mirar los grabados en una revista y beber jugo de naranja es también una gran diversión. A los
> (5) norteamericanos les satisface todo y gozan de todo. Encontrarse en la calle a Peter Lorre es un gran entretenimiento; platicar con una hórrida jamona en un fonducho de mala muerte es magnífico; presenciar un buen accidente automovilístico en la calle es demasiado maravilloso para describirlo con palabras.

1. Ante el espectáculo de los norteamericanos tratando de divertirse en todo momento, ¿cuál de las siguientes emociones muestra el tono del narrador?

    (A) Aburrido
    (B) Entretenido
    (C) No afectado
    (D) Asombrado

Respuesta

Pregunta 1: B

The narrator shows a certain detached amusement for the phenomenon he is describing, as is shown in the words he chooses to name his topic: "El primordial objeto de la vida . . . ." Among the basic human drives, entertainment does not usually rank alongside self-preservation. The overstatement indicates that this narrator is somewhat detached. He is not commenting on what entertainment means to him, but rather on what it means to the people he is observing. He then enumerates things that he thinks North Americans find entertaining, a list that culminates with the sight of an automobile accident. Any spectacle is entertaining. Choice (C) is a possible answer, but not the best answer. One does not get the impression from this passage that the writer is entirely indifferent to the subject matter; if he found it entertaining enough to write about, he is not totally indifferent.

Práctica 2

Read the passage and select the best answer to the question that follows.

> Al sol, ya se sabe, hay que acercarse con las espaldas bien cubiertas. Ninguna imprudencia nos está permitida, pues este astro, que posee una memoria de elefante, puede pasarnos factura cuando menos lo esperamos. Sirve que nosotros lo tengamos en cuenta al comprar un bronceador. Vale que busquemos
>
> *Línea* uno que nos ofrezca seguridad total de los efectos de rayos ultravioleta. Ahora protegernos del sol vera-
> *(5)* niego traspasa cuestiones estéticas.

1. ¿Cuál es la idea principal de esta selección?

   (A) Lo bueno de broncearse durante el verano
   (B) Los efectos que el sol puede tener en la piel
   (C) La importancia de seleccionar bien una crema protectora
   (D) Lo que hay que hacer en caso de que uno sufra una quemadura

Respuesta

Pregunta 1: C

This selection informs the reader about the importance of protecting oneself from the sun. The main recommendation is to select a good sunblock. It highlights that protection is more important than aesthetics. The words that have a common connection that support the main idea are "cubiertas," "bronceador," "seguridad total," and "protegernos."

Práctica 3

Read the passage and select the best answer to the question that follows.

> En el trayecto que se me había encomendado recorrer, hay un puente, en el que a intervalo de un minuto, debían circular por una vía única dos trenes: el que yo manejaba y un tren de mercancías. Sabiendo el peligro de estos cruces, se me habían hecho mil recomendaciones, inútiles, por otra parte, pues es de suponer la atención que pondría yo en las señales luminosas.
>
> *Línea*
> *(5)* Al acercarnos al puente en cuestión, divisé claramente la luz verde, que me daba libre paso, y respirando aliviado, aumenté un poco la velocidad de nuestra marcha, no mucho sin embargo, dado que había que cruzar un puente y podría resultar peligroso.
>
> Segundos después se sintió una sacudida intensísima y se oyó un ruido horrible: los dos trenes chocaron, se incendiaron y se desmenuzaron. Hubo cientos de muertos y miles de heridos. Por una rara
> *(10)* casualidad yo quedé ileso. ¡Ojalá hubiera muerto!
>
> Nunca podré olvidar un espectáculo tan espantoso. Como siempre sucede en las catástrofes, la sensación de espanto no es simultánea con el choque; sólo al cabo de algunos minutos, cuando vi las llamas de los coches que ardían, cuando distinguí las dos locomotoras semi-erguidas como dos hombres que luchan por derribarse, cuando oí los lamentos de los heridos y vi las ambulancias que acudían a levantar
> *(15)* las víctimas, sólo entonces me di cuenta de lo que acababa de suceder.

1. ¿Qué se narra en este trozo?

   (A) Un encuentro entre amigos
   (B) Un desastre natural
   (C) Una colisión
   (D) La circulación de trenes

Respuesta

Pregunta 1: C

This selection narrates the event of a collision between two trains. The words that have a common connection are "sacudida intensísima," "ruido horrible," "chocaron," "muertos," "heridos," "espantoso," and "catástrofes."

Understand Details

After the main idea of the passage has been identified, there will be a variety of questions that ask about specific information contained in the text. These details can relate to setting or origin (where); time (when); character, definition, or identification (who or what); purpose and reason (why); or manner (how). Many times these questions can be easily recognized by focusing on a particular word or phrase, but the answer will most often be a rephrasing of a word or string of words in the text.

Práctica

Read the passage and select the best answer for each question that follows.

> Sin apenas tiempo para disfrutar de su viaje de novios, Carlos Sainz ha vuelto a tomar el volante de su Toyota Celica GT4 para afrontar una nueva prueba del Campeonato del Mundo de Rallys.
>
> En efecto, en la mañana del 12 de mayo Sainz y su mujer empezaron su viaje a las islas Bermudas, que
>
> *Línea* (5)
>
> duró muy poco. Después de una semana de descanso, ya estaba el piloto madrileño en Grecia junto con su copiloto Luis Moya, realizando el recorrido de entrenamiento de la 34 edición del Acrópolis, una carrera que se destaca entre las más duras del campeonato, pero que para Carlos Sainz tiene un significado muy especial, ya que allí consiguió su primera victoria en una prueba del Mundial, concretamente hace ahora dos años.

1. ¿Quién dirigirá el equipo en la competencia?

   (A) La señora Sainz
   (B) Luis Moya
   (C) Carlos Sainz
   (D) Un entrenador griego

2. ¿Qué tipo de competencia es?

   (A) Una carrera de caballos
   (B) Una carrera aérea
   (C) Una carrera de coches deportivos
   (D) Un partido de campeonato de la Copa Mundial

3. ¿Por qué estuvo Carlos Sainz en las Islas Bermudas?

   (A) Para celebrar su primera victoria
   (B) Es donde decidió pasar su luna de miel
   (C) Para entrenarse para la próxima competencia
   (D) Para recuperarse mental y físicamente

Respuestas

Pregunta 1: C

Carlos, as the subject of the phrase "ha vuelto a tomar el volante," is identified as the driver, or "piloto," about which the passage speaks. Luis Moya and la señora Sainz are secondary figures, and there is no Greek trainer.

Pregunta 2: C

Toyota Celica GT4 and Rally both refer to car racing, to which Sainz has returned. Choices (A), (B), and (D) are based on distracting factors. "Piloto" is the subject of the verb in "estaba el piloto madrileño en Grecia," but nowhere in the passage is any association made with anything other than cars. The word "Mundial" is also a distractor in choice (D), since there is a possible confusion with the World Cup in soccer competition. However, the word Copa never appears, nor are there any references to soccer.

Pregunta 3: B

This is a classic example of rephrasing of words or a series of words in the text. "Luna de miel" and "viaje de novios" are synonyms, and they both mean "honeymoon."

Determining the Intended Reader

The reading passages that appear on the AP Spanish Language and Culture exam represent a wide variety of sources. Most often the intended reader of a passage can be determined by the content of the reading itself. The intended reader is anyone who is interested enough to pick up the literature to read it. In some cases, the writer addresses the reader directly, and from context provided within the passage, the reader can identify him or herself. In other cases, the passage may be an essay that tries to convince a particular kind of reader to take a certain position. Read the following passage and think about the type of reader to whom it is directed.

Práctica

Quien desee comer una manzana y tenga ante sí un manzano de su propiedad, cargado de manzanas maduras al alcance de la mano, no tiene problema alguno para hacerse con ellas. Coge una manzana y, con ello, ha conseguido lo que pretendía. Los problemas comienzan cuando las manzanas cuelgan tan

Línea altas que resulta difícil alcanzarlas. El objetivo, cogerlas, no cabe lograrlo sin dificultades. Se tropieza

(5) con un óbice en el logro de nuestro objetivo. ¿Cómo se podrá comportar uno ante esta nueva situación?

Se puede renunciar a las manzanas, si la necesidad de comerlas no es muy acuciante o si se sabe por experiencia que no se halla preparado para tal situación, es decir, si no se siente uno con fuerzas suficientes para coger una manzana de un árbol elevado.

Pero también cabe la posibilidad de que comience uno a intentar conseguir su objetivo, o dicho de

(10) otro modo, de que trate de buscar, sin plan previo alguno, los medios y métodos apropiados para lograrlo. Intenta uno sacudir violentamente al árbol de un lado para otro y se da cuenta de que su tronco resulta demasiado grueso para poderlo mover. Arroja piedras a las manzanas y comprueba que para esto le falta la práctica requerida. Echa mano de un palo y trata de alcanzar con él las manzanas, pero el palo resulta demasiado corto.

(15) Muchos intentos, muchos fracasos. Tal vez—tras largo esfuerzo—un éxito fortuito.

Pero también se puede proceder de la siguiente manera: se sienta uno y reflexiona sobre la situación.

1. ¿A quién parece estar dirigido este pasaje?

   (A) A un campesino hambriento
   (B) A un chico pequeño
   (C) A una persona perezosa
   (D) A una persona pragmática

Respuesta

Pregunta 1: D

The correct answer is choice (D) because the purpose of this passage is to interest the reader in learning how to solve everyday problems. This writer appeals to the reader's reason by presenting a concrete example of a problem and then offering a variety of solutions, none of which is the most efficient manner of solving the problem. This writer is addressing a reader who wants to learn how to think logically when confronted by problems and not act impulsively. A pragmatic person is one who will analyze the situation and then take the most appropriate action, which in this case is to sit and contemplate the situation.

Making Predictions

Making predictions is a skill that should be applied throughout the reading process. You can make predictions about the content of a reading selection simply by reading its title. You should continue to make predictions while you are reading as to what will happen next. Predictions are always based on prior knowledge, and, therefore, tend to be more accurate as knowledge increases. On the exam, the questions asking you to make predictions will generally present a hypothetical scenario and then ask you to make a prediction of the most probable outcome of the scenario. For example, a question might ask you to determine what the title of a book would be that you would check out if you wanted to further your understanding of the topic addressed in the reading source, or what would be an appropriate title for an essay based on the reading. In each case, there is nothing in the reading itself that will answer these questions, and you must rely on your overall understanding of the text. These types of questions will generally come at the end of the question series for any given text, and as they are presenting a hypothetical situation, the conditional mood will probably be used (¿Cuál de las siguientes preguntas sería . . . ?, ¿Qué libro buscarías . . . ?, etc.). You can expect no more than one question of this type per reading selection.

Práctica

Read the passage and answer the question that follows.

> INGREDIENTES (para 4 personas)
> 1½ litro de leche
> 75 gramos de arroz
> *Línea* 2 sobres de café soluble (o descafeinado soluble)
> *(5)* 50 gramos de azúcar
> La piel de medio limón
> 1 palo de canela
> Canela en polvo
>
> En una cazuela mezclamos un litro de leche, la piel de limón, el palo de canela y el arroz. Removemos
> *(10)* todo con una espátula de madera y lo cocemos a fuego suave durante 45 minutos.
>
> A media cocción, añadimos poco a poco el resto de la leche al café soluble y al azúcar disueltos, y dejamos que siga cociendo hasta que quede cremosa la mezcla. Lo servimos en boles individuales espolvoreado con canela en polvo.
>
> El arroz con leche es un postre muy popular y fácil de elaborar. La leche aporta al postre proteínas y
> *(15)* diferentes minerales como el calcio, mientras que el arroz es buen fuente de hidratos de carbono complejos. En esta receta se presenta una variante de este postre, ya que se añade un poco de café soluble, que va a dar al plato un toque de color y sabor diferente.

1. Si quisieras investigar más información basándote en el tema de esta lectura, ¿cuál de las siguientes publicaciones te sería más útil?

   (A) Postres típicos del mundo hispano
   (B) Recetas sencillas, deliciosas y saludables
   (C) Sea el perfecto anfitrión
   (D) Por qué estudiar gastronomía

Respuesta

Pregunta 1: A

The text obviously refers to cooking, and the reader should be able to identify that the dish being described is some sort of dessert. Not only does the word postre appear in the reading itself, but so do many ingredients associated with desserts (azúcar, piel de limón, canela). The theme of this particular reading is a dessert, making (A) the best answer. Both (B) and (D) deal with cooking, but you can eliminate (B) because of saludable, as most of the ingredients in this dish would not make it necessarily healthy, and choice (D) refers more to a study program, to which this text does not refer. Choice (C) is easily eliminated because it deals more with hosting a party or event but does not necessarily have anything to do with cooking.

Understanding Meaning

Besides testing how much vocabulary you already know, the examination also tests your ability to deduce the meaning of words and idioms from the context in which they appear. It is not uncommon for even the most advanced Spanish speaker to encounter unfamiliar words while reading. For most native speakers, however, unfamiliar vocabulary generally does not present a problem because they are able to extract plenty of information from context to effectively understand the passage and, in most cases, they are likely capable of giving you a probable meaning of the words they do not know. On the other hand, students of Spanish too often tend to get hung up on vocabulary they do not recognize, and some feel they cannot continue reading without knowing the meaning of the unfamiliar word. In such cases, the first reaction often is to turn to a bilingual dictionary to help learn its meaning. The use of dictionaries, however, is not permitted on the examination, and therefore it is important to learn other strategies that you can use to help you work with unfamiliar vocabulary when reading.

Inferring the Meaning of Unfamiliar Words Using Context Clues

Being able to infer the meaning of unfamiliar words or idioms using context clues is a powerful tool that can boost your interpretive ability. However, it is important to remember that you do not have to understand all words in a reading passage to be an effective reader. In many cases you won't need to worry about the words you do not recognize in order to extract all the information you will need from a text. However, there are times when unfamiliar words and idioms may play a pivotal role in your understanding of a particular sentence, and in these cases you should use the following strategies to help you make an educated guess to their meaning:

1. **READ THE ENTIRE SENTENCE OR PARAGRAPH.** You have to have a frame of reference to understand unfamiliar vocabulary.
2. **IDENTIFY THE PART OF SPEECH OF THE WORD.** Is it a noun, adjective, verb, adverb, etc.?
3. **USE CONTEXT CLUES.** To what other words does the unfamiliar word relate? If the word is an adjective, what noun is it modifying? If the word is a verb, who is the subject?
4. **DO YOU KNOW WORDS OF THE SAME FAMILY?** Often a word that may be unfamiliar is of the same family of a word you already know. For example una docena (a dozen) includes the number doce (twelve). Break up prefixes and suffixes to help you as well.
5. **IDENTIFY COGNATES AND PRONOUNCE WORDS.** For example, the Spanish verb facilitar is a cognate of the English to facilitate. Sometimes pronouncing a word can help identify its meaning.

Mastering this ability requires patience and practice, and the more you apply these strategies to your daily reading, the more comfortable you will become in your ability to read. Remember, it is not important to know the exact definition of the words; simply approximating the meaning is enough in most cases.

Práctica

Read the following text and predict the meaning of the underlined words. The entire text forms part of a story that is also an example of a product from the Spanish-speaking world.

Introducción:

El siguiente cuento es una leyenda de España. Es una adaptación de la leyenda publicada en 2008 en el boletín titulado Materiales, publicado por el Ministerio de Educación, Política Social y Deporte de España.

La leyenda del *cuélebre*

Hace muchos, muchos, años vivía en un <u>bosque</u> verde y <u>frondoso</u> un animal fantástico que se llamaba *cuélebre*. Tenía el cuerpo de serpiente y las <u>alas de</u> <u>murciélago</u>. Su cuerpo era enorme y tenía una larga <u>cola</u>. El *cuélebre* vivía en el norte de España, muy cerca de las <u>orillas</u> de los ríos. Su trabajo era de proteger su precioso <u>tesoro</u>.

Línea (5)

Una tarde lluviosa, cuando el *cuélebre* se despertó, estaba tan hambriento que decidió tomar una merienda. Sabía dónde encontrarla porque, siempre cuando tenía hambre, <u>se alimentaba</u> de personas y <u>ganado</u>. Así que <u>se deslizó</u> por los árboles del bosque hasta que llegó a la orilla de un lago. Allí, al otro lado, vio a una <u>ovejita</u> que comía hierba. El *cuélebre* <u>se acercó</u> sigilosamente hasta alcanzar a la ovejita por detrás, abrió su boca y <u>se la tragó</u> de un solo bocado. Al haber satisfecho su hambre, decidió tomarse una siestita.

(10)

La mañana siguiente, un niño que paseaba por allí vio al *cuélebre* que dormía y <u>se asustó</u> tanto que tuvo que correr para que el *cuélebre* no lo viera. El niño llamó a unos <u>cazadores</u>, y les llevó hasta donde estaba la bestia, todavía durmiendo junto al lago. Entonces, los cazadores abrieron su enorme boca para que la ovejita pudiera salir. Luego, recogieron unas rocas que estaban cerca y las pusieron en la boca del *cuélebre*.

(15)

Unas horas después, cuando el *cuélebre* se despertó, se sintió tan mal que comenzó a <u>arrastrarse</u> hasta llegar al mar. Allí, por el peso de las rocas en su estómago, <u>se ahogó</u> y descansó para siempre, en el fondo del océano.

Respuestas

bosque
(línea 1)   The first step is to identify that this word is a noun, as evidenced by the indefinite article. This means that it is either a person, place, thing, or idea. The next contextual clue is that the verb *vivir* and the preposition *en* indicates that the subject of the sentence, the c*uélebre,* lived here, which gives us evidence that "bosque" is a place. When we consider that the *cuélebre* is an "animal fantástico," then this place is likely rural and not urban. The adjective "verde" is another clue, and when we think of a rural place that is green in which an animal might live, we likely would think of a forest, which is what this word means.

frondoso (1)   The first step again is to identify the part of speech, and this word is an adjective. We know this because it follows the conjunction "y" and, since this conjunction does not introduce a new clause, its function is to link the word "frondoso" with "verde." Since "verde" describes "bosque," and we now know that "bosque" is a forest, then "frondoso" is another adjective that is describing the forest. This information would be sufficient for general comprehension, but if we wanted to be more precise, we could think of another adjective that would describe a forest. If you thought of *leafy* or *dense*, then you would be correct.

alas de murciélago (2–3)	This is a structure in which we have two nouns, where "murciélago" is modifying "alas." When we look at the context, we can see that it too follows the conjunction "y" and, just like in the previous example, the conjunction is linking these nouns to the nouns beforehand. The previous nouns "cuerpo" and "serpiente" are describing the body of the *cuélebre,* and therefore we can safely assume that the nouns "alas" and "murciélago" are doing the same. To be more precise, "alas" is referring to a body part just like "cuerpo" does beforehand, and since "serpiente" is a type of animal, then we can safely assume that "murciélago" is an animal as well. There is not enough context to tell us exactly *what* body part or animal these words mean, but this information is enough to establish sufficient comprehension. In case you are wondering, "alas" means *wings*, and "murciélago" means *bat*. However, this information is not vital to understand what is happening in the story.
cola (3)	We see that this word is a noun. It also follows the conjunction "y" and the conjugated verb "tenía," so it is part of a new clause, but it does relate to the clause before the conjunction. When we look at the first clause in this sentence, we see that it again describes the body of the animal. This means that the second clause is likely doing the same thing, so we can safely assume that "cola" is part of the body of the animal. When we consider the adjective "larga," it tells us that this body part is long and, when we remember that we already know this animal had a body of a serpent, then likely this word means "tail."
orillas (4)	We identify that this word is a noun. Further context clues tell us that this noun relates to the verb "vivía," so "orillas" is a place. We already know that the *cuélebre* lived in a forest, so this particular place must be somewhere inside the forest. Further digging tells us that "ríos" is modifying the word "orillas," and since the lack of preposition "en" rules out that it lives *in* the river, it must be somewhere nearby, which gives us words like *edge* or *shore*, which is the meaning of this word.
tesoro (5)	This word is a noun, and it is the direct object of the verb "proteger." We also know that this object is "precioso," which looks and sounds like *precious* in English. This is a clue that "tesoro" must be something of value, which makes sense because the *cuélebre* is protecting it. If you guessed that it means *treasure*, you are correct.
se alimentaba (8)	We easily identify that this word is a verb in the imperfect tense, and the subject is the *"cuélebre."* We also see that this verb follows the expression *"tenía hambre,"* which is sufficient evidence to infer that "se alimentaba" probably means *ate*.
ganado (8)	As we begin to feel more comfortable inferring meaning, let's not be tempted to skip steps in the process. This is an example of how that can backfire. The word looks like the past participle of the verb *ganar*, but it is not. Like in several previous examples this word follows the conjunction "y" and thus relates to what comes before the conjunction, which in this case is the noun "personas." This tells us that "ganado" is a noun. Further investigation shows us that both "personas" and "ganado" are the direct objects of the verb "se alimentaba," which we now know means "ate." This tells us that the *cuélebre* ate both people and "ganado," and we can safely infer that "ganado" is a type of food. Thinking about it more, we easily reach the conclusion that "ganado" is likely some sort of animal rather than a plant, for if the *cuélebre* eats people, then it is likely not a vegetarian. In fact, "ganado" means *livestock*.

se deslizó (8)	We identify that this is a verb in the preterit tense, and the subject is *cuélebre*. Further context shows us that the *cuélebre* did this action "por los árboles" and that it then "llegó a la orilla de un lago" (to the shore of a lake). Therefore, the verb "se deslizó" is likely a verb of movement, bringing the *cuélebre* from where it woke up to the lake. This is sufficient to understand the text, but if we were to take it a step further, when we remember that the *cuélebre* has the body of a snake and therefore no legs or feet, then we see that "se deslizó" probably means *to slither* or *slide*.
ovejita (10)	We quickly identify that this word is a noun, and that it is also the direct object of the verb "vio" (*saw*). Another important clue is the preposition "a," which is often used before a direct object that denotes a human being or an animal, so we know that the noun probably is one of those two things. Further investigation shows us that the "ovejita" is eating "hierba" on the other side of the lake. The word "hierba" looks and sounds like *herbs*, so we assume that it probably is an animal and that it is grazing. We don't have enough information to say exactly what type of animal it is, but that is not vital to understand enough to comprehend the story. In case you are curious, "ovejita" means *small sheep* or *lamb*.
se acercó (10)	This word is a verb in the preterit tense and the subject of this verb is *cuélebre*. There is no direct object, but there is the preposition "hasta" (*until*) that precedes another verb "alcanzar" and the direct object "la ovejita." So you know that the *cuélebre* did something until it did something else to the "ovejita" . . . but what? As we look further, we see in the next clause that the *cuélebre* "abrió su boca" (*opened its mouth*). This gives us enough information to know what "se acercó" probably means. Working backwards from "abrió su boca," we deduce that the *cuélebre* opened its mouth to eat the "ovejita," but before being able to do so, the *cuélebre* must have caught or reached the "ovejita," and this is probably what "alcanzar" means. But since we know from the previous sentence that the sheep was on the other side of the lake, the *cuélebre* had to move toward it first. Therefore, "se acercó" means *approached*. Another way to confirm this is to change the verb to the infinitive form, which is *acercarse*. In this word, we see the preposition "cerca" (*near*), which gives us further evidence that our supposition is correct.
se la tragó (11)	We quickly identify that this word is a verb in the preterit tense, and again the subject is the *cuélebre*. Since this is the third verb in the preterit in this sentence, it is the third action in the sequence of events. We know that right before this verb, the *cuélebre* opened its mouth. This should be sufficient information to infer that "se la tragó" means *ate* or *swallowed*.
se asustó (14)	Again we start by identifying that this word is a verb in the preterit tense. This time, however, the subject is "un niño." It is also the second of three verbs in this sentence that are conjugated in the preterit tense, and all three have the same subject. The first and last actions in the sequence contain the basic verbs "vio" (*saw*) and "correr" (*ran*), so logically, the boy likely became scared after seeing the enormous *cuélebre* that was sleeping, and thus ran away, which is what "se asustó" means.
cazadores (15)	We identify that this word is a noun and is the direct object of the verb "llamó." An important clue again is that it follows the preposition "a," which means that this noun is either a human being or an animal. Since the subject of the verb "llamó" is the young boy, and he calls the "cazadores" after running away from the *cuélebre*, it makes sense that "cazadores" must be people, and people that can help him. This is sufficient information to establish understanding. In case you are still curious, "cazadores" are *hunters*.

arrastrarse (20)   This word is a verb, and it is in the infinitive form because it follows the conjugated verb "comenzó a." The subject is *cuélebre*. In this context, we know that the *cuélebre* woke up, felt sick, and "comenzó a arrastrarse" until it reached the sea. We have sufficient information to infer that this is a verb of motion, which is correct and sufficient for understanding the text. Thinking through it further, if we remember that the *cuélebre* felt sick because the sheep in its stomach was replaced with rocks, then we likely are visualizing movement to the sea that is labored and difficult. If this leads you to infer that this verb probably means *to drag*, you are correct.

se ahogó (21)   This word is also a conjugated verb and the subject is *cuélebre*. We know that this action occurred after the *cuélebre* reached the ocean and that, following this action, the beast rested for eternity at the bottom of the ocean. This information, paired with our prior knowledge that its stomach was filled with rocks, helps us infer that this verb means *drowned*.

As you practice inferring meaning of unfamiliar words using context clues, do not worry too much if you are not able to infer the exact meaning. Often, simply getting in the ballpark is good enough. The goal is to understand ideas, and if you are able to infer enough to understand correctly the overall idea being presented, you will perform well on most interpretive tasks.

Culture and Content Across Disciplines

Culture

When talking about culture, one has to consider the products, practices, and perspectives (for more detailed information, refer to the section on culture in Chapter 1). Sometimes the questions regarding culture will pertain to a certain attitude that is presented within the text, or it may ask you about a particular expression that is used and why.

Práctica

Read the passage and answer the questions that follow. As you read, try to identify some of the practices and perspectives that are demonstrated.

A las cuatro merendamos juntos, pan y pasas, sentados en el sofá, y cuando nos levantamos, no sé por qué, mi padre no quiso que limpiara el espaldar que el albañilito había manchado de blanco con su chaqueta; me detuvo la mano y lo limpió después sin que lo viéramos . . .

Línea
(5)   —¿Sabes, hijo mío, por qué no quise que limpiara el sofá? Porque limpiarle mientras tu compañero lo veía era casi hacerle una reconvención por haberlo ensuciado. Y esto no estaba bien: en primer lugar, porque no lo había hecho de intento, y en segundo lugar, porque le había manchado con ropa de su padre, que se la había enyesado trabajando; y lo que se mancha trabajando no ensucia; es polvo, cal, barniz, todo lo que quieras, pero no suciedad. El trabajo no ensucia. No digas nunca de un obrero que sale de su trabajo: "Va sucio." Debes decir: "Tiene en su ropa las señales, las huellas del trabajo." Recuér-
(10)   dalo. Quiero mucho al albañilito: primero, porque es compañero tuyo, y además, porque es hijo de un obrero. —Tu padre.

---

1. ¿De qué se trata esta selección?

  (A) De la conducta apropiada de un anfitrión
  (B) De los modos de mantenerse limpio en casa
  (C) De la conducta apropiada de un huésped
  (D) De los modos de disciplinar a un hijo

2. ¿Por qué no quería el papá que su hijo limpiara el sofá de inmediato?

    (A) No quería que el albañilito viera a su hijo trabajando.

    (B) Quería que la madre lo hiciera.

    (C) Quería que el albañilito viera lo que había hecho.

    (D) No quería parecer descortés al invitado.

3. En las línea 9, ¿qué quiere decir ". . . lo que se mancha trabajando no ensucia"?

    (A) Indica que no puede ensuciarse trabajando.

    (B) Significa que el padre no vio que la chaqueta estaba sucia.

    (C) Significa que trabajar no es una desgracia.

    (D) Quiere decir que el padre se sentía superior a los obreros.

Respuestas

Pregunta 1: A

The predominant cultural perspective that stands out is the importance of being a good host. The narrator is obviously young and still in the process of learning the importance of hospitality. This perspective is highlighted not only by what the father tells his son, but also by certain actions he takes, such as not cleaning the chalk stain left on the sofa.

Pregunta 2: D

As in the question prior, the action is not taken because the father does not want his guest to feel uncomfortable. This is indeed a cultural practice—not doing a particular action that may make someone feel uncomfortable.

Pregunta 3: C

This question asks you to reflect on the use of language in order to understand a particular cultural perspective. In this case, you must go beyond what the words are literally saying and focus on the general idea within the context. The father is teaching his son why it is important to respect those who work, regardless of the work they do. The saying also conveys a cultural perspective.

Content Across Disciplines

You can expect that the reading selections on the AP Spanish exam will deal with a number of topics pertaining to different disciplines. As you prepare for the exam, it is important to diversify your readings as much as possible in order to expose yourself to the vocabulary and ideas that pertain to different topics. Do not panic if you find yourself in front of a selection on a topic about which you know very little. Consider this as an opportunity to grow your knowledge of that particular subject.

Práctica

Read the passage and answer the questions that follow. As you read, try to identify (1) the subject matter to which the passage pertains, and (2) key vocabulary words that are common when talking about the subject.

En verano se ven menos horas de televisión, según los estudios de audiencia. Los días son más largos. Los espectadores encuentran elementos sustituidores de ocio fuera de su hogar habitual. La publicidad floja y disminuye la presión competitiva. Este año, sin embargo, y a excepción de Antena 3, que apenas *Línea* modificará su programación, la lucha por ganar más cuota de pantalla no baja la guardia. La más agre- *(5)* siva es Telecinco, que prepara las maletas para situarse en las playas. En la de Marbella ya ha contratado a su alcalde para que haga de presentador.

Para los jóvenes, Telecinco ha preparado una versión reducida de La quinta marcha, que se emitirá al mediodía desde distintos emplazamientos turísticos y playeros. En esta misma línea de seguimiento a la audiencia consumidora de discos y refrescos, se mueve Hablando se entiende la basca, una versión del *(10)* programa de Coll que se realizará en el mismo escenario de Hablando se entiende la gente, el teatro de la ONCE de Madrid. Chavales entre 10 y 17 años ofrecerán diariamente su espectáculo conducido por unos de los presentadores de La quinta marcha.

---

1.   1. ¿Qué tendencias se han notado entre los televidentes españoles?

(A) Durante el invierno miran menos porque están tan ocupados.

(B) Durante el verano miran menos porque prefieren disfrutar del tiempo fuera de casa.

(C) No hay diferencia entre el número de horas que miran en verano y en invierno.

(D) Depende más de la edad del televidente cuánto miran en el verano.

2. ¿De dónde procede este trozo?

(A) Es un folleto del Consejo de Turismo sobre la televisión.

(B) Es un guión para los televidentes.

(C) Es de una revista que investiga las novedades en la televisión.

(D) Es de una obra literaria mostrando la vida moderna.

Respuestas

Pregunta 1: B

The correct answer can be found in the first three sentences of the passage, where the main idea is basically restated verbatim.

Pregunta 2: C

The information presented in the passage is simply stating the facts as they appear. There is no reference to any other programming besides the three that are mentioned in the article (eliminating choice (B)), and it is too specific to be choice (A) or (D).

Practice Reading Comprehension Passages

In addition to reading comprehension, you should have identified that this article was about television and programming. There is a lot of vocabulary that can be extracted from this article that you can use when talking about television in general. These words include: audiencia, espectadores, ocio, publicidad, programación, cuota de pantalla, presentador, emitir, programa, escenario, teatro, and espectáculo, as well as the name of two television stations, Antena 3 and Telecinco. This information can be helpful to demonstrate your knowledge of Spanish culture. Looking at the questions, you could have also picked up on the word televidente. As you are making a list of vocabulary on any particular topic, remember to identify its function (verb, noun, adjective), and think about possible words in the same family (espectáculo, espectacular, espectador; presentador, presentar, presentación, and so on).

Finally, be sure to use the text to your advantage. Too often students make mistakes by not noticing the small details that can help them in their overall communication. For example, you should have noted that the word programa is masculine (line 11, ". . . versión del programa"), whereas the word programación is feminine. Although in this article there is no way to tell the gender of programación, later in the passage you will find the word "versión" preceded by una, which should be enough to tell you that programación is also a feminine noun, since both words end in -ión. Also, you should have identified that Antena 3 and Telecinco are television stations in Spain by the mention of two Spanish cities, Marbella (line 7) and Spain's capital, Madrid (line 13).

Reading Graphs, Tables, and Charts

You can expect to have three graphs, tables, and/or charts as part of the exam. The first will be in Section I, Part A, the second in the Print and Audio Texts (combined) portion of Section I, Part B, and lastly as part of the Section II, Task 2 (Argumentative Essay). In each case these graphs, tables, or charts will relate thematically to the article that precedes them and/or to the audio that follows. These require a slightly different approach than reading texts. In most cases, they make complex information easier to understand, but they can lead to confusion when they are misinterpreted. Below are some strategies you can use.

- Read the introduction and title of the graph, table, or chart.
- Read the labels on the graph, table, or chart, if applicable.
- Pay attention to any pattern printed on each section of a graph or pie chart, and use the key to understand what each pattern represents.
- Analyze the information gathered from the graph, table, or chart. Ask yourself what conclusions you can make from these and how they relate to the article seen beforehand and/or predict how they will relate to the audio that follows.

One of the more common mistakes students make when working with graphs, tables, or charts is to force a point of view that cannot be supported by the image. Often these graphics simply present information objectively and do not have a positive or negative point of view on the topic.

Bar Graphs

Bar graphs show the relationship between groups or different categories. When reading a bar graph, make sure to:

- Read the introduction and title.
- Read the label on each axis.
- Determine the value that each bar represents.
- Analyze the relationship between each bar in the graph and how they compare or contrast with each other.

Práctica: El siguiente gráfico presenta la principal actividad que realizan los usuarios de internet en México. Se basa en datos compilados por INFOTEC en 2018.

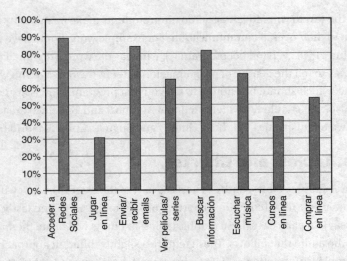

This graph presents data objectively, and there are several conclusions that can be made:

- Most people surveyed use the internet to access social media.
- The top reasons to use the internet is for communication and information rather than entertainment.
- It is apparent, since the combined percentages exceed 100%, that the people surveyed use the internet for more than one purpose, such as chatting with friends, shopping, and accessing music and movies.
- Fewer than half the people surveyed use the internet to play videogames or to take online courses.

Pie Charts

Pie charts show how different elements relate to a whole. Generally, the information presented in pie charts is measured with percentages, with the sum of the parts equal to 100 percent. A pie chart will be divided in sections with different colors and/or patterns with a key to indicate what each color and pattern means. When reading a pie chart, make sure to:

- Read the introduction and title.
- Read the label for each part of the pie.
- Understand what each part represents and how they relate to each other.
- Analyze each part in relation to the whole.

Práctica: El siguiente gráfico presenta el tipo de basura que se tira en la Patagonia, Argentina. Se basa en datos compilados por el gobierno de Argentina en 2018.

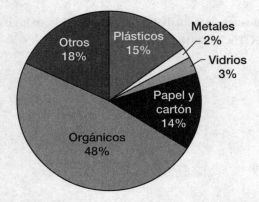

Like the previous bar graph, this pie chart presents information quite objectively. The main conclusion that can be drawn is that a higher percentage of trash thrown is organic, meaning that the original product came from a living being (plant, animal, and so on), while plastic trash is a distant third. It is unclear what "otros" may refer to, but we know what it is not (organic trash, plastic, paper, metal, or glass).

Tables

Unlike graphs and pie charts, tables list data about a specific subject. The data is lined up in columns and rows, with headings identifying each of the categories. When reading a table, you should:

- Read the introduction and title.
- Read the row and column headings.
- Determine the value of each of the numbers in the table (percentages, in tens, thousands, etc.).
- Read down from the left and then across to the right.

Práctica: La siguiente tabla presenta la tasa de abandono escolar prematuro de la población total de jóvenes entre 18 y 24 años. La información se basa en datos compilados por el Instituto Vasco de Estadística.

País	2013	2014	2015	2016	2017
Alemania	11,9	11,2	11,0	10,7	10,6
Francia	9,7	9,0	9,2	8,8	8,9
España	23,6	21,9	20,0	19,0	18,3
Italia	16,8	15,0	14,7	13,8	14,0
Reino Unido	12,4	11,8	10,8	11,2	10,6

As with the previous two graphs, this table presents data objectively. Several ideas that can be extracted from this table are the following:

- Of the five countries, France consistently has had the lowest dropout rates and Spain the highest.
- Both Italy and France experienced a slight increase in dropout rates between 2016 and 2017.
- Since 2013 and 2017, Spain had the biggest decrease in dropout rates.

Avoid Forcing Interpretation from Graphs, Tables, and Charts

As mentioned earlier, a common mistake is for students to force meaning or a point of view from the graph, table, or chart that cannot be supported by the image. Almost always, the information presented in tables, graphs, and charts will be objective and neutral. Avoid the temptation to suggest that these images are trying to present a particular point of view unless it is clear that this is what they are doing.

For example, the bar graph simply presents the types of activities that internet users do when using the internet. It never suggests that people prefer to use the internet to watch movies or listen to music, so making that claim would be incorrect.

Let's try another example with the pie chart. As mentioned earlier, the pie chart simply presents information about the type of trash that is thrown away. However, when we look at vidrio, glass, the percentage is quite low. Why is that? Do people in the region of Patagonia use less glass? Do they recycle glass more often than other products? We don't have enough information to answer these questions, so to make any of these claims would be an incorrect statement because it cannot be supported by the information in the chart.

Finally, the table presents dropout rates in several European countries between 2013 and 2017. One thing it does not show is why students dropped out, so one cannot make a statement as to why based solely on information from this table.

ANSWER SHEET
Reading Comprehension

Selección 1
1. Ⓐ Ⓑ Ⓒ Ⓓ
2. Ⓐ Ⓑ Ⓒ Ⓓ
3. Ⓐ Ⓑ Ⓒ Ⓓ
4. Ⓐ Ⓑ Ⓒ Ⓓ
5. Ⓐ Ⓑ Ⓒ Ⓓ
6. Ⓐ Ⓑ Ⓒ Ⓓ
7. Ⓐ Ⓑ Ⓒ Ⓓ

Selección 2
1. Ⓐ Ⓑ Ⓒ Ⓓ
2. Ⓐ Ⓑ Ⓒ Ⓓ
3. Ⓐ Ⓑ Ⓒ Ⓓ
4. Ⓐ Ⓑ Ⓒ Ⓓ
5. Ⓐ Ⓑ Ⓒ Ⓓ
6. Ⓐ Ⓑ Ⓒ Ⓓ
7. Ⓐ Ⓑ Ⓒ Ⓓ
8. Ⓐ Ⓑ Ⓒ Ⓓ
9. Ⓐ Ⓑ Ⓒ Ⓓ
10. Ⓐ Ⓑ Ⓒ Ⓓ
11. Ⓐ Ⓑ Ⓒ Ⓓ

Selección 3
1. Ⓐ Ⓑ Ⓒ Ⓓ
2. Ⓐ Ⓑ Ⓒ Ⓓ
3. Ⓐ Ⓑ Ⓒ Ⓓ
4. Ⓐ Ⓑ Ⓒ Ⓓ
5. Ⓐ Ⓑ Ⓒ Ⓓ

Selección 4
1. Ⓐ Ⓑ Ⓒ Ⓓ
2. Ⓐ Ⓑ Ⓒ Ⓓ
3. Ⓐ Ⓑ Ⓒ Ⓓ
4. Ⓐ Ⓑ Ⓒ Ⓓ
5. Ⓐ Ⓑ Ⓒ Ⓓ
6. Ⓐ Ⓑ Ⓒ Ⓓ
7. Ⓐ Ⓑ Ⓒ Ⓓ

Selección 5
1. Ⓐ Ⓑ Ⓒ Ⓓ
2. Ⓐ Ⓑ Ⓒ Ⓓ
3. Ⓐ Ⓑ Ⓒ Ⓓ
4. Ⓐ Ⓑ Ⓒ Ⓓ
5. Ⓐ Ⓑ Ⓒ Ⓓ
6. Ⓐ Ⓑ Ⓒ Ⓓ
7. Ⓐ Ⓑ Ⓒ Ⓓ

Selección 6
1. Ⓐ Ⓑ Ⓒ Ⓓ
2. Ⓐ Ⓑ Ⓒ Ⓓ
3. Ⓐ Ⓑ Ⓒ Ⓓ
4. Ⓐ Ⓑ Ⓒ Ⓓ
5. Ⓐ Ⓑ Ⓒ Ⓓ
6. Ⓐ Ⓑ Ⓒ Ⓓ
7. Ⓐ Ⓑ Ⓒ Ⓓ

Selección 7
1. Ⓐ Ⓑ Ⓒ Ⓓ
2. Ⓐ Ⓑ Ⓒ Ⓓ
3. Ⓐ Ⓑ Ⓒ Ⓓ
4. Ⓐ Ⓑ Ⓒ Ⓓ
5. Ⓐ Ⓑ Ⓒ Ⓓ
6. Ⓐ Ⓑ Ⓒ Ⓓ
7. Ⓐ Ⓑ Ⓒ Ⓓ
8. Ⓐ Ⓑ Ⓒ Ⓓ
9. Ⓐ Ⓑ Ⓒ Ⓓ
10. Ⓐ Ⓑ Ⓒ Ⓓ
11. Ⓐ Ⓑ Ⓒ Ⓓ

Selección 8
1. Ⓐ Ⓑ Ⓒ Ⓓ
2. Ⓐ Ⓑ Ⓒ Ⓓ
3. Ⓐ Ⓑ Ⓒ Ⓓ
4. Ⓐ Ⓑ Ⓒ Ⓓ
5. Ⓐ Ⓑ Ⓒ Ⓓ
6. Ⓐ Ⓑ Ⓒ Ⓓ
7. Ⓐ Ⓑ Ⓒ Ⓓ

Selección 9
1. Ⓐ Ⓑ Ⓒ Ⓓ
2. Ⓐ Ⓑ Ⓒ Ⓓ
3. Ⓐ Ⓑ Ⓒ Ⓓ
4. Ⓐ Ⓑ Ⓒ Ⓓ
5. Ⓐ Ⓑ Ⓒ Ⓓ
6. Ⓐ Ⓑ Ⓒ Ⓓ
7. Ⓐ Ⓑ Ⓒ Ⓓ

Selección 10
1. Ⓐ Ⓑ Ⓒ Ⓓ
2. Ⓐ Ⓑ Ⓒ Ⓓ
3. Ⓐ Ⓑ Ⓒ Ⓓ
4. Ⓐ Ⓑ Ⓒ Ⓓ
5. Ⓐ Ⓑ Ⓒ Ⓓ

Selección 11
1. Ⓐ Ⓑ Ⓒ Ⓓ
2. Ⓐ Ⓑ Ⓒ Ⓓ
3. Ⓐ Ⓑ Ⓒ Ⓓ
4. Ⓐ Ⓑ Ⓒ Ⓓ
5. Ⓐ Ⓑ Ⓒ Ⓓ

Selección 12
1. Ⓐ Ⓑ Ⓒ Ⓓ
2. Ⓐ Ⓑ Ⓒ Ⓓ
3. Ⓐ Ⓑ Ⓒ Ⓓ
4. Ⓐ Ⓑ Ⓒ Ⓓ
5. Ⓐ Ⓑ Ⓒ Ⓓ
6. Ⓐ Ⓑ Ⓒ Ⓓ
7. Ⓐ Ⓑ Ⓒ Ⓓ

Selección 13
1. Ⓐ Ⓑ Ⓒ Ⓓ
2. Ⓐ Ⓑ Ⓒ Ⓓ
3. Ⓐ Ⓑ Ⓒ Ⓓ
4. Ⓐ Ⓑ Ⓒ Ⓓ
5. Ⓐ Ⓑ Ⓒ Ⓓ
6. Ⓐ Ⓑ Ⓒ Ⓓ
7. Ⓐ Ⓑ Ⓒ Ⓓ

Selección 14

1. Ⓐ Ⓑ Ⓒ Ⓓ
2. Ⓐ Ⓑ Ⓒ Ⓓ
3. Ⓐ Ⓑ Ⓒ Ⓓ
4. Ⓐ Ⓑ Ⓒ Ⓓ
5. Ⓐ Ⓑ Ⓒ Ⓓ
6. Ⓐ Ⓑ Ⓒ Ⓓ
7. Ⓐ Ⓑ Ⓒ Ⓓ

Selección 15

1. Ⓐ Ⓑ Ⓒ Ⓓ
2. Ⓐ Ⓑ Ⓒ Ⓓ
3. Ⓐ Ⓑ Ⓒ Ⓓ
4. Ⓐ Ⓑ Ⓒ Ⓓ
5. Ⓐ Ⓑ Ⓒ Ⓓ
6. Ⓐ Ⓑ Ⓒ Ⓓ
7. Ⓐ Ⓑ Ⓒ Ⓓ

Selección 16

1. Ⓐ Ⓑ Ⓒ Ⓓ
2. Ⓐ Ⓑ Ⓒ Ⓓ
3. Ⓐ Ⓑ Ⓒ Ⓓ
4. Ⓐ Ⓑ Ⓒ Ⓓ
5. Ⓐ Ⓑ Ⓒ Ⓓ
6. Ⓐ Ⓑ Ⓒ Ⓓ
7. Ⓐ Ⓑ Ⓒ Ⓓ
8. Ⓐ Ⓑ Ⓒ Ⓓ
9. Ⓐ Ⓑ Ⓒ Ⓓ
10. Ⓐ Ⓑ Ⓒ Ⓓ
11. Ⓐ Ⓑ Ⓒ Ⓓ

Selección 17

1. Ⓐ Ⓑ Ⓒ Ⓓ
2. Ⓐ Ⓑ Ⓒ Ⓓ
3. Ⓐ Ⓑ Ⓒ Ⓓ
4. Ⓐ Ⓑ Ⓒ Ⓓ
5. Ⓐ Ⓑ Ⓒ Ⓓ
6. Ⓐ Ⓑ Ⓒ Ⓓ
7. Ⓐ Ⓑ Ⓒ Ⓓ

Selección 18

1. Ⓐ Ⓑ Ⓒ Ⓓ
2. Ⓐ Ⓑ Ⓒ Ⓓ
3. Ⓐ Ⓑ Ⓒ Ⓓ
4. Ⓐ Ⓑ Ⓒ Ⓓ
5. Ⓐ Ⓑ Ⓒ Ⓓ

Selección 19

1. Ⓐ Ⓑ Ⓒ Ⓓ
2. Ⓐ Ⓑ Ⓒ Ⓓ
3. Ⓐ Ⓑ Ⓒ Ⓓ
4. Ⓐ Ⓑ Ⓒ Ⓓ
5. Ⓐ Ⓑ Ⓒ Ⓓ
6. Ⓐ Ⓑ Ⓒ Ⓓ
7. Ⓐ Ⓑ Ⓒ Ⓓ

Selección 20

1. Ⓐ Ⓑ Ⓒ Ⓓ
2. Ⓐ Ⓑ Ⓒ Ⓓ
3. Ⓐ Ⓑ Ⓒ Ⓓ
4. Ⓐ Ⓑ Ⓒ Ⓓ
5. Ⓐ Ⓑ Ⓒ Ⓓ
6. Ⓐ Ⓑ Ⓒ Ⓓ
7. Ⓐ Ⓑ Ⓒ Ⓓ

Selección 21

1. Ⓐ Ⓑ Ⓒ Ⓓ
2. Ⓐ Ⓑ Ⓒ Ⓓ
3. Ⓐ Ⓑ Ⓒ Ⓓ
4. Ⓐ Ⓑ Ⓒ Ⓓ
5. Ⓐ Ⓑ Ⓒ Ⓓ
6. Ⓐ Ⓑ Ⓒ Ⓓ
7. Ⓐ Ⓑ Ⓒ Ⓓ
8. Ⓐ Ⓑ Ⓒ Ⓓ
9. Ⓐ Ⓑ Ⓒ Ⓓ
10. Ⓐ Ⓑ Ⓒ Ⓓ
11. Ⓐ Ⓑ Ⓒ Ⓓ

Selección 22

1. Ⓐ Ⓑ Ⓒ Ⓓ
2. Ⓐ Ⓑ Ⓒ Ⓓ
3. Ⓐ Ⓑ Ⓒ Ⓓ
4. Ⓐ Ⓑ Ⓒ Ⓓ
5. Ⓐ Ⓑ Ⓒ Ⓓ
6. Ⓐ Ⓑ Ⓒ Ⓓ
7. Ⓐ Ⓑ Ⓒ Ⓓ

Selección 23

1. Ⓐ Ⓑ Ⓒ Ⓓ
2. Ⓐ Ⓑ Ⓒ Ⓓ
3. Ⓐ Ⓑ Ⓒ Ⓓ
4. Ⓐ Ⓑ Ⓒ Ⓓ
5. Ⓐ Ⓑ Ⓒ Ⓓ
6. Ⓐ Ⓑ Ⓒ Ⓓ
7. Ⓐ Ⓑ Ⓒ Ⓓ
8. Ⓐ Ⓑ Ⓒ Ⓓ

Selección 24

1. Ⓐ Ⓑ Ⓒ Ⓓ
2. Ⓐ Ⓑ Ⓒ Ⓓ
3. Ⓐ Ⓑ Ⓒ Ⓓ
4. Ⓐ Ⓑ Ⓒ Ⓓ
5. Ⓐ Ⓑ Ⓒ Ⓓ
6. Ⓐ Ⓑ Ⓒ Ⓓ
7. Ⓐ Ⓑ Ⓒ Ⓓ

Section I, Part A

To briefly review the steps for reading:

When reading print texts

1. Read the introduction
2. Understand the format of the text
3. As you read
   a. underline key words that will remind you of the main ideas being presented
   b. identify people, places, and events
   c. use context clues to infer the meaning of unfamiliar words that you feel are important, and
   d. make note of any cultural elements (products, practices, or perspectives).

4. After you finish, evaluate the information to
   a. determine the tone and mood,
   b. determine the intended reader, and
   c. draw conclusions and make predictions based on the text.

When reading graphs, charts, or tables

1. Read the introduction
2. Read tables and graphs from the left column and move across
3. Remember that most graphics present information objectively, so don't try to force an interpretation that cannot be supported by the data

When answering questions

1. Carefully read the question and options
2. Select the option whose idea best reflects the information presented in the text

Finally, after most reading activities you will find a "Cultural Awareness" section that highlights the cultural product(s), practice(s), and perspective(s) mentioned in the texts. This is an opportunity to reflect on these aspects of culture in different countries, and how they are similar to or differ from those in your own community. This reflection is important to prepare for Task 4 (Cultural Comparison). If you are not aware of the practices, products, and perspectives in your own community on these topics, it is an opportunity for you to research them.

Selección 1

Tema curricular: Las familias y las comunidades

El siguiente informe trata de una exposición en España sobre el uso de las redes sociales. Fue publicado por la Oficina de Comunicaciones del Gobierno de Cantabria, España, en febrero de 2022.

Pablo OZuloaga señala la importancia de la exposición de AMAT para informar a los jóvenes sobre los riesgos de determinadas conductas en las redes sociales

El vicepresidente y consejero de Universidades, Igualdad, Cultura y Deporte, Pablo Zuloaga, ha señalado la importancia de la exposición de la asociación AMAT, instalada en la plaza Ángel Menéndez de Torrelavega, para informar y dar a conocer a los jóvenes y a toda la sociedad los riesgos que existen en *Línea* las redes sociales como consecuencia de determinadas conductas y actitudes.

(5) Tanto los hijos como los padres, ha indicado, deben tomar conciencia de los riesgos que existen detrás de un 'like' y 'me gusta' que se realiza a una persona desconocida o ante la petición de determinados comportamientos poco razonables.

En la presentación de este proyecto de la asociación AMAT sobre relaciones afectivas en jóvenes a través de medios digitales y redes sociales, Zuloaga ha asegurado que los jóvenes de Cantabria van a disponer *(10)* con esta muestra de herramientas para detectar manipulaciones y los riesgos en las redes sociales, garantizando un uso seguro y fiable de internet.

Junto al vicepresidente, en la presentación de la exposición han participado la directora general de Juventud, Alicia Renedo; el alcalde de Torrelavega, Javier López Estrada; la concejala de Juventud, Igualdad y Festejos, Patricia Portilla; y Alberto Marchante, gerente de la asociación AMAT.

(15) El alcalde de Torrelavega ha puesto en valor el trabajo de la asociación AMAT para hacer frente a los riesgos y adicciones a los que se enfrenta la sociedad actual, sobre todo vinculados a las nuevas tecnologías. En este sentido, ha considerado importante trasladar a los jóvenes cuáles son estos riesgos, así como sus causas y consecuencias, para poder hacer frente a los problemas que pueden derivarse de estas situaciones.

(20) Alberto Marchante ha destacado la importancia de este proyecto para informar y dar a conocer los riesgos y las adicciones que pueden estar presentes detrás del uso de dispositivos móviles, como la búsqueda de aprobación social, la realización de prácticas socioafectivas o el desconocimiento que se puede tener de la persona que se encuentra detrás de la pantalla.

Sobre la exposición, que permanecerá en Torrelavega durante la primera quincena de diciembre, ha *(25)* indicado que tendrá un carácter itinerante y que pretende acercarse a los centros educativos que lo demanden para trabajar en talleres los distintos contenidos.

La muestra se compone de cuatro tótems que incluyen paneles informativos muy visuales con contenidos dirigidos a difundir los tipos de conducta y riesgos que existen hoy en día en las relaciones afectivas y en especial con los jóvenes, con prácticas como subida de contenidos a redes para conseguir más 'me *(25)* gusta', cibercontrol de la pareja o desaparecer sin dejar rastro.

1. ¿Cuál es el tema central de este texto?

(A) La importancia de establecer límites en el uso de las redes sociales para los jóvenes
(B) Los peligros asociados al uso irresponsable de las redes sociales
(C) Las influencias de las redes sociales en la autoestima de los adolescentes
(D) Unas estrategias para aumentar la popularidad en línea

2. ¿Cuál es el público objetivo de este texto?

(A) Profesionales de la industria tecnológica interesados en la seguridad en línea
(B) Psicólogos y consejeros especializados en salud mental de los jóvenes
(C) Educadores que buscan desarrollar programas de concienciación sobre comportamientos en línea
(D) Padres y adolescentes preocupados por los riesgos del comportamiento en línea

3. ¿Cuál es uno de los objetivos de la exposición?

    (A) Promover la desconexión total de las redes sociales
    (B) Concienciar sobre los peligros y adicciones relacionados con el uso de tecnologías digitales
    (C) Crear conciencia sobre la importancia de la ciberseguridad en las transacciones en línea
    (D) Impulsar prácticas de relaciones afectivas más tradicionales

4. ¿Qué prácticas se mencionan como inseguras, según el texto?

    (A) Compartir intereses comunes y actividades recreativas
    (B) Realizar actividades físicas juntos y mantener una comunicación abierta
    (C) Subir contenidos a redes para obtener más 'me gusta'
    (D) Enviar menajes de apoyo a través de las redes sociales.

5. ¿Qué significa la palabra "cibercontrol" (línea 33) en el contexto que se usa en el texto?

    (A) Controlar las actividades en línea de alguien
    (B) Controlar su propio uso de tecnología
    (C) Controlar la seguridad cibernética en redes sociales
    (D) Controlar la transmisión de datos a través de la web

6. Considerando el propósito de la exposición, ¿qué tipo de actividades podrían llevarse a cabo en los talleres que se mencionan?

    (A) Enseñanza de técnicas de meditación para manejar el estrés
    (B) El impacto psicológico de las redes sociales y estrategias para mantener la salud mental
    (C) Resolución de conflictos y habilidades de comunicación efectiva
    (D) Exploración de la historia y evolución de las redes sociales

7. Necesitas más información relevante a este evento. ¿Cuál de las siguientes opciones sería más apropiada para formular?

    (A) ¿Cuál es el horario exacto de la exposición?
    (B) ¿Cómo puedo participar en otros eventos culturales que patrocina el ayuntamiento?
    (C) ¿Qué restaurantes se encuentran cerca de la plaza Ángel Menéndez?
    (D) ¿Quién crees es el bloguero más influyente y qué prácticas recomienda él?

Cultural Awareness

Cultural practice: The article presents a common practice in Spain: paying under the table in cash for a number of products and services and thus avoid paying taxes on the product or service.

Cultural perspective: This article is also an opinion piece, and the author clearly feels that this continued practice will hinder Spaniards from reaching global economic prosperity.

Are the practice and/or perspective mentioned in this article similar to or different from what you have observed in your own community?

Selección 2

Tema curricular: Los desafíos mundiales

Fuente 1: El siguiente artículo presenta información sobre los esfuerzos en una comunidad para maximizar su seguridad alimentaria frente al cambio climático. Fue escrito por Muy Waso y publicado en Global Voices en agosto de 2023.

'Cosechar agua': Mujeres guaraníes del Chaco boliviano lideran producción alimentaria como respuesta al cambio climático

Cosechar agua

Ir al mercado, comprar tus alimentos y preparar tus comidas no son tareas sencillas. Pero es aún más complicado si vives en el Chaco boliviano: sin agua, a casi 40 grados de temperatura y lejos de los centros urbanos.

Línea

(5) Ese es el contexto que amenaza la seguridad alimentaria de los habitantes del Chaco boliviano, en especial la de sus comunidades indígenas. Durante los últimos años, el chaco boliviano experimentó niveles críticos de sequía.

El Gran Chaco es una región geográfica ubicada en América del Sur, que se extiende por partes de varios países, incluyendo Argentina, Paraguay, Bolivia y Brasil. Es una de las áreas de mayor biodi-

(10) versidad de la región y está caracterizada por su ecosistema único. Varias comunidades indígenas habitan esta región, como los Guarayos, Ayoreos, Chiquitanos y Guaraníes.

El cambio climático está azotando al Gran Chaco, que ha visto incendios forestales devastadores en los últimos años y sequías severas que ponen en riesgo la seguridad hídrica y alimenticia de la población. Como alternativa, en la comunidad de Timboy Tiguasú, durante el último año se implementó un

(15) modelo de producción sostenible de alimentos. Se trata de una respuesta local a la crisis climática, reflejada en una baja producción agrícola. Timboy Tiguasú es una comunidad guaraní al sur de Bolivia, en el Departamento de Tarija.

Más de 120 mujeres guaraníes de esta comunidad lideraron la producción orgánica de alimentos para tener dietas más saludables y nutritivas. Ahora, ellas trabajan a diario en sus huertos, cosechan ocho

(20) tipos de cultivos hortícolas, los echan en sus ollas y los sirven en sus platos.

El manejo de los cultivos tuvo énfasis en los policultivos con sentido familiar y resiliente. Algo así como una ensalada de hortalizas en las parcelas de tierra. Una fila con una variedad de verduras y otra con otro tipo.

Esta distribución de los cultivos logró que el 87% de las plagas y enfermedades sean controladas y

(25) prescindir de los pesticidas.

La cosecha de agua, una aliada de la agricultura familiar

Además, esta propuesta de Modelo Productivo Agrícola contó con el manejo eficiente del agua. Un proceso que implica la cosecha, almacenamiento y distribución de agua de lluvia por temporadas. Se excavaron zanjas para recolectar agua de la lluvia, luego se almacenó y se distribuyó en sistemas de riego por aspersión. Este sistema de riego consiste en aplicar el agua al suelo por medio de tuberías,

(30) simulando la lluvia.

"En la comunidad no tenían acceso a las verduras para preparar sus alimentos. Con este proyecto logramos demostrar que a través de un modelo de producción agroecológica se puede cosechar alimentos sanos en el Chaco y frente a la crisis climática", cuenta Ricardo Paita, responsable del proyecto y la organización Centro de Estudios Regionales para el Desarrollo de Tarija (CERDET).

(35) La acción climática puede ser impulsada desde diferentes experiencias de producción, distribución y consumo alternativo de alimentos saludables y sostenibles frente a los efectos del cambio climático. Actualmente, unidades educativas y otras comunidades indígenas replican este modelo productivo y ponen sobre la mesa la necesidad de producir alimentos sin pesticidas y de manera sostenible.

Fuente 2: La siguiente tabla presenta la huella hídrica de los alimentos, y representa la cantidad de agua requerida para la producción de un kilogramo de los alimentos seleccionados (en litros).

Carne vacuna	15.400
Carne de oveja / cabra	8.800
Legumbres	4.100
Cereales	1.600
Carne de cerdo	6.000
Carne de pollo	4.300
Frutas	960
Hortalizas	320

1. ¿Cuál es la idea principal del texto?

   (A) Una comunidad de Timboy Tiguasú implementa un modelo agrícola sostenible.
   (B) El cambio climático amenaza la seguridad alimentaria en el Gran Chaco.
   (C) Unas comunidades indígenas ignoran la crisis climática y continúan con prácticas agrícolas tradicionales.
   (D) Mujeres guaraníes lideran producción orgánica sin pesticidas.

2. Según el texto, ¿qué problema enfrentan las comunidades del Chaco boliviano?

   (A) Pérdida de biodiversidad debido al cambio climático
   (B) Falta de acceso a mercados donde comprar alimentos
   (C) Desafíos en la preservación de su cultura
   (D) Escasez de agua, agravada por el cambio climático

3. ¿Qué técnica de cultivo se destaca como una alternativa para controlar las plagas y enfermedades en los cultivos?

   (A) El uso de pesticidas químicos
   (B) El cultivo simultáneo de diversas especies vegetales
   (C) Implementación de sistemas de riego tradicionales
   (D) Cultivo de plantas genéticamente modificadas

4. ¿Qué importancia tiene la cosecha de agua?

   (A) Ayuda a controlar plagas y enfermedades.
   (B) Aumenta la producción de cultivos.
   (C) Reduce el uso de pesticidas.
   (D) Garantiza el acceso al agua en épocas de sequía.

5. Según el contexto del texto, ¿qué significa «azotando» en la frase "El cambio climático está azotando al Gran Chaco" (línea 11)?

   (A) Abandonando
   (B) Desarrollando poco a poco
   (C) Afectando severamente
   (D) Ignorando por completo

6. ¿Qué significa "policultivos con sentido familiar y resiliente" (línea 22) en el contexto del texto?

   (A) Cultivar varias especies de plantas en una parcela pequeña

   (B) Cultivar especies que se adaptan bien a las condiciones y que son sostenibles

   (C) Cultivar plantas que son familiares para la comunidad local

   (D) Utilizar técnicas agrícolas basadas en conocimientos familiares

7. ¿Qué importancia tendría la replicación de este modelo en otras comunidades?

   (A) Ayudaría a combatir la sequía.

   (B) Contribuiría a la seguridad alimentaria.

   (C) Permitiría aumentar la producción de alimentos.

   (D) Promovería la producción con pesticidas.

8. ¿Qué información presenta la tabla?

   (A) La eficiencia en el uso de agua para la producción de alimentos

   (B) La cantidad de agua necesaria para la producción de varios alimentos

   (C) Los alimentos que más impactan la escasez de agua

   (D) El impacto que tiene la disponibilidad de agua en la elección de alimentos y prácticas agrícolas

9. ¿Qué representan los números en la tabla?

   (A) La cantidad de agua necesaria para producir un kilogramo de diferentes tipos de alimentos

   (B) Los kilogramos de diferentes tipos de alimentos que se pueden producir por litro de agua

   (C) Los kilogramos de agua necesarios para la producción de un litro de alimento

   (D) Los litros de agua que producen diferentes tipos de alimentos

10. ¿Cuál de las siguientes declaraciones se puede comprobar con información del artículo y la tabla?

   (A) Por su alta huella hídrica, no hay una cultura de ganadería en el Gran Chaco.

   (B) La comunidad de Timboy Tiguasú cultiva hortalizas porque tienen una menor huella hídrica.

   (C) Las comunidades del Chaco prefieren comer verduras que carne.

   (D) Las mujeres guaraníes no cultivan cereales o legumbres por escasez de agua.

11. Para obtener más información sobre los temas presentados en el artículo y la tabla, ¿cuál de las siguientes opciones sería más útil?

   (A) Un informe sobre cómo maximizar la seguridad alimentaria

   (B) Un artículo sobre técnicas de riego eficientes en la agricultura

   (C) Un libro de recetas que únicamente usan ingredientes con baja huella hídrica

   (D) Un estudio científico sobre la biodiversidad en las regiones afectadas por sequías

---

Cultural Awareness

Cultural practice: The article presents a particular practice in Bolivia to maximize the production of crops during severe droughts. Do you know of a similar practice in your own community?

Selección 3

Tema curricular: La belleza y la estética

Introducción: El siguiente anuncio es para un evento de baile en Lima, Perú. Fue publicado en la página web del Ministerio de Cultura de Perú.

MUNICIPALIDAD DE LIMA TE INVITA AL XIII CONCURSO NACIONAL DE MARINERA LIMEÑA 2018

Con el propósito de preservar y revalorar las expresiones culturales de nuestra ciudad, la Gerencia de Cultura de la Municipalidad de Lima, organiza el XIII Concurso Nacional de Marinera Limeña 2018, el domingo 22 de julio en el Anfiteatro Nicomedes Santa Cruz del Parque de la Exposición.

Línea

(5)   Este evento reunirá a más de 100 parejas de bailarines, de reconocidas escuelas de bailes de nuestro país, en seis distintas categorías: INFANTIL (8 a 11 años), PREJUVENILES (12 a 17 años), JUVENILES (18 a 21 años), ADULTOS (22 a 34 años), PREMAYORES (35 a 49 años) y MAYORES (50 años a más), quienes se disputarán premios que van desde los S/ 500 hasta S/ 5,000 soles, además de escapulario, bandas, trofeo y diplomas de honor.

Asimismo, se presentará la competencia de la categoría Campeón de Campeones, en la que partici-

(10)   parán todos los campeones de los concursos de Marinera Limeña realizados por la Municipalidad de Lima, excepto los ganadores de los dos últimos años de la categoría Campeón de Campeones.

Esta actividad se realiza con el fin de motivar a la población y que se encuentre con sus raíces y manifestaciones populares como lo son los bailes costumbristas y típicos del Perú, los mismos que constituyen el patrimonio inmaterial de la Humanidad, fortaleciendo y hacia la identidad nacional.

(15)   **Lugar:** Anfiteatro Nicomedes Santa Cruz, Parque de la Exposición

Dirección: Av. 28 de Julio, Cercado de Lima

Fecha: 22 de julio

Hora: 9:00 am

Ingreso libre

1. **¿A quiénes se dirige principalmente este anuncio?**

   (A) A estudiantes de baile

   (B) A bailarines profesionales

   (C) Al público limeño

   (D) A ganadores de concursos anteriores

2. ¿Cuál es la meta principal de este evento?

   (A) Seleccionar a los mejores bailarines del país

   (B) Conservar y apreciar un aspecto importante de la cultura peruana

   (C) Motivar a los espectadores a participar en el baile

   (D) Crear una identidad nacional

3. ¿Qué pueden ganar los concursantes?

   (A) Un premio monetario

   (B) Un trofeo o diploma

   (C) La oportunidad de competir en la categoría Campeón de Campeones en el futuro

   (D) La oportunidad de ganar cualquiera de làs opciones mencionadas en opciones A, B y C

4. ¿Quiénes pueden competir en la categoría Campeón de Campeones?

   (A) Los campeones de cualquier concurso de baile anterior que nunca han ganado esta categoría

   (B) Los que han ganado su categoría y que también han participado en esta categoría en años recientes

   (C) Los que han ganado un concurso del mismo patrocinador y que no han ganado esta categoría recientemente

   (D) Únicamente los campeones de categoría de este concurso que aún no han ganado esta categoría

5. Si quisieras más información de este evento, ¿cuál de las siguientes preguntas sería más apropiada para formular?

   (A) No veo la hora de este evento. ¿Cuál es la parada de autobús más cercana?

   (B) Me gustaría llevar a mi familia. ¿Cuánto nos costaría asistir?

   (C) Mi hija es bailarina y vivimos justo al lado del teatro. ¿Puede ella participar también?

   (D) Quiero inscribirme en un curso de baile para mantenerme en forma. ¿Qué tipo de baile me convendría más?

Cultural Awareness

Cultural product: This advertisement promotes an event in Lima, Perú, whose purpose is to celebrate a typical Peruvian dance, the *baile marinera*.

Cultural perspective: This advertisement also highlights the importance of preserving and appreciating traditional dances in Perú.

Does your community sponsor events similar to the one mentioned in this advertisement?

Selección 4

Tema curricular: Las familias y las comunidades

En la siguiente carta, Pablo le escribe a su amigo de una fiesta que experimentó cuando estuvo en México.

Querido Javier,

Espero que todo te vaya bien. Acabo de pasar unas semanas en México para celebrar el día de los Reyes Magos con mis tíos y quería contarte de cómo me fue. Me divertí un montón, especialmente
Línea disfrutando de la rosca de Reyes. No sé si la has probado, pero es absolutamente deliciosa.

(5)   La rosca de Reyes es un bizcocho fino que contiene en promedio tres figuras de plástico en forma de niño y que simbolizan al hijo de Dios. Según me contó mi tía, es una tradición que vino de España en los primeros años del Virreinato y formó parte de las festividades de año nuevo para recordar la llegada a Jerusalén de los Reyes Magos. Desde entonces la rosca de Reyes es el centro de atención de la fiesta de cada seis de enero por ser una de las tradiciones más antiguas de la iglesia católica que
(10)   recuerda este evento. Esto es muy distinto de lo que hacemos en Estados Unidos, donde la celebración es típicamente el veinticinco de diciembre.

Según la religión católica, quién encuentre la figura deberá vestir y presentar al niño Dios en la iglesia durante la fiesta del Día de la Candelaria el 2 de febrero para celebrar los 40 días de su nacimiento. Mi hermano la encontró, pero se la dio a nuestro primo para que él lo entregara, dado que ya había-
(15)   mos vuelto a casa. Mi tío nos dijo que desde la Edad Media las familias españolas acostumbraban a servir una merienda en la cual se partía la rosca de Reyes y que unos historiadores aseguran de que se trata de una costumbre romana que tomó la iglesia católica y la unió a la Navidad.

Los comerciantes aprovechan esta ocasión para incrementar sus ganancias mediante la venta de roscas de todos tamaños, pero mi tía nos la preparó y te aseguro que la de mi tía es la mejor rosca que
(20)   hayas comido jamás. Ella la elaboró cuidadosamente con harina, azúcar, mantequilla y huevos hasta tener una pasta fina y después la puso en un molde y la adornó con trozos de fruta seca. Te aseguro que no has comido mejor bizcocho en tu vida.

Aunque tuvimos que volver a casa, la festividad continúa hasta el Día de la Candelaria, cuando las familias se reúnen nuevamente para celebrar la presentación del niño Dios en la iglesia. En ese
(25)   momento se preparan y se comen tamales verdes, rojos y de dulce acompañado con atole de maíz. ¡Cuánto me encantaría estar de nuevo allí para gozar de ellos! Pero mi tía me dijo que esta tradición ha perdurado generaciones y que seguramente podré disfrutar de ella en el futuro.

Bueno, me despido de ti. Lo he pasado súper bien con mis tíos, y espero que un día tengas también la oportunidad de experimentar esta fiesta tan bonita. Cuídate y nos veremos en la escuela.

(30)   Un abrazo,
Pablo

---

1. ¿Qué es una rosca de Reyes?

    (A) Es una figura pequeña que se presenta a la iglesia el 6 de enero.
    (B) Es un tipo de postre con pequeñas figuras escondidas adentro.
    (C) Es un tipo de regalo traído por los Reyes Magos.
    (D) Es una fiesta que tiene la familia durante el mes de enero.

2. ¿Cuándo se celebra esta tradición?

   (A) El veinticinco de diciembre
   (B) El seis de enero
   (C) El dos de febrero
   (D) Cuarenta días después del dos de febrero

3. ¿En qué consiste la costumbre?

   (A) Los miembros de la familia se visten con trajes romanos para ir a la iglesia.
   (B) Todos compran regalos para presentar al niño Jesús el Día de la Candelaria.
   (C) Todos compran o preparan una rosca para la fiesta en casa.
   (D) Se celebra el Día de los Reyes Magos visitando la iglesia con comida especial.

4. ¿Qué tiene que hacer el que encuentra la figura del niño?

   (A) Tiene que vestirse con traje romano para ir a la iglesia.
   (B) Tiene que preparar la fiesta para el Día de la Candelaria.
   (C) Tiene que llevarla a Belén.
   (D) Tiene que presentarse a la iglesia con la figura.

5. ¿De dónde procede la tradición de la rosca?

   (A) Tiene raíces en la época colonial de México.
   (B) Empezó con el Nacimiento.
   (C) Tiene raíces en las costumbres de la iglesia católica medieval.
   (D) Los romanos empezaron la costumbre con una fiesta pagana.

6. ¿Qué permite esta costumbre?

   (A) Que toda la familia se reúna para ayudar a los comerciantes.
   (B) Que los comerciantes disfruten de un descanso de su negocio.
   (C) Que la iglesia estreche las relaciones con la comunidad comercial.
   (D) Que los niños se sientan parte de la comunidad religiosa.

7. ¿Por qué se molesta Pablo al fin de la carta?

   (A) Quiere poder entregar el niño en la iglesia.
   (B) No quiere perderse otra cena maravillosa.
   (C) No se va a repetir esta celebración por unos años.
   (D) No quiere volver a las clases.

Comparación cultural

Cultural Awareness

Cultural product: The article presents the *rosca de Reyes*, a dish that is typical of the Christmas season in Mexico.

Cultural practice: The article also presents a number of religious and family activities that are performed during the Christmas season.

How are the products and practices similar to or different from those in your own community? Hint: if you are not familiar with *King Cake*, you may want to look it up.

Selección 5

Tema curricular: La vida contemporánea

El siguiente fragmento del libro Corazón: Diario de un niño, de Edmundo de Amacis, relata un evento que experimentó el narrador con un joven obrero.

A las cuatro merendamos juntos, pan y pasas, sentados en el sofá, y cuando nos levantamos, no sé por qué, mi padre no quiso que limpiara el espaldar que el albañilito había manchado de blanco con su chaqueta; me detuvo la mano y lo limpió después sin que lo viéramos. Jugando, al albañilito se le cayó
Línea   un botón de la cazadora, y mi madre se le cosió; él se puso encarnado, y la veía coser; muy admirado y
(5)   confuso, no atreviéndose ni a respirar. Después le enseñé el álbum de caricaturas, y él, sin darse cuenta, imitaba los gestos de aquellas caras, tan bien, que hasta mi padre se reía. Estaba tan contento cuando se fue, que se olvidó de ponerse al andrajoso sombrero, y al llegar a la puerta de la escalera, para manifestarme su gratitud, me hacía otra vez la gracia de poner el hocico de liebre.

    —¿Sabes, hijo mío, por qué no quise que limpiara el sofá? Porque limpiarle mientras tu compa-
(10)   ñero lo veía era casi hacerle una reconvención por haberlo ensuciado. Y esto no estaba bien: en primer lugar, porque no lo había hecho de intento, y en segundo lugar, porque le había manchado con ropa de su padre, que se la había enyesado trabajando; y lo que se mancha trabajando no ensucia; es polvo, cal, barniz, todo lo que quieras, pero no suciedad. El trabajo no ensucia. No digas nunca de un obrero que sale de su trabajo: "Va sucio." Debes decir: "Tiene en su ropa las señales, las huellas del trabajo."
(15)   Recuérdalo. Quiero mucho al albañilito: primero, porque es compañero tuyo, y además, porque es hijo de un obrero. —Tu padre.

1. ¿De qué trata esta selección?

   (A) De la conducta apropiada de un anfitrión
   (B) De los modos de mantenerse limpio en casa
   (C) De la conducta apropiada de un huésped
   (D) De los modos de disciplinar a un hijo

2. Al levantarse del sofá, ¿qué le molestaba al hijo?

   (A) Que la ropa del visitante estaba sucia
   (B) Que se vieron algunas huellas del trabajo en el sofá
   (C) Que en la chaqueta del albañilito faltaba un botón
   (D) Que la chaqueta mostraba señales del trabajo

3. ¿Cómo se sentía el albañilito cuando observó a la mamá reparando la ropa?

   (A) Estaba muy triste.
   (B) Se avergonzó.
   (C) Se enojó.
   (D) Se arrepintió.

4. En la línea 15, ¿qué quiere decir ". . . lo que se mancha trabajando no ensucia"?

   (A) Indica que no puede ensuciarse trabajando.
   (B) Significa que el padre no vio que la chaqueta estaba sucia.
   (C) Significa que trabajar no es una desgracia.
   (D) Quiere decir que el padre se sentía superior a los obreros.

5. ¿Por qué no quería el papá que su hijo limpiara el sofá de inmediato?

   (A) No quería que el albañilito viera a su hijo trabajando.
   (B) Quería que la madre lo hiciera.
   (C) Quería que el albañilito viera lo que había hecho.
   (D) No quería parecer descortés al invitado.

6. ¿Qué determina la diferencia entre el hijo y el albañilito?

   (A) Los aspectos socio-económicos de los dos
   (B) El nivel de formación educativa de los dos
   (C) Las características personales de los dos
   (D) La edad de los dos

7. ¿Cómo es la relación entre el papá y el hijo?

   (A) Parece que el padre es muy exigente.
   (B) Parece que los dos gozan de relaciones muy estrechas.
   (C) Parece que el chico no le hace mucho caso al padre.
   (D) El chico parece ser muy mimado por su padre.

Cultural Awareness

Cultural perspective: In this fragment, the mother and father demonstrate the right conduct of being a good host, and the father takes the time to explain this importance to his son.

How is the perspective presented in this text similar to or different from your own community?

Selección 6

Tema curricular: Los desafíos mundiales

En la siguiente carta, Susana, una joven española, le cuenta a su amiga una preocupación que ella tiene.

Querida Susana,

Ya se están aproximando las vacaciones de verano, y no puedo decirte cuánto me alegra poder descansar un poco. Las clases han ido bien, pero todavía tengo los exámenes del fin de curso . . .

Línea ¡qué rollo!

(5) Gracias por tu última carta en que me informaste de que habías adoptado un cachorro. ¿Por fin le has dado un nombre? Supongo que requiere mucha responsabilidad pero igual te llena de alegría. Me gustaría también tener un perrito, pero mi padre dice que tengo que enfocarme en los estudios y que volveremos a discutirlo en el otoño.

Hablando de mascotas, es el tema de mi proyecto de investigación para la clase de ciencias socia-

(10) les. Me entristeció enterarme de que este país encabeza la lista en abandono de mascotas, con más de cien mil perros abandonados anualmente. Para mí, no hay ningún motivo válido que justifique el abandono de estos pequeños seres de cuatro patas.

Muchos creen que es durante el período estival cuando se da el mayor número de abandonos, pero hay que desmentir esta creencia (aunque sí, es cierta para los gatos). Hoy en día se mantiene estable

(15) a lo largo del año, siendo factores económicos el principal motivo seguido por camadas no deseadas. Si no quisie-ron una camada, ¿por qué no esterilizar a los perros para evitar que se abandonen a sus crías? ¡Y casi el diez por ciento de los casos de abandono es por la pérdida de interés! ¿Puedes creerlo?

¿Cómo crees que podemos reducir este problema? Seguro que hay que afrontarlo desde varios frentes, como mejorar la legislación. Pensando en este asunto, creo también que hay que poner

(20) en marcha más campañas, como unas de este-rilización para evitar camadas no deseadas y que fomenten la adopción de animales. ¿Qué opinas?

¿Y tú? ¿Qué vas a hacer con tu cachorro cuando vayas de vacaciones? ¿Lo vas a llevar contigo o tienes a alguien que lo va a cuidar? Desde hace varios años ha habido portales en que amantes de animales anuncian su disponibilidad de acoger a una mascota durante los días de vacaciones. Pero,

(25) ¿sabes qué?, también hay hoteles que han tomado la iniciativa de permitir la entrada de animales domésticos por un pequeño suplemento. Seguramente ya lo tienes todo pensado y planeado . . . simplemente quería pasarte unas ideas en caso de que las necesitaras.

Bueno, eso es todo que te voy a contar por ahora porque tengo que irme. Lo siento por haberme ido por las ramas con este asunto. Como puedes ver, me ha tocado bastante. Te prometo que en la

(30) próxima carta volveré al tema de la pregunta que me hiciste. Mientras tanto, espero que el fin del año escolar te vaya bien y aprovecho esta oportunidad para despedirme con un gran abrazo y beso.

Saludos a tu familia,
Alicia

1. ¿Con qué propósito le escribe Alicia a Susana?

   (A) Para informarla de su proyecto

   (B) Para continuar a corresponder con ella

   (C) Para cambiar el tema de una conversación previa

   (D) Para despedirse de ella

2. Según Alicia, ¿cuál es la principal razón para el abandono de los perros?

   (A) Las familias van de vacaciones y no pueden cuidarlos.

   (B) No tienen suficiente dinero para mantenerlos.

   (C) Se deteriora la afección que tienen por ellos.

   (D) Los perros tienen muchas crías.

3. Según la carta, ¿cómo se compara la situación del abandono de mascotas en España con la de otros países europeos?

   (A) Es menor que el de otros países.

   (B) Es igual que el de otros países.

   (C) Es mayor que el de otros países.

   (D) No tiene los datos para hacer una comparación.

4. ¿De dónde parece provenir la información que Alicia le presenta a su amiga?

   (A) Es resultado de su investigación.

   (B) Es su propia opinión del tema.

   (C) Es sentido común.

   (D) Es resultado de entrevistas.

5. ¿Cuál de las siguientes declaraciones mejor describe la solución al problema?

   (A) Hay que castigar a los que abandonan las mascotas.

   (B) Hay que concienciar más a la gente del problema.

   (C) Hay que hacerle frente desde múltiples ángulos.

   (D) Hay que crear más plataformas para el cuidado responsable de mascotas.

6. ¿Qué novedad menciona Alicia puede ayudar a reducir la tasa de abandono durante el período estival?

   (A) Una nueva campaña que promueve la esterilización de las mascotas

   (B) Una plataforma en la que las personas indican su capacidad de cuidar a las mascotas cuando el dueño está de vacaciones

   (C) Establecimientos de alojamiento que permiten la entrada de animales

   (D) Un movimiento que promueve la adaptación durante el período de vacaciones

7. ¿Qué comunica Alicia en el cierre de su carta cuando dice que se había ido « . . . por las ramas» (línea 35)?

   (A) Que se había desviado del tema de discusión anterior

   (B) Que este asunto no tiene una solución fácil

   (C) Que este es un tema que le importa mucho

   (D) Que es una persona bastante sensible

Cultural Awareness

Cultural practice: This correspondence presents an unfortunate practice in Spain: how many pets are abandoned and the reasons for this abandonment. Unlike most cultural practices, this one is accidental, meaning that it is a result of circumstances rather than desire. There are other practices mentioned in this text, including the emergence of pet sitting opportunities and hotels that now have designated rooms for pets.

Cultural perspective: This correspondence also presents the view shared by many in Spain regarding the abandonment of pets, and how it is frowned upon and considered cruel.

How do the practices and perspectives presented in this text compare to those in your own community?

Selección 7

Tema curricular: La ciencia y la tecnología

Fuente 1: El siguiente artículo se trata del uso de las diferentes redes sociales en España. Fue publicado en 2018 por DigitalNewsReport.es.

Facebook y WhatsApp siguen liderando en redes pero YouTube, Twitter e Instagram crecen entre los jóvenes

Casi la mitad de la población conectada en España continúa empleando Facebook (48%) para seguir, comentar o compartir noticias, al menos semanalmente. La popular red social, objeto de polémicas en el último año por la filtración de datos personales de usuarios a terceros, mantiene su

Línea

(5) liderazgo en uso informativo en todas las franjas de edad, seguido por el servicio hermano WhatsApp, que usa en relación con la actualidad informativa al menos uno de cada tres internautas de cualquier edad, y que continúa siendo el sitio o la aplicación más popular en uso general.

Los mayores crecimientos en uso de redes sociales y las mayores diferencias por edad están en YouTube (pasa de 67% a 74%), Twitter (sube del 33% al 39%) e Instagram (del 29%, llega al 36%). Las tres suben, en uso general, entre seis y siete puntos porcentuales en un año; esto sitúa a YouTube a la

(10) par de Facebook en uso general.

La encuesta del Digital News Report ha encontrado similitudes y diferencias en el uso que se hace de dos servicios de la misma empresa, Facebook y Whats-App, en relación con las noticias, tomando como base los internautas que han respondido que empleaban cada plataforma con finalidad informativa o de debate y opinión en torno a las noticias. No existe una distinción radical entre Facebook

(15) y WhatsApp, pero sí se observa cómo el consumo más pasivo de noticias (ver titulares y vídeos y hacer clic en enlaces), así como las interacciones más sencillas, como los 'me gusta' o compartir directamente una publicación, tienden a producirse con más frecuencia en Facebook, mientras que WhatsApp concentra la participación proactiva, dentro de grupos creados al efecto y debates privados.

La fuente de la noticia es el principal criterio que emplean los usuarios para decidir si leen o ven

(20) una información que encuentran en redes sociales. Sendas mayorías del 57% también consideran importantes aspectos tan distintos como, por una parte, el titular y la imagen con los que se presenta cada información, y por otra parte, la persona que comparte la noticia. Por último, las opiniones están divididas en cuanto a la relevancia del número de interacciones ('me gusta,' comentarios o veces que se ha compartido) a la hora de determinar el interés de una información: casi una tercera parte lo

(25) considera importante, y son algunos más quienes no lo tienen en cuenta.

Fuente 2: La siguiente tabla presenta el porcentaje de usuarios de internet en España por tipo de actividad realizada en 2018. Los datos provienen del Instituto Nacional de Estadística.

Hombres y mujeres en España de 16 a 74 años		
Actividad realizada	**Mujeres**	**Hombres**
Recibir o enviar correos electrónicos	81,1	79,3
Telefonear o videollamadas a través de internet	37,3	39,0
Participar en redes sociales	64,4	70,5
Jugar o descargar juegos	36,0	31,1
Ver contenidos de video de sitios para compartir (p. ej. YouTube)	76,8	74,9
Vender bienes o servicios	14,8	11,4

1. ¿Cuál es el propósito del artículo?

   (A) Informar de los hábitos de uso de las redes sociales en España
   (B) Explicar las razones por las cuales los usuarios usan las redes sociales
   (C) Analizar cuáles son las redes sociales que más se usan para encontrar y compartir noticias
   (D) Informar de los resultados de una encuesta sobre los efectos del uso de las redes sociales

2. ¿Qué información presenta el artículo sobre Facebook?

   (A) Su uso ha bajado
   (B) Su uso ha generado controversia
   (C) Es el sitio predilecto para encontrar noticias
   (D) Es mayormente usado por los adultos

3. Según el artículo, ¿qué red social es la más usada por los jóvenes para dar y recibir noticias?

   (A) Facebook
   (B) YouTube
   (C) Twitter
   (D) Instagram

4. Según la información presentada en el artículo, ¿cuál es la red social más usada en uso general?

   (A) Facebook
   (B) WhatsApp
   (C) YouTube
   (D) Twitter

5. ¿Cómo se destacan YouTube, Twitter e Instagram en cuanto a su uso general?

   (A) Todas tienen el mismo nivel de importancia.
   (B) Han experimentado un crecimiento continuo.
   (C) Son tan populares como Facebook.
   (D) Su uso se ha incrementado entre los jóvenes.

6. Según el artículo, ¿cómo se diferencian Facebook y WhatsApp como fuente de noticias?

   (A) No hay ninguna diferencia.

   (B) Los usuarios de WhatsApp tienden a interactuar más con otros usuarios.

   (C) Los usuarios de Facebook divulgan más noticias.

   (D) Las noticias se encuentran más fácilmente por WhatsApp.

7. ¿A qué se refiere el artículo cuando dice «La fuente de la noticia . . . » (línea 24)?

   (A) A la procedencia de la noticia

   (B) Al tipo de noticia

   (C) A la fiabilidad de la noticia

   (D) Al contenido de la noticia

8. Según el artículo, ¿qué impacto tienen los comentarios de otros en determinar el interés de una noticia?

   (A) Tienen un impacto enorme.

   (B) Tienen un impacto mínimo.

   (C) No tienen ningún impacto.

   (D) Para algunos son importantes y para otros no tanto.

9. ¿Qué información presenta la tabla?

   (A) Las acciones que realizan los usuarios de redes sociales en línea

   (B) El número de personas que realizan diferentes actividades por internet

   (C) Las actividades típicas que ambos sexos efectúan por internet

   (D) Las acciones preferidas por hombres y mujeres en internet

10. Según la información en la tabla, ¿cuál de las siguientes opciones mejor describe la actividad realizada más frecuentemente en línea?

   (A) Efectuar operaciones económicas

   (B) Comunicarse con otros

   (C) Entretenerse

   (D) Compartir fotos y videos

11. Si fueras a investigar el tema presentado en el artículo y en la tabla, ¿cuál de las siguientes publicaciones tendría la información que buscas?

   (A) La conquista global de Facebook

   (B) La evolución de las comunidades virtuales en la península Ibérica

   (C) Redes sociales e internet: cómo usarlos para impulsar tu negocio

   (D) Siete motivos para usar internet y redes sociales en tu vida

---

Cultural Awareness

Cultural practice: The article presents current habits in Spain regarding use of social media to access news, while the table presents current habits regarding use of the internet in general.

How do these compare to the use of social media and the internet in your community?

Selección 8

Tema curricular: Las identidades personales

El siguiente fragmento, del libro Tiempo Mexicano por Carlos Fuentes publicado en 1973, relata el cambio social que ocurrió en México en el siglo XX.

Línea

(5)

(10)

(15)

(20)

Entre los jóvenes de clase media, y a veces de clase obrera que con grandes sacrificios llegan a los estudios superiores, tiene lugar, por otra parte, la transformación cultural más interesante de la década. Quizás la historia cultural del México independiente pueda dividirse en tres etapas. La primera, hasta finales de la dictadura de Díaz, muestra una marcada tendencia—que las grandes excepciones, de Fernández de Lizardi a Posadas, no alcanzan a suprimir—a los que Antonio Caso llamó "la imitación extralógica": una cultura importada, como las mansardas que en las casas de la Colonia Juárez esperaban inútilmente la ventisca invernal. Pero a fines del Porfiriato, las novelas de Rabasa y Frías, la poesía de Othón, los grabados de Posada anunciaban un descubrimiento: el de México por sí mismo. La Revolución, en esencia un paso del no ser, o del ser enajenado, al ser para sí, fue el acto mismo de ese descubrimiento—los actos coinciden con las palabras y la apariencia con el rostro: la máscara cae y todos los colores, voces y cuerpos de México brillan con su existencia real. Un país dividido en compartimientos estancos entra en contacto con sí mismo. Las formidables cabalgatas de la División del Norte y del Cuerpo del Noroeste por todo el territorio de la república son un abrazo y un reconocimiento: los mexicanos saben por primera vez cómo hablan, cómo cantan, cómo ríen, cómo aman, cómo beben, cómo comen, cómo injurian y cómo mueren los mexicanos.

Del choque revolucionario surgió una doble tendencia cultural, positivo en cuanto permitió a los mexicanos descubrirse a sí mismos, y negativa en cuanto llegó a un extremo chauvinista, tipificado popularmente en la frase "Como México no hay dos" que sólo acentúa nuestra forzosa relación bilateral con los Estados Unidos. Curiosa y suicida coincidencia de cierta izquierda y de la derecha cierta: la xenofobia, la afirmación de la singularidad mexicana, la invención estimágtica de "ideas exóticas" para denigrar, sencillamente, las ideas que no se comprenden o se juzgan peligrosas para la ortodoxia de los unos o las ganancias de los otros.

1. ¿Cómo se diferencian los jóvenes modernos de los de la época del Porfiriato?

   (A) Creen que saben más.
   (B) No tienen identidad auténtica.
   (C) Son más artísticos.
   (D) Disfrutan de más oportunidades.

2. ¿Qué pasó en la primera etapa de la gran transformación mexicana?

   (A) Estalló la rebelión contra la dictadura de Porfirio Díaz.
   (B) Los mexicanos imitaron las modas ajenas.
   (C) El pueblo se escondió tras máscaras regionales.
   (D) El país se dividió en varios departamentos.

3. ¿Cómo empezaron algunos a mostrar su independencia?

   (A) Unos artistas iniciaron unas nuevas tendencias artísticas.
   (B) La División del Norte se encontró con el Cuerpo del Noroeste.
   (C) Mexicanos de todas partes se juntaron en contra de Porfirio Díaz.
   (D) Unos mexicanos empezaron a pensar de una manera no muy lógica.

4. ¿Qué es lo que se veía al caer la máscara?

   (A) Se veían muchos colores brillantes.
   (B) Descubrieron que eran xenofóbicos.
   (C) Reconocieron sus diferencias regionales.
   (D) Se enteraron de cómo eran sus compatriotas.

5. ¿Qué aspecto positivo tiene la doble tendencia cultural mexicana?

   (A) Los mexicanos reconocieron sus semejanzas.
   (B) Supieron que tenían que juntarse para luchar contra los Estados Unidos.
   (C) Descubrieron el valor de la cultura autóctona.
   (D) Descubrieron que a todos les gustaban los colores vivos.

6. En las líneas 22–23, ¿qué quiere decir la frase "Como México no hay dos?"

   (A) Hay sólo una raza mexicana.
   (B) No se pueden permitir influencias extranjeras en México.
   (C) No hay diferencias políticas entre los mexicanos.
   (D) Todas las regiones de México gozan de oportunidades iguales.

7. Por último ¿en qué consiste la transformación discutida en esta selección?

   (A) El fomento de revolución artística
   (B) La creación de regiones únicas
   (C) Un proceso de autoidentificación mexicana
   (D) El reconocimiento de la superioridad cultural mexicana

---

Cultural Awareness

Cultural perspective: In this fragment, the Mexican author Carlos Fuentes connects several key episodes in Mexican history to the formation of the culture and identity of its people.

Can you think of an event in recent history that had an effect on the identity and culture in your own community? How is the perspective of history impacting culture and identity similar to or different from that in your own community?

Selección 9

Tema curricular: La belleza y la estética

En esta carta, Pablo le escribe a su amigo, Javier, sobre una experiencia que tuvo en México D.F.

Querido Javier,

Espero que te encuentres bien. Te escribo para contarte sobre mi increíble visita al museo Trick Eye en la Ciudad de México. ¡Fue una experiencia fuera de este mundo!

Línea   Cuando entré en el museo, me quedé impresionado por las increíbles exhibiciones de realidad aumentada. Las pinturas y escenarios eran tan realistas que sentí que estaba entrando en un mundo
(5)   mágico. Tuve la oportunidad de sumergirme en pinturas surrealistas y escenarios oníricos, algo que nunca había experimentado antes. Además, pude interactuar con dragones, explorar ambientes subacuáticos y presenciar erupciones volcánicas, ¡fue alucinante!

Lo más asombroso fue la forma en que pude ver las obras de artistas famosos como Vincent van Gogh. La tecnología utilizada en Trick Eye realmente les dio vida de una manera completamente
(10)   nueva. Fue como si estuviera caminando dentro de las pinturas mismas.

La aplicación TrickEye AR fue mi compañera durante toda la visita. Era fácil de usar y me permitió activar los efectos de realidad aumentada en cada escenario. También, tuve la oportunidad de tomarme fotos interactivas con las obras, lo cual fue muy divertido.

En resumen, mi visita a Trick Eye fue inolvidable. No puedo dejar de hablar de esta experiencia a
(15)   mis amigos y familiares. Si alguna vez tienes la oportunidad de venir a la Ciudad de México, definitiva-mente te recomiendo que visitemos juntos este museo. ¡No te arrepentirás!

Espero verte pronto para contarte más detalles en persona. Cuídate mucho y nos vemos pronto.

Con cariño,
(20)   Pablo

---

1. ¿Cuál es el motivo de la carta de Pablo a Javier?

    (A) Contarle sobre su visita a un parque temático en la Ciudad de México
    (B) Invitarlo a un evento especial en su ciudad
    (C) Compartir detalles sobre una experiencia que tuvo
    (D) Pedirle su opinión sobre unas atracciones en la Ciudad de México

2. ¿Por qué dice Pablo que su experiencia fue "fuera de este mundo"?

    (A) Porque visitó un lugar especial en las afueras de la ciudad.
    (B) Porque participó en un evento espacial.
    (C) Porque las exhibiciones fueron increíbles.
    (D) Porque tuvo un encuentro con seres mágicos.

3. Según la carta, ¿qué tipos de obras hay en el museo?

    (A) Obras tradicionales enmarcadas que se pueden apreciar desde lejos
    (B) Obras que cobran vida y se vuelven interactivas
    (C) Obras en exhibición que solo se pueden ver a través de pantallas
    (D) Obras que se pueden tocar y manipular libremente

4. ¿Qué permitió a Javier disfrutar al máximo su experiencia?

   (A) La ayuda de un guía especializado
   (B) La posibilidad de tomar fotos de las obras
   (C) Un programa que activó efectos en cada escenario
   (D) Las figuras y criaturas utilizadas en las exhibiciones

5. Según la carta, ¿cuál de las siguientes afirmaciones describe mejor la relación entre Javier y Pablo?

   (A) Son buenos amigos y se ven a menudo
   (B) Son amigos cercanos que comparten los mismos intereses
   (C) Son compañeros de clase que se reúnen ocasionalmente
   (D) Tienen una relación cercana pero viven en distintas ciudades

6. Después de recibir la carta, Pablo quiere encontrar más información sobre el tema. ¿Cuál de las siguientes publicaciones le sería más útil?

   (A) Un libro sobre la evolución de los museos en México
   (B) Un informe sobre las tendencias de la tecnología en América Latina
   (C) Una revista que destaca las últimas exhibiciones en museos de la ciudad
   (D) Un catálogo de aparatos y dispositivos tecnológicos

7. Según la carta, ¿cuál de los siguientes adjetivos mejor describe la personalidad de Pablo?

   (A) Es tímido y retraído.
   (B) Es valiente y aventurero.
   (C) Es entusiasta de lo innovador.
   (D) Es fornido y competitivo.

Cultural Awareness

Cultural perspective: This letter talks about an art museum in Mexico City that incorporates technology to enhance the visitor's experience and ability to engage with the works on display.

Are there similar in your community that incorporate innovation to enhance the way one experiences art?

Selección 10

Tema curricular: La belleza y la estética

El siguiente anuncio es para un evento en el Municipio de Bahía Blanca, Argentina. Fue publicado en 2022 por el Municipio de Bahía Blanca.

La Fonola Tango
DESCRIPCIÓN

Comenzaron a tocar juntos en el 2022. Buscan amalgamar la poesía y armonías de los Tangos Tradicionales y "nuevas voces" que

Línea describen realidades urbanas de hoy sin

(5) perder de vista la esencia que le dio vida al género.

Natalia Otero (voz) viene del folclore, de la canción de autor, rock fusión. Guillermo Ocejo (guitarra), del jazz y el tango.

(10) Así buscan dar un toque personal a esta música ciudadana que, como Bahienses, los representa, por ser una ciudad de fuerte raíz tanguera. Aquí nacieron Cobián, Di Sarli.

Afiches, Tinta Roja, Corazón al Sur, Mari-

(15) posita, etc. son algunos de los clásicos que podrán escuchar.

Que sea el 18 octubre esta presentación es un motivo de celebración ya que se cumple un año del primer concierto de La Fonola Tango

Entrada General: $3000

(20) Promociones: 25% de descuento para jubilados y afiliados UMSur.

* Las promociones son solo por boletería del teatro.

HORA *(Miercoles) 21:00*
Teatro Municipal
Alsina 425
PULSE AQUÍ PARA ADQUIRIR TU ENTRADA EN LÍNEA

1. ¿Cuál de las siguientes declaraciones mejor describe las canciones de La Fonola Tango?

   (A) Historias de amor y desamor tradicionales del tango
   (B) Una combinación del tango tradicional y asuntos contemporáneos
   (C) Una fusión de distintos géneros de música latinoamericana con temas urbanos
   (D) Un homenaje a los músicos tangueros tradicionales de Bahía Blanca

2. ¿Cuál es la razón específica para la selección de la fecha de esta actuación?

   (A) Se conmemora el aniversario del Teatro Municipal
   (B) Es un día que celebra los clásicos del tango
   (C) Honra el aniversario de la primera actuación del grupo
   (D) Es su primer concierto este año

3. ¿Dónde se pueden adquirir las entradas para jubilados?

   (A) Solo en la taquilla del Teatro Municipal

   (B) Exclusivamente en línea

   (C) En línea y en la taquilla del Teatro Municipal

   (D) En otros puntos de venta

4. ¿Qué aspecto resalta sobre la ciudad en la que se llevará a cabo el concierto?

   (A) Es un centro cultural reconocido por sus presentaciones musicales

   (B) Es conocida por sus festivales de música tanguera.

   (C) Se caracteriza por sus eventos culturales únicos.

   (D) Ha sido cuna de reconocidos músicos del tango.

5. Si quisieras saber más información sobre el evento, ¿qué pregunta sería más apropiada formular?

   (A) ¿Cuál es la ubicación del evento?

   (B) ¿Cuál es el programa detallado del evento?

   (C) ¿Qué grupo será cabeza de cartel?

   (D) ¿Hay descuentos disponibles para las entradas?

Cultural Awareness

Cultural product: This advertisement presents a tango concert in Bahía Blanca.

Cultural practice: In addition to preserving the elements of traditional tango, the artists also include contemporary themes into their music.

Are there musical groups in your community that combine traditional music and contemporary themes into their music?

Selección 11

Tema curricular: Las familias y las comunidades

Este anuncio promueve una tradición típica de Venezuela. Fue publicado en *http://Venezuelatuya.com*.

La hallaca

Uno de los platos más reconocidos y elaborados que se presenta en la gastronomía venezolana es sin lugar a dudas la hallaca. Esta obra maestra de nuestra culinaria es el más tradicional de los platos que engalanan las festividades navideñas en nuestra Venezuela.

Línea
(5)

La hallaca es el resultado del proceso histórico que ha vivido nuestra sociedad.

Desde su cubierta de hojas de plátano hasta los detalles que adornan y componen su guiso, pasando por su ingrediente primordial, la masa de maíz coloreada con onoto, la hallaca es la expresión más visible del mestizaje del venezolano. Cada ingrediente tiene sus raíces: la hoja de plátano, usada tanto por el negro africano como por el indio americano, es el maravilloso envoltorio que la cobija; al descubrirla, traemos al presente nuestro pasado indígena, pues la masa de maíz coloreada

(10)

con onoto es la que nos recibe con su esplendoroso color amarillo; luego, en su interior se deja apreciar la llegada de los españoles a estas tierras, carnes de gallina, cerdo y res, aceitunas, alcaparras, pasas . . . todo picado finamente, guisados y maravillosamente distribuidos se hacen parte de un manjar exquisito. Sus ingredientes, todos partes de diferentes raíces se complementan armoniosamente en la hallaca, expresión del mestizaje y colorido del que es parte nuestro pueblo.

(15)

La palabra "Hallaca" proviene del guaraní y deriva de la palabra "ayúa" o "ayuar" que significa mezclar o revolver, de estas palabras se presume que "ayuaca" sea una cosa mezclada, que por deformación lingüística paso a llamarse "ayaca." Otra versión presume que la palabra procede de alguna lengua aborigen del occidente del país, cuyo significado es "envoltorio" o "bojote."

Sea cual sea el origen de esta palabra, sabemos que "la hallaca" es completamente venezolana,

(20)

tanto por su nombre como por su confección y es orgullo de nuestra cocina, pues ella sin distinciones sociales se presenta espléndida en la mesa navideña de todos los venezolanos, aportando un toque de maravilloso gusto y sabor a nuestra navidad.

En el mes de diciembre cuando las fiestas navideñas desbordan la alegría del venezolano, la hallaca es parte importante de la celebración, se intercambian, se regalan, se venden . . . en fin, en las fiestas

(25)

de navidad para el venezolano no puede faltar la tan reconocida hallaca.

Para su preparación existen diversas recetas, pues en cada región del país hay recetas tradicionales, además como en la mayoría de los platos venezolanos cada familia le aporta su sazón y varía su confección.

1. ¿Qué simboliza la hallaca?

   (A) La integración intercultural del país
   (B) La cultura de los indígenas en Venezuela
   (C) La llegada de los españoles a tierra venezolana
   (D) La variedad de ingredientes autóctonos del país

2. Según el artículo, ¿cuál es el ingrediente principal de la hallaca?

   (A) Las hojas de plátano
   (B) La masa de maíz
   (C) La carne
   (D) El guisado

3. ¿A qué se refiere el autor cuando escribe ". . . se deja apreciar la llegada de los españoles" (línea 13)?

   (A) A que los españoles tuvieron el mayor impacto en la creación de la hallaca
   (B) A que los españoles trajeron nuevas técnicas culinarias
   (C) A que los españoles contribuyeron ingredientes no endémicos
   (D) A que los españoles disfrutaron de las tierras venezolanas

4. ¿Cuántas culturas son representadas en la preparación de la hallaca?

   (A) Dos
   (B) Tres
   (C) Cuatro
   (D) Más de cuatro

5. ¿Qué significa la frase "ella sin distinciones sociales se presenta espléndida en la mesa" (líneas 26–27)?

   (A) Que las cocina venezolana es magnífica pero modesta
   (B) Que las cenas navideñas suelen ser muy ricas
   (C) Que toda clase de gente goza de este plato
   (D) Que la hallaca es la más bella de todas las comidas venezolanas

---

Cultural Awareness

Cultural product: This reading presents a typical dish served during Christmas time in Venezuela and its origins.

How is the product presented in this article similar to or different from one in your own community?

Selección 12

Tema curricular: Las identidades personales y públicas

Este fragmento de la novela Rosaura a las diez, del escritor argentino Marcos Denevi, relata las primeras impresiones que tienen unas chicas al conocer a otra persona por primera vez.

Entonces comenzaron entre ellas una de esas conversaciones en que a mí, aunque esté presente, no me dan intervención, porque van a decir cosas que saben que yo no he de admitirles, y hablando entre ellas y diciéndolo todo ellas ligerito, quieren convencerme antes de que yo les ataje la palabra en

Línea   la boca.

(5)   —Y no parece que tenga veintiséis años.

—No ha hablado en ningún momento.

—¡Nos miraba, y en qué forma!

—Parecía asustada.

—No, asustada no. Sorprendida, maravillada, estupefacta.

(10)   —Y mucha desenvoltura no aparenta tener.

—Les digo que es una santita que nunca salió de su casa. Por eso ahora
        anda así.

—Y se vino vestida bien modestamente.

—Tenía una media corrida.

(15)   —Y los zapatos llenos de polvo.

—El collar es una fantasía de dos por cinco.

—Oigan, ¿no será sorda? ¿No será que no oye lo que se le dice y por eso nos miraba así?

—Pero no, si cuando yo le pregunté . . .

—Pues algo raro hay en ella. Todavía no sé lo que es, pero ya lo sabré. Déjenme estudiarla.

(20)   Y yo me acordé de aquellas manchas rojas en el antebrazo de Rosaura, ¡y sentí una indignación!

—¡Vean qué tres serpientes he traído yo al mundo!—exclamé, mirándolas con furia—. La señorita Eufrasia, al lado de ustedes, es Santa Eufrasia. No quería decirles nada, pero veo que es necesario. La pelea de Rosaura con el padre fue como para llamar a la policía. Tiene los brazos llenos de cardenales. Me miraron, horrorizadas.

1. ¿Quién narra lo que pasa en este trozo?

   (A) La señorita Eufrasia
   (B) Una de las chicas
   (C) La mamá de las chicas
   (D) Una chica huérfana

2. ¿De qué hablan?

   (A) De una joven que está visitando a la familia.
   (B) De una chica que es compañera de clase en la escuela.
   (C) De una santa que visitaba la casa.
   (D) De una joven pobre que visitaron en su casa.

3. ¿Con qué intenciones hablan las tres chicas?

   (A) Para conocer mejor a la chica
   (B) Para adivinar la identidad de la chica
   (C) Están chismeando
   (D) Les interesa ayudarle

4. En la línea 25, ¿qué quiere decir la frase "La señorita Eufrasia, al lado de ustedes, es Santa Eufrasia"?

(A) Que las chicas son tan buenas como si fueran santas.
(B) Que a la narradora le parece que las tres chicas son muy crueles.
(C) Que la narradora cree que cualquier persona puede ser santa.
(D) Que la narradora no cree que la señorita Eufrasia sea santa.

5. ¿Qué quiere la narradora que hagan las tres chicas?

(A) Que ellas se callen.
(B) Que ellas sean más piadosas.
(C) Que las chicas la conozcan mejor.
(D) Que las tres le muestren más respeto.

6. ¿Por qué se quedan horrorizadas las tres chicas?

(A) No pueden creer que les hable la narradora con tanta franqueza.
(B) Les ofende que haya intervenido la narradora en sus conversaciones.
(C) Dudan que la narradora les haya dicho la verdad.
(D) Les escandalizan los hechos del caso que acaba de decirles la narradora.

7. ¿Qué puede ser el pensamiento central de este trozo?

(A) A las mujeres les gusta chismear todo el tiempo.
(B) Los pobres no tienen ningunos derechos.
(C) No se debe juzgar sin saber todos los datos del caso.
(D) La intolerancia tiene raíces en la falta de comunicación.

Cultural Awareness

Cultural perspective: This fragment presents a classic situation in which people from different backgrounds meet each other for the first time. The young girls' comments about Rosaura's appearance anger their mother, who reprimands them for their insolence. The perspective presented here is to not pass judgment of others without knowing who they are.

How is the perspective presented in this fragment similar to or different from one in your own community?

Selección 13

Tema curricular: La vida contemporánea

El siguiente artículo se trata del uso de videojuegos en la enseñanza en Aguascalientes, México. Fue publicado por la página web CienciaMx en 2015.

> ### Videojuegos y matemáticas en el aula
> **Por Lidia Vázquez**
>
> El cuerpo académico de Investigación de Objetos de Aprendizaje e Ingeniería de Software de la Universidad Autónoma de Aguascalientes (UAA) ha desarrollado más de 30 videojuegos con patrones interactivos y móviles para la enseñanza de matemáticas en estudiantes de 5o y 6o grados de primaria.
>
> *Línea*
> (5)
> En entrevista para la Agencia Informativa Conacyt, el doctor Francisco Javier Álvarez Rodríguez, investigador académico de la UAA, explica los objetivos, resultados y desafíos inherentes a la implementación de tecnología lúdica como herramienta didáctica en los últimos dos grados de educación básica. "La creación y desarrollo de un videojuego didáctico requiere de una especialidad en el área y una serie de expertos que ayuden a producir un juego con elementos de acción, que sea atractivo para el usuario y además contenga elementos didácticos, que generen un proceso que permita poner todos
> (10)
> estos elementos para poder producir estos videojuegos y reforzar su aprendizaje en esta materia", aseguró Álvarez Rodríguez, quien es miembro nivel III del Sistema Nacional de Investigadores (SNI).
>
> Explicó que la competencia es ligada a un videojuego para que los niños, a través de este y de las interacciones con que se maneja, desarrollen habilidades de las enseñanzas de las matemáticas. Entre los videojuegos ya desarrollados se encuentran PokeMath, MathChallenge, SpaceMath, Fracciones,
> (15)
> GeoBodies, CubeLand, Regla de Tres, Marcianos, Perimeters y Kaxan.
>
> Brecha digital entre maestros y alumnos
>
> Uno de los grandes retos a los que se enfrenta el equipo de la UAA, aseguró el investigador, es el hecho de que varios de los docentes del nivel básico prefieren los métodos tradicionales de enseñanza, situación que se suma al "choque generacional" con una tecnología a la que se le niega su
> (20)
> importancia como herramienta didáctica moderna y práctica.
>
> Es importante mencionar que el proyecto de la UAA tiene cinco años de desarrollo. Inició con un análisis profundo del proceso de enseñanza individual, que permitió el desarrollo de dos juegos con el fin de ver cómo se interrelacionaban los elementos de videojuego con las cuestiones educativas y tener esta experiencia de ensamble y, posteriormente, la definición de procesos para realizar una
> (25)
> producción más ordenada. Una vez definido esto, el objetivo principal fue generar un proceso con patrones interactivos que permitiera producir los juegos.
>
> Dijo que estos videojuegos se han probado en escuelas de educación básica en lugares semirrurales, y se comprobó que los videojuegos sirven para elevar la calidad y reforzar el proceso de enseñanza-aprendizaje de las matemáticas.
> (30)
> Recalcó que los niños están inmersos en la tecnología, razón por la que si se aprovecha la brecha digital, tener videojuegos a la disposición de los niños en la escuela, la casa, durante periodos vacacionales o fines de semana, podría ayudar a reforzar los aprendizajes de un ciclo escolar y disminuir los niveles de reprobación..

1. ¿Cuál es el propósito principal del texto?

   (A) Argumentar a favor del uso exclusivo de tecnologías educativas modernas
   (B) Detallar el proceso de desarrollo de videojuegos para un público especializado en programación
   (C) Criticar la efectividad de los videojuegos en el aprendizaje matemático
   (D) Informar sobre una iniciativa de integrar videojuegos en la enseñanza

2. ¿A qué público está dirigido principalmente el texto?

   (A) Expertos en tecnología y desarrollo de videojuegos
   (B) Estudiantes de primaria que utilizan videojuegos en su aprendizaje
   (C) Profesionales y académicos en el campo de la educación y la pedagogía
   (D) Padres de familia interesados en las nuevas metodologías de enseñanza

3. ¿Qué característica destacada se menciona sobre los videojuegos didácticos?

   (A) Son creados únicamente por expertos en matemáticas.
   (B) Contienen elementos de acción y son atractivos para los usuarios.
   (C) Se enfocan únicamente en los aspectos teóricos de las matemáticas.
   (D) Son diseñados sin la intervención de expertos en educación.

4. Según el texto, ¿cuál es un desafío en la implementación de los videojuegos en la educación?

   (A) La falta de interés de los estudiantes en la tecnología
   (B) La preferencia de algunos docentes por métodos tradicionales
   (C) La inaccesibilidad de los videojuegos en áreas rurales
   (D) La falta de apoyo del gobierno

5. ¿Qué beneficio potencial se menciona sobre el uso de videojuegos en la enseñanza?

   (A) Reducir los costos educativos
   (B) Eliminar los libros de texto
   (C) Elevar la calidad y reforzar el aprendizaje de matemáticas
   (D) Aumentar el tiempo de juego en la escuela

6. En el contexto del texto, ¿qué se puede inferir sobre el término "brecha digital" (línea 18)?

   (A) La disparidad en la familiaridad de tecnologías digitales entre distintas generaciones
   (B) Una división ideológica sobre la importancia de la tecnología en los métodos educativos modernos
   (C) La diferencia en la calidad y tipo de videojuegos utilizados en la enseñanza entre diferentes regiones geográficas
   (D) Una referencia a la falta de infraestructura tecnológica en el ámbito educativo

7. Según la información del texto, ¿cuál de las siguientes parece más probable para el futuro?

   (A) Los videojuegos serán reemplazados gradualmente por métodos de enseñanza más tradicionales.
   (B) La integración de videojuegos en la enseñanza de matemáticas se expandirá y diversificará.
   (C) El uso de videojuegos en educación se limitará solo a áreas urbanas.
   (D) Los docentes se resistirán completamente a la incorporación de tecnología en el aula.

Cultural Awareness

Cultural product & practice: This article presents the creation of videogames (product) to help teach math (practice) to young students.

What innovations or innovative techniques exist in your community to help teach complex subjects to students?

Selección 14

Tema curricular: La belleza y la estética

En esta carta, Javier le escribe a su amigo sobre una experiencia que tuvo la noche anterior.

Querido Pablo,

    ¿Cómo estás? Te quería escribir anoche, pero estaba demasiado metido en mis propios pensamientos. Fui al cine con Sebastián y unos amigos suyos de la secundaria. Ya sabes cuánto me

Línea
(5) gusta ver películas, pero la verdad es que esta vez no disfruté la experiencia. Para empezar, nosotros llegamos tarde y las butacas estaban casi llenas. Afortunadamente pudimos encontrar suficiente asientos, pero tuvimos que separarnos y me quedé con dos jóvenes muy parlanchines: no dejaron de platicar durante toda la película . . . ¡qué horror! Además, la película fue una tontería: demasiado énfasis en la acción y efectos especiales y ninguna consideración en desarrollar la trama. Y para colmo, al juntarse de nuevo el grupo, todos la alababan como si fuera la mejor del año. Yo me quedé

(10) quieto durante el camino a casa porque no quería ser aguafiestas.

    Al llegar a casa empecé a pensar en cómo los gustos de cada uno son tan distintos. Para mí, ir al cine es una experiencia íntima que empieza el momento en que entro la sala. No entiendo cómo a alguien no le molestaría llegar tarde y perderse los tráilers. Además, no soporto cuando la gente habla durante la película. Me encanta poder discutir las películas, pero se debería hacer después de que

(15) haya terminado. Esta reflexión me hizo pensar en qué opinan otros de su experiencia en el cine. Pensé en que seguramente para los dos jóvenes a mi lado, el compañerismo era una parte de su diversión, y que ver una película en el cine es un evento que compartes con los que te rodean. Por eso no se molestaron por el hecho de que la película ya había empezado y disfrutaron de ella, aunque me pareció pésima.

(20)   A causa de esta reflexión, me di cuenta de que posiblemente mi experiencia podría haber sido diferente si hubiera cambiado mi actitud. Al contemplar la película de nuevo, pude ver elementos graciosos en ella, y me pregunté si no disfruté de la película por ser mala, o simplemente porque estaba tan frustrado de antemano que no iba a gozarla de todas formas. Creo que lo que he aprendido es que la diversión es distinta para cada persona, y cuando un grupo decide hacer algo juntos es

(25) imposible complacer a todos, y el fraternizar es una parte intrínseca de la experiencia así que hay que abandonar las expectativas personales y no frustrarse tanto si algo sale diferente de lo que uno quiere. ¿Qué piensas tú? Lo siento por escribirte una carta tan filosófica, pero me ayuda poder vocalizar mis pensamientos y compartirlos.

    Bueno, me despido de ti y espero tu respuesta. Salúdale a toda tu familia y espero que nos

(30) veamos pronto.

¡Un abrazo!
Javier

---

1. Según la carta, ¿qué se puede afirmar sobre la relación entre Javier y las personas con quienes fue al cine?

    (A) El vínculo de amistad es bastante fuerte.

    (B) Son todos amigos de la escuela.

    (C) Los demás no se llevan bien con Javier.

    (D) Javier se siente un poco apartado del grupo.

2. ¿Qué hicieron los dos jóvenes durante la película?

   (A) Conversaron.
   (B) Lucharon.
   (C) Se durmieron.
   (D) Se enfermaron.

3. ¿Por qué no participó Javier en la discusión después de la película?

   (A) Porque estaba demasiado enojado.
   (B) Porque no quería ser pesimista.
   (C) Porque estaba cansado.
   (D) Porque no le caía bien el grupo.

4. Según la reflexión personal de Javier, ¿cuál de las siguientes afirmaciones mejor refleja su opinión de la experiencia de ir al cine?

   (A) Es más divertido ir con un grupo.
   (B) Es algo profundo y personal.
   (C) Es una experiencia que hay que hacer con otras personas.
   (D) Es un evento que se disfruta más solo.

5. ¿Por qué cree Javier que los otros gozaron más la experiencia que él?

   (A) Porque les gustan las películas de acción
   (B) Porque la película tuvo buenos efectos especiales
   (C) Porque la compartieron con sus amigos
   (D) Porque son más optimistas que él

6. En la carta, ¿cuál es el significado de la frase "todos la alababan" (línea 11)?

   (A) Todos debatían la película.
   (B) Todos celebraban la película.
   (C) Todos criticaban la película.
   (D) Todos maldecían la película.

7. Con base en su reflexión, ¿qué cambio se nota en Javier?

   (A) Llega a ser más comprensivo.
   (B) Aumenta su frustración.
   (C) Se deprime un poco.
   (D) Siente vergüenza por su actitud.

Cultural Awareness

Cultural perspective: This fragment presents a perspective of a young man in regards to the movies and to certain behaviors exhibited by his friends.

How are the perspectives presented in this correspondence similar to or different from those in your own community?

Selección 15

Tema curricular: Las identidades personales y públicas

En el siguiente fragmento, el narrador habla de su experiencia en Guatemala.

Patrocinado por el Instituto de Cultura e invitado por el Instituto

Guatemalteco, vengo a pasar un mes en Guatemala. A mi regreso, todos, amigos, parientes, colegas y hasta simples conocidos, me han asediado con su curiosidad por este país, del que por desgracia tan poco se conoce en Europa. Un mes, por modo cierto, es muy poco tiempo para llegar al conocimiento
Línea de cualquier cosa importante y desde luego mucho menos para captar las esencias tan complejas y los
(5) matices tan variopintos de un país como Guatemala.

En todos los medios sociales en los que me he desenvuelto, la cortesía natural y algo más importante y sincero, como es la cordialidad, son la regla. En cada momento de mi vida allí, he tenido la sensación entrañable de encontrarme en mi propio país y también de que "el solo hecho de ser español" ya era algo importante en Guatemala. Esto no implica, ni mucho menos, en el nativo o residente,
(10) servilismo ni ausencia de un lógico y acertado orgullo nacional, sino que si los "peninsulares" nos colocamos en la natural posición de hermanos, ellos como hermanos nos acogen.

Lo que no aceptan, y hacen muy bien, es la actitud más o menos veladamente "paternalista" y protectora, que el desconocimiento de la realidad hace adoptar a muchos de los que intentan "españolear" en América. Creo sinceramente que la única razón de los alientos que los guatemaltecos han
(15) prodigado a mis modestas actuaciones públicas se ha debido a mi sentir, sinceramente expresado, de que tanto más tenía yo que aprender de ellos, como ellos de mí.

El intelectual guatemalteco es curioso de todos los saberes, hábil conversador, que sabe escuchar y decir—cada cosa a su tiempo—y de una cultura extensa e intensa, sin el mal de la pedantería. Como uno de los más gratos recuerdos de esta mi entrañable Guatemala, tengo el del "redescubrimiento" del
(20) apacible coloquio—hoy casi olvidado entre nosotros—con el designio más de aprender que de enseñar, el sentido de la mutua comprensión y la tolerancia liberal que preside toda mente selecta.

---

1. ¿Quién es el autor de este trozo?

   (A) Es un guatemalteco que actualmente vive en España.
   (B) Es un turista casual en Guatemala.
   (C) Es el embajador cultural español en Guatemala.
   (D) Es un peninsular invitado por una organización guatemalteca.

2. ¿Qué actitud mostraba este autor?

   (A) Se sentía muy superior por ser español entre guatemaltecos.
   (B) Se sentía bien acogido.
   (C) Se sentía muy humillado porque los guatemaltecos eran tan inteligentes.
   (D) Se sentía muy dispuesto a regresar a su país cuanto antes.

3. ¿Qué característica de los guatemaltecos le impresionó más?

   (A) La envidia que le tenían porque era europeo.
   (B) Lo pedante que eran los guatemaltecos intelectuales.
   (C) Su gran curiosidad intelectual en cuanto a todo el mundo.
   (D) Su soberbia que no les permitió admitir la superioridad española.

4. ¿Qué crítica implícita hay en lo que dice este autor?

    (A) Critica a sus propios compatriotas.
    (B) Critica a los europeos con negocios en Guatemala.
    (C) Critica a los guatemaltecos por ser tan serviles.
    (D) Critica la pereza guatemalteca.

5. ¿Qué revela la actitud de los guatemaltecos en cuanto a las relaciones con los españoles?

    (A) Los guatemaltecos siempre han entendido mejor a los españoles que al revés.
    (B) Los guatemaltecos siempre han entendido peor a los españoles que al revés.
    (C) Las dos nacionalidades siempre se han tratado como iguales.
    (D) Nunca se han entendido bien.

6. ¿Qué sugiere que se aprenda de los guatemaltecos?

    (A) Sugiere que se aprenda a apreciar el arte de no hacer nada.
    (B) Sugiere que todo el mundo imite la sinceridad de los guatemaltecos.
    (C) Sugiere que todos viajen a Guatemala para experimentar esta cultura.
    (D) Sugiere que todos los intelectuales sean más pedantes, tal como los guatemaltecos.

7. ¿Cómo sería posible caracterizar a este escritor?

    (A) Muy sincero pero ingenuo.
    (B) Muy pensador.
    (C) Intenso.
    (D) Es un mentiroso.

Selección 16

Tema curricular: La vida contemporánea

Fuente 1: El siguiente artículo se trata del precio de la electricidad en España. Fue publicado en la página web Cantabria 24 Horas en abril de 2023.

El precio de la electricidad sigue bajando gracias a la apuesta del Gobierno por las energías renovables

Abril cierra con buenas noticias para los consumidores del mercado regulado de la luz, pues el mes ha cerrado con un precio medio de 73 euros el megavatio hora.

Unos niveles mucho más bajos que en meses anteriores y lejos de aquellos valores medios superi

Línea ores a 100 y a 200 euros el MWh.

(5) La mayor participación de las energías renovables y el tope al gas (medida aplicada por el gobierno que consiste en poner un tope, o límite, al precio máximo de gas) ha permitido que el precio de la electricidad haya caído de forma paulatina en los últimos meses y ya sitúe en niveles de 2020.

Según los datos de la Comisión Nacional de los Mercados y la Competencia (CNMC), para una potencia de 4,4 KW y un consumo de 250 KWh al mes (distribuido en los tramos punta, valle y llano),

(10) el precio medio de la factura de abril será de 48 euros. Segunda factura más baja desde 2021. Se trata del segundo precio más bajo desde febrero de 2021, cuando la factura media se situó en 47 euros. Y si lo centramos en el presente 2023, abril ha cerrado con la factura más baja de los primeros 4 meses del año.

El auge de las renovables ha provocado que durante varias jornadas el pool eléctrico marcase 0

(15) euros el MWh, una situación que se ha repetido hasta en 19 ocasiones. Por ello el precio de la electricidad en abril se ha reducido notablemente. Si se compara con los valores de hace 1 año, el coste de la luz era 120 euros más caro ya que en 2022 abril cerró con una media de 191,78 euros el megavatio hora. Hace 12 meses la factura media de la luz fue de 124 euros, la quinta más cara de la serie histórica en aquel momento.

(20) La mayor aportación de energía solar y eólica durante el mes ha sido clave y al no poder almacenarse implica poder tener un coste cero en el mercado mayorista, lo que ha propiciado los precios a la baja. De hecho, el buen aprovechamiento de las renovables ha hecho posible que, por segundo mes consecutivo, no se haya tenido que aplicar el tope al gas.

Fuente 2: La siguiente tabla presenta parte de la estructura de la generación eléctrica en España en gigavatio-hora (GWh). Fue compilada usando datos de la Red Eléctrica (REE.ES).

Fecha	2018	2019	2020	2021	2022
Hidráulica	34.117	24.719	30.632	29.626	17.907
Carbón	37.277	12.671	5.021	4.983	7.765
Motores diesel	3.178	2.836	2.399	2.517	2.548
Turbina de gas	1.049	671	407	424	657
Ciclo combinado (combinación de turbina de gas y de vapor de condensación)	30.044	55.242	44.023	44.500	68.137
Eólica	49.581	54.245	54.906	60.526	61.194
Solar fotovoltaica	7.766	9.252	15.302	20.981	27.902
Generación total	260.982	260.829	251.399	260.011	276.413

*Un gigavatio-hora es equivalente a mil (1.000) megavatios horas (MWh)

1. ¿Cuál es el tema del artículo?

   (A) El aumento en el precio de la electricidad
   (B) La inestabilidad del mercado eléctrico en España
   (C) La disminución del precio de la electricidad debido a energías renovables
   (D) Nuevas regulaciones gubernamentales sobre energía

2. ¿Cuál fue el precio medio del megavatio hora en abril?

   (A) 100 euros
   (B) 200 euros
   (C) 47 euros
   (D) 73 euros

3. ¿Qué medida gubernamental tuvo un impacto en el precio de la electricidad?

   (A) Incremento en la producción de carbón
   (B) Poner un tope al precio del gas
   (C) Reducción de impuestos a la energía
   (D) Importación de energía

4. Según el artículo, ¿cuál fue la factura media de electricidad en 2023?

   (A) 124 euros
   (B) 48 euros
   (C) 191,78 euros
   (D) 47 euros

5. ¿Cuál de las siguientes afirmaciones es verdadera según el artículo?

   (A) El precio de la electricidad ha sido constante en los últimos años.
   (B) El pool eléctrico nunca marcó 0 euros el MWh.
   (C) Abril de 2023 tuvo la factura más baja en los primeros 4 meses del año.
   (D) El tope al gas se aplicó todos los meses.

6. ¿Qué papel jugaron las energías renovables en la reducción de precios?

   (A) Contribuyeron a bajar el precio.
   (B) Incrementaron el costo de la electricidad.
   (C) Solo la energía solar tuvo impacto.
   (D) No tuvieron influencia.

7. ¿Cuál fue la contribución de la energía solar y eólica?

   (A) Aumentaron la capacidad de almacenamiento de energía, reduciendo así la dependencia de combustibles fósiles.
   (B) Contribuyeron a estabilizar los precios de la electricidad al diversificar las fuentes de energía.
   (C) Facilitaron la reducción de precios en el mercado debido a su incapacidad de almacenamiento.
   (D) Mejoraron la eficiencia energética global, pero no tuvieron un impacto directo en la reducción de los precios de la electricidad.

8. ¿Cómo se compara el precio de la luz de abril 2023 con abril 2022?

    (A) Era más barato en 2022.

    (B) No hubo cambios significativos.

    (C) Era más caro en 2022.

    (D) Era más barato en 2023.

9. ¿Qué muestra la tabla en el documento?

    (A) Precios de diferentes tipos de energía.

    (B) Las fuentes de creación eléctrica en España.

    (C) Consumo de electricidad en hogares, por fuente.

    (D) Costo de producción de electricidad.

10. Según la información en la tabla, ¿cómo se compara la evolución de la generación de energía solar con la energía eólica entre 2018 y 2022?

    (A) Ambas fuentes han experimentado un crecimiento, pero la solar ha mostrado una tasa de aumento más acelerada.

    (B) Ambas energías han incrementado su producción, pero la solar ha duplicado su capacidad respeto a la eólica.

    (C) Ambas energías han incrementado su producción, pero la eólica ha mostrado un incremento proporcionalmente mayor.

    (D) Ambas fuentes de energía han tenido una disminución en su producción.

11. ¿Cuál de las siguientes declaraciones se puede comprobar con información del artículo y de la tabla?

    (A) La disminución del precio de la electricidad

    (B) El aumento en la producción de energía hidráulica

    (C) El incremento en el uso de energías renovables

    (D) La eficiencia de la energía solar en comparación con otras fuentes

---

Cultural Awareness

Cultural perspective: The article and table show the use of role of renewable energies in generating electricity in Spain.

What is the role of renewable energies in generating electricity in your community?

Selección 17

Tema curricular: La vida contemporánea

En el siguiente fragmento, del libro Y van dos . . . de Marcelo Menasche, el narrador narra las experiencias que tuvo después de tomar una decisión importante.

> Cuando vi a Dora por tercera vez en brazos de un amigo diferente no esperé más. Y tomé una decisión: no la volvería a ver en mi vida.
>
> Dicen que el mejor remedio para estas cosas es viajar; hasta tal punto debe ser cierto que tuve una
>
> *Línea*
>
> (5) vez una novia que, después de haberme hecho sufrir como inocente en el infierno me recomendó ella misma el cambio de lugar. Cosa que me inspiró el doble temor de que esa mujer me estaba tomando por imbécil y tenía comisión por envío de clientes a un balneario.
>
> Como estábamos en pleno febrero bien podía elegir Mar del Plata, "la aristocrática playa." La vida agitada y tonta del balneario me haría olvidar.
>
> Reuní unos pesos, unas camisas y saqué un boleto "fin de semana." Subí al vagón, no sin pensar un
>
> (10) poco, involuntariamente, en la posible aventura de viaje.
>
> Es realmente asombroso, pero es el caso que los "magazines" ilustrados y las escritoras america-nas tienen una pasión morbosa por ese tema: Irremediablemente, sube al tren "momentos antes de la salida" (¡qué gracia! bueno fuera "momentos después de la salida"), el joven escritor, elegante, atlético y famoso. La casualidad quiere que la bella y misteriosa viajera lea en ese mismo instante su última
>
> (15) novela. (Un detalle siempre es "su última novela"; podría suceder, tratándose de un escritor prolífico y famoso, que la hermosa joven leyese la penúltima o la antepenúltima. Pero según parece hay un con-sorcio de escritores de esta categoría y nadie puede introducir innovaciones al estilo de la sociedad que es intangible). Una conversación se entabla pronto, sobre todo cuando los dos interlocutores son jóvenes.

1. ¿Por qué decidió visitar Mar del Plata?

    (A) Porque todos los aristócratas iban allí en el invierno.
    (B) Porque habría mucha actividad para pasar el tiempo.
    (C) Porque todos los escritores estarían allí.
    (D) Porque podría leer muchos libros.

2. ¿Qué desea olvidar este narrador?

    (A) Una novela que leyó
    (B) Un negocio fracasado
    (C) Una relación amorosa
    (D) Una joven que leyó su novela

3. ¿En qué tema tienen las escritoras americanas una pasión morbosa?

    (A) Los amores fracasados
    (B) La posibilidad de aventuras inesperadas
    (C) Conversaciones casuales en trenes
    (D) Viajes ferrocarrileros con autores famosos

4. ¿Qué hizo al subir al vagón?

   (A) Entabló una conversación con un escritor.
   (B) Observó el encuentro de otros dos pasajeros.
   (C) Empezó a leer una novela a una joven.
   (D) Imaginó una aventura entre dos personas.

5. ¿Qué parece opinar el narrador del joven escritor?

   (A) Admira su atleticismo.
   (B) Envidia su popularidad.
   (C) Se enoja que tenga tanto éxito.
   (D) Lo odia porque es famoso.

6. En las líneas 18–19, ¿cuál es el tono de las palabras "que la hermosa joven leyese la penúltima o la antepenúltima?"

   (A) Sarcástico
   (B) Irónico
   (C) Trágico
   (D) Chismoso

7. ¿Cuál es la actitud del narrador en este trozo?

   (A) Está deprimido.
   (B) Parece muy desilusionado.
   (C) Está muy enamorado.
   (D) Tiene buen sentido del humor.

Cultural Awareness

Cultural perspective: This fragment presents a perspective of an Argentine male narrator following a lost love affair. During part of his narration, he ridicules the idyllic world that he feels American magazines present.

How are the perspectives presented in this fragment similar to or different from those in your own community?

Selección 18

Tema curricular: Las familias y las comunidades

El siguiente texto se trata de un evento académico promovido por las instituciones educativas de la Asociación para la Enseñanza en Cali, Colombia, en 2010.

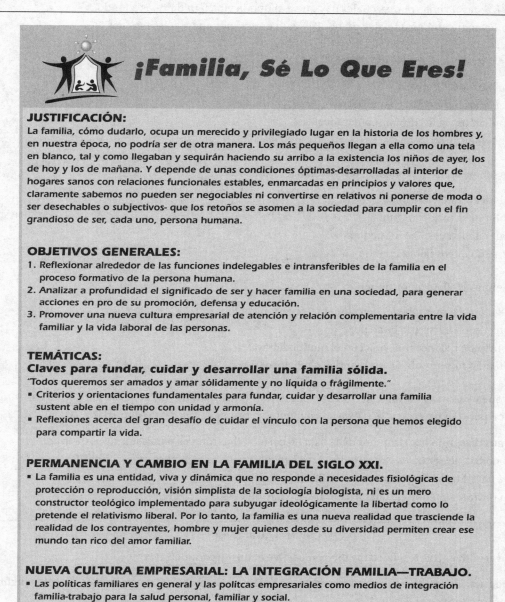

¡Familia, Sé Lo Que Eres!

JUSTIFICACIÓN:

Línea
(5)
La familia, cómo dudarlo, ocupa un merecido y privilegiado lugar en la historia de los hombres y, en nuestra época, no podría ser de otra manera. Los más pequeños llegan a ella como una tela en blanco, tal y como llegaban y seguirán haciendo su arribo a la existencia los niños de ayer, los de hoy y los de mañana. Y depende de unas condiciones óptimas-desarrolladas al interior de hogares sanos con relaciones funcionales estables, enmarcadas en principios y valores que, claramente sabemos no pueden ser negociables ni convertirse en relativos ni ponerse de moda o ser desechables o subjectivos- que los retoños se asomen a la sociedad para cumplir con el fin grandioso de ser, cada uno, persona humana.

(10)
OBJETIVOS GENERALES:

1. Reflexionar alrededor de las funciones indelegables e intransferibles de la familia en el proceso formativo de la persona humana.
2. Analizar a profundidad el significado de ser y hacer familia en una sociedad, para generar acciones en pro de su promoción, defensa y educación.
(15)
3. Promover una nueva cultura empresarial de atención y relación complementaria entre la vida familiar y la vida laboral de las personas.

TEMÁTICAS:
Claves para fundar, cuidar y desarrollar una familia sólida.
"Todos queremos ser amados y amar sólidamente y no líquida o frágilmente."
(20)
▪ Criterios y orientaciones fundamentales para fundar, cuidar y desarrollar una familia sustent able en el tiempo con unidad y armonía.
▪ Reflexiones acerca del gran desafío de cuidar el vínculo con la persona que hemos elegido para compartir la vida.

PERMANENCIA Y CAMBIO EN LA FAMILIA DEL SIGLO XXI.
(25)
▪ La familia es una entidad, viva y dinámica que no responde a necesidades fisiológicas de protección o reproducción, visión simplista de la sociología biologista, ni es un mero constructor teológico implementado para subyugar ideológicamente la libertad como lo pretende el relativismo liberal. Por lo tanto, la familia es una nueva realidad que trasciende la realidad de los contrayentes, hombre y mujer quienes desde su diversidad permiten crear ese
(30)
mundo tan rico del amor familiar.

NUEVA CULTURA EMPRESARIAL: LA INTEGRACIÓN FAMILIA—TRABAJO.
▪ Las políticas familiares en general y las polítcas empresariales como medios de integración familia-trabajo para la salud personal, familiar y social.

1. ¿Cuál es el propósito de este evento?

   (A) Explorar la función de los padres en el ámbito familiar y exponer cómo hay que criar a los hijos
   (B) Definir y promover los valores inherentes de la familia, su impacto en el ser humano
       y su importancia social
   (C) Justificar las razones por las cuales hay que explorar la vida familiar más a fondo
   (D) Promocionar cambios sociales y laborales para darles más apoyo a las familias

2. ¿A quiénes parece ser dirigido este folleto?

   (A) A miembros del gobierno
   (B) A matrimonios, novios y educadores
   (C) A empleados y jefes de compañías locales
   (D) A funcionarios de la iglesia

3. ¿A qué se refiere la frase "como una tela en blanco" (líneas 3–4)?

   (A) A la inocencia de los niños
   (B) Al color de la tez de los niños
   (C) A cómo deben vestirse los pequeños
   (D) Al tamaño de los bebés cuando nacen

4. ¿Cómo define el folleto a una familia?

   (A) Es algo que va más allá del pensamiento preestablecido.
   (B) Es una unión necesaria biológica.
   (C) Es vital para balancear la vida con el mundo laboral.
   (D) Es un pilar importante de los mandatos religiosos.

5. Imagina que necesitas más información del seminario y que le mandas un mensaje por correo electrónico a la
   Asociación para la Enseñanza. ¿Cuál de las siguientes preguntas sería más apropiada?

   (A) Buenos días, ¿me podría quitar de la lista de correos electrónicos para estos tipos de eventos?
   (B) ¿Me podría decir cuáles van a ser los temas en los que se va a enfocar este seminario?
   (C) ¿Qué hay? Mi esposa y yo estaremos allí. Nos vemos entonces.
   (D) A mi novia y a mí nos gustaría asistir. ¿Acaso hay un costo?

Cultural Awareness

Cultural perspective: This text presents the perspective of the importance of family.

Cultural product: This text presents an event that took place in Colombia in which participants are taught to reflect on the importance of family.

How are the products and perspectives presented in this text similar to or different from those in your own community?

Selección 19

Tema curricular: Los desafíos mundiales

La siguiente carta es de una estudiante a su profesor en la que habla de un artículo que leyó que le llamó la atención.

Profesor Sánchez,

Ante todo quiero agradecerle por ser un profesor tan inspirador. Verdaderamente disfruté mucho su clase y estoy más interesada que nunca en el servicio social y en buscar oportunidades en las que
Línea yo pueda ayudar a los menos afortunados. Por eso quisiera comentarle de un proyecto que descubrí
(5) que me ha dejado muy entusiasmada y me gustaría poder compartirlo con usted.

El otro día estaba leyendo el periódico y leí un artículo de una organización que se llama "Payasos sin Fronteras." ¿Los conoce? Estuve muy conmovida por los logros de este grupo y el impacto que ha tenido durante los últimos veinte años. El grupo toma la iniciativa de darles apoyo emocional a las poblaciones refugiadas de todo el mundo mediante la risa. Hasta ahora ha hecho más de diez mil
(10) actuaciones en casi cien países, haciéndoles reír a más de tres millones de niños y niñas.

Después de leer el artículo, decidí investigarlos más. Descubrí que empezaron en 1993, cuando un grupo de estudiantes de una escuela en Barcelona le invitaron a un payaso a que les acompañara a un campo de refugiados en Croacia, durante la guerra de los Balcanes. Desde aquel día, este grupo ha crecido hasta contar con secciones en varios países europeos, Estados Unidos, Canadá y Sudáfrica.
(15) Los miembros son típicamente artistas profesionales que han llevado un largo recorrido en los circos, teatros, u otras disciplinas y que trabajan como voluntarios en los proyectos internacionales y aunque la organización les paga todos los gastos para llevar a cabo la labor, no reciben ninguna compensación ni salario.

El artículo me dejó muy emocionada, y me pregunté si se pudiera llevar a cabo un proyecto pare-
(20) cido o formar una sección en nuestra comunidad. Sé que muchos están sufriendo ahora por la crisis económica, y un proyecto como éste podría por lo menos brindarles a los niños más impactados unos momentos de alivio. ¿Conoce usted a alguien que pueda ayudarme con esta iniciativa? ¿Tiene unos consejos para ayudarme? También, sería un gran honor si usted pudiera participar de alguna forma, aunque sea de forma mínima. Su curso y su pasión por los desafortunados me han dado la motivación
(25) de buscar estas oportunidades, y nada me haría más feliz que poder trabajar a su lado.

Le agradezco por todo lo que ha hecho por mí y espero que considere mi invitación y que me pueda ayudar de cualquier forma posible.

Atentamente,
(30) Luisa Ramírez

---

1. ¿Con qué propósito le escribe Luisa a su profesor?

   (A) Para agradecerle su ayuda
   (B) Para informarle de algo que descubrió
   (C) Para pedirle ayuda
   (D) Para informarle de algo y pedirle ayuda

2. ¿Cuál es la función primaria Payasos sin Fronteras?

   (A) Llamar la atención a los problemas mundiales
   (B) Recaudar fondos para ayudar a los refugiados
   (C) Hacerles reír a todos los niños del mundo
   (D) Traer humor y felicidad a los que están sufriendo

3. ¿Qué les provee la organización a los payasos que deciden participar?

    (A) Reembolso de los gastos personales y de viaje
    (B) Pagamento de producción y de transporte
    (C) Apoyo emocional y moral
    (D) Entrenamiento profesional

4. ¿Quiénes suelen ser los voluntarios de esta organización?

    (A) Artistas de todos tipos de disciplinas
    (B) Gente experimentada en diferentes espectáculos para niños
    (C) Estudiantes universitarios con ganas de viajar
    (D) Personas interesadas en desarrollar proyectos internacionales

5. ¿Cómo se puede describir la relación entre Luisa y el profesor?

    (A) Es una relación bastante fría.
    (B) Se conocen personalmente.
    (C) Son amigos.
    (D) Ella ha sido estudiante de él.

6. Si Luisa quisiera investigar más los impactos de esta organización que menciona
    en su carta, ¿cuál de las siguientes publicaciones le ayudaría más?

    (A) La solidaridad caminando de la mano de la risa
    (B) Desplazamiento y conflictos globales
    (C) El que ríe vive mejor
    (D) Los retos de ser payaso

7. Según la carta, ¿cuál de los siguientes adjetivos mejor describe el estado emocional de Luisa?

    (A) Inspirada
    (B) Desilusionada
    (C) Preocupada
    (D) Frustrada

Cultural Awareness

Cultural product: This correspondence presents a group from Spain whose mission is to help bring emotional support to people who have been displaced.

How are this group and its mission similar to or different from non-profit groups in your own community?

Selección 20

Tema curricular: La belleza y la estética

El siguiente artículo trata de un baile tradicional. Fue publicado en la página web de la Alcaldía de Ibagué en Colombia.

El Sanjuanero

El Sanjuanero tolimense, más que una danza es un lenguaje representativo de la idiosincrasia del departamento. Su nombre original es el *Contrabandista*, melodía oficializada en 1988 como la danza

Línea insignia del departamento. Fue compuesto por el maestro *Cantalicio Rojas*.

(5)   La coreografía del *Sanjuanero Tolimense* es el resultado de la investigación de Inés Rojas Luna (QEPD), quien recogió diferentes representaciones folclóricas de todo el Tolima. Rojas Luna logró mezclar los rajaleñas que se bailan en el sur del departamento con los bambucos característicos del norte, en municipios como Líbano, Fresno y Villahermosa. Esta danza representa las estrategias de conquista y el idilio que vivían los campesinos tolimenses en las épocas de antaño.

(10)   Empieza con el coqueteo, pasa por el enamoramiento y termina con el símbolo del matrimonio. Es una coreografía mestiza, en la que se combinan pasos indígenas (movimientos suaves sobre la tierra) con la influencia española (pasos fuertes, donde se levantan los cuerpos).

En otros tiempos, los hombres utilizaban este baile para estar cerca de la mujer a la que amaban y para formalizar el noviazgo en medio de la fiesta.

(15)   **Historia**

Nadie sabe con exactitud dónde, cuándo, ni cómo se inició la antiquísima celebración sanjuanera que nos llama a los tolimenses en el mes de junio. Todos conocemos la historia moderna de la festividad a partir de 1959 cuando el patriarca conservador Adriano Tribín Piedrahita, decidió crear el Festival Folclórico, casi como una extensión de la Alianza por la Paz, iniciativa que propuso como

(20)   elemento catalizador para alcanzar la convivencia y reconciliación de las convulsionadas regiones del país.

Pero para llegar a ese punto de la historia moderna del *San Juan* muchos acontecimientos históricos, económicos, políticos y sociales debieron sucederse; no exactamente en Ibagué, sino en el llano tolimense, en las encomiendas, haciendas y caseríos tornados en poblaciones, localizadas estas a

(25)   orillas del río Grande de la Magdalena. Lo cierto es que el *San Juan* como celebración llega a estas tierras con el influjo español, se entremezcla con las tradiciones aborígenes, amalgamado por la evangelización de las misiones católicas, con el propósito de convertir a los pueblos nativos considerados paganos. La relación estrecha surgida entre conquistadores y conquistados, luego entre encomenderos y encomendados, y posteriormente entre señores y jornaleros, hizo que el *San Juan* iniciara su

(30)   camino hacia la modernidad y la festividad que hoy observamos.

---

1. Según el artículo, ¿qué representa el Sanjuanero Tolimense?

   (A) Las diversas lenguas que se hablan en esta región
   (B) Las investigaciones hechas por una antropóloga famosa
   (C) Los rasgos y el carácter de la provincia
   (D) La historia de la conquista de esta parte del país

2. ¿Qué escenifica el baile?

   (A) Las tradiciones de la gente indígena y los españoles
   (B) Un cortejo típico del pasado
   (C) Unos cuentos folklóricos
   (D) Los bailes característicos del norte y del sur de Colombia

3. ¿Qué es "bambuco" (línea 9)?

    (A) Es un tipo de música.

    (B) Es un departamento del país.

    (C) Es una representación teatral.

    (D) Es un conjunto de pueblos.

4. Según el artículo, ¿cuál fue el propósito original del Festival Folclórico?

    (A) Servir de evento unificador para diversas facciones en conflicto

    (B) Darle homenaje a la cultura del departamento

    (C) Llamar la atención a diversos asuntos políticos y económicos

    (D) Representar la llegada de los españoles en el siglo XVII

5. ¿A qué se refiere la palabra "tornados" (línea 30) en el texto?

    (A) A los tumultos que existían en aquel entonces

    (B) A la ubicación de diversos pueblos

    (C) A la peculiaridad de la tierra colombiana

    (D) Al crecimiento de habitantes en una parte de la provincia

6. ¿Qué adjetivo mejor describe la fiesta de San Juan?

    (A) Religiosa

    (B) Moderna

    (C) Heterogénea

    (D) Pagana

7. Al escribir un ensayo sobre el tema del artículo, quisieras buscar más información. ¿Cuál de las siguientes publicaciones te serviría más?

    (A) Ferias y fiestas del Tolima

    (B) Bailes folclóricos españoles

    (C) Una historia concisa de América Latina

    (D) Guía práctico del altiplano colombiano

Cultural Awareness

Cultural product: This text presents a type of dance in Colombia.

How is this dance similar to or different from those in your own community?

Selección 21

Tema curricular: La vida contemporánea

Fuente 1: El siguiente artículo trata del tema de ser vegetariano. Fue publicado en *www.laopinion.com*.

Hasta qué punto conviene ser vegetariano. La Opinión Digital

(*www.laopinion.com/salud/salud_nutrition.html*)

Realmente, la carne, como cualquier otro alimento excepto la leche materna para su descendiente en el primer período de la vida de los mamíferos, no es indispensable para la nutrición del hombre, pero es un valioso componente de gran riqueza nutritiva en las dietas de muchas personas que

Línea gozan de buena salud y no ejerce en los sujetos normales los efectos nocivos que el vegetarianismo le

(5) atribuye. Existe la creencia popular de que la alimentación vegetariana es más saludable que una que incluya carne u otros productos derivados de animales.

Lo cierto es que todo tipo de alimentación cuenta con beneficios nutritivos y puede también presentar aspectos problemáticos.

La selección de alimentos que escoge la persona es el factor que determina si una alimentación es

(10) saludable o no. Si se elige una alimentación vegetariana, es importante asegurarse de ingerir cantidades suficientes de vitamina B_{12} y calcio, especialmente durante la adolescencia.

Una alimentación vegetariana bien planeada tiende a incluir niveles menores de grasa saturada y colesterol, así como niveles más altos de fibra y elementos nutrientes derivados de las plantas que una alimentación no vegetariana.

(15) Especialistas en nutrición del programa de Extensión Cooperativa de la Universidad de California citan diversas investigaciones que indican que una alimentación con tales características puede reducir el riesgo de desarrollar diabetes, presión arterial alta, problemas del corazón y obesidad.

Sin embargo, los beneficios mencionados pueden obtenerse también con una alimentación que incluya productos animales. Con una planificación cuidadosa y el consumo de carnes magras y

(20) productos animales con poca grasa, así como frutas y verduras, se puede llevar una alimentación con poca grasa saturada y colesterol y rica en fibra y nutrientes derivados de plantas.

Además, el consumo de productos animales facilita obtener las cantidades recomendables de calcio, zinc, hierro y vitamina B_{12}.

Fuente 2: La siguiente tabla presenta una guía para una dieta vegetariana. Fue publicado en la página web *www.macroestetica.com* en 2009.

Grupo de alimentos	Raciones diarias sugeridas	Tamaños de la ración
Panes, cereales, arroz y pasta	6 o más	1 rebanada de pan, ½ bollo, ½ taza de cereal cocido, arroz o pasta, 30g de cereal seco
Vegetales	4 o más	½ taza cocidos o 1 taza crudos, ½ taza jugo de verduras
Frutas	3 o más	1 pieza de fruta, ½ taza de jugo de fruta, ½ taza de fruta enlatada o cocida
Leguminosas y otros sustitutos de carne	2 a 3	½ de leguminosas cocidas, 120g de tofú, 240 ml de leche de soja, 45g de queso de soja, 2 cucharadas de crema de cacahuate, 90g de hamburguesa de tofú
Productos lácteos (opcional)	No más de 3	1 taza de leche o yogur, 45g de queso natural, 60 g de queso procesado
Huevos (opcional)	3 a 4 a la semana	1 huevo o 2 claras, ½ taza de sustituto de huevo
Grasas, dulces y alcohol	Pocas cantidades	Aceite, margarina y mayonesa, aderezos para ensalada, gaseosas, dulces, cerveza, vino y bebidas destiladas

1. ¿Cuál es el propósito del artículo?

    (A) Persuadir a que los lectores sigan una dieta vegetariana

    (B) Analizar cómo una dieta vegetariana puede reducir el riesgo de contraer unas enfermedades

    (C) Criticar la creencia de que seguir una dieta vegetariana es más saludable que otras dietas

    (D) Presentar información de lo que uno debe tener en cuenta al pensar en ser vegetariano

2. ¿Qué técnica usa el autor del artículo para apoyar una de sus ideas?

    (A) Cita varias anécdotas de su propia experiencia.

    (B) Incluye resultados de unos estudios.

    (C) Hace referencia a unas estadísticas.

    (D) Incorpora varios dichos y proverbios.

3. ¿Cuál de las siguientes afirmaciones mejor resume la opinión presentada en el artículo en cuanto al consumo de carne?

    (A) Perjudica tanto como acusa el pensamiento vegetariano.

    (B) Es esencial para obtener ciertas vitaminas y minerales.

    (C) Aunque provee algún beneficio, causa muchos más problemas a la salud.

    (D) Forma parte de una dieta saludable, siempre que sea baja en grasa.

4. Según el artículo, ¿qué alimento es absolutamente necesario para el ser humano?

    (A) Comidas ricas en fibra durante la edad adulta

    (B) Alimentos que contienen mucho calcio durante la juventud

    (C) La leche materna durante la primera parte de la vida

    (D) Frutas y verduras en la vejez

5. ¿A qué se refiere "la selección de alimentos" (línea 10) en cuanto a su impacto a llevar una dieta saludable?

    (A) A elegir una determinada cantidad de comida

    (B) A seleccionar solo comidas de alta calidad

    (C) A escoger diversas comidas con una variedad de valores nutritivos

    (D) A evitar las comidas con grasa

6. Según el artículo, ¿qué beneficio aporta el consumo de carne?

    (A) Provee la grasa necesaria en una dieta.

    (B) Aprovisiona ciertas vitaminas y minerales.

    (C) Reduce el riesgo de algunas enfermedades.

    (D) Suministra fibra y otros nutrientes que se encuentran también en plantas.

7. ¿Qué información presenta la tabla?

    (A) Un menú diario típico de una persona vegetariana

    (B) Los tipos y cantidades de comidas que forman una saludable dieta vegetariana

    (C) El valor nutritivo de ciertos alimentos en relación a otros

    (D) Los alimentos más saludables para llevar una dieta balanceada

8. Si fueras de seguir la tabla al pie de la letra, ¿cuál es la cantidad mínima de pan, cereales, pasta y arroz que deberías consumir en un día?

    (A) Dos bollos y una taza de pasta
    (B) Una rebanada de pan, un bollo y una taza de cereal cocido
    (C) Dos rebanadas de pan y una taza de arroz
    (D) Dos tazas de arroz y una rebanada de pan

9. Según la tabla, ¿cuál de los siguientes alimentos no se debería consumir diariamente?

    (A) Una naranja
    (B) Huevo duro
    (C) Queso fresco
    (D) Un sándwich de crema de cacahuete

10. ¿Cuál de las siguientes afirmaciones del artículo se puede verificar en la tabla?

    (A) El consumo de carne en poca cantidades es beneficioso para la salud.
    (B) No es indispensable el consumo de carne para la nutrición.
    (C) Hay que consumir una variedad de alimentos vegetarianos.
    (D) La alimentación vegetariana es más saludable que una que incluye carne.

11. Al preparar una presentación para tu clase sobre el mismo tema del artículo y la tabla, quisieras buscar más información. ¿Cuál de las siguientes publicaciones te ayudaría más en tu preparación?

    (A) Los beneficios ecológicos de ser vegetariano
    (B) 10 efectos nocivos del consumo de carne y otros productos animales
    (C) La ética de matar por comida
    (D) La dieta vegetariana: una opción posible, sana y científica

---

Cultural Awareness

Cultural perspective: The article presents an opinion on certain considerations one should make when considering becoming a vegetarian, while the table presents suggested daily intake of a vegetarian diet.

How are the perspectives presented in these texts similar to or different from those in your own community?

Selección 22

Tema curricular: La ciencia y la tecnología

En la siguiente carta, un estudiante le escribe a su profesor acerca de un artículo que leyó.

Estimado Profesor Morales,

Le escribo para agradecerle por haberme recibido ayer en su oficina y comentarle que disfruté mucho la charla que tuvimos sobre la ética de modificar células. Al volver a casa investigué más el
Línea asunto y encontré un artículo que me hizo pensar más en el tema y quería compartir mis pensamien-
(5) tos con usted.

El autor relata la historia de una niña de cuatro años que padece leucemia y sus padres decidieron traer al mundo otra hija para ser la donante de células madre provenientes de su cordón umbilical. La pregunta esencial es que si se pudiera salvar a un hijo al manipular células, ¿lo haría?

Entiendo que modificar células presenta muchos problemas. Por un lado, la Iglesia Católica está
(10) completamente en contra de la idea porque cada persona es un don de Dios, y al modificar las células una persona pierde su dignidad inhe-rente. Por otro lado, esta modificación le puede salvarle la vida a la niña, y podría curar otras enfermedades.

Otra idea que surgió es el hecho de cómo se sentiría la otra niña, la que nació para salvarle a su hermana. ¿Cómo le van a justificar los padres la razón por la cual vino al mundo? ¿Fue porque querían
(25) otra hija o porque fue por el ansia del bienestar de la otra?

Temo que no haya una respuesta correcta o fácil a este asunto. Algunos científicos ven una distin-ción entre una persona y un conjunto de células. Argumentan que aunque el embrión tiene la potencialidad de transformarse en persona, no lo es, y esto es diferente de cuando es feto que sí ya tiene vida. Creo que todos compartimos la misma opinión de que crear un feto para hacer uso de sus
(20) órganos y después descartar el individuo es una idea espantosa. La cuestión es que si hay que poner un conjunto de células en la misma categoría.

Personalmente tengo más preguntas que respuestas. Por un lado entiendo el argumento de los científicos y la razón de los padres, pero también comprendo el peligro y el dilema ético que el desa-rrollo de estas prácticas puede llevar. ¿Dónde ponemos el límite? ¿Tenemos el derecho de usar la
(25) ciencia para cambiar nuestro destino? ¿Quién decide si es permisible o no?

Este tema es algo que seguramente me va a seguir rondando en la cabeza y no veo la hora de poder discutirlo más a fondo con usted. Otra vez, agradezco el tiempo que tuvo para mí.

Atentamente,
Julio Benavides

1. ¿Por qué le escribe el estudiante al profesor?

   (A) Para informarle de un acontecimiento en el mundo de la medicina
   (B) Para presentarle los resultados de una investigación
   (C) Para continuar una conversación que tuvieron
   (D) Para debatir un asunto que le causó molestia

2. ¿Qué historia le relata el estudiante al profesor?

   (A) De los avances científicos en la modificación de células
   (B) De la decisión que tomó una familia
   (C) De la polémica que existe en a la torno a la modificación de células
   (D) De las complicaciones médicas que tuvo una pequeña niña

3. ¿A qué se refiere el autor de la carta cuando dice que para la Iglesia Católica cada persona es un "don de Dios" (línea 12)?

   (A) A que cada persona es tal y como debería ser.

   (B) A que las personas son muy religiosas.

   (C) A que los científicos deben tener más fe.

   (D) A que también las personas enfermas son gente digna.

4. ¿Qué dilema presenta el autor de la carta que posiblemente van a enfrentar los padres mencionados?

   (A) Decidir si quieren tomar medidas para salvarle la vida a su hija

   (B) Proveer para dos hijas, una de las cuales es enferma

   (C) Explicarle a una hija el motivo de traerla al mundo

   (D) Determinar si la modificación de células es una práctica ética

5. ¿Qué debate presenta el autor de la carta en cuanto al uso de células?

   (A) Si las células que se usan efectivamente ya tienen vida.

   (B) Si el embrión se puede convertir en persona.

   (C) Si hay que crear un feto para usar los órganos.

   (D) Si las personas son formadas de un grupo de células.

6. ¿Qué quiere comunicar el autor de la carta cuando dice que el tema le "va a seguir rondando" (línea 31)?

   (A) Que este tema le está causando dolor de cabeza.

   (B) Que no puede dejar de pensar en él.

   (C) Que no tiene la capacidad de pensar más.

   (D) Que el tema es demasiado complejo para él.

7. ¿Cuál de las siguientes afirmaciones describe mejor al autor de la carta?

   (A) A pesar de que acaba de enterarse de este tema, tiene las ideas bien claras.

   (B) Es un experto del tema, aunque no tiene opiniones muy fuertes.

   (C) Le fascina el asunto y quiere aclarar sus propias ideas.

   (D) Le interesa el tema, pero necesita ayuda para poder explicarse mejor.

Cultural Awareness

Cultural perspective: This text presents the perspective of a student in regards to the ethics of stem cell research and cloning cells in general.

How is the perspective presented in this text similar to or different from those in your own community?

Selección 23

Tema curricular: La ciencia y la tecnología

El siguiente artículo trata sobre los acuarios. El artículo original fue publicado en Eroski Consumer en 2010.

Los acuarios proliferaron en plena fiebre científica de comienzos del siglo veinte en las ciudades costeras. Cien años más tarde se llaman oceanarios y su misión de acercar el mundo marino, exhibiendo una recreación natural de su fauna y su flora, se ha afianzado. Cumplen además la triple

Línea function de conservar, investigar y concienciar de la necesidad de proteger el planeta. Con el conven-
(5) cimiento de que se salvaguarda mejor lo que se conoce, el espectador de estos escaparates acuáticos contempla el resultado de un trabajo preciso de biólogos y profesionales que velan por el funciona-miento perfecto unas instalaciones complejas y una organización eficaz. Todo para lograr acercar la biodiversidad de los mares y mostrar el ecosistema, el patrimonio universal que se esconde debajo del agua.

(10) A primera hora de la mañana comienza la actividad en el complejo laberinto de zonas privadas y espacio público. La parte franca, la que disfrutan los visitantes, la conforman salas de cristal recorri-das por pasillos. Antes de que estos accedan, se inspeccionan los acrílicos y el metacrilato, se observa el agua y se comprueba que reine la armonía dentro de ella. En el otro lado del cristal la actividad se multiplica. Se toman pruebas de agua, se controlan los filtros, los sensores, los vasos, las tuberías y los
(15) comprensores, las tomas de mar y las bombas que permiten el intercambio del agua. Pese a que todo el sistema está informatizado, la inspección visual es constante.

Los miles de animales y plantas que pueblan las aguas llegan del mar o son criados en cautividad, pero sea cual sea su procedencia, antes de pasar a convivir en la reproducción oceánica del ocean-ario salvan una cuarentena. A pesar de que la imitación es perfecta y flora y fauna viven en un habitat
(20) idéntico, las nuevas incorporaciones pueden suponer un peligro de alteración de los ácidos y microor-ganismos. Para evitarlo, todas las especies, grandes o pequeñas, viven sus primeros días en el acuario en pequeños tanques esperando el momento de pasar a las aguas definitivas. La cuarentena es un proceso complicado pero de vital importancia porque es donde se consigue que los peces se acli-maten, se acostumbren al alimento que recibirán, y también donde se les desparasita y se les cura las
(25) heridas. Cuando el pez está en óptimas condiciones puede pasar a la exposición.

En el acuario no hay corrientes que limpien las aguas, ni los animals pueden huir de un foco intoxi-cado. La limpieza es clave. Todos los días se sifona la suciedad del fondo, ya sean excrementos, algas o restos de comida. Se realiza de manera mecánica con herramientas específicas para cada espa-cio, pero cuando el tamaño del vaso impide la manipulación de mangueras son los buzos quienes se
(30) encargan de mantener la higiene de paredes, suelo y decorados.

Visitar un acuario es tener la oportunidad de imaginar un viaje en el submarino del capitán Nemo, el protagonista de 20.000 leguas de viaje submarino. Tras los cristales reina la vida inalcanzable del fondo de los océanos. Pero un acuario no es solo la suma de recipientes con millones de metros cúbicos de agua en los que se expone el ciclo de animales y plantas, en los que se pueden ver peces
(35) tropicales, corales, atunes, medusas, tortugas. También son centros científicos que realizan labores de investigación y conservación de la fauna y la flora marina. Se desarrollan proyectos medioambientales ahora más necesarios que nunca, porque vivimos un tiempo en que la salud de algunos mares, dete-riorada por la actividad humana, pone en riesgo la salud de todo el planeta.

(revista.consumer.es/web/es/20100501/actualidad/informe1/75560.php)

1. ¿Cuál será el propósito de un acuario?

   (A) Crear la ilusión de la vida submarina en la superficie del mar
   (B) Rescatar a animales marítimos heridos por pescadores deportivos
   (C) Enseñar al público de su responsabilidad para cuidar del ecosistema oceánico
   (D) Atraer al público para enriquecer la ciudad donde está el patrimonio universal

2. ¿Qué es la cuarentena (líneas 23 y 28)?

   (A) Un tipo de vaso en el que se guardan animales para observarlos.
   (B) Un tipo de tratamiento que recibe un animal enfermo para curarlo.
   (C) El tiempo necesario para preparar el acuario para recibir el animal.
   (D) Un modo mediante el cual se acierta a que se adapte el animal al medio ambiente nuevo.

3. ¿Cómo se limpia el vaso grande del acuario?

   (A) Hay peces que comen materias dañosas en el acuario.
   (B) Hay buceadores encargados de mantener la limpieza.
   (C) Hay herramientas mecánicas que se utilizan para limpiarlo.
   (D) Hacen correr chorros de agua para intercambiar las aguas.

4. ¿Cómo se mantiene todo un sistema tan complejo en el acuario?

   (A) Con mucha tubería
   (B) Por inspección visual
   (C) Por ciencia de ordenador
   (D) Con bombas y mangueras

5. ¿Por qué le gusta tanto al público visitar el acuario?

   (A) Lo inaccesible y secreto siempre le fascinan al público.
   (B) Le gusta visitar al Capitán Nemo cuando visita el acuario.
   (C) Al público le encanta la idea de ser animal acuático.
   (D) Le atrae la oportunidad de aprender sobre el alimento procedente del mar.

6. ¿Qué importancia tiene el acuario?

   (A) Es la única manera de salvar las especies en peligro de desaparecer.
   (B) No hay otro lugar donde se puede observar inutilidad de la vida marina.
   (C) Las indagaciones científicas logradas allí son imprescindibles.
   (D) Al visitar el acuario los niños se entusiasman por hacerse científicos.

7. Según el artículo, ¿a qué se atribuye el deterioro del mar?

    (A) Al descuido del ser humano

    (B) Al calentamiento global de las aguas

    (C) Al maltrato del océano por los marineros

    (D) A la sobreproducción de la industria pescadera

8. ¿Cuál de las siguientes frases sería el mejor título para este artículo?

    (A) Guía básica para montar un acuario

    (B) Cómo cuidar a tus peces

    (C) El mar entre cuatro paredes

    (D) Ventajas y desventajas de un acuario

Cultural Awareness

Cultural product: This text presents information about aquariums and how they function.

How are the aquariums presented in this text similar to or different from those in your own community?

Selección 24

Tema curricular: Las familias y las comunidades
Introducción: La siguiente selección trata de un festival en Valencia, España.

El origen de la fiesta de las Fallas se sitúa en los últimos años del siglo XV, cuando los carpinteros de la ciudad, en vísperas de la fiesta de su patrón San José, quemaban frente a sus talleres, en las calles y plazas públicas, los trastos inservibles junto con los artilugios de madera que empleaban para elevar *Línea* los candiles que les iluminaban mientras trabajaban en los meses de invierno.

(5) En la actualidad, son más de 350 las fallas que se queman en la ciudad de Valencia la noche del 19 de marzo, durante la tradicional cremà. Estos impresionantes monumentos de cartón piedra que invaden las calles tras la plantà, el 15 de marzo, compiten en ingenio y belleza, desde unas estructuras piramidales que garantizan una perfecta caída y posterior conversion en cenizas, satirizando sobre los últimos acontecimientos de la vida política, social y cultural.

(10) Las fallas van tomando poco a poco la ciudad transformándola en un auténtico espectáculo que cobra más fuerza a medida que se acerca su fin. Quien visite Valencia durante los días previos a la llamarada final se verá irremediablemente envuelto por la fiesta. Tendrá ocasión de pasearse entre las fallas que se instalan en cada esquina mientras escucha la música de las bandas o come chocolate con buñuelos; sentir que los cimientos retumban todos los días a las 14,00 horas, con la mascletà que se

(15) dispara desde la plaza del Ayuntamiento; ver una corrida de toros; asistir a la ofrenda a la Virgende los Desamparados, el 17 y el 18 de marzo, que convierte la fachada de la Basílica en un auténtico tapiz de flores y la plaza de la Virgen en un jardín; o disfrutar de la magia de los castillos de fuegos artificiales que llegan a su punto culminante la noche del 18 de marzo, nit del foc.

(www.pueblos-espana.org/comunidad+valenciana/valencia/valencia/)

1. ¿A quién(es) está dirigido este informe?

    (A) A gente que busca participar en un festival tranquilo.
    (B) A los que sufren de piromanía.
    (C) A turistas que quieren experimentar un evento local.
    (D) A jóvenes aficionados de los fantoches.

2. ¿Cuál fue el origen de las Fallas?

    (A) La gente quería honrar al alcalde de la ciudad de Valencia.
    (B) Tuvo origen en la dedicación de candiles en la Basílica durante la cremà.
    (C) Unos carpinteros quemaron sus desperdicios y otros objetos en público.
    (D) Alguna gente hizo fuegos en las calles para iluminar la ciudad de noche.

3. Actualmente, ¿cómo se hacen las fallas?

    (A) Los artesanos las hacen de cartón.
    (B) Los carpinteros las hacen de madera.
    (C) Los valencianos las producen con piedras.
    (D) La gente las construye de artilugios.

4. ¿Dónde se sitúan las fallas?

   (A) En la plaza del Ayuntamiento
   (B) En los jardines
   (C) En la Basílica
   (D) En las esquinas

5. ¿Con qué motivo se construyen las fallas?

   (A) Para mostrar la dedicación religiosa
   (B) Para conmemorar figuras sacadas de la historia
   (C) Para burlarse cómicamente de personas actuales
   (D) Para satírizar las grandes figuras religiosas de hoy y del pasado

6. ¿Qué es la mascletà (línea 18)?

   (A) Fuegos artificiales diurnos
   (B) Una corrida de toros
   (C) Fuegos artificiales nocturnos
   (D) Un desfile de carrozas

7. ¿Qué pasa durante la última noche?

   (A) Toda la gente se reúne en la plaza de la Basílica y del Ayuntamiento.
   (B) Hay un espectáculo tremendo de fuegos artificiales.
   (C) La Virgen aparece vestida de flores delante de la Basílica.
   (D) Hay obras de magia en los castillos de fuegos artificiales.

Cultural Awareness

Cultural practice: This text presents a festival that happens in Valencia, Spain, in March.

Cultural product: In addition to the festival, the text mentions the creation of structures that are a key part of the festival.

How are the practices and products presented in this text similar to or different from those in your own community?

Answers Explained

Selección 1

1. **(B)** This information can be found throughout the reading, and it is first introduced in lines 4-5 when the author references the risks that exist in social media that come as a consequence of certain behaviors and attitudes.

2. **(D)** The target audience is young users of social media, and this idea is reinforced throughout the text. Parents are also included as a target audience in line 6 ("Tanto los hijos como los padres...").

3. **(B)** This is the best answer, as nowhere in the text does it dissuade users from using social media, but rather aims to teach younger users how to use it more responsibly and make them aware of the possible risks that can come with certain behaviors.

4. **(C)** This information is stated in line 25, where one of the risks is when young people use social media to achieve "aprobación social" (social approval), and again in the last line, where this idea is stated more explicitly.

5. **(A)** The word "cibercontrol" is used with "de la pareja", meaning that the control is of a romantic partner using cyber means. This is one of the risks presented in the article, making it the best option.

6. **(B)** This is the best answer because it aligns with the objectives of the exposition, which are to raise awareness of the risks associated with the use of social media and digital technologies and social-emotional habits. The workshops ("talleres") could focus on talking about the psychological impacts and offer strategies for a healthier and safer use of social media.

7. **(A)** This option is the most relevant to this particular event. The article mentions the days that the exposition will happen, but not the times. Option (D) is not the best option because determining the most influential blogger is a matter of opinion and beyond the scope of the exposition.

Selección 2

1. **(A)** The text principally presents how a community of Bolivia is implementing a sustainable agricultural model in order to face the challenges of climate change, such as the lack of water. This makes Option A the best answer.

2. **(D)** The text specifically mentions in lines 11-13 the challenges related to the lack of water and the high temperatures that are exasperated by climate change.

3. **(B)** The text mentions in line 22 the use of polyculture (the raising of more than one species of plant at the same time and place) as an effective strategy to control plagues and to reduce the dependency on pesticides.

4. **(D)** The "harvesting" of water is vital to guarantee access of water during periods of drought. This makes Option D the best answer.

5. **(C)** In the context of climate change, the word "azotando" means to have a severe negative impact, making Option C the clear answer.

6. **(B)** In the text, this is referring to the practice of cultivating different species of plants in the same plot. This is a sustainable and adaptive strategy in an area that is affected by climate change.

7. **(B)** The replication of this sustainable model in other communities can significantly contribute to their food security, especially in regions that are affected by climate change.

8. **(B)** The table presents the water footprint of different foods. In other words, the amount of water necessary for their production. Make sure to always read the introduction of the sources, for this is where helpful information can be found to accurately interpret graphs and tables.

9. **(A)** As stated in the introduction, the numbers in the table represent the amount of water (in liters) that is needed to produce one kilogram of the food type, making Option (A) the best answer.

10. **(B)** Considering the low water footprint of vegetables in the table compared to other foods, and the cultivation practice in Timboy Tiguasú, Option (B) is the statement that can best be verified.

11. **(A)** When making predictions based on information from multiple sources, make sure to select the   option? [to avoid close repetition] that best answers the question. Given the text's focus on sustainable agricultural practices and water management and the table's information on the water footprint of many different types of foods, including meat, the report mentioned in Option (A) would be very useful to better understand these topics in a broader context. One might be tempted to select Option (B), but its focus is on irrigation, not on food security.

Selección 3

1. **(C)** The advertisement is for the general public since the dancers have already been selected. The adjective limeño refers to a resident of Lima, Perú.

2. **(B)** The answer to this question is clearly found in lines 1 and 2, and then restated in lines 20–23. Some might be tempted to select answer (A), for in this competition there will be winners. However, the stated goal of the advertisement is not to pick the best dancers in the nation, but rather to preserve a cultural practice.

3. **(D)** There are a number of prizes that are mentioned in lines 13 through 15. These include monetary prizes as well as diplomas and trophies. In addition, lines 16–17 present the Campeón de Campeones category, which is where the winners of past competitions compete. Although the text never says what each category winner receives, one can safely assume that the winner will win one of the prizes mentioned in lines 13–15 and qualify to compete in an upcoming Campeón de Campeones event.

4. **(C)** The answer is found in lines 16–19, where it states that any champion of a contest sponsored by the Municipalidad de Lima can compete except for those who have won this category sometime in the past two years.

5. **(A)** When answering questions that force you to think beyond the text, a good idea is to think of the most logical option. In this case, option (A) is logical because the text does give information about the location of the event, but nothing about how to get there. Option (B) is not logical because the text says that the cost is free (line 28). Option (C) is incorrect because this text is inviting the general public, not looking for dancers. Option (D) is also not a good option because the author of this text would not necessarily know how to answer this, nor does it have anything to do with the event that the author is promoting.

Selección 4

1. **(B)** The answer to this question is found in lines 6–7, where it states that the rosca is ". . . un bizcocho fino . . . que contiene en promedio tres figures de plástico . . . ." The adjective "delicioso" in line 5 proves that the "bizcocho" is a type of food, therefore making option (B) the correct answer because it is the only option that mentions a type of food ("postre").

2. **(B)** This information is found in lines 10–11, which says that the rosca is ". . . el centro de atención de la fiesta de cada seis de enero . . . ." The other dates make reference to different activities, but not the eating of this food.

3. **(D)** Pay close attention to this question, for unlike questions 1 and 2, it refers now to the event, not the food. Although there are two events mentioned in this text (el Día de los Reyes Magos and el Día de la Candelaria), the main event is el Día de los Reyes Magos because the author of this letter was not able to stay long enough to experience the second celebration. El Día de los Reyes Magos, or Epiphany as it is known in English, is an event that celebrates the arrival of the three kings (also known as wise men) to Bethlehem to visit the infant Jesus. Although the text itself does not explicitly say what actions are taken besides eating the rosca de Reyes, you can infer that the family goes to church because in lines 30–31, when talking about the actions surrounding el Día de la Candelaria, it says that families ". . . se reúnen nuevamente para celebrar la presentación del niño

Dios en la iglesia." The key word is "nuevamente" (once again), meaning that they had met earlier to do a similar celebration, which is celebrating with food and going to church. Option (A) is incorrect because the only reference to Romans is in line 21, where it states that some historians believe that this tradition has Roman origins. Option (B) is incorrect because in lines 15–16 it says that only the person who finds the plastic figure in the rosca de Reyes has to dress up and present gifts, not everyone. Option (C) is incorrect because not everyone prepares or purchases a rosca; only one is made per family.

4. **(D)** This information is found in lines 15–16, where it says, ". . . quien encuentre la figura deberá vestir y presentar al niño Dios en la iglesia . . . ."

5. **(C)** You can find the answer in lines 19–20, where it speaks to how long this current tradition has been in place. Some might be tempted to select option (D), and although some historians believe that it has Roman origins, it is not clear if the current Catholic religious celebration began in Roman times since Romans were pagans, thus making option (D) an answer difficult to prove.

6. **(D)** This is another question in which process of elimination can help you clearly identify the correct answer. There is nothing explicitly stated in the text that will help you answer this question. Rather you have to consider the message as a whole. Does this tradition make it so that families come together to help merchants? Not really, so option (A) can be eliminated. Does this celebration allow merchants to take a break? No, because they actually take advantage of this time to expand their earnings (lines 23–24); thus option (B) can be eliminated. Does this celebration tighten relations between the church and merchants? No. Merchants take advantage of this celebration to gain more money, but the church almost definitely is not using this as a financial gain, but rather to celebrate an important part of its history (eliminate option (C)). Does this celebration allow children to feel a part of the religious community? Well, yes. They get to remember an important religious event and eat delicious food, and, if they find the plastic figure, they will

have to present it at church. By the process of elimination, option (D) is the clear answer.

7. **(B)** The penultimate paragraph contains this information. Pablo mentions all the foods that will be prepared for the Día de la Candelaria, and is upset that he will not be there to partake. Option (A) is incorrect because Pablo did not find the plastic figure—his brother did—and therefore Pablo could not present it even if he wanted to. Option (C) is incorrect because this celebration is a yearly event. Option (D) is incorrect because he never mentions not wanting to return to school. In fact, he simply states that he will see his friend in school, and one could infer that he could be looking forward to it.

Selección 4—Más Práctica

When answering these questions, consider how you and your family celebrate a religious holiday during the months of December and January. Consider the products used (food, gifts, etc.), the practices (do you go to a religious establishment, home of a family member, etc.), and perspectives (why do you and your family do these activities?). If you don't know about the King Cake in New Orleans, you may want to do some research on it and compare/contrast it to the rosca de Reyes mentioned in the text. This will give you an example of how communities in the United States and in Spanish-speaking countries celebrate important events.

Selección 5

1. **(A)** To answer this question, you have to read the entirety of the passage. The passage talks about the visit of a construction worker or bricklayer (albañil) to the house of the narrator. The family treats this guest with the utmost respect, and the father stops his son from cleaning the back of the sofa where the worker was sitting and accidentally stained in white (probably due to having dust on his clothes from being at work earlier that day). The father keeps the son from cleaning the back of the couch because he does not want his guest to feel bad for having stained it. Therefore, option (A) is the best answer because it refers to the proper conduct of a host (anfitrión) when he has a guest.

2. **(B)** The answer is found in lines 2–3 where the narrator says, ". . . no quiso que limpiara el espaldar que el albañilito había manchado de blanco . . ." (He did not want me to clean the back of the couch that the guest had stained in white). The word "huellas" means footprints or remnants, and, in this case, refers to the white dust that came off the jacket of the guest as he was sitting at the couch.

3. **(B)** This may be a difficult question to answer if you don't know the vocabulary in the options. However, these are words that you should know and learn if you don't. Avergonzarse means to be embarrassed, enojarse means to be upset/angry, and arrepentirse means to be regretful or sorry. In line 5 of the text, the albañilito becomes "encarnado," or red faced, meaning he is embarrassed. The word encarnar comes from the prefix en and the noun carne (meat). In other words, encarnar means to turn the color of meat, or flesh colored (red).

4. **(C)** This is a quote that you cannot take literally and have to understand it in context to find out its true meaning. The father is trying to communicate to his son why he did not want him to clean up the stain left by the guest. He says that any dirt or dust on the worker is a result of hard work, and therefore should not be considered a disgrace or embarrassment, but rather a source of pride because that person has put in a tough day.

5. **(D)** This answer follows the same train of thought throughout the story. The hosts do not want to embarrass the guest, for that would be rude ("descortés").

6. **(A)** Throughout the text you can tell there is a definite socioeconomic class difference between the two characters. The albañilito is dusty and dirty, has buttons falling off his clothes, and has a raggedy hat ("andrajoso sombrero"). The family, on the other hand, cares for their belongings, such as the immediate impulse to want to clean the couch once it was stained and sewing the button back on the jacket. There is nothing in the text that can be used to evaluate the level of education between the son and the worker because they could be both of school age and attending the same school, making options (B) and (D) not the best choices. Option (C) is not the best answer because it is inferred that the boy and the worker are friends, and therefore there are no major personality differences.

7. **(B)** The fact that the father takes the time at the end of the passage to explain to his son why he did not want him to clean the couch shows a true devotion from the father to his son. The fact that his son writes about this memory of his father shows that the son really respects his father, therefore making option (B) the best answer. Option (A) is incorrect because the father is not demanding; he just wants to teach his son the right etiquette in a non-confrontational way. Options (C) and (D) are incorrect because the son does learn from his father, and there is nothing in the text to suggest that he is spoiled by his father.

Selección 6

1. **(B)** The answer is clearly found in line 5, where Alicia informs the reader that this is in response to a letter that Susana previously wrote. Options (A) and (C) are not correct, for even though she does change the topic of discussion and does inform Susana of her project, this is not the reason for this exchange.

2. **(B)** The answer can be found in line 15, where Alicia says that factores económicos are the main reason. Therefore, one can safely assume that the family does not have enough money to care for the animals.

3. **(C)** Line 10 says that her country encabeza la lista. If we look carefully at the verb, we see that it includes the noun cabeza, which means head. Therefore, this verb means at the top of or leads the list.

4. **(A)** Although Alicia never mentions explicitly where she got her information, she delves into this topic because she is working on a research project for one of her classes. All the facts that she provides about animal abandonment are quite specific, and therefore we can safely assume that she knows this as a result of her investigation.

5. **(C)** Lines 19–22 show the reader that there is not one solution to this problem, making option (C) the best answer.

6. **(C)** The key word here is "novedad," which means that it is something new, and the only novelty that Alicia mentions is that certain hotels are now offering rooms in which pets are allowed, making option (C) the best answer. Don't be tempted to select option (B), for Alicia says that this platform has been around for several years, and therefore is not a novelty.

7. **(A)** The expression irse por las ramas means to go off on a tangent. We can clearly see this is what Alicia does in this letter, especially because she apologizes for having dedicated the majority of this correspondence on animal abandonment and for not addressing the question Susana asked in her previous letter (line 31).

Selección 6—Más Práctica
It is always a good idea to note how interpersonal writings are structured and the tone that is used throughout. This is an informal correspondence, so both the greeting ("Querida") and goodbye ("Saludos a tu familia") are appropriate for this context as well as the use of "tú" throughout. Also note the division. First is the opening, where Alicia talks briefly about her school and asks a question about Susana's puppy. Next comes the body, which fills lines 9 through 28. Finally comes the closing, in lines 29–33. Not only is this correspondence organized by being divided into paragraphs, but there is also organization of thought throughout. One idea leads to another, which helps the reader follow the train of thought. It is a good idea to notice the structural and organizational elements of correspondences, as they will help you become a better writer in the Free Response Task 1: Email Reply portion of the exam.

Selección 7

1. **(C)** In line 2 the article clearly presents that the angle it is investigating is which social media sites are used in regards to the news and all activities that surround it (sharing, commenting, and so on).

2. **(C)** Lines 3–4 show that Facebook still leads in terms of its uso informativo (to become informed). The article also mentions that Facebook has encountered some controversy, but that is a side bar and not the main data presented in the text.

3. **(A)** Be careful not to jump to premature conclusions, for although the title of the article says that the use of YouTube, Twitter, and Instagram is growing among younger people, the article also states in line 4 that the use of Facebook for informative purposes leads in all age ranges (todas las franjas de edad), which is what the question is asking.

4. **(B)** The answer is found in line 6–7, where it says that WhatsApp continues to be the most popular in terms of general use.

5. **(D)** The answer to this question is clearly seen in the title, where it states that the use of these sites is increasing in young people. Option (A) is not correct, for all three sites have different percentages of usage. Option (B) is also incorrect, for we are only presented with the data for this past year, and there is no way of knowing if this growth is similar or different than in previous years. Option (C) is also incorrect because, although the text does say that YouTube is as popular as Facebook when it comes to general use, the text does not say the same about the other two social media platforms.

6. **(B)** The answer to this question can be found in lines 16–20, where the text states that interactions in Facebook tend to be more passive, while in WhatsApp the participants tend to engage each other in debates, and so on.

7. **(A)** The word fuente refers to the source, which is where the news comes from.

8. **(D)** The answer can be found in lines 25–27, where the author says that opinions are divided in terms of whether the number of likes or interactions a news story gets has a direct effect on user interest in the story. For some people it does, while for many more it does not.

9. **(C)** Be careful with this question, for although the article talks about social media platforms, the introduction to this table clearly states that it is presenting what types of activities internet users do on the internet. This rules out option (A) because it refers exclusively to social media platforms, and not the internet in general. Option (B) is incorrect because the table gives percentages, not number of people. Option (D) is incorrect because the table simply presents what internet users do and does not present whether they enjoy doing these activities or not.

10. **(B)** The activity that has the highest percentage is sending and receiving emails, which is a type of communication. Some may argue that if we were to combine some of these categories, other options could also be correct. However, be careful when doing so, for one of the pitfalls some students fall into is when they try to force an interpretation that cannot be backed up by the evidence given. For example, some students may argue that Option (C) (entretenerse) could be correct if we were to combine playing videogames, participating in social media sites, and watching videos like on YouTube. However, the graph never says that the use of social media and watching videos is for entertainment purposes. It could be that people watch videos as part of a homework assignment or for research. It could be that people use social media for business purposes or to maintain contact with family. They may not necessarily enjoy it, but do it because it is a necessity. Therefore, unless a graph or table explicitly tells you why people do the actions they are doing, we cannot force our own interpretation and have to simply accept the data as presented to us.

11. **(B)** Both sources specify use of the internet and social media in Spain, making option (B) the best answer. Option (A) is all about Facebook, which the table does not mention. Option (C) refers to

using these tools for business purposes, which is never mentioned in the article. Option (D) is incorrect because both the article and table present objective data and are not trying to persuade a habit.

Selección 8

1. **(D)** The passage talks about the social evolution of Mexico during part of the 20th century, and how a compartmentalized society now has become more integrated. The first few lines speak to the changes that have happened, one of which is that both middle-class and working-class youth can go on to study in the university ("estudios superiores"). This, along with the information in lines 14–15, where the text mentions "Un país dividido en compartimientos . . . entra en contacto con sí mismo," implies that the unification and discovery of their own country gives the Mexican people more opportunities to learn about themselves.

2. **(A)** The Mexican revolution is the event that began the great transformation, for it broke with the cultural history that existed up to that point. Option (B) refers to part of the culture before the transformation began, and since it is not part of the transformation itself, it is an incorrect option. The revolution was an act of self-discovery, and therefore the masks of isolation that existed beforehand fell (lines 13–14), thus making option (C) incorrect. Option (D) is incorrect because there is nothing in the text to support the division of Mexico into states during this period.

3. **(A)** The theme throughout this passage is the self-discovery of Mexico as a nation comprised of many colors, cultures, and people. The passage says that the beginning of this self-identity came through art (lines 9–11), in which authors and artists started seeing Mexico for what it really was.

4. **(D)** Don't be limited to the information in lines 13 and 14, which mention the mask falling ("la máscara cae"). The "colores, voces y cuerpos de México" refer to the recognition of who the Mexican people really are, as described later in lines 17–19.

5. **(C)** This answer may be difficult if you don't know the meaning of the word "autóctona" (autochthonous, or native to a land or area), and if this is the case, then it is a good word to learn. However, you can use the process of elimination to find the right answer. The "doble tendencia" referenced in the question is found in line 20, where the author says that a positive aspect was that the Mexicans were able to discover themselves ("descubrirse a sí mismos"). You can eliminate option (A) because the discovery implies learning something new, not recognizing similarities. Option (B) can be eliminated because there is nothing in the text to suggest an impending battle with the United States, and the only time the United States is mentioned is in the negative aspect of the "doble tendencia," not the positive aspect that this question asks. Finally, option (D) can be eliminated because there is nothing to suggest that they liked the same colors, and the "colores" mentioned refer to the diversity of the people.

6. **(B)** The idea behind the saying is that there is no equal to Mexico, there is only one. The author introduces the saying by stating that it typifies a chauvinist extreme that came as a result of the great transformation. The use of the word "chauvinista" implies that one feels superior to another, and in this case, the "other" are those outside of Mexico, or foreign influences ("influencias extranjeras"), thus making option (B) the best answer. Some may be tempted to select option (A), but it is not correct because Mexican is not a race, but rather a community formed of many different races.

7. **(C)** By this point, this answer should be pretty clear. The transformation is the discovery of Mexico as a country comprised of many different people and accepting this as the new reality. Yes, art did play a part in this self-discovery, but it is not the focus of the transformation that this passage discusses, therefore making option (A) incorrect. Option (D) is incorrect because, although there is a sense of superiority as a result of this self-discovery, the passage is focused on the process of self-discovery, not the consequences afterward. There is nothing in the text to support option (B) as a viable answer.

Selección 9

1. **(C)** Pablo writes this letter to share ("compartir") details about the experience he had at the Trick Eye Museum in Mexico City and the impressions it left on him, making Option (C) the best choice.

2. **(C)** The expression is the same in Spanish as it is in English, and means "out of this world". Pablo uses this phrase to describe the extraordinary nature of the augmented reality exhibitions and how he felt being immersed in them.

3. **(B)** In lines 6-9 and again in 11-12, Pablo mentions that he could interact with the works, like exploring environments and seeing famous artworks come to life through augmented reality.

4. **(C)** Pablo mentions the use of the TrickEye AR application (lines 13-15), which was easy to use and enabled the augmented reality effects. This significantly enhanced his museum experience.

5. **(D)** In lines 16-19, Pablo expresses his wish to share more about his experience when they see each other and suggests visiting the museum together if Javier comes to Mexico City. This implies that they live in different places but that they also maintain a close relationship.

6. **(C)** Given Pablo's interest in museum exhibitions and how he experienced them, a magazine covering the latest exhibitions would be the publication most relevant and of interest to him.

7. **(C)** Given the excitement that Pablo expresses of having this experience, one can safely infer that he prefers innovative, modern experiences, making Option (C) the best answer.

Selección 10

1. **(B)** This is the correct answer because it most completely and accurately reflects the themes of the group's songs. This information can be found in the first paragraph in which the group looks to combine ("amalgamar") traditional tango with new voices ("nuevas voces") that describe urban realities.

2. **(C)** In lines 15-16 texts note the significance of the concert date, tying it to the anniversary of their first performance. This is a common way for

groups to celebrate milestones in their history. There is no evidence in the text to suggest that any of the other options are correct.

3. **(A)** Be careful when answering this question, because it asks specifically where tickets for retirees are available. This information can be found in lines 18-19, where the asterisk in line 19 specifies that the theater's box office is a unique point of sale for discounted tickets.

4. **(D)** This information can be found in lines 11-12, in which it talks about the city being the birthplace of famous tango musicians. Although this information is included to add cultural context and appeal to the event, there is no evidence in the text to suggest that it presents multiple musical presentations, festivals or unique cultural events. This makes Option (D) the best choice because it can clearly be validated by the text.

5. **(B)** The text covered basic information including the venue, date, and how to purchase tickets. It does not specify the concert's schedule or performances. Asking for a detailed program is a logical next step for someone seeking more in-depth information about what the event will entail.

Selección 11

1. **(A)** The hallaca symbolizes the "mestizaje del venezolano," which is comprised of "el negro africano," "el indio americano," and "la llegada de los españoles." Remember that the word mestizo means of mixed race.

2. **(B)** The three main ingredients are the banana leaf, the masa de maíz (corn dough), and the guiso (stew), which is a combination of meats, olives, capers, and raisins. However, a careful reading will show that the banana leaf is only used as a wrapper ("envoltorio"); therefore, it cannot be the main ingredient. The meat and guiso are one and the same, because the meat is part of the guiso, which also includes other ingredients. Therefore, the only lone ingredient that stands out is masa de maíz.

3. **(C)** The context in which this line is used talks about the contributions each community made to the creation of this dish. The arrival of the

Spaniards contributed capers, raisins, and olives. One can safely assume that these ingredients were not found in Venezuela before the arrival of the Spaniards, making option (C) the best answer.

4. **(B)** This question elaborates on the information you should have already learned in order to answer question 1. The three cultures are African, European, and indigenous.

5. **(C)** ". . . sin distinciones sociales . . ." means without social distinctions. Therefore, people from all social classes and races can enjoy this meal.

Selección 11—Más Práctica

You may want to think about dishes that you and your family eat during holidays or celebrations and what cultures influenced the creation of these dishes. For instance, most people will eat turkey during Thanksgiving, and you may want to research why turkey and not another animal is eaten. Also, the side dishes may differ somewhat in different parts of the country. Why? You already have information regarding a dish served in Venezuela and its influences, now you simply need to dig a little deeper into dishes that you and your community enjoy during celebrations, and you will have two great examples to use on any oral presentation pertaining to cultural significance of food and/or how people celebrate different types of celebrations.

Selección 12

1. **(C)** Passages that tend to come from works of literature can always be tricky, so it is best to read the entire passage first before answering the questions. The answer to this question can be found in line 24, when the narrator exclaims, "¡Vean qué tres serpientes he traído yo al mundo!" The expression traer al mundo means to give birth, so that means that the narrator is the mother of the three girls who are gossiping.

2. **(A)** The verb "hablaban" in the question refers to what the girls were talking about earlier in the passage. A careful reading will show at the end that this person is Rosaura, and she had a physical altercation with her father that has left her with bruises on her arms ("brazos llenos de cardenales"). You can then assume that Rosaura must have come to the narrator's home, who is now

taking care of her, and her three daughters are talking about their first impressions of Rosaura.

3. **(C)** By reading the dialogue, you can tell that the girls are gossiping about Rosaura. They talk about her clothes and how she looked scared, and one of the girls at the end of the dialogue wants to "estudiarla" (study her more) because there is something strange about Rosaura ("algo raro hay en ella").

4. **(B)** Although we don't know who Eufrasia is based solely on this fragment, when the mother says that compared to how her daughters are acting now (which is not very nice) Eufrasia could be a saint, we can infer that Eufrasia probably is not a very nice person. Therefore, the intent of this declaration is to emphasize how cruel the girls are being at this moment.

5. **(B)** The adjective piadoso means pious or compassionate. You can infer based on the mother's reaction that she is not appreciative of the way her daughters are talking about Rosaura, and when she mentions the bruises on her arm, she wants the girls to understand that this is a person who has suffered and therefore needs some compassion. Some would argue that option (D) is also a possibility, but it is not the best answer because the mother does not necessarily want the daughters to respect Rosaura. She simply does not want them to criticize her without knowing all the hardship that she has suffered.

6. **(D)** The girls are "horrorizadas" immediately following the revelation that Rosaura has bruises all over her arms from the horrible fight with her father. One might argue that option (A) is a possibility, but the girls would have to be pretty spoiled to react that way, and we don't have enough background knowledge in this fragment alone to say whether this is the case. Also, the fact that the mother reprimanded them suggests that she is not afraid to draw the line when it comes to unacceptable behavior, and therefore it is quite probable that the girls have been scolded before.

7. **(C)** Based on the fragment and all the explanations for the previous answers, this should be pretty clear. The girls in this fragment are making

fun of someone's appearance and peculiarities without knowing all the facts.

Selección 13

1. **(D)** The text primarily describes the project of the University of Aguascalientes in integrating video games into mathematics teaching. It does not solely argue in favor of modern educational technologies Option (A), detail game development processes for a programming audience Option (B), or critique the effectiveness of video games in learning Option (C). Instead, it informs about the use of video games in an educational context.

2. **(C)** The text discusses the implementation of video games in an educational context and addresses topics like implementation challenges and pedagogical benefits. It does not specifically target technology experts Option (A), primary school students Option (B), or parents Option (D).

3. **(B)** The text highlights that the educational video games developed contain action elements and are designed to be attractive to users (lines 9-10). It does not mention that they are created only by mathematics experts, focus solely on the theoretical aspects of mathematics, or are designed without the involvement of education experts.

4. **(B)** The text mentions in lines 20-21 that a challenge is the preference of some teachers for traditional teaching methods, which implies resistance to modern educational methods.

5. **(C)** The text indicates in lines 30-31 and 34-35 that one of the observed benefits of using video games in teaching is the improvement in the quality and reinforcement of mathematics learning. It does not mention reducing educational costs Option (A), eliminating textbooks Option (B), or increasing playtime at school Option (D) as benefits.

6. **(A)** The "digital divide" is mentioned in the context of a "generational clash" (line 21) between teachers and students, suggesting a difference in familiarity and comfort with digital technologies between different generations.

7. **(B)** Given the demonstrated effectiveness and the focus of the project, it seems likely that the integration of video games in teaching will expand

and diversify. The text does not suggest that video games will be gradually replaced by more traditional methods, limited to urban areas, or that teachers will completely resist technology integration.

Selección 14

1. **(D)** In the first paragraph of the correspondence, Javier talks about being separated from Sebastián and some of his friends, and that he did not enjoy the film as much as the rest of the group, so he could not partake in the conversation that followed. All this confirms that Javier felt a little excluded from the rest of the group during this outing.

2. **(A)** The verb platicar in line 8 is a synonym of hablar or charlar. The adjective parlanchín used in line 7 is similar to the English noun "parlance," meaning the way or manner in which one speaks. If you could not figure out what this verb means in context, you probably could easily eliminate options (C) (they fell asleep) and (D) (they became ill) because they probably would not have been something they would have done repeatedly throughout the entire movie. If you are able to eliminate two options, you have raised your chances of being correct if you need to guess.

3. **(B)** In lines 8–9 Javier describes the movie as being a "tontería," yet the rest of the group he is with acted as if it were "la mejor del año." Therefore, he did not speak because he did not want to be a spoilsport ("aguafiestas"). The word aguafiestas literally means water on a party, like raining on a party, and means something that ruins a fun event.

4. **(B)** The answer to this question is found in the first half of the second paragraph, where Javier talks about his personal reflection on the event once he arrived home. He says, "ir al cine es una experiencia íntima," meaning that, for him, it is a very personal and meaningful experience. His frustration with the other moviegoers is enough information to easily eliminate options (A) and (C) from the list. However, he never states that he prefers to go alone, and in fact he says that he really enjoys talking about the movie after it has

ended, so one can safely assume that he enjoys going with other people, as long as they like to arrive on time and don't talk during the movie. Based on this information, you can comfortably eliminate option (D).

5. **(C)** Although Javier has a very particular idea of what the movie-going experience should be like, the reader can see that as he is writing, he is coming to the realization that not everyone is made the same, and maybe he should have had a different reaction to the events that transpired. Line 20 shows his realization that maybe the others had more fun simply because they were enjoying the experience of being together.

6. **(B)** In order to answer this question correctly, you will need to use context clues to figure out the meaning of this verb. In the previous sentence, you can see that the narrator disliked the film by calling it "una tontería." On the other hand, the rest of the group reacted ("la alababan") as if it were the best movie of the year. Therefore, you can safely assume that the verb alabar means something positive, so you can eliminate options (C) and (D) for being negative. You could also eliminate option (A) because if they were debating about the film, Javier probably would have engaged in this debate. In case you have not already figured it out, the verb alabar means to praise.

7. **(A)** You can tell in the final paragraph that Javier's tone changes as he becomes more understanding of the experience he had. You can see this change when he uses words like aprender (line 28) and "abandonar las expectativas personales no frustrarse tanto" (lines 31–32). One may be tempted to choose option (D), but the tone that comes across is not necessarily one of embarrassment, but rather of understanding, therefore making option (A) the best answer.

Selección 15

1. **(D)** The introduction to this text clearly states that this person is not from Guatemala; therefore, you could eliminate option (A) without even having read a single word of the text itself. We don't know much about the narrator except that, based

on the title, he was invited to spend a month in Guatemala. Therefore, option (B) is not correct because he is visiting the country on a more official capacity than simply being a tourist. This leaves options (C) and (D), and the only thing to suggest the profession of the narrator is in lines 18–19 where he refers to his own "modestas actuaciones públicas," which could suggest that he is a performer of some sort. However, we don't have enough information to say that he is a cultural ambassador, but we do know that he was invited by the Instituto de Cultura, a Guatemalan organization, so we have enough evidence to comfortably select option (D).

2. **(B)** The adjective acogido means accepted or embraced, and this is clearly seen when he talks about the "cortesía natural" and "cordialidad" he experienced, and how the Guatemalans "nos acogen" (line 14). One may be tempted to select option (C), but although he may have felt a little humbled, it is not because the Guatemalans were so much smarter than him.

3. **(C)** This is another example where the process of elimination can help tremendously. The narrator is highly impressed with the Guatemalan people, and therefore options (A) and (D) can quickly be dismissed because they both refer to negative attributes (envy and arrogance). Even if you do not know what soberbia means, the rest of the sentence in option (D) that says "no les permitió admitir la superioridad española" should be enough to convey a negative attribute. Option (B) can be quite complicated, especially if you don't know what the word pedante means. However, if you look at line 23 in the text, the narrator says, "sin el mal de la pedantería," and therefore you could infer that pedantería is a negative noun. Pedante means pretentious, and the adjective "pedant" also exists in English.

4. **(A)** The narrator praises the Guatemalan people and on several occasions makes indirect criticisms about his own country. This is seen in statements such as how little Guatemala is known in Europe and how he rediscovered the art of conversing, which, says the narrator, is almost forgotten in his country. You could easily

eliminate options (C) and (D) since they criticize Guatemala, and there is no mention of economics, so you can safely eliminate option (B).

5. **(A)** The narrator speaks of the peninsulares and Guatemalans as hermanos, so they clearly have a bond. However, one can clearly infer that Guatemalans have a much better understanding of the world outside of them than the outside world has of them. This can be seen in the statements "por desgracia tan poco se conoce en Europa" (line 3) and "no aceptan . . . la actitud . . . protectora, que el desconocimiento de la realidad hace adoptar a muchos de los que intentan 'españolear' en América" (lines 15–17). Based on the latter statement alone, you can easily eliminate option (C), and because they do have a bond, you can eliminate option (D).

6. **(B)** Here is another example where the process of elimination can be helpful. The word pedante makes another appearance here, and if you learned anything from question 3, then you can safely eliminate option (D) from contention. You can also eliminate option (A) because it really has nothing to do with the overall message of the text. Option (C) could be a possibility, but it really does not answer the question. The question asks what does the narrator suggest we learn, and the answer is not that one learns to travel to Guatemala, but rather how to apply some of the positive qualities in their own life.

7. **(B)** You probably easily eliminated options (C) and (D) because the narrator is clearly not intense nor does he appear to be a liar. A careful reading of option (A) indicates why it too should be eliminated. The narrator may be sincere, but he is not naïve. Option (B) is clearly the best choice, for he is reflecting on his experience and writing quite eloquently.

Selección 16

1. **(C)** The title and line 5 discuss the impact of renewable energies on reducing electricity prices. These sources, being more cost-effective, lead to a decrease in reliance on expensive fossil fuels, thus driving down electricity costs.

2. **(D)** This information is stated directly in line 2, indicating the average price for megawatt-hour in April as 73 euros. This reflects the market conditions and impact of renewable energy and government policies.

3. **(B)** Lines 5-8 mention the government's intervention to cap gas prices, a significant factor influencing electricity prices. This is a strategy used in Spain to control energy costs.

4. **(B)** According to line 11, the average electricity bill in April 2023 is expected to be 48 euros.

5. **(C)** This information can be found in lines 13-14, noting that April 2023 recorded the lowest electricity bill in the first four months, signaling a downward trend in electricity pricing.

6. **(A)** Lines 15 and 21-23 indicate that renewable energies, particularly their increased supply, played a role in reducing electricity prices by affecting the marginal cost of power generation.

7. **(C)** Option (C) is the correct answer because it mentions the inability of solar and wind energy ("energía solar y eólica") to be stored. This leads to times when these renewable energy sources generate an excess of energy, and since it cannot be easily stored and needs to be used, it often leads to a reduction in electricity prices.

8. **(C)** The text indicates in lines 16-20 that the price of electricity in April 2023 was significantly lower than in April 2022, by as much as 120 euros.

9. **(B)** This option is correct because, as the title of the table states, the table provides detailed data on how electricity is generated in Spain, measured in gigawatt-hours (GWh).

10. **(A)** Based on the table, it is evident that both solar and wind energy sources have seen growth in their contribution to electricity generation. However, solar energy has exhibited a more rapid rate of increase, almost quadrupling in four years. Careful with Option (C), for it is not the best answer because it states that the increase in use is proportionately higher. Even though wind power continues to be a greater source of energy in Spain than solar, its use has not increased at a quicker rate than that of solar energy.

11. **(C)** This option is correct because both the information in the text and the data in the table collectively demonstrate the trend of increased use of renewable energy sources, which have contributed to the trend of decreasing electricity prices.

Selección 17

1. **(B)** The narrator wants to go on a trip because he wants to forget his girlfriend. In lines 8–9, he says that he chooses Mar del Plata because the "vida agitada" will help him forget. One can assume that the agitated life he is referring to means a lot of frivolous activities. Don't be tempted to pick option (A) simply because of the word "aristócratas." Mar del Plata is known as "la playa aristócrata," but it does not mean that many aristocrats will be there, nor is that the reason the narrator is going.

2. **(C)** As in the previous explanation, the narrator wants to go to forget about his ex-girlfriend, whom he saw in the arms of a "friend" too many times.

3. **(B)** The narrator boards a train to his destination and immediately starts imagining a possible encounter between a young writer and a young lady. In line 11, the narrator states, "no sin pensar un poco" (not without thinking a little) in a possible adventure. The imagined story is of a writer who boards the train at the last minute, and as he enters the coach, he sees a young lady reading his last novel. The "pasión morbosa" refers to the type of story, which is a chance encounter on a train that may lead to an amorous relationship, which is often written about but hardly ever happens in real life.

4. **(D)** As in the previous explanation, all the events from the end of line 13 on are part of the imagination of the narrator.

5. **(B)** As the narrator imagines this chance encounter, he goes off on a tangent about how these types of stories always have the young lady reading the last novel, and therefore the young author obviously has to be a famous prolific writer. One can note that there is a condescending tone, which is likely due to a sense of envy. To say the narrator

hates or is angry at the character he has created is probably too harsh. Remember that the narrator is imagining this story, and he is probably projecting the type of fame he wishes he could have.

6. **(A)** As with the previous example, the narrator questions why in these types of stories the young lady is always reading the latest novel. If the author was so famous and prolific, why could it never be the second-to-last or third-to-last novel? Obviously the narrator is not searching for an answer; he is simply poking fun at the convenience of it all.

7. **(B)** When considering the passage as a whole, option (B) becomes the obvious choice. The narrator has his heart broken, wants to leave to forget, boards a train, and imagines a chance encounter between two young individuals. One gets the sense that the narrator is ridiculing the story he is imagining, and therefore the prevailing mood is that this probably won't happen (although the narrator probably secretly wishes that it would happen to him). This makes desilusionado the best option because there is a sense of loss of hope for the author. To say that he is depressed (option (A)) is a little too severe an emotion for this story, and there is nothing to suggest that he is still in love or that he has a good sense of humor about losing his girlfriend, therefore eliminating options (C) and (D).

Selección 18

1. **(B)** The answer to this is found in the section titled Objetivos generales, where each of the bullet points states the objectives of this publication. The text simply is trying to define the importance of family values and how they benefit individual humans and society as a whole.

2. **(B)** This is another question where the process of elimination is key. The text obviously is directed at families, as per its title. Therefore, you can safely eliminate options (A), (C), and (D).

3. **(A)** ". . . como una tela en blanco . . ." literally means a white canvas. This refers to the innocence of children, since the proverbial canvas will

be painted by the experiences they have as they grow.

4. **(A)** The text is trying to promote a deeper understanding of what it means to have a family and its role in both the individual and society. Lines 25–30 speak to its importance and how it goes beyond the simple unification of bride and groom, therefore having a deeper meaning and importance than simply a union.

5. **(D)** With these types of questions, you have to identify what is not in the text. In the introduction to the text, it states that this is promoting an event, and therefore if you were interested in attending this seminar, you might want to know if there is a fee, making option (D) the best answer.

Selección 19

1. **(D)** Make sure that you read all options before making your selection. Some individuals may stop at (B) without realizing that option (C) is also correct. Option (D) is correct because it has both answers. Luisa writes to inform her professor about a program that she has discovered, and she asks him if he would be interested in helping her.

2. **(D)** This is the best answer because it addresses the scope of Payasos sin fronteras, which is to give emotional support to refugee populations around the world. Options (A) and (C) are incorrect because they cover too wide a scope, and option (B) is incorrect because the text never mentions raising money as a primary goal, although it certainly could help their cause.

3. **(B)** This information can be found in lines 20–21, where the text says that the organization pays all expenses to cover the production. This would include transportation and production costs, but not personal expenses.

4. **(B)** In lines 17 through 19, the text shows that the volunteers are professional artists who have worked in circuses, theater, and other performance disciplines. Of the options, option (B) is the best because it speaks of shows and performances. Be careful if considering option (A) because "todos tipos de artistas" also could

include painters, sculptors, musicians, etc., and this group is almost solely performance artists.

5. **(D)** This is clearly seen in the opening of the correspondence, where Luisa remembers how inspiring her teacher was to her. They probably don't know each other on a friendly basis because she still refers to him as Profesor, which implies a more formal relationship, therefore eliminating options (B) and (C).

6. **(A)** The goal of this organization is to provide emotional support and solidarity to refugees through laughter, making option (A) the clear answer. Option (B) could deal with causes for refugees, but it does not achieve the goal of the investigation, which is to learn more about the organization Payasos sin fronteras. Options (C) and (D) are too generic and have nothing to do with the goal of this organization.

7. **(A)** If you read the entire card, it is clear that Luisa is inspired, for she wants to create her own project to help the youth in her community.

Selección 19—Más Práctica
To answer these questions, think about service and volunteer programs in your community. Some ideas can include soup kitchens, English as a second language classes that are given to immigrants, etc. If you don't know of any programs, you can research some online.

Selección 20

1. **(C)** The first sentence of the text speaks to how the dance is "representativo de la idiosincrasia del departamento." The word idiosincrasia means trait. Don't be confused by the word lengua, for it is still a dance, but one that "communicates" the qualities and peculiarities of this part of Colombia.

2. **(B)** Lines 13–14 explain what the dance dramatizes. It includes all parts of an amorous union, from flirting to the wedding.

3. **(A)** This is a tricky answer to figure out, but it can be done! A dance typically includes two aspects: movement and music. The choreography of the dance as created by mixing the dance, or movement, from a type of dance in the south of the

state, with the bambuco, from the north. In this context, the options could be dance, music, or both. When you look at the options, it is evident that options (B) and (D) can be eliminated, and since the bambuco refers to a part of how the choreography was created, it probably is not a theatrical representation, therefore eliminating option (C).

4. **(A)** This information is found in lines 22–26, where it says that the creation of the festival was to achieve coexistence and reconciliation between the regions of the country that were in turmoil.

5. **(D)** Don't be influenced by the English word tornado. Use the context to figure out the meaning of this word. In line 30, the text mentions the haciendas (ranch) and caseríos (village) that turned into poblaciones (large settlements)—in other words, became larger.

6. **(C)** Lines 31–37 describe how the celebration began from Spanish influence, but then it combined with local traditions and, throughout the generations, kept evolving as a mixture of elements from populations from different extremes (conquerors and those conquered, aristocrats and day workers). Therefore, the best description of the San Juan celebration is that it is a combination of a variety of influences, making it heterogeneous, or varied and mixed.

7. **(A)** The Sanjaunero is unique to the state of Tolima, as stated in the first two paragraphs. Therefore, to find out more information about celebrations in this area, it only makes sense to find a publication based on this region.

Selección 21

1. **(D)** This passage presents the pros of having a vegetarian diet, but it also argues that eating meat in moderation has its merits. The author is not necessarily trying to convince the reader of one diet over another, but says that if the reader chooses to follow a vegetarian diet, he/she should also supplement with vitamins and minerals (lines 11–12).

2. **(B)** Lines 17–20 are where the author introduces the results of several investigations on the benefits

of having a specific type of diet. The author summarizes the results, and because he/she does not present any actual data from the investigation, option (C) cannot be a possibility.

3. **(D)** Although the article states that by eating animal products ". . . facilita obtener las cantidades recomendables de calcio, zinc, hierro y vitamina B12," the author never mentions that this is the only place one can get these vitamins and minerals, only that consuming meat is a good source of these. Therefore, option (B) is not the best answer. The author does say that eating lean meats along with fruits and vegetables is a healthy diet.

4. **(C)** The information needed for this answer is in lines 1–3. Be careful when reading because the author says that meats and other foods with exception of mother's milk is not essential for human nutrition. Options (A), (B), and (D) are all true for a generally healthy diet, but they are not absolutely essential, which is what the question is asking.

5. **(C)** This fragment follows the sentence in lines 8–9 where the author says that all foods have benefits but could also have problematic areas. Therefore, selección de alimentos refers to the types of foods that are being selected, and one should consider supplementing the food with something else in case the food does not contain the vitamins and minerals that one should have (an idea presented in lines 11–13).

6. **(B)** As with the explanation for question 3 in this section, in lines 26–27 the author says that eating animal products is a good source of minerals and vitamins. One can misread the information contained in lines 23–25 and think that fiber is derived from meat, and thus be tempted to select option (D), but the article here (and in lines 15–16) says that the fiber necessary is derived from fruits and vegetables, not meats.

7. **(B)** Again, with questions of purpose, one has to always read the introduction first. The introduction says that this is a guide (guía), and the first two columns give general examples and guidelines. This is definitely not a menu, nor does it provide the nutrient content of the foods listed;

therefore, you can easily eliminate options (A) and (C). Because the table gives general examples of foods in each category, and foods that absolutely have to be consumed, option (D) can also be eliminated.

8. **(A)** The table says that for breads and cereals, one should consume 6 or more portions. The third column provides an example of what a portion should be. Option (A) is the only choice that provides 6 or more portions. Let's do the math: 2 bollos = 4 portions (½ bollo is one portion) + 1 taza de pasta = 2 portions (½ taza de pasta is one portion) = 6 portions. Following this example, you will see that all other options fall short of the 6 recommended portions per day.

9. **(B)** This should be a pretty simple question to answer, for not only are huevos optional, but the guide also suggests that they only be consumed 3 or 4 times a week. Although milk products are also optional, they can be consumed daily, just no more than 3 servings per day. If you don't know what cacahuete is, it means peanut, and crema de cacahuete is peanut butter and is located in the Leguminosas y otros sustitutos de carne category.

10. **(B)** The table never mentions meat, and eggs are not considered meat. Therefore, you can easily eliminate options (A) and (D), because there would have to be information in the table to suggest that meat is either beneficial or not for one of these options to be true. Option (C) is not the best answer. The table does give a list of various vegetarian products, but remember that the question asks what statement made in the article can be supported by the table. Since the article never mentions that one has to consume a variety of vegetarian products, option (C) is not correct. The article does explicitly state that consumption of meat is not essential for human nutrition, and the table does provide a list of non-meat foods that one can consume to hit all the nutritional needs. You can therefore use the information in the table to validate the statement in the article, and this is why option (B) is the best answer.

11. **(D)** This should have been pretty straightforward. Options (A) and (C) are obviously out of place for neither the article nor the table talk about envi-

ronmental benefits or ethical reasons for being a vegetarian. The article does mention briefly that consumption of meats high in fat content can be bad for your health, but it is by no means the overall message of the text. In addition, this cannot be verified by any information in the table, so option (B) can be safely eliminated. Both the article and the table provide information on guidelines that one should follow if he or she is considering becoming vegetarian, making option (D) the correct answer.

Selección 22

1. **(C)** In the opening of the letter, Julio refers to a conversation that he had with the professor, and that led to his research sometime thereafter. Since he is continuing to talk about the same topic of the original discussion, this is a continuation, and therefore option (C) is the best answer.

2. **(B)** The historia that the question references refers to that of the family who made a certain decision in order to try and save their daughter's life. The daughter indeed has medical issues, but her issues are not the story, but rather the actions that the family took to address these issues. Therefore, option (D) is not an option. Although the author also mentions the controversy (polémica), he does not summarize the story of this controversy, so option (C) cannot be considered an option.

3. **(A)** You probably could figure out that the word don is part of the verb donar (to gift) and adjective donación (a gift). Therefore, the expression means that everyone is a gift from God, and therefore should accept himself or herself as he or she is.

4. **(C)** The information needed to answer this question can be found in lines 15–19. This is where the author continues his thoughts on the moral dilemma that the family in question will probably face. The family has already made the decision they did, so options (A) and (D) can be eliminated because they speak of actions that have already happened as if they hadn't yet. Option (B) is incorrect because there is nothing in the text to suggest that the family will feel burdened from having to raise two young girls.

5. **(A)** The answer to this question can be found in the fifth paragraph, where the author is debating whether cells do have life and should be considered human. Option (B) is incorrect because the author states that scientists believe this to be true already, and he later rejects the statement that option (C) makes. Option (D) is irrelevant because the author never brings up this question.

6. **(B)** The word rondar means to wander or to haunt. By using context clues, you could figure this out on your own. In the previous paragraph, he mentions that he has ". . . más preguntas que respuestas . . . ," and he closes his letter by saying, ". . . no veo la hora de poder discutirlo más a fondo . . . ," therefore implying that he has not achieved closure on this issue. Therefore, you could infer that rondar means something that has not gone away, which is close enough to deduce that (B) is the best answer.

7. **(C)** By now you should comfortably be able to eliminate options (A) and (B) from this list. He is obviously no expert on the subject and still has questions about it. Option (D) is not the best answer because of the statement ". . . necesita ayuda para explicarse mejor." His issue is not that he can't explain himself; it is that he still does not know what side of the argument he is willing to support.

Selección 23

1. **(C)** Be careful with this question, for it is not asking what the purpose of the article is, but rather what the purpose of an acuario is. Although options (A) and (B) are certainly true of aquariums, they are not the purpose mentioned in the text. Aquariums are spaces intended to ". . . conservar investigar y concienciar de la necesidad de proteger el planeta," therefore making option (C) the best answer.

2. **(D)** You may have guessed from context that cuarentena is Spanish for quarantine. As stated in lines 28–30, la cuarentena is a process, so option (A) can be excluded since that refers to an object. Option (B) is partially correct because it is part of the process, but option (D) is the best answer because it inherently comprises two elements of

the process (adapting to the new environment and to the new food). Option (C) is incorrect because the period is solely to treat the animal, not the space that the animal will occupy.

3. **(B)** The word buzo is a scuba diver, and they are the ones responsible for cleaning the larger tanks (lines 37–38). The word buceador is a synonym, and the verb is bucear. It is a good word to add to your vocabulary in case you did not already know it. If you did not know it, then you still could have figured out the correct answer by the process of elimination, and by seeing the similarities between the two words buzo and buceador. Remember that the letter "c" when next to the letters "e" or "i" has a soft sound, like the letter "s." When next to the vowels "a," "o," or "u," it has a sound like the letter "k." In the case of the word buzo, the letter "c" changes to "z" in order to keep the soft sound.

4. **(B)** Lines 15–20 contain all the information you need to answer this question. Although there are mechanized systems in place, visual inspection is key to ensuring that all aspects of the operation are functioning well. Options (A), (C), and (D) all include parts of the operation, but option (B) is the one that oversees all those parts.

5. **(A)** The information needed to answer this question is in lines 39–41. They speak about the opportunity to visit the depths of the ocean, like Captain Nemo. Don't be tempted to select option (B) simply because it references the captain; he is not at the aquarium. Options (C) and (D) may be individual preferences, but they are not mentioned in the text.

6. **(C)** The word imprescindible means essential and communicates the same idea presented in line 46 that scientific projects done at aquariums are "más necesarios que nunca." Don't be tempted to select option (B), for the noun inutilidad makes this statement completely false.

7. **(A)** This answer is almost taken verbatim from lines 47–48. Options (C) and (D), although possibly true, are too specific, and the article does not go into specifics.

8. **(C)** Although nowadays there are aquariums of all shapes and sizes, your basic aquarium will probably be square shaped. Therefore, the four paredes refer to the see-through walls of the aquarium, making this the best answer. Options (A) and (B) are not appropriate because they are geared to setting up an aquarium at home, and this article does not deal with this topic. Option (D) is not correct because the article does not give any information on this topic.

Selección 24

1. **(C)** The text is about las Fallas, a celebration in Valencia, Spain. Since the reading gives a brief history and overview of the festivities, it is most likely aimed to attract tourists to the area. By no means is it a tranquil celebration, so you can easily eliminate option (A), and if you suffer from pyromania and you know it, you probably don't want to go to this celebration and be surrounded by flames, thus eliminating option (B). Option (D) is incorrect because the fantoches, or puppets, are burned at the end.

2. **(C)** Lines 2–4 give the history of the fallas. The carpenters would burn scraps of wood and left-over contraptions on the eve of the celebration of San José.

3. **(A)** Line 8 says that the constructions are made out of "cartón piedra," or paper mache (plasterboard). Note that the word piedra modifies the word cartón, so it is not the main material used, thus eliminating option (C).

4. **(D)** You can find the answer in lines 15–16, where it says that these structures ". . . se instalan en cada esquina. . . ."

5. **(C)** This might be a little difficult to understand if you don't pay attention to punctuation. The answer you seek begins in line 9 and continues in lines 10–11. In line 9, it says that the structures compete with each other in ingenuity and beauty while satirizing the latest political, social, and cultural events. The information in between describes how the structures are shaped, thus ensuring a smooth fall and burning. Pay attention

to the use of punctuation so that you can keep track of the ideas being communicated.

6. **(A)** In the text, the mascletà is the object of the passive voice form of the verb disparar (shoot). Therefore, the mascletà is something that is shot every day at 2:00 p.m., which is what option (A) communicates. The word diurno means during the daytime.

7. **(B)** The "castillos de fuegos artificiales" that the text mentions at the end refers to the size of the fireworks, not that they are in castles. This is why option (D) is incorrect. If you identified that it was some sort of spectacle with fireworks, you could then easily have eliminated options (A) and (C).

PART 3
Listening Comprehension

3

General Considerations

The listening comprehension part of the exam consists of two parts: Print and Audio Texts (combined) and Audio Texts. The questions and multiple-choice answers for all questions in this section will be printed in your test booklet. Before each audio selection is played, you will be given time to read the introduction and preview the questions and multiple-choice options. The audios all come from authentic sources, and can include interviews, presentations, advertisements, and so on. Each audio will be played twice.

Format of the Exam

The listening comprehension part of the exam is divided into the following parts:

Print and Audio Texts (combined)—This portion includes two reading and listening activities and a total of 17 questions. The first activity will pair an article with a listening source; the second will be a graph, table, or chart paired with a listening source.

- **Article and audio** (10 questions): For this first activity you will have 4 minutes to read the article and then two additional minutes to read the introduction to the audio source and preview the questions. After the audio plays once, you will then have one minute in which you start answering the questions before the audio is played again. Following the second playing of the audio, you will have 15 seconds per question to finish answering the questions. You can expect to have 10 questions on this section: 4 questions about information in the article, 4 about information in the audio, and 2 relating to both sources. This means that you will have a total of 2 minutes and 30 seconds after the second listening of the audio to finish answering the questions.

- **Graph, table, chart and audio** (7 questions): For this activity you will have one minute to read the graph, table, or chart, and then have one additional minute to read the introduction to the audio source and preview the questions. After the audio plays once, you will have one minute in which you start answering the questions before the audio is played again. Following the second playing of the audio, you will have 15 seconds per question to finish answering the questions. You can expect to have 7 questions in this section: 3 about information in the graph, table, or chart; 3 about information in the audio; and 1 relating to both sources. This means that you will have a total of 1 minute and 45 seconds after the second listening to finish answering the questions.

Audio Texts—This portion includes three listening activities and a total of 18 questions. Before each activity, you will be given one minute to read the introduction and to preview the questions and multiple-choice answers. Following the first listening of the audio, you will have one minute to start answering the questions. Following the second listening of the audio, you will have 15 seconds per question to finish answering the questions. You can expect the following types of audio files: interview (5 questions), instructions (5 questions), and a presentation (8 questions).

Types of Questions

The types of questions in this section are very similar to those in Part A, Reading Comprehension. You can expect the following types of questions in the listening section.

- **UNDERSTAND CONTENT.** Identify the main idea and details.
- **THINK CRITICALLY.** Identify the purpose of the text, the target audience, point of view of its author, the tone or attitude, and how the author communicates his/her ideas; be able to separate fact from opinion and make predictions based on information presented in the text.
- **UNDERSTAND MEANING.** Infer the meaning of unfamiliar words and expressions using context clues; comprehend a wide variety of vocabulary, idioms, and cultural expressions.
- **UNDERSTAND CULTURE AND CONTENT ACROSS DISCIPLINES.** Identify practices, products, and perspectives of Hispanic cultures as well as information pertaining to other disciplines, such as science, geography, history, art, and so on.

Strategies for Listening Comprehension

Before You Listen

- **READ THE INTRODUCTION AND TITLE.** All listening selections will have a brief introduction about the text and its source. This information is helpful to get you thinking about what information will be presented, as well as the possible point of view of the author and intended audience.
- **READ THE QUESTIONS AND MULTIPLE-CHOICE ANSWERS.** You will have plenty of time to read the questions and preview the answers. Use this time to gather as much information about the selection as possible.

During the First Listening

- **IDENTIFY THE MAIN IDEA.** Listen for repetition of words or phrases and for words that are topically related.
- **VISUALIZE WHAT YOU HEAR.** Imagine in your mind's eye what is being said. This will help you understand the overall ideas.
- **IMAGINE.** If the topic deals with an unfamiliar subject matter, try to imagine what it would be like to be in that situation or to experience the setting or event that is discussed.
- **FOCUS ON WHAT YOU DO KNOW AND NOT ON WHAT YOU DON'T KNOW.** Don't get hung up on single words you don't understand. Focus on what you do understand and use contextual clues to help you figure out the gist of ideas that may not be entirely clear.
- **EVALUATE THE INFORMATION BEING PRESENTED.** Is the speaker trying to persuade the listener? Is the speaker stating facts or opinions? What evidence, if any, does the speaker present?
- **FOCUS ON THE MESSAGE, NOT THE DISTRACTIONS.** Often there will be background noise as you listen or in the audio itself. These noises can include traffic sounds or music. Don't let the background noises distract you from focusing on the message that is being delivered.

During the Second Listening

- **TAKE NOTES OF KEY WORDS.** You will have space in your exam book to take notes. However, limit these notes to individual words and not phrases. Make sure that the words you do write down will help you remember the main ideas of the listening passage.

- **CONFIRM AND CLARIFY.** You should already have understood the main idea of the listening passage, so during the second listening you want to focus on identifying a few details that support the main idea. You can also use this time to confirm the information you understood the first time and to help clarify any doubts that you may have had.

Strategies for Improving Listening Comprehension

Like reading, the best way to become a better listener is to practice regularly. Here are a couple of suggestions that will make you a better listener.

- **LISTEN TO A LOT OF AUTHENTIC SPANISH.** Nothing improves listening comprehension than a lot of practice, so listen to as much Spanish as you can. Make sure that you listen to authentic audio sources that were produced for a Spanish-speaking audience. Do not shy away from audios that include a lot of visual and/or audio distractions, such as background noises and music. The more you become accustomed to listening to Spanish with distractions in the background, the better prepared you will be for this exam.
- **VISUALIZE AS YOU LISTEN.** If you can picture what the words say, you are more likely to remember them. If you practice with a video source, try listening to the video first with your eyes closed and see if you visualized correctly what you heard.
- **TAKE NOTES OF KEY WORDS.** Practice taking notes of key words that will help you remember the main ideas of the listening passage. Avoid writing down whole sentences or phrases, because this will take a lot of time and it may cause you to not hear part of the audio.4

Section I, Part B—Listening Comprehension: Print and Audio Texts (Combined)

The first section of the test includes both print and audio texts. You will be given the theme of the activity and a brief introduction to each source. The print source will be either an article or some sort of image, table, or graph to study before listening to the audio source. You will be given four minutes to read the article or one minute to look over any graphs or tables before the audio begins. While reading, you should implement all of the reading strategies that are highlighted in the Reading Comprehension portion of this book. The audio source will either be a dialogue, narrative, or some other type of speech sample. Before listening to the audio file the first time, you will have an additional minute to read a preview of the selection and look over the questions that you will be asked. After listening to the audio selection, you will have an additional minute to begin answering the questions. After the selection has played the second time, you will have 15 seconds per question to finish answering them. You may take notes during the audio section, but they will not be scored.

Strategies for Reading

- Understand the format of the print text.
- Read the introduction and scan the passage to get the general idea. Predict what the selection may be about.
- Reread more carefully to
    - identify key vocabulary words (underline them),
    - identify characters,
    - identify the setting, and
    - understand what is happening.
- Use background knowledge.
- Evaluate the information you have gleaned from the piece to
    - determine the tone and mood of the piece,
    - determine the intended reader, and
    - draw conclusions about the piece.
- Read the chart from the left column and then across.

Strategies for Listening

- Read the introduction and questions to each sample.
- Concentrate while you listen.
- Evaluate the information being presented.
- Follow the thread of the conversation.
- Visualize, if you can.
- Take note of key words that lead to ideas.
- Focus on what you understand and don't get hung up on what you don't understand. Use contextual clues to help you understand unfamiliar words or phrases.
- Remember that you will hear the audio twice. Listen the first time for overall theme and general ideas, and use the second listening to take notes on specific details.

ANSWER SHEET
Print and Audio Texts

Selección 1

1. Ⓐ Ⓑ Ⓒ Ⓓ
2. Ⓐ Ⓑ Ⓒ Ⓓ
3. Ⓐ Ⓑ Ⓒ Ⓓ
4. Ⓐ Ⓑ Ⓒ Ⓓ
5. Ⓐ Ⓑ Ⓒ Ⓓ
6. Ⓐ Ⓑ Ⓒ Ⓓ
7. Ⓐ Ⓑ Ⓒ Ⓓ

Selección 2

1. Ⓐ Ⓑ Ⓒ Ⓓ
2. Ⓐ Ⓑ Ⓒ Ⓓ
3. Ⓐ Ⓑ Ⓒ Ⓓ
4. Ⓐ Ⓑ Ⓒ Ⓓ
5. Ⓐ Ⓑ Ⓒ Ⓓ
6. Ⓐ Ⓑ Ⓒ Ⓓ
7. Ⓐ Ⓑ Ⓒ Ⓓ
8. Ⓐ Ⓑ Ⓒ Ⓓ
9. Ⓐ Ⓑ Ⓒ Ⓓ
10. Ⓐ Ⓑ Ⓒ Ⓓ

Selección 3

1. Ⓐ Ⓑ Ⓒ Ⓓ
2. Ⓐ Ⓑ Ⓒ Ⓓ
3. Ⓐ Ⓑ Ⓒ Ⓓ
4. Ⓐ Ⓑ Ⓒ Ⓓ
5. Ⓐ Ⓑ Ⓒ Ⓓ
6. Ⓐ Ⓑ Ⓒ Ⓓ
7. Ⓐ Ⓑ Ⓒ Ⓓ

Selección 4

1. Ⓐ Ⓑ Ⓒ Ⓓ
2. Ⓐ Ⓑ Ⓒ Ⓓ
3. Ⓐ Ⓑ Ⓒ Ⓓ
4. Ⓐ Ⓑ Ⓒ Ⓓ
5. Ⓐ Ⓑ Ⓒ Ⓓ
6. Ⓐ Ⓑ Ⓒ Ⓓ
7. Ⓐ Ⓑ Ⓒ Ⓓ
8. Ⓐ Ⓑ Ⓒ Ⓓ
9. Ⓐ Ⓑ Ⓒ Ⓓ
10. Ⓐ Ⓑ Ⓒ Ⓓ

Selección 5

1. Ⓐ Ⓑ Ⓒ Ⓓ
2. Ⓐ Ⓑ Ⓒ Ⓓ
3. Ⓐ Ⓑ Ⓒ Ⓓ
4. Ⓐ Ⓑ Ⓒ Ⓓ
5. Ⓐ Ⓑ Ⓒ Ⓓ
6. Ⓐ Ⓑ Ⓒ Ⓓ
7. Ⓐ Ⓑ Ⓒ Ⓓ

Selección 6

1. Ⓐ Ⓑ Ⓒ Ⓓ
2. Ⓐ Ⓑ Ⓒ Ⓓ
3. Ⓐ Ⓑ Ⓒ Ⓓ
4. Ⓐ Ⓑ Ⓒ Ⓓ
5. Ⓐ Ⓑ Ⓒ Ⓓ
6. Ⓐ Ⓑ Ⓒ Ⓓ
7. Ⓐ Ⓑ Ⓒ Ⓓ

Selección 7

1. Ⓐ Ⓑ Ⓒ Ⓓ
2. Ⓐ Ⓑ Ⓒ Ⓓ
3. Ⓐ Ⓑ Ⓒ Ⓓ
4. Ⓐ Ⓑ Ⓒ Ⓓ
5. Ⓐ Ⓑ Ⓒ Ⓓ
6. Ⓐ Ⓑ Ⓒ Ⓓ
7. Ⓐ Ⓑ Ⓒ Ⓓ
8. Ⓐ Ⓑ Ⓒ Ⓓ
9. Ⓐ Ⓑ Ⓒ Ⓓ
10. Ⓐ Ⓑ Ⓒ Ⓓ

Selección 8

1. Ⓐ Ⓑ Ⓒ Ⓓ
2. Ⓐ Ⓑ Ⓒ Ⓓ
3. Ⓐ Ⓑ Ⓒ Ⓓ
4. Ⓐ Ⓑ Ⓒ Ⓓ
5. Ⓐ Ⓑ Ⓒ Ⓓ
6. Ⓐ Ⓑ Ⓒ Ⓓ
7. Ⓐ Ⓑ Ⓒ Ⓓ
8. Ⓐ Ⓑ Ⓒ Ⓓ
9. Ⓐ Ⓑ Ⓒ Ⓓ
10. Ⓐ Ⓑ Ⓒ Ⓓ

Selección 9

1. Ⓐ Ⓑ Ⓒ Ⓓ
2. Ⓐ Ⓑ Ⓒ Ⓓ
3. Ⓐ Ⓑ Ⓒ Ⓓ
4. Ⓐ Ⓑ Ⓒ Ⓓ
5. Ⓐ Ⓑ Ⓒ Ⓓ
6. Ⓐ Ⓑ Ⓒ Ⓓ
7. Ⓐ Ⓑ Ⓒ Ⓓ

Selección 10

1. Ⓐ Ⓑ Ⓒ Ⓓ
2. Ⓐ Ⓑ Ⓒ Ⓓ
3. Ⓐ Ⓑ Ⓒ Ⓓ
4. Ⓐ Ⓑ Ⓒ Ⓓ
5. Ⓐ Ⓑ Ⓒ Ⓓ
6. Ⓐ Ⓑ Ⓒ Ⓓ
7. Ⓐ Ⓑ Ⓒ Ⓓ
8. Ⓐ Ⓑ Ⓒ Ⓓ
9. Ⓐ Ⓑ Ⓒ Ⓓ
10. Ⓐ Ⓑ Ⓒ Ⓓ

Print and Audio Texts (Combined) Practice Exercises

Selección 1

Tema curricular: Los desafíos mundiales

Primero tienes un minuto para leer la fuente número 1

Fuente 1: Los siguientes datos presentan la brecha salarial y el trato igualitario y ausencia de discriminación en distintos países. Fueron compilados por datos publicados por la Biblioteca del Congreso Nacional de Chile (BCN).

Brecha salarial de género	
País	**2020**
Chile	21,1
Colombia	11,1
Costa Rica	3,7
Estados Unidos	18,9
México	16,7

La brecha salarial de género indica, en porcentajes, la remuneración menor que reciben las mujeres con trabajo a tiempo completo que los hombres.

Trato igualitario y ausencia de discriminación	
País	**2020**
Chile	0.55
Colombia	0.54
Costa Rica	0.67
Estados Unidos	0.67
México	0.37

El Trato igualitario y ausencia de discriminación mide si los individuos están libres de discriminación motivada por condiciones socioeconómicas, género, etnicidad, religión, país de origen, orientación sexual, o identidad de género, con respecto a servicios públicos, empleo, procesos judiciales y el sistema de justicia. 0 = más discriminación, 1 = menos discriminación.

Tienes dos minutos para leer la introducción y prever las preguntas.

Fuente 2: El siguiente audio, titulado *Diferentes épocas y una misma lucha: la igualdad de la mujer* fue publicado en 2016 por TeleToledo (España).

Track 1

1. ¿Qué tipo de información presenta la primera tabla?

   (A) El porcentaje de mujeres que trabajan a tiempo completo.
   (B) Los resultados de una encuesta de opinión de mujeres de esperada remuneración anual.
   (C) El porcentaje de menos dinero que ganan las mujeres que los hombres.
   (D) El número de mujeres que trabajan que reciben un salario menor que los hombres.

2. En la segunda tabla, ¿qué país tiene más trato igualitario?

    (A) Chile
    (B) Colombia
    (C) Costa Rica
    (D) México

3. Según la información contenida en las dos tablas, ¿cuál de las siguientes afirmaciones es correcta?

    (A) En Chile hay poca brecha salarial pero más discriminación.
    (B) En Costa Rica hay mucha brecha salarial pero menos discriminación.
    (C) En Colombia tanto la brecha salarial como la discriminación son relativamente bajas.
    (D) En México tanto la brecha salarial como el trato igualitario son altos.

4. Según la fuente auditiva, ¿cuál de las siguientes afirmaciones es correcta?

    (A) Históricamente la mujer ha logrado más que los hombres.
    (B) Las mujeres han tenido que luchar para hacerse un lugar en la sociedad y en la historia.
    (C) La radiología y la radiografía fueron inventadas por mujeres.
    (D) Las mujeres han disfrutado de derechos iguales desde hace muchos años.

5. Según el audio, ¿qué campo no se menciona como una contribución de las mujeres mencionadas?

    (A) Astronomía y filosofía
    (B) Deportes y atletismo
    (C) Política y activismo social
    (D) Cine y artes visuales

6. Según la fuente auditiva, ¿cuál de las siguientes opciones sigue siendo un tema de preocupación?

    (A) La falta de oportunidades educativas para las mujeres.
    (B) La discriminación en el ámbito laboral.
    (C) La violencia contra la mujer.
    (D) El acceso limitado a servicios de salud para las mujeres.

7. ¿Qué información de la tabla se puede comprobar en la fuente auditiva?

    (A) La brecha salarial entre mujeres y hombres sigue estando vigente.
    (B) La brecha salarial se está reduciendo.
    (C) El trato igualitario y la ausencia de discriminación no han mejorado en los últimos años.
    (D) En algunos países hay menos discriminación que en otros.

Cultural Awareness

Cultural practice & perspective: The table represents how women are treated in the labor force and in general in Spanish-speaking countries. The audio reaffirms some of these treatments and presents the perspective that women are just as capable as men, and highlights the contributions of several women throughout history.

The table also represents data from the United States. How are these practices and perspectives similar or different from what you have observed in your own community?

Selección 2

Tema curricular: La belleza y la estética

Primero tienes cuatro minutos para leer la fuente número 1.

Fuente 1: El siguiente artículo trata de un barrio en Buenos Aires, Argentina. Fue publicado en la página web *http://Alojargentina.com*.

La Boca
(*http://Alojargentina.com*)

En un barrio típico de inmigrantes de los más distintos orígenes, entre los que se destacan griegos, yugoslavos, turcos e italianos, sobre todo genoveses. La calle Caminito, de apenas 100 metros de longitud, es peatonal. Es una calle tan pequeña como particular. En ella no hay puertas. Algunas
Línea ventanas, algún balcón lleno de plantas y de ropas colgadas a secar. Sus paredes pintadas de diferentes
(5) colores recuerdan a Venecia. En ellas hay todo tipo de murales, cerámicas y distintos adornos. Al principio era simplemente un ramal del ferrocarril, llena de tierra, yuyales y piedras. Al lugar se lo llamaba "la curva," la que luego se convirtió en "un caminito" que acortaba distancias. Ese fue el famoso "caminito" por el que transitaba a diario Juan de Dios Filiberto, quien luego escribió el tango que lleva su nombre. La iniciativa de ponerle ese nombre a la calle surgió nada menos que de su
(10) amigo Benito Quinquela Martín. Hoy es una calle turística, no sólo visitada por los extranjeros, sino por argentinos de todo el país, orgullosos de ese lugar tan pintoresco. El Club Atlético Boca Juniors, ubicado en Brandsen 805, es uno de los clubes de fútbol más importantes del país y fue fundado por cinco jóvenes habitantes del barrio de la Boca en 1905. El nombre de la institución fue tomado directamente del barrio, pero se le agregó la palabra "Juniors" que le daba a la denominación algo más
(15) de prestigio, contrastando con la fama de "barrio difícil" que se había ganado la Boca por aquel entonces. Su estadio de fútbol tiene capacidad para 50.000 espectadores y en su barrio social y deportivo se practican otras disciplinas deportivas.

Tienes dos minutos para leer la introducción y prever las preguntas.

Fuente 2: Esta grabación trata de un pueblo en México. Fue publicada en la página web *www.mexicodescono-cido.com.mx*.

Track 2

1. ¿Cuál es el propósito del artículo?

   (A) Contar la historia de un equipo de fútbol profesional
   (B) Comentar sobre el desarrollo de una calle de Buenos Aires
   (C) Describir cómo se ha evolucionado un barrio porteño
   (D) Relatar la influencia de los inmigrantes en la capital argentina

2. ¿Cómo se podría describir la calle Caminito?

   (A) Peculiar
   (B) Común
   (C) Simple
   (D) Rústica

3. ¿Cómo recibió la calle el nombre "caminito"?

   (A) Por su forma de línea recta
   (B) Por ser una calle que abreviaba la ruta de muchos
   (C) Por ser un destino turístico
   (D) Por su apariencia pintoresca

4. Según toda la información presentada en el artículo, ¿cómo se podría describir la gente que vive en este barrio?

   (A) Muchos se sentirán molestos por la cantidad de turistas.
   (B) Será gente diversa pero orgullosa de su barrio.
   (C) Los residentes serán grandes aficionados del fútbol.
   (D) Los habitantes serán expertos en bailar el tango.

5. ¿Cuál es el propósito de la fuente auditiva?

   (A) Narrar la historia de Santa Clara del Cobre
   (B) Explicar las razones por las cuales fue nombrada Pueblo Mágico
   (C) Describir el pueblo como destino turístico
   (D) Detallar el proceso de producción de artesanía

6. Según la fuente auditiva, ¿cómo se distingue esta comunidad?

   (A) Por sus viviendas y plazas
   (B) Por tener una influyente comunidad indígena
   (C) Por su producción de objetos hechos de cobre
   (D) Por haber inventado una nueva técnica de elaborar el metal

7. ¿A qué se refiere la fuente auditiva cuando afirma que un techo "se ilumina con los rayos del sol"?

   (A) A que hay una representación del sol encima.
   (B) A que el techo brilla como el sol.
   (C) A que refleja la luz del sol.
   (D) A que ilumina como si fuera de día.

8. ¿A quiénes les interesaría más visitar este pueblo?

   (A) A empresarios y fabricantes
   (B) A artistas y excursionistas
   (C) A indígenas y extranjeros
   (D) A funcionarios y empresas inmobiliarias

9. ¿Qué tienen en común las dos fuentes?

   (A) Las dos resaltan las características del lugar.
   (B) Las dos destacan los productos de cada comunidad.
   (C) Tanto el audio como el artículo muestran los cambios que han ocurrido a través de los años.
   (D) Las dos fuentes señalan la influencia de varias culturas en el desarrollo de la comunidad.

10. Si fueras a escribir sobre la información de las dos fuentes, ¿cuál sería el mejor título para tu ensayo?

   (A) La magia del color local
   (B) Características de un pueblo latinoamericano
   (C) Ventajas de vivir en una comunidad autóctona
   (D) El crisol cultural argentino

Cultural Awareness

Cultural product: Both these texts present peculiar places in Argentina and Mexico and how they reflect the character of the people who live there.

How are these places similar to or different from those in your own community?

Selección 3

Tema curricular: La vida contemporánea

Tienes un minuto para leer la fuente número 1.

Fuente 1: Esta tabla presenta algunas ventajas e inconvenientes de asistir a una universidad grande.

¿Por qué elegir una universidad grande?	
Ventajas	**Inconvenientes**
• Conocer y convivir con todo tipo de gente y gente de distintas carreras • Variedad de instalaciones de acuerdo a las necesidades de cada carrera • Buen ambiente debido a la variedad de estudiantes • El prestigio, tratándose de una universidad que abarca mucho puede ser muy fuerte, y por ende un arma importante al egresar • Gran variedad de oportunidades sociales y de trabajo • Mucha gente conocerá la universidad, y por ende es una carta de presentación reconocida por todos • Los profesores suelen ser de alta calidad	• Las clases son muy grandes • Muchos profesores se interesan más por sus propias investigaciones que en enseñar las clases • Muchos cursos, especialmente los preliminares, suelen ser enseñados por asistentes de profesores • Posibilidad de no destacarse por la gran cantidad de estudiantes • Más burocrático que personal • Más competición para las becas

Tienes dos minutos para leer la introducción y prever las preguntas.

Fuente 2: La siguiente grabación trata de unos beneficios de asistir a una universidad pequeña. Está basada en información publicada en la página web *www.collegeboard.com*.

Track 3

1. Según la información proveída en la tabla, ¿cuál es un beneficio de asistir a una universidad grande?

   (A) No hay que preocuparse de perderse en la muchedumbre.
   (B) Los cursos básicos suelen ser más fáciles porque los catedráticos no los suelen enseñar.
   (C) Hay más ocasiones de participar en ferias y seminarios.
   (D) Todo está más al alcance del estudiante.

2. Basándote en la información de la tabla, ¿cuál sería un reto de asistir a una universidad grande?

   (A) La variedad de eventos sociales puede afectar negativamente los estudios.
   (B) Sería más difícil desarrollar amistades verdaderas por la gran cantidad de estudiantes.
   (C) Los asistentes de los profesores no están capacitados para controlar sus clases.
   (D) Hay más barreras y limitaciones relacionados con la inscripción y diseño de los estudios.

3. ¿Para qué tipo de persona sería apropiado asistir a una universidad grande?

   (A) Una persona autónoma que, aunque le gusta socializar, prefiere ser más incógnita que el ombligo del mundo.
   (B) Una persona introvertida que frecuentemente necesita ayuda de consejeros y profesores por una variedad de asuntos.
   (C) Una persona a quien le encanta entablar debates con su profesor y otros estudiantes durante las clases.
   (D) Una persona que quiere que su universidad tenga un fuerte sentido de comunidad y ambiente unido.

4. Según la fuente auditiva, ¿cuál es un beneficio de asistir a una universidad pequeña?

   (A) Hay amplias oportunidades de formar parte de diferentes grupos sociales.
   (B) Existe una relación más personal entre los docentes y los estudiantes.
   (C) Las carreras son menos competitivas que en las grandes universidades.
   (D) Los profesores suelen enseñar sus clases mejor que los de las universidades grandes.

5. ¿Cómo se distinguen las universidades pequeñas en cuanto a las carreras que ofrecen?

   (A) Hay tantas carreras como las que ofrecen las universidades grandes.
   (B) Los estudiantes tienden a seguir varias carreras de estudio.
   (C) Se animan a los estudiantes a que personalicen sus investigaciones.
   (D) Los profesores y estudiantes trabajan juntos para crear las distintas carreras que se ofrecen cada año.

6. ¿Qué recomendación ofrece la grabación para una persona que esté preocupada en un aspecto de asistir a una universidad pequeña?

   (A) Conversar con estudiantes actuales para informarse de las oportunidades de ocio
   (B) Conocer bien a los profesores y asesores para enterarse del apoyo que la universidad ofrece
   (C) Buscar en el catálogo de cursos unas carreras de estudio que le interesan
   (D) Investigar si las universidades efectivamente son capaces de cumplir con los intereses de los estudiantes

7. Según la tabla y la fuente auditiva, ¿cuál de las siguientes afirmaciones es correcta?

   (A) Las universidades grandes suelen ser de renombre, mientras las más pequeñas son de menos prestigio.
   (B) Hay tantas oportunidades de formar parte de un grupo social en las universidades pequeñas como en las grandes.
   (C) En las universidades grandes, los profesores son más experimentados que los de las universidades pequeñas.
   (D) El entorno en los dos tipos de universidades es igualmente agradable, según la personalidad del estudiante.

Cultural Awareness

Cultural perspective: The print and audio texts present certain perspectives on making a decision on what type of college or university to attend.

How are the perspectives presented in these texts similar to or different from what you have observed in your own community?

Selección 4

Tema curricular: La belleza y la estética

Tienes cuatro minutos para leer la fuente número 1.

Fuente 1: El siguiente artículo trata de un tipo de música popular en México. Fue publicado en la página web *http://InfoMorelos.com.*

El corrido
(*http://InfoMorelos.com*)

El corrido es una parte central de la música popular mexicana. Se ha convertido en una de las fuentes más eficientes para la difusión de las historias heroicas o románticas. Estas historias, frecuentemente se ubican en el ambiente de la revolución de 1910; sin embargo, ahora también se abarcan

Línea
(5) temas como el narcotráfico y la política contemporánea. Los temas más populares y difundidos son el amor engañado, la queja del débil frente al poderoso, el énfasis en actos guerreros, la habilidad especial en el manejo de las armas y el desafío después de haber sufrido alguna injusticia.

En los tiempos de la revolución, los cantantes viajeros recitaban los corridos en las calles o las plazas públicas, para comunicar novedades acerca de los acontecimientos importantes, así como lo habían hecho los trovadores de la Edad Media. La fuerte difusión de los corridos también tiene que ver
(10) con la venta de los textos impresos en papel de colores en las ferias y fiestas populares. Estas impresiones frecuentemente estaban ilustradas por el entonces totalmente desconocido artista José Guadalupe Posada. Estas hojas servían frecuentemente para la difusión de ideas revolucionarias. Eran algo así como celdas de lo subversivo que, normalmente, fueron ignoradas por parte de la censura, ya que estas hojas se consideraban como "asuntos del populacho" sin importancia.

(15) El musicólogo Vicente T. Mendoza opina que el primer corrido fue "Macario Romero," que data del año 1898 y surgió en el estado de Durango. El texto relata un acontecimiento del año 1810.

El corrido es recitado o cantado y tiene parte de sus raíces en la música popular española. La voz principal a veces es apoyada por un refrán cantado por un coro. El acompañamiento consiste principalmente en instrumentos de cuerda, tales como la guitarra, el violín y el guitarrón. A veces también
(20) tocan instrumentos de viento, sobre todo trompeta.

Sin embargo, frecuentemente una guitarra basta para cantar los corridos, presentando historias de infidelidad, borracheras, tragedias familiares, atrevidas aventuras y amores a un público que escucha sorprendido, admirado o indignado.

Además existen diferentes concursos para la composición y representación de corridos. Hoy en día,
(25) Chabela Vargas, Amparo Ochoa, Cuco Sánchez, Vicente Fernández y otros son los intérpretes más destacados de los corridos tradicionales, mientras que los Tigres del Norte son el representante más conocido del corrido contemporáneo.

Tienes dos minutos para leer la introducción y prever las preguntas.

Fuente 2: La siguiente grabación trata de la música clásica. Se basa en un artículo publicado en la página web *www.buscarinformación.com.*

Track 4

1. Durante la revolución, ¿cuál era la función primaria de los corridos?

   (A) Entretener a la gente
   (B) Investigar la historia de México
   (C) Proveer noticias de diferentes sucesos
   (D) Criticar varios aspectos de la sociedad mexicana

2. ¿Cuál es uno de los temas de los corridos?

   (A) El comercio de libros y textos
   (B) Las injusticias cometidas durante la revolución
   (C) La vida y las obras de diferentes héroes
   (D) Las fiestas y ferias populares de México

3. ¿Qué otro impacto tuvieron los corridos?

   (A) Causaron una polémica que llevó a la censura de algunos corridos.
   (B) Inspiraron una representación gráfica de las letras de algunas canciones.
   (C) Cambiaron los gustos y filosofía de la sociedad.
   (D) Hicieron que la gente aprendiera más de la música española.

4. ¿Cuál es una característica del corrido?

   (A) Es una mezcla de varios estilos musicales de América Latina.
   (B) Sólo hay una persona que canta.
   (C) Se usan instrumentos acústicos y eléctricos.
   (D) Es cantada por un conjunto cuyos miembros tocan y cantan.

5. Según la grabación, ¿qué tipo de música se puede denominar "música clásica"?

   (A) Música que une varios instrumentos en una orquesta
   (B) La música compuesta entre la Edad Media y el barroco
   (C) Sólo la música compuesta por Bach y Beethoven
   (D) La música que incorpora los estilos de diferentes épocas

6. ¿Cómo se caracteriza la música clásica?

   (A) Es compleja y resulta difícil de entender.
   (B) Es melancólica por tratar de temas serios.
   (C) Es elegante y asequible, pero merece profunda atención.
   (D) Es principalmente para los adinerados.

7. Según la fuente auditiva, ¿quiénes gozan de la música clásica?

   (A) Los aficionados de la época medieval
   (B) Generalmente la gente mayor
   (C) Tanto los mayores como los jóvenes
   (D) Principalmente la juventud

8. ¿Cómo se destacó la música clásica?

   (A) Por lograr unir varios instrumentos distintos para una representación
   (B) Por ser la primera en perfeccionar la unión entre el canto e instrumentos
   (C) Por ser la primera rama musical que creó obras dramáticas
   (D) Por su capacidad de ser relevante en diferente épocas

9. ¿Qué tienen en común la música clásica y los corridos?

   (A) Los dos tienen sus orígenes antes del siglo XIX.
   (B) Los dos incorporan una gran variedad de instrumentos de todos los tipos.
   (C) Los dos presentan historias de la antigüedad.
   (D) Los dos gozan de bastante popularidad en el presente.

10. ¿Por quiénes parecen ser adaptados los dos estilos musicales?

   (A) Los corridos son para la clase obrera, y la música clásica es para los más
       educados.
   (B) La música clásica es para los catedráticos, y los corridos son para los guerreros.
   (C) Los corridos son para los que les gusta festejar, y la música clásica es
       para los que favorecen lo dramático.
   (D) La música clásica es para los que tienen gustos más refinados, y los corridos
       son para la gente que busca romance.

Cultural Awareness

Cultural product: The print text presents a type of music that is famous in Mexico.

How is this particular music similar to or different from what you have observed in your own community?

Selección 5

Tema curricular: Los desafíos sociales

Tienes un minuto para leer la fuente número 1.

Fuente 1: El siguiente anuncio trata de unas razones para participar en una manifestación. Se basa en un anuncio publicado por la UGT, una organización sindical obrera de España.

Razones para participar este sábado ¡Juntos podemos hacer una diferencia!	
Las reformas laborales del gobierno hacen el despido más fácil, más rápido y más barato.	Impulsa la privatización de los servicios públicos, como el transporte, educación y sanidad.
El empresario tiene todo el poder, la flexibilidad interna facilita la movilidad, la modificación de jornada, horario y modificación de salarios.	Perjudican el empleo público, incrementan la jornada, reducen días libres, nos quitan la paga de navidad . . .
Fomenta la inestabilidad de los jóvenes, que los condena al subempleo y al desempleo.	Reduce las prestaciones por desempleo, elimina subsidio y reduce la prestación desde el 6° mes.
Seguro que tienes más razones . . . ¡ponlas aquí!	

Tienes dos minutos para leer la introducción y prever las preguntas.

Fuente 2: En la siguiente conversación, dos amigos hablan de un evento que quieren preparar.

Track 5

1. ¿Cuál es el propósito principal de esta manifestación?

    (A) Proponer cambios a los beneficios que ofrecen las empresas

    (B) Criticar las injusticias en el mundo del trabajo

    (C) Pedir aumentos de sueldo y cantidad de tiempo libre

    (D) Impulsar reformas de la gestión pública

2. ¿Cuál parece ser la queja global de los manifestantes?

    (A) Los jóvenes no tienen tantas oportunidades como los demás.

    (B) El gobierno no les está prestando atención a los deseos del público.

    (C) Las compañías privadas tienen demasiado dominio.

    (D) La legislación laboral es anticuada.

3. ¿Qué quieren los organizadores de esta manifestación?

    (A) Quieren que los participantes dejen sus trabajos.

    (B) Invitan a que la gente añada sus propias quejas.

    (C) Mandan que los empresarios no despidan a tanta gente.

    (D) Proponen que se dé un sobresueldo durante los días festivos.

4. En la conversación, ¿qué están planeando estos hombres?

   (A) Una huelga
   (B) Un carnaval
   (C) Una lucha
   (D) Una feria

5. ¿Por qué están insatisfechos los dos?

   (A) Los dos hombres piensan que no pueden mejorar su situación.
   (B) Ellos opinan que merecen más pago.
   (C) La empresa está por quebrar y no puede pagarles.
   (D) Los otros empleados no desean cooperar con su plan.

6. ¿Qué resolución proponen los dos?

   (A) Proponen que la compañía les permita trabajar la semana que viene.
   (B) Proponen que la compañía les reembolse por el tiempo de trabajo perdido.
   (C) Recomiendan que la compañía acepte el ascenso de cincuenta dólares.
   (D) Sugieren que el árbitro les permita regresar al empleo sin contrato para que puedan mantener la producción.

7. ¿Qué tienen en común la fuente escrita y la auditiva?

   (A) Las dos buscan aumento de sueldo.
   (B) Las dos buscan una solución lo más antes posible.
   (C) Las dos se quejan de la falta de contratos.
   (D) Las dos buscan armar un grupo para luchar contra las injusticias.

Cultural Awareness

Cultural practice: The print and audio texts present a common practice in many Spanish-speaking countries: going on strike or holding a social protest.

How is the practice presented in these texts similar to or different from what you have observed in your own community?

Selección 6

Tema curricular: La ciencia y la tecnología

Tienes cuatro minutos para leer la fuente número 1.

Fuente 1: La siguiente tabla presenta medidas de prevención ante un terremoto.

Consejos y medidas de prevención ante un sismo		
Antes	**Durante**	**Después**
• Identifique y marque las zonas más seguras en casas, escuelas, oficinas, edificios y calles para ubicarse en ellas. • Aléjese de ventanales y cables de alta tensión. • Identifique lugares seguros cercanos para la concentración de personas, como parques o casas de familiares. Póngase de acuerdo con los familiar para ubicarse en ellos. • Identifique las rutas de evacuación y realice si-mulacros preventivos de comportamiento. • Coloque los muebles de manera que los pasillos queden despejados. • Tenga un botiquín, botellas de agua, lámparas y pilas y un radio, siempre a la mano.	• Mantenga la calma y ayude a que otros hagan lo mismo. • No corra, no grite y no empuje a nadie, muchas veces hay más accidentes durante la evacuación, que por efectos del sismo. • Colóquese bajo los escritorios, mesas fuertes o en los sitios marcados como seguros como son los marcos de puertas y junto a pilares de contención de edificios. • Aléjese de ventanas que puedan romperse con el movimiento. • Si es posible salir a la calle, colóquese en lugares alejados de cables de alta tensión.	• Salga de los edificios y casas y permanezca un buen rato fuera de ellos. • Revise los daños externos antes de entrar nuevamente y los internos antes de que su familia entre. • No utilice gas, aparatos eléctricos ni encienda cerillos. • Encienda un radio de pilas, para mantenerse informado. Atienda las indicaciones del personal de protección civil siempre. • Esté preparado para las réplicas, a veces estas son menores y frecuentemente con mayores consecuencias. • Evite saturar las líneas telefónicas, para que los servicios de emergencia puedan atender las llamadas de urgencia.

Tienes dos minutos para leer la introducción y prever las preguntas.

Fuente 2: En la siguiente conversación, dos mujeres hablan de un evento que ocurrió la noche anterior.

Track 6

1. Según la información en la tabla, ¿qué preparativos puedes hacer en la casa?

   (A) Determinar la mejor forma de salir de la casa en caso de un sismo

   (B) Comprar reservas de comestibles en caso de que quede atrapado

   (C) Identificar los edificios públicos en su barrio para poder refugiarse en ellos

   (D) Situar los muebles para que no obstruyan el paso de salida

2. ¿Por qué hay que mantener la calma durante un sismo?

   (A) Porque el desorden puede aumentar el número de heridos.

   (B) Porque el nerviosismo puede causarles mucha tensión a los demás.

   (C) Porque la tranquilidad ayuda a que se encuentren lugares de refugio.

   (D) Porque la calma ayuda a que otros se tranquilicen.

3. ¿Por qué hay que quedarse afuera de los edificios después de un sismo?

   (A) Porque es más fácil que los socorristas te encuentren.

   (B) Porque es posible que el personal de protección necesite tu ayuda.

   (C) Porque es probable que la estructura haya sido dañada.

   (D) Porque es más fácil revisar los daños desde el exterior.

4. Según la conversación ¿qué acontecimiento comentan estas mujeres?

   (A) La noche anterior lanzaron muchos cohetes.

   (B) La noche anterior sufrieron un bombardeo.

   (C) La noche anterior hubo una plaga de insectos.

   (D) La noche anterior hizo muy mal tiempo.

5. ¿Qué molestia adicional ha sufrido la segunda narradora?

   (A) No tiene electricidad en la casa.

   (B) No tiene agua corriente en la casa.

   (C) No tiene plantas en el huerto.

   (D) No tiene gotas.

6. ¿Qué remedio hay para el problema de la segunda narradora?

   (A) Todo estará arreglado pronto, ese mismo día.

   (B) El ayuntamiento le ha prometido hacer reparaciones mañana.

   (C) Ella esperará hasta que brille el sol para colgar la ropa al aire.

   (D) No hay remedio, tendrá que esperar mucho tiempo.

7. Según la conversación y la información de la tabla, ¿qué preparativos deberían haber hecho las dos mujeres que les habrían ayudado durante este evento?

   (A) Localizar el lugar de refugio seguro en su casa

   (B) Tener guardados una linterna, botellas de agua y radio

   (C) Colocar los muebles de manera que queden despejados los pasillos

   (D) Identificar las rutas de evacuación y realizar simulacros preventivos

---

Cultural Awareness

Cultural perspectives: The print and audio texts present how different communities prepare for and react to environmental challenges, such as earthquakes or a bad storm.

How are the perspectives presented in these texts similar to or different from what you have observed in your own community?

Selección 7

Tema curricular: La vida contemporánea
Tienes cuatro minutos para leer la fuente número 1.

Fuente 1: El siguiente texto se trata de la Feria Apícola en Campoo de Yuso, un municipio de Cantabria, España. Fue publicado por la Oficina de Comunicación del Gobierno de Cantabria en 2022.

Línea

El pabellón deportivo municipal de La Población acogerá el 15 de octubre una nueva edición, la XVI, de la Feria Apícola de Campoo de Yuso, que reunirá a expertos apícolas en torno a unas jornadas técnicas internacionales y ofrecerá las mejores mieles de la comarca y del resto de la región en un mercado alimentario que se complementará con talleres, actuaciones musicales y la entrega del

(5) premio 'Miel Solidaria 2022', que recaerá en la residencia de ancianos San Francisco de Reinosa.

Organizada por el Ayuntamiento de Campoo de Yuso, en colaboración con la Asociación Española de Cría de Abejas Reinas (AECRIA) y la Asociación de Apicultores Campurrianos (APICAM) y el patrocinio del Gobierno regional, a través de la Consejería de Desarrollo Rural, Ganadería, Pesca, Alimentación y Medio Ambiente, la Feria comenzará a las 9:00 horas en el salón de acto del polide-

(10) portivo para, a continuación, dar paso a las exposiciones de las jornadas técnicas que se desarrollarán por la mañana, con expertos de diferentes regiones del país.

Ya por la tarde, se celebrarán talleres simultáneos y la entrega del premio 'Miel Solidaria 2022', basado en una recaudación de miel de los diferentes puestos, además de un mercado agroalimentario con 20 productores para la exposición y venta de productos alimentarios con la asistencia de empresas

(15) de material apícola y actuaciones musicales.

Así lo han explicado hoy el consejero de Desarrollo Rural, Ganadería, Pesca, Alimentación y Medio Ambiente, Guillermo Blanco, y el alcalde de Campoo Yuso, Eduardo Ortiz, durante la presentación de un evento en el que participará una veintena de productores agroalimentarios, tales como quesos, embutidos, orujos, repostería, cosméticos naturales, sidras, zumos y miel, además de fabricantes de

(20) material apícola para mostrar las últimas novedades del sector.

Durante su intervención, el consejero ha destacado la importancia de la miel como un producto con "innegables" beneficios para la salud que contribuye "de manera decidida" al mantenimiento del medio ambiente y de la biodiversidad de la Comunidad Autónoma.

Ha reafirmado el compromiso de su departamento con el sector apícola, al que el Gobierno de

(25) Cantabria destina de manera anual ayudas para la producción y comercialización de la miel y prima de polinización, y que se reparten entre los titulares de explotaciones apícolas.

El titular de Desarrollo Rural también se ha comprometido a seguir apoyando al sector para hacer frente a las amenazas que afectan a las explotaciones apícolas y a sus profesionales, tales como plaguicidas, parásitos, cambio climático, sistemas de manejo, sobreexplotación y, especialmente, la invasión

(30) de especies exóticas, como la avispa velutina.

Finalmente, ha destacado la importancia de las ferias agroalimentarias para promocionar y difundir la excelente calidad de los productos cántabros, como la miel, y ejercer como "escaparate ideal" para hacer llegar las producciones agroalimentarias al consumidor.

Por su parte, el alcalde de Campoo de Yuso ha agradecido la colaboración de todas las asociaciones

(35) e instituciones y ha insistido en la apuesta del Ayuntamiento por preservar todo tipo de especies como la abeja que tiene beneficios no sólo para la biodiversidad y el medio ambiente, sino también a nivel alimenticio, logrando un producto de "gran calidad".

Tienes dos minutos para leer la introducción y prever las preguntas

Fuente 2: Este audio se trata de la importancia de las abejas para el medio ambiente. Fue publicado por Medicina y Salud Pública (Puerto Rico) en febrero de 2022.

Track 7

1. ¿Cuál es el propósito del artículo?

   (A) Informar sobre una celebración y los eventos relacionados a ella
   (B) Promover la importancia de la apicultura en la región
   (C) Anunciar las actividades culturales en Campoo de Yuso
   (D) Presentar a los expertos apícolas que participarán en la feria

2. ¿Cómo se determina el ganador del premio Miel Solidaria 2022?

   (A) Por votación del público asistente
   (B) Por la recaudación de miel de los diferentes puestos
   (C) Por elección del alcalde de Campoo de Yuso
   (D) Por los miembros de la residencia de ancianos

3. ¿Cuál es una de las estrategias para apoyar y proteger el sector apícola?

   (A) Fomentar la importación de miel
   (B) Combatir las amenazas a las explotaciones apícolas
   (C) Reducir las ayudas económicas
   (D) Aumentar los impuestos a los productores de miel

4. Según el artículo, ¿cuál es la mayor amenaza para la apicultura?

   (A) Plagas y parásitos
   (B) Cambio climático y sobreexplotación
   (C) Sistemas de manejo
   (D) Invasión de especies exóticas

5. Según el audio, ¿cuál es el papel de las abejas en nuestros ecosistemas?

   (A) Son los únicos insectos que pueden polinizar plantas y alimentos.
   (B) Son los principales polinizadores, y el reino vegetal no podría evolucionar sin ellos.
   (C) Únicamente polinizan plantas y alimentos en ciertas regiones del mundo.
   (D) Tienen un papel pequeño en la polinización de plantas y alimentos.

6. Según el audio, ¿qué impacto tendría la posible extinción de las abejas en los humanos?

   (A) Las plantas no podrían reproducirse o evolucionar.
   (B) No habría animales en los ecosistemas.
   (C) No tendríamos alimentos.
   (D) Serían atacados por otros insectos.

7. Según el audio, ¿qué se puede hacer para crear conciencia y cuidar a las abejas?

   (A) Incrementar el uso de pesticidas en la agricultura

   (B) Despreocuparse por la importancia de los ecosistemas

   (C) Participar en campañas de conservación enfocadas en las abejas

   (D) Fomentar la urbanización en áreas donde las abejas prosperan

8. Según la grabación, ¿qué se recomienda hacer si nos encontramos con un enjambre de abejas?

   (A) Atacarlo y dañarlo tanto como sea posible

   (B) Llamar a las autoridades de emergencia

   (C) Beber un vaso de agua con azúcar

   (D) Informar a las autoridades ambientales y mantener la calma.

9. ¿Qué tienen en común las dos fuentes?

   (A) Incluyen información sobre eventos relacionados con la apicultura y la producción de miel.

   (B) Presentan iniciativas para promocionar y difundir productos agroalimentarios.

   (C) Resaltan la importancia de las abejas y su papel en el medio ambiente.

   (D) Destacan los beneficios de las abejas en la salud y la industria alimentaria.

10. ¿Qué información de la fuente auditiva no se puede comprobar en el texto?

   (A) La importancia de hacer frente a las amenazas de las abejas

   (B) El mayor peligro para las abejas

   (C) El impacto del cambio climático en las abejas

   (D) Concienciación como una herramienta para proteger las abejas

---

Cultural Awareness

Cultural product, practice & perspectives: The article and audio present the perspective that bees are important. The article also presents a practice of protecting bees, and a town in Spain created an entire fair around celebrating apiculture (product).

What is the perspective in your community in terms of the importance of bees? Are there certain practices that are done to protect bees, such as beekeeping and bekeeping clubs? If not, are there practices to protect other plants or animals?

Selección 8

Tema curricular: La ciencia y la tecnología

Tienes cuatro minutos para leer la fuente número 1.

Fuente 1: El siguiente artículo trata de la energía eólica. Fue publicado en la página web *www.enbuenas-manos.com*.

¿Qué es la energía eólica?

La energía eólica es la energía producida por el viento. La utilización de este tipo de energía por el hombre no es nada nuevo pues se viene haciendo desde tiempos remotos.

Las ventajas de la energía eólica ya eran aprovechadas por los babilonios y los chinos hace más de
Línea 4.000 años para bombear agua para regar los cultivos y en la Edad Media era el viento el encargado de
(5) mover los molinos para moler el grano y, por supuesto, era la energía utilizada por los barcos.

Hoy día se aprovecha esta energía para, mediante un generador, transformarla en electricidad.

Son muchas las ventajas de la energía eólica, estas son algunas de ellas:

- Los costes de producción de este tipo de energía son relativamente bajos, pueden competir en rentabilidad con otras fuentes de producción de energía: centrales térmicas de carbón, centrales
(10) de combustible, etc.
- Otra de las ventajas de la energía eólica es que es una energía limpia, para su producción no es necesario un proceso de combustión. Es un proceso limpio que no perjudica a la atmósfera, la fauna, la vegetación y no contamina el suelo ni las aguas.
- Los modernos molinos de viento pueden ser instalados en zonas remotas, no conectadas a la
(15) red eléctrica, para conseguir su propio suministro.
- Una de las mayores ventajas de la energía eólica es que es inagotable, sostenible y no contaminante.
- La utilización de la energía eólica para la generación de electricidad no incide sobre las características fisicoquímicas del suelo, ya que no se produce ningún contaminante que le perju-
(20) dique, ni tampoco vertidos o grandes movimientos de tierras.
- La energía eólica no altera los acuíferos y la producción de electricidad a partir de esta energía no contribuye al efecto invernadero, no destruye la capa de ozono ni genera residuos contaminantes.

A pesar de todas las ventajas de la energía eólica esta también tiene algunas desventajas:
(25)
- La fuerza del viento es muy variable, por lo que la producción de energía no es constante.
- Los modernos molinos de viento son estructuras grandes y todavía bastantes caras.
- Hay quien está en contra de los aerogeneradores porque producen una alte-ración sobre el paisaje.
- Las turbinas son ruidosas.
(30)
- Los parques eólicos son un peligro para las aves, las palas de los molinos han matado a muchas de ellas.
- Hoy por hoy las empresas de energía eólica dependen de subsidios de los gobiernos pues todavía no son competitivas.

Tienes dos minutos para leer la introducción y prever las preguntas.

Fuente 2: La siguiente fuente auditiva trata de los beneficios de la energía solar. Se basa en un artículo de David Dickson, director de SciDiv.net.

Track 8

1. ¿Cuál es el propósito del artículo?

   (A) Contar la historia del uso de energía eólica
   (B) Mostrar los efectos positivos y problemas del viento
   (C) Presentar los pros y contras del uso de energía producida por el viento
   (D) Convencer a que se hagan cambios en nuestras fuentes de energía

2. ¿Cómo se usaba el viento en la antigüedad?

   (A) Para poder sacar agua potable de la tierra.
   (B) Ayudaba con la agricultura.
   (C) Se usaba para cosechar los granos.
   (D) Se usaba en la fabricación de naves y barcos.

3. ¿Cuáles son unos beneficios de la energía eólica?

   (A) Es barato producir e instalar los molinos.
   (B) La energía producida es constante y abundante.
   (C) No produce ningún contaminante y no contribuye a la huella de carbono.
   (D) No afecta negativamente ni a la fauna ni al medioambiente.

4. Según la información proveída en el artículo, ¿quién estaría más dispuesto a usar energía eólica?

   (A) Un jubilado que acaba de comprarse una cabaña en las montañas para poder disfrutar de la vista y la tranquilidad.
   (B) Una pareja que quiere mudarse al campo y piensa construirse una casa autosuficiente, apartada de la red eléctrica.
   (C) Una persona que piensa trasladar su empresa a una zona remota y necesita una fuente fiable de energía.
   (D) Un grupo de ornitólogos que necesita energía para su nueva instalación de observatorios, los cuales se encuentran en la ruta de aves migratorias.

5. Según la fuente auditiva, ¿qué quiere comunicar el locutor acerca de la energía solar cuando dice que es "el último recurso de energía renovable"?

   (A) Que se debe usar después de agotar todos los otros recursos.
   (B) Que dura más tiempo que otras energías.
   (C) Que es la más reciente de las energías renovables.
   (D) Que es la energía renovable con más uso variado.

6. ¿Qué papel desempeña Fondo Clima Verde?

   (A) Suministra apoyo financiero para extender el uso de energías renovables en países en vías de desarrollo.
   (B) Provee dinero para combatir el calentamiento global y la pobreza.
   (C) Participa en conferencias para alcanzar mayor conciencia del medio ambiente y energías renovables.
   (D) Presiona a las compañías de energía y al gobierno a que integren planes de energía renovable en el desarrollo del país.

7. ¿Qué problema todavía existe con la energía solar?

   (A) La tecnología todavía está en su infancia.
   (B) El proceso de convertir la luz del sol en energía no es muy rápido.
   (C) Los paneles solares son poco eficientes.
   (D) El precio de los dispositivos sigue siendo demasiado alto.

8. ¿Qué obstáculo se encuentra en cuanto a la difusión de la energía solar globalmente?

   (A) Los grupos de presión y ayuda gubernamental todavía favorecen el uso de energía de recursos tradicionales.
   (B) No hay suficiente evidencia de que puede ser una forma alternativa viable.
   (C) Esta energía beneficia mayormente a los países que se encuentran en la línea ecuatorial.
   (D) Todavía no resulta claro qué beneficios medioambientales ofrece esta alternativa.

9. ¿Qué tienen en común las dos fuentes?

   (A) Hacen referencia a las ventajas y desventajas de usar estos tipos de energía renovable.
   (B) Presentan los beneficios que estas energías aportan a la flora y fauna.
   (C) Muestran algunos de los desafíos que todavía enfrentan estas energías alternativas.
   (D) Resaltan la creciente popularidad de tratar de incorporar estas energías.

10. ¿Qué tienen en común las dos formas de energía alternativa?

   (A) Ofrecen un bajo coste de producción.
   (B) No proveen energía constante.
   (C) Necesitan una forma de batería para almacenar la energía que producen.
   (D) Benefician a abundantes fuentes de energía.

Cultural Awareness

Cultural perspective: The print and audio texts present certain perspectives on alternative energy.

How are the perspectives presented in these texts similar to or different from what you have observed in your own community?

Selección 9

Tema curricular: Los desafíos mundiales

Tienes un minuto para leer la fuente número 1.

> **Fuente 1:** El siguiente gráfico representa las razones por las cuales los jóvenes entre 10 y 17 años abandonan los estudios escolares en seis países de América Latina. Se basa en datos de SITEAL publicados en 2010.

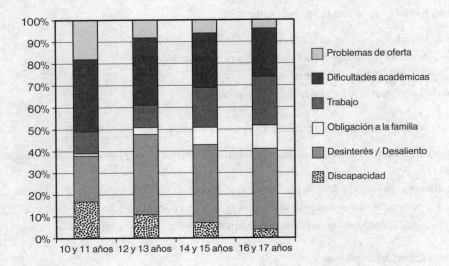

Tienes dos minutos para leer la introducción y prever las preguntas.

> **Fuente 2:** El siguiente reportaje trata del asunto de la preparación de jóvenes latinoamericanos para entrar en el mundo laboral. El reportaje fue publicado en Radio Naciones Unidas en 2012. La grabación dura aproximadamente cuatro minutos.

Track 9

1. Entre los estudiantes de 12 y 13 años, ¿cuál es la razón principal para abandonar los estudios?

   (A) No entienden las materias académicas.

   (B) Necesitan apoyar a la familia económicamente.

   (C) Prefieren perseguir otras actividades que el estudio.

   (D) Les resulta difícil llegar a las escuelas.

2. ¿Qué factor ha incrementado más durante los años?

   (A) Los jóvenes tienen que asumir roles típicamente reservados para los padres.

   (B) Los estudios tienden a ser más difíciles.

   (C) Los estudiantes tienen menos tiempo para dedicarse a los estudios.

   (D) Les falta interés a las familias para que sus hijos continúen con los estudios.

3. Según el gráfico, ¿qué les ayudaría más a los estudiantes entre 10 y 11 años para continuar con los estudios académicos?

    (A) Introducción de programas de becas y subsidios

    (B) Programas de apoyo y fortalecimiento académico

    (C) Mayor involucramiento de los padres

    (D) Mejoramiento de la disponibilidad de escuelas en zonas rurales

4. Según la fuente auditiva, ¿cuántos en América Latina carecen de las destrezas básicas para cumplir el trabajo?

    (A) El 25% de la población latinoamericana

    (B) El 50% de la población latinoamericana

    (C) 200 millones de jóvenes

    (D) Un cuarto de la población joven

5. Según Marisol Sanjinés, ¿qué hay que hacer para mejorar el problema?

    (A) Mandar que todos los jóvenes se queden en las escuelas hasta cumplir la secundaria

    (B) Aumentar la inversión de 1 dólar por persona a 10 a 15 dólares por persona

    (C) Proveer oportunidades a los que abandonaron los estudios para que puedan conseguir ciertas habilidades

    (D) Proporcionar equipo a los agricultores para facilitarles el trabajo en el campo

6. Al final de la entrevistas, ¿qué comunica la cita de la joven en cuanto a la situación en la que se encuentran muchos jóvenes?

    (A) Que los jóvenes son incapaces de controlar sus propios destinos

    (B) Que están a la merced de las acciones o inactividad de la generación actual

    (C) Que están sufriendo y los mayores hacen muy poco para ayudarlos

    (D) Que son mayormente ignorados por la generación anterior

7. ¿Qué se puede afirmar sobre el gráfico y la fuente auditiva?

    (A) Los dos presentan unas causas para el abandono escolar en América Latina.

    (B) Los dos exponen unas consecuencias por abandonar los estudios.

    (C) La fuente auditiva presenta unas soluciones para reducir las causas que presenta el gráfico.

    (D) El gráfico presenta las razones que llevan a la situación que la fuente auditiva trata de solucionar.

Cultural Awareness

Cultural practice: The print text presents the reasons students in several Latin American countries drop out of school, while the audio presents the preparedness of young Latin Americans entering the workforce.

How are the practices presented in these texts similar to or different from what you have observed in your own community?

Selección 10

Tema curricular: La vida contemporánea

Tienes cuatro minutos para leer la fuente número 1.

Fuente 1: El artículo trata de unas razones por las cuales una persona no recibe un contrato después de tener una entrevista. Se basa en un artículo publicado en la página web *www.pymex.pe*.

---

10 razones por las que no es contratado después de una entrevista laboral

Si está desempleado o ya tiene un empleo pero decide cambiarlo, sea cual sea su opción, la búsqueda y selección de personal son su asunto principal ahora. Muchas veces luego de una entrevista (en la que todo parecía andar bien) el resultado no es el esperado y pues no lo llaman. Debe continuar buscando hasta que logre el puesto de trabajo deseado.

Línea

(5)   Los paradigmas de selección para los encargados de recursos humanos no son los mismos, pero si coinciden en muchos aspectos. Veamos algunas razones por las cuales no fue seleccionado, luego de ello podrá reflexionar y tendrá más claro cuales son sus áreas a mejorar:

1. **Llegó tarde**—La puntualidad es una de las cualidades que todo empleador busca en sus candidatos.

(10)
2. **Su CV no está bien redactado**—Las faltas de ortografía y mala redacción juegan un punto en contra y lo toman como falta de profesionalismo.

3. **La información consignada no es verdadera**—Las personas encargadas de recursos humanos muchas veces contrastan la información o solicitan referencias. El día que encuentren algo que no coinciden no se detendrán a preguntarle por qué mintió, simplemente no lo llamarán.

(15)
4. **No sabe nada de la empresa**—Es conveniente antes de asistir a una entre-vista de trabajo conocer al menos la información básica de la empresa: rubro, años en el mercado, premios, etc.

5. **Mala reputación online**—Puede que esté a punto de obtener el trabajo tan esperado, pero a la persona encargada de selección se le ocurrió buscar su nombre en Google. Depende de Ud. que los resultados de la búsqueda no lo perjudiquen.

(20)
6. **Dio comentarios negativos de sus anteriores <u>trabajos</u>**—No hay nada de malo decir los motivos de salida de otros centros laborales, lo malo es extenderse demasiado y hacer de esta respuesta una forma de desprestigio total a la institución que alguna vez le dio trabajo.

7. **Mostrar excesivo interés por el sueldo**—Es necesario saber cuanto será el monto del salario entre otras condiciones, pero si muestra solo interés en el dinero su entrevistador puede tomarlo
(25)   como la única motivación por la cual Ud. accedió a una entrevista.

8. **8. No tiene <u>experiencia</u>**—Si aun no tiene una experiencia relevante pues manténgase activo y trate de involucrarse en proyectos de corto plazo al menos. Más de uno o dos meses sin trabajar deja una impresión negativa en los encargados de selección de personal.

9. **Se mostró desinteresado**—No muestre desesperación, pero demostrar un poco de interés en la
(30)   oferta no le cae mal a nadie. Trate de ser cordial y respetuoso.

10. **Su presentación personal no estuvo acorde a la entrevista**—La primera impresión sí cuenta en estas ocasiones, busque una vestimenta y accesorios sobrios.

Tienes dos minutos para leer la introducción y prever las preguntas.

Fuente 2: En la siguiente fuente auditiva, el psicólogo Dr. Esteban Prado ofrece unos consejos para una entrevista de trabajo. La grabación fue publicada por el periódico El Comercio y dura aproximadamente 3 minutos y 10 segundos.

Track 10

1. A quién está dirigido este informe?

   (A) A los jefes de grandes empresas que buscan ampliar su personal
   (B) A empleados que están pensando en dejar su trabajo
   (C) A estudiantes que van a graduarse de la universidad
   (D) A solicitantes que activamente están buscando trabajo

2. ¿Qué no se debería divulgar durante una entrevista?

   (A) La información que sabe de la empresa
   (B) La antipatía que tiene por el empleo previo
   (C) La razón por la cual quiere la entrevista
   (D) Su interés acerca de cualquier oferta que reciba

3. Según la información presentada en el informe, ¿cómo puede el entrevistado prepararse mejor de antemano?

   (A) Saber cuánto paga el puesto para no hacer esa pregunta durante la entrevista
   (B) Revisar el currículum para averiguar que esté bien escrito y que los datos sean verídicos
   (C) Pasar unos meses únicamente buscando el puesto perfecto
   (D) Publicar en redes sociales la mala experiencia que tuvo en su trabajo previo

4. ¿Qué comunica el autor de la ropa que se debe llevar a una entrevista?

   (A) Que debe llamar la atención
   (B) Que debe mostrar su personalidad
   (C) Que debe ser de última moda
   (D) Que debe ser moderada

5. Según la fuente auditiva, ¿a qué se refiere la "película" que menciona el Dr. Prado?

   (A) A cómo el candidato quiere ser recordado después de la entrevista
   (B) A la representación visual de las cualificaciones del candidato
   (C) Al hecho de que las entrevistas suelen ser filmadas
   (D) A que muchos entrevistadores son gente famosa

6. Según el Dr. Prado, ¿en qué aspecto es mejor equivocarse en una entrevista?

   (A) En la forma en que se presenta al entrevistador
   (B) En el tono que usa para referirse al entrevistador
   (C) En las preguntas que se hacen al entrevistador
   (D) En el volumen con que se habla al entrevistador

7. Según el Dr. Prado, ¿qué habilidad tienen muchos entrevistadores?

    (A) Son capaces de saber si alguien está contando falsedades.
    (B) Casi nunca se equivocan en el uso de *tú* y de *usted.*
    (C) Tienen la capacidad de crear un ambiente relajante.
    (D) Saben hacer las preguntas adecuadas en cada situación.

8. Según la fuente auditiva, ¿qué debe hacer el entrevistado durante la entrevista?

    (A) Cerrar la entrevista debidamente
    (B) Engrandecer las experiencias que tuvo en los trabajos previos
    (C) Participar activamente, tanto en hacer como en contestar preguntas
    (D) Ocultar los miedos y bajo autoestima que tiene

9. ¿Qué información tienen en común las dos fuentes?

    (A) La importancia de mostrar interés por el puesto y la compañía
    (B) La importancia de vestirse bien para la entrevista
    (C) El beneficio de tener experiencia
    (D) La forma en qué uno debe actuar durante la entrevista

10. Con base en la información del informe y de la fuente auditiva, ¿qué pregunta sería más apropiada para terminar una entrevista?

    (A) ¿Cuáles son los desafíos que enfrenta la organización en este momento?
    (B) ¿Cuánto paga el puesto y puedo trabajar desde mi casa?
    (C) ¿En cuánto tiempo puedo recibir un ascenso?
    (D) ¿A qué se dedica exactamente esta empresa?

Cultural Awareness

Cultural perspective: The print and audio texts present certain perspectives on how to best be prepared to get a job.

How are the perspectives presented in these texts similar to or different from what you have observed in your own community?

Answers Explained

Selección 1

1. **(C)** The first table presents data about the gender wage gap, percentage of remuneration that full-time working women receive less when compared to men. In this table the higher the number, the higher the gap between pay.

2. **(C)** According to the second table, Costa Rica has the highest score (0.67) for equal treatment and absence of discrimination. Based on the description on the side, this means that there is less discrimination compared to other listed countries. Unlike the table above, a higher number means less discrimination.

3. **(C)** Colombia has a relatively lower gender wage gap (11.1%) and a relatively high score for (0.54) for equal treatment and absence of discrimination, indicating both lower wage gap and discrimination when compared to all countries on the list except Costa Rica. None of the other statements are true based on information found in these tables.

4. **(B)** The audio source discusses the challenges women have faced in making a place for themselves in society and history, highlighting various female figures who have made significant contributions.

5. **(D)** The audio source mentions contributions in fields like astronomy, philosophy, science (radiology), sports (marathon running), and social activism, but there is no mention of contributions in cinema and visual arts.

6. **(C)** At the end of the audio, it mentions ongoing issues such as violence against women, highlighting it as ongoing concerns. The audio also mentions wage disparities, but Option (B) is not the best answer because even though it refers to discrimination, it does not specifically mention pay discrimination. There are also other forms of discrimination, such as not offering a job or promotion based on gender. This makes Option (C) the best answer for this question.

7. **(A)** The audio source corroborates the ongoing issue of the gender wage gap, which is illustrated in the table. This makes Option (A) the clear answer.

Selección 1—Más práctica

Análisis literario: **(C)** apóstrofe. In this literary device, the speaker (*voz poética*) addresses all men. This direct reference to men in general, and not to one specific person, makes it an example of apostrophe. You have probably learned several literary devices from your English class, and they are helpful to know, especially if you want to take AP Spanish Literature and Culture down the road.

Selección 2

1. **(C)** The text deals with the neighborhood known as *La Boca* in Buenos Aires. The majority of the text describes the peculiarities and characteristics of this area. Don't be tempted to select option (D) simply because of the word *inmigrantes*, as this answer refers to their influence in all of Buenos Aires, whereas the text only deals with a particular neighborhood in Buenos Aires.

2. **(A)** The text describes this street as having multicolored buildings but without any doors. This would make it quite odd or unique, thus making option (A) the correct answer.

3. **(B)** In line 9, the text says that the street was named as such because ". . . acortaba distancias." The verb *acortar* means to make shorter, a synonym of the verb *abreviar*.

4. **(B)** Because this neighborhood is so peculiar and unique, one must infer that the people who live there are too, or would have to be. In addition, they probably feel a sense of pride for their neighborhood, therefore making option (B) the best answer.

5. **(B)** At the very beginning of the audio, the speaker says that the town was recently named *pueblo mágico*. Therefore, the purpose of this audio is to explain why it received this honor.

6. **(C)** The word *cobre* appears several times in the audio. It means copper, and it has been used in this area for many generations. The copper is found in artisanal works and living structures, and there is also a museum dedicated to this metal.

7. **(C)** Read the answers carefully to distinguish the difference in meaning from one to the other. The roofs illuminate because they reflect light, making option (C) the best answer. All the other options suggest that there is something embedded in the roof itself that gives it light or an image. In other words, the light is produced from the roof, and not by reflecting light.

8. **(B)** One gets the impression from this audio that this is a small town that is very close knit and proud of their history and artisanal culture. Therefore, it is unlikely that businessmen and large corporations would be attracted, making options (A) and (D) incorrect. Option (C) could be a possibility, but it is quite exclusive, meaning that it does not include people who are not either indigenous or foreigners. Option (B) is the best choice because it refers to travelers and artists, and that comprises the majority of people (both local and foreign) who would be interested.

9. **(A)** Both the audio and the text describe the peculiarities of a small town and neighborhood. Although there is mention of the products from Santa Clara del Cobre, there is no mention of original products from La Boca, making option (B) incorrect. Furthermore, option (D) is incorrect because the audio does not talk about the influences from different cultures.

10. **(A)** The text and audio use the word *color* in their presentations, and the word *color* can also refer to sights, sounds, and people from the area. Option (B) is incorrect because La Boca is not a town. Option (C) is incorrect because neither the text nor the audio want to persuade the audience to move to these areas by citing their benefits, and option (D) is incorrect because Santa Clara del Cobre is not in Argentina.

Selección 3

1. **(C)** This is a question where the process of elimination can help. Options (A) and (B) can be eliminated because they are in the *Inconvenientes* section of the text. Option (D) is not the best answer because it says that everything is within reach, and one can assume that in a big university, this probably isn't the case. Option (C) is the best answer because the text says that there are a variety of opportunities in bigger universities, and that can include the events mentioned in option (C).

2. **(D)** This answer suggests that classes cannot be personalized based on the need of the student, which is true and falls under the category of bureaucracy. All the other options, although possible, are on an individual level, not across the board, whereas option (D) is probably true for all students.

3. **(A)** This question requires you to consider all of the qualities of the personalities presented. A benefit mentioned in the text of a large university is the social opportunities, and a negative is the possibility of not standing out as a person. The student described in option (A) is someone who likes to socialize, but not stand out, thus making this the best answer. All other profiles include a trait that would make this person encounter some difficulty based on the information presented in the text.

4. **(B)** The audio says that a benefit of small universities includes ". . . los asesores conocen muy bien a los estudiantes . . . ." Remember that the word *docente* means teacher. All other options are negated in the audio.

5. **(C)** Toward the end of the audio, the speaker says that small schools offer the opportunity for students to ". . . desarrollar especialidades creativas, individuales enfocadas en áreas de interés específicas," which is the same idea communicated in option (C).

6. **(A)** Midway through the audio, the speaker says that students should speak with other students in order to learn more about social life and what non-academic activities are available (". . . hablen

con estudiantes para entender cómo es la vida social y qué tipo de actividades no académicas existen").

7. **(D)** Remember that to answer these questions, you have to have proof from both sources. There is nothing to suggest that smaller schools are not prestigious. The text says that larger schools tend to be more prestigious, but option (A) is incorrect because it says that they are all prestigious. This absolute declaration makes it incorrect. Option (B) is incorrect because the audio explicitly refutes this idea. Option (C) is incorrect because there is nothing in the audio or text that references the experience of the teachers. Option (D) is correct. Both the audio and text present pros to large and small schools, so it is ultimately up to the student to decide what is best according to his or her personality.

Selección 4

1. **(C)** Lines 9–12 have all this information. In line 10, it says, "comunicar novedades" (to communicate news), which is a synonym of the word *suceso* in the answer.

2. **(C)** You can find this information at the beginning of the first paragraph, where it says that the *corrido* has become one of the most efficient ways to spread heroic and romantic stories. Be careful with option (B), for it is not correct because of the word *injusticia*. There is nothing in the text to suggest that the *corridos* criticized the revolution, but rather simply communicated events.

3. **(B)** In lines 12–15, you can read about how the *corridos* were associated with the sale of "textos impresos . . . ilustradas por . . . José Guadalupe Posada." Option (A) is incorrect because in lines 16–18 we see that these texts were ignored by the censors due to the subtlety in the way that they conveyed pro-revolution messages.

4. **(D)** The key information is found in paragraph 4, where it mentions how there is a main voice accompanied by a chorus, and that there are several instruments used. Although in the following paragraph the text says that often a *corrido* only

needs a singer with a guitar, there is nothing to suggest that this is the norm.

5. **(A)** Be careful when answering this question, for you may be tempted to select option (B) or (C). Option (B) is incorrect because the audio states at the beginning that classical music is often referred to as music that was composed from medieval to contemporary times, and option (B) limits itself to only two time periods within this range. Option (C) is incorrect because the audio presents this as the idea of some purists, but does not argue this as being the case. The audio does define classical music as ". . . la unión de varios instrumentos para dar paso al desempeño de una orquesta . . . ," thus making option (A) the best answer.

6. **(C)** About halfway through the audio, the speaker says that classical music is ". . . seria, para un oido especial o más refinado . . . ," and continues with ". . . no en el sentido de ser grave e inaccesible." One can then understand that the audio argues that classical music is refined and elegant, but accessible to all listeners. Option (A) is wrong because it communicates the opposite idea of the audio text. Option (B) is incorrect because it uses the word *serio* out of context and, therefore, communicates a different idea than what the audio text means to communicate. At the end of the audio, the speaker mentions ". . . las personas más cultas . . ." and ". . . la élite . . . ," but if you listen carefully, you will hear that the speaker says the music was arranged by them ". . . adaptada por las personas más cultas . . . ," not *for* them (*para* ellos). The difference between the preposition *por* and *para* in this case is what makes option (D) incorrect.

7. **(C)** Be careful with this question, for although it comes later in the list, the information needed to answer it is in the beginning of the audio. The audio text says that classical music ". . . siempre ha contado con un gran número de seguidores y entusiastas de todas las edades," meaning young and old alike. Don't assume that all questions will always follow in the order of the audio or print text. The comprehension portion of the exam will test how well you have understood the entirety of the passage.

8. **(B)** At the beginning of the second half of the audio, the speaker describes classical music as being "... la primera rama musical que unió perfectamente el despempeño de los instrumentos con las voces de personas," thus making option (B) the only correct answer.

9. **(D)** Both the print and audio texts mention that this music is still prevalent in today's society. Option (A) is incorrect because classical music has much older origins. Option (B) is incorrect because the *corrido* includes only a few different instruments, while classical music has a bunch. Finally, option (C) is incorrect because classical music does not necessarily tell stories from antiquity.

10. **(A)** As with the explanation for question 6 in this section, the key word is the preposition *por*. Classical music was arranged by the upper class, while you can tell that the origins of the *corridos* were from members of the working class. All other options, although maybe true for individual tastes, do not satisfy the overarching ideas that both the print and audio texts present.

Selección 4—Más Práctica
If you are having trouble thinking of a style of music in your own community, consider hip-hop, rap, country, and metal music. Although most of these styles, except country music, are quite different, you may be surprised to learn how their origins are not far removed from those of the corrido.

Selección 5

1. **(B)** By reading this advertisement, you will quickly see that all statements are negative toward labor reforms. Therefore, the purpose of this document is to criticize as a way to promote change.

2. **(C)** Read carefully in order to select the best answer. Options (B) and (D) are incorrect because in the former it is not known whether the government is paying attention to the group's desires, and there is nothing to confirm that the current legislation is antiquated. Option (A) is tricky because the text says that "... fomenta la inestabilidad ..." (encourages instability), but it is not clear whether or not this instability is a reality at

the time of publication of this document. What is clear is that this group believes that the business owner has all the power, and that can lead to a number of other issues.

3. **(B)** At the very bottom of the advertisement, the group invites the reader to add additional reasons to participate in this protest. Some may opt for option (C), but note that, although this may be an inherent desire, what the group is trying to achieve with this protest is labor reforms.

4. **(A)** The word *huelga* is a strike, which is when people stop working to protest conditions and to try to achieve their demands.

5. **(B)** Toward the end of the dialogue, one of the speakers mentions "Pidamos un ascenso de cincuenta dólares al mes como mínimo ...," which proves that they are not happy with the money they are being paid. There is nothing in the audio to suggest that the company is going belly up, so option (C) is not a correct choice.

6. **(C)** As in the explanation for question 5, the two speakers want a raise, and if they get it, they both agree to "... empezar de nuevo el martes por la mañana."

7. **(D)** Option (A) is incorrect because the ad never mentions wanting an increase in salary. Option (B) is incorrect because there is no time frame in the ad indicating when they want this to be accomplished, and option (C) is incorrect because, once again, the ad does not mention contracts.

Selección 6

1. **(D)** The key word in the question is *preparativos*, meaning that you can find this information in the first column of the table. The fifth bullet has all the information you need to answer this question. If you carefully read all the other options, you will see that there is nothing in this column to support their claims.

2. **(A)** Again, the key word is *durante*, so this means you have to look at the second column. The second bullet says to remain calm because disorder is the leading cause of accidents during an earthquake.

3. **(C)** The third column does not give this information explicitly, but one can easily infer from the second bullet that the reason to leave the building is because it may be damaged. The second bullet says that one needs to check the building for damage, which implies that it may have become structurally unsound. Option (A) could easily be removed, for there is nothing in the text to support it, and option (B) is incorrect because, although the text does say to help others, this is not the main reason for leaving a building. Option (D) is incorrect because, although it is probably true that one can better observe any structural damage from outside, the main reason to leave the building is to avoid the chance that it may fall on you. Once outside, then you can start looking at it more carefully to see if it is safe to re-enter.

4. **(D)** This should be pretty straightforward, for the two speakers mention the *tormenta* right from the beginning. The "espectáculo pirotécnico" one of the speakers refers to is used to describe the lightning during the storm.

5. **(B)** Toward the very end of the dialogue, one speaker asks the other if water has been restored. The other responds negatively, but says that she hopes it will soon because she has a lot of laundry to do.

6. **(A)** The last person to speak says that she called the municipality and they would take care of it ". . . esa misma mañana." Therefore, the solution will be taken care of that same day.

7. **(B)** Since the event that took place in the audio is not an earthquake, you must consider which of the preparations in the table would be most logical for a family before a thunderstorm. The best choice is option (B), for a storm could cut electricity, and the family would need a radio to be able to hear any important news announcements.

Selección 7

1. **(A)** The article mainly details the organization and events of the *Feria Apícola de Campoo de Yuso*, including various activities like technical sessions, a market, and workshops. This makes it

clear that the purpose of the article is to inform about a celebration and its associated events.

2. **(B)** The article mentions that the 'Miel Solidaria 2022' award is based on honey collection from different stalls, indicating that the winner is determined by this criterion.

3. **(B)** In lines 28-31 the text states that the Rural Development Department is committed to supporting the apiculture sector by addressing threats to beekeeping operations, making this the correct answer.

4. **(D)** In lines 30-31 the article specifically mentions the threat posed by exotic species such as the vespa velutina (Asian hornet) to beekeeping, identifying it as a significant threat.

5. **(B)** The audio emphasizes the critical role of bees as the primary pollinators and states that without them, the plant kingdom would struggle to evolve.

6. **(C)** The audio notes that a third of our food relies on bees for pollination, indicating that their extinction would severely impact human food sources.

7. **(C)** Towards the end of the audio, the speaker suggests participating in conservation campaigns focused on bees as a way to raise awareness and care for them.

8. **(D)** In the final parts of the end of the audio, the recommendation in the event of encountering a swarm of bees is to remain calm and inform environmental authorities.

9. **(C)** Both the article and the audio emphasize the significance of bees and their crucial role in the environment.

10. **(B)** The text does not explicitly mention awareness as a tool for protecting bees, which is discussed in the audio.

Selección 8

1. **(C)** This should be pretty clear-cut because the article is largely divided into two sections: *ventajas* and *desventajas* (pros and cons).

2. **(B)** This information can be found in lines 4 and 5, where the text speaks about how the ancient

Chinese and Babylonians used wind to help pump (*bombear*) water for their crops.

3. **(C)** Be careful when making this selection. Although the text says that the cost is relatively low, it continues by saying that it is on par with coal-fired power stations, which is not cheap for the common user, therefore making option (A) incorrect. Options (B) and (D) are in the *desventajas* section, so they too should be eliminated.

4. **(B)** This is the best option because it includes benefits mentioned in the text. Read carefully through the other options, and you will clearly see that they include at least one element from the *desventajas* section of the text.

5. **(C)** The word *último* means latest, as in the most recent. Do not be tricked by the false cognate *ultimate* into translating this word as meaning *the best*. If you think about it, solar energy technology has not been around that long in relation to wind and water energy.

6. **(A)** In the first third of the audio text, the speaker mentions *Fondo Clima Verde* and says, ". . . busca recaudar y distribuir alrededor de US$30 mil millones . . . para ayudar a los países en desarrollo."

7. **(D)** The speaker mentions two issues with solar technology: poor efficiency and high costs. However, the speaker continues by saying that technology has debilitated the technology barrier, whereas at the end of the audio the speaker says, ". . . los costos de capital de los dispositivos solares siguen siendo considerables . . . ," meaning that their cost is still a problem.

8. **(A)** The information needed to answer this question comes at the very end of the audio, where the speaker says that government subsidies frequently still follow the interests of traditional energy companies (such as coal and oil).

9. **(C)** Remember that the correct answer has to include information from both sources. The audio source does not present the pitfalls of using solar energy (except for price, which is only one, not multiple), thus eliminating option (A). The audio does not mention the direct benefits to animals, so option (B) can safely be eliminated as well.

Option (D) is also incorrect because there is no reference in either text as to the popularity increase.

10. **(D)** Both the text and audio speak to the abundance of energy that can be harnessed using these technologies. Neither one is cheap (eliminate option (A)), and although wind energy may be inconsistent, it is unclear whether or not the same is true for solar (eliminate option (B)). Finally, there is no mention in the text that wind energy has some sort of battery.

Selección 9

1. **(C)** The graph shows that the leading cause for abandoning school in this age group is because of disinterest. Therefore, it can safely be assumed that these students are interested in pursuing other activities (whether legal or illicit).

2. **(A)** If you look at all the categories, only one has increased significantly, and that is the white part of the column, or *Obligación a la familia*. One can safely assume that this obligation is some sort of help to the family, a role and responsibility that is traditionally that of the parents.

3. **(B)** The biggest area of concern for this age group is that they are struggling with their studies. Therefore, the biggest help would be tutoring and programs to help the students overcome these difficulties.

4. **(D)** Be careful when answering this question. The audio says, ". . . 25% de esos jóvenes están trabajando en situaciones donde se les paga muy poco . . . nos muestra que los jóvenes salen al mercado del trabajo sin las destrezas necesarias. . . ." 25% of youth is one fourth of the youth population, therefore making option (D) the only correct answer.

5. **(C)** About halfway through the audio, Marisol Sanjinés mentions that young people ". . . necesitan una segunda oportunidad u otras vías para ir adquiriendo estas competencias o destrezas necesarias para poder tener un empleo . . . ." Don't be tempted to select option (B) simply because the same numbers are mentioned. The audio text says that every dollar invested in education gives a return of $10–$15 over the productive lifetime of

that person. It does not say that they need to raise the investment from $1 to $10 or $15.

6. **(B)** The young person at the end of the audio says that they can either be victims of the failure of the generation that preceded them, or they can be protagonists of their own destiny. In other words, she is asking for help and says that the previous generation is the one that needs to take action by providing the means for young people to succeed academically and in life.

7. **(D)** The sole function of the graph is to present the reasons for abandoning studies, and the audio presents what needs to be done to rectify the issue, making option (D) the best answer. Options (A) and (B) are incorrect because, in the first case, the audio does not say why young people abandon their studies, and, in the second case, the graph does not show the consequences that this abandonment has. Option (C) is incorrect because it is the opposite of what the graph and audio present.

Selección 10

1. **(D)** The title gives all the information you need. The target audience is someone who has just had an interview but has not been hired. Remember that the word *solicitante* means applicant or candidate.

2. **(B)** Line 25 explicitly says that making negative comments about previous work experience is a reason that one was not hired. The word *antipatía* means dislike and is the opposite of *simpatía*.

3. **(B)** The second item in the list makes reference to the writing of the résumé. Poor spelling and editing show lack of professionalism by the candidate.

4. **(D)** The last item on the list refers to the dress that a candidate has to consider wearing. The word *sobrio* may be a little problematic, but you can overcome this obstacle with a little ingenuity. There is not a whole lot of context to help you with meaning, so the best strategy is the process of elimination. The first option says clothing that draws attention. A candidate probably does not want his clothing to garner more attention than his or her credentials, and also clothing that draws

attention may be positive or negative. Option (B) is probably not a good choice because, depending on one's personality, there could be many types of dress, and this could cause issues in an interview. Option (C) says that it has to be of the latest style and trend. Well, this may be true for certain types of jobs, like in the fashion industry, but is probably not true for most job interviews. In addition, option (C) is too similar to option (A), for they both will draw attention. The last option has the adjective *moderada*, which you probably already inferred to mean moderate. This means that it is neither flashy nor underdressed, which is a safe bet for any type of interview.

5. **(A)** Although *película* does mean movie, in this context it refers to the image or memory that the interviewer has of the candidate following the interview.

6. **(B)** In the first third of the audio, the speaker says that it is better ". . . equivocarse usando el usted que el tú . . . ." As you probably already know, it is better to be overly polite at the beginning than to come across as rude.

7. **(A)** Toward the end of the audio, the speaker mentions that many interviewers are trained to study body behavior and can tell if someone is "fingiendo," or pretending. Therefore, it is always best to tell the truth.

8. **(C)** Halfway through the audio, the speaker says that it is best that the interviewee ask questions that are appropriate within the context. Remember that these comprehension questions will not necessarily always go in order, so make sure that you listen to the entirety of the passage before beginning to answer.

9. **(A)** Both the audio and the text make reference to showing interest in the position, albeit in different ways. The text shows that being disinterested (number 9 in the list) could be a reason that one was not hired, and therefore one should show interest. The audio says that it is important that the candidate ask appropriate questions, and inherently this will demonstrate that the candidate is interested in the work and in learning more about what the job entails.

10. **(A)** When considering these options, ask yourself what would be the most appropriate question to ask in this situation. A good question is presented in option (A), for the candidate may be interested in some of the challenges that the company faces as a way to determine whether or not he or she can help overcome these challenges. Options (B) and (C) are not good choices because they show too much interest in compensation and advancement, and that is something the text explicitly says is a negative. Option (D) is also not a good option because it shows that the candidate has no background knowledge on the company, and hence probably would not be hired.

5

Section I, Part B—Listening Comprehension

Section I, Part B of the test consists of up to three selections that will be a combination of long narratives, interviews, short lectures, instructions, or some other type of speech sample. These selections will be between two and five minutes in length. You may take notes on this section, but they will not be scored.

You should practice before taking the exam to see if you do better taking notes, or if you do better simply trying to recall information from memory. The advantage of notes is that you have a cue to jog your memory about the content of the speech sample. However, you should avoid writing whole sentences. Instead, practice identifying and writing down key words that will help you recall the ideas presented in the sample.

Some of the following selections are longer than those you will see on the AP exam, but they will allow you to practice your ability to listen for main ideas and details.

Strategies for Listening

- Read the introduction and questions to each sample.
- Concentrate while you listen.
- Evaluate the information being presented.
- Follow the thread of the conversation.
- Visualize, if you can.
- Take notes of key words that lead to ideas.
- Focus on what you understand and don't get hung up on what you don't understand. Use contextual clues to help you understand unfamiliar words or phrases.
- Remember that you will hear the audio twice. Listen the first time for the overall theme and general ideas, and use the second listening to take notes on specific details.

ANSWER SHEET
Audio Texts

Selección 1

1. Ⓐ Ⓑ Ⓒ Ⓓ
2. Ⓐ Ⓑ Ⓒ Ⓓ
3. Ⓐ Ⓑ Ⓒ Ⓓ
4. Ⓐ Ⓑ Ⓒ Ⓓ
5. Ⓐ Ⓑ Ⓒ Ⓓ
6. Ⓐ Ⓑ Ⓒ Ⓓ
7. Ⓐ Ⓑ Ⓒ Ⓓ

Selección 2

1. Ⓐ Ⓑ Ⓒ Ⓓ
2. Ⓐ Ⓑ Ⓒ Ⓓ
3. Ⓐ Ⓑ Ⓒ Ⓓ
4. Ⓐ Ⓑ Ⓒ Ⓓ
5. Ⓐ Ⓑ Ⓒ Ⓓ
6. Ⓐ Ⓑ Ⓒ Ⓓ
7. Ⓐ Ⓑ Ⓒ Ⓓ
8. Ⓐ Ⓑ Ⓒ Ⓓ

Selección 3

1. Ⓐ Ⓑ Ⓒ Ⓓ
2. Ⓐ Ⓑ Ⓒ Ⓓ
3. Ⓐ Ⓑ Ⓒ Ⓓ
4. Ⓐ Ⓑ Ⓒ Ⓓ
5. Ⓐ Ⓑ Ⓒ Ⓓ

Selección 4

1. Ⓐ Ⓑ Ⓒ Ⓓ
2. Ⓐ Ⓑ Ⓒ Ⓓ
3. Ⓐ Ⓑ Ⓒ Ⓓ
4. Ⓐ Ⓑ Ⓒ Ⓓ
5. Ⓐ Ⓑ Ⓒ Ⓓ

Selección 5

1. Ⓐ Ⓑ Ⓒ Ⓓ
2. Ⓐ Ⓑ Ⓒ Ⓓ
3. Ⓐ Ⓑ Ⓒ Ⓓ
4. Ⓐ Ⓑ Ⓒ Ⓓ
5. Ⓐ Ⓑ Ⓒ Ⓓ
6. Ⓐ Ⓑ Ⓒ Ⓓ
7. Ⓐ Ⓑ Ⓒ Ⓓ
8. Ⓐ Ⓑ Ⓒ Ⓓ

Selección 6

1. Ⓐ Ⓑ Ⓒ Ⓓ
2. Ⓐ Ⓑ Ⓒ Ⓓ
3. Ⓐ Ⓑ Ⓒ Ⓓ
4. Ⓐ Ⓑ Ⓒ Ⓓ
5. Ⓐ Ⓑ Ⓒ Ⓓ
6. Ⓐ Ⓑ Ⓒ Ⓓ
7. Ⓐ Ⓑ Ⓒ Ⓓ

Selección 7

1. Ⓐ Ⓑ Ⓒ Ⓓ
2. Ⓐ Ⓑ Ⓒ Ⓓ
3. Ⓐ Ⓑ Ⓒ Ⓓ
4. Ⓐ Ⓑ Ⓒ Ⓓ
5. Ⓐ Ⓑ Ⓒ Ⓓ
6. Ⓐ Ⓑ Ⓒ Ⓓ
7. Ⓐ Ⓑ Ⓒ Ⓓ
8. Ⓐ Ⓑ Ⓒ Ⓓ

Selección 8

1. Ⓐ Ⓑ Ⓒ Ⓓ
2. Ⓐ Ⓑ Ⓒ Ⓓ
3. Ⓐ Ⓑ Ⓒ Ⓓ
4. Ⓐ Ⓑ Ⓒ Ⓓ
5. Ⓐ Ⓑ Ⓒ Ⓓ
6. Ⓐ Ⓑ Ⓒ Ⓓ
7. Ⓐ Ⓑ Ⓒ Ⓓ

ANSWER SHEET
Audio Texts

Selección 9

1. Ⓐ Ⓑ Ⓒ Ⓓ
2. Ⓐ Ⓑ Ⓒ Ⓓ
3. Ⓐ Ⓑ Ⓒ Ⓓ
4. Ⓐ Ⓑ Ⓒ Ⓓ
5. Ⓐ Ⓑ Ⓒ Ⓓ
6. Ⓐ Ⓑ Ⓒ Ⓓ

Selección 10

1. Ⓐ Ⓑ Ⓒ Ⓓ
2. Ⓐ Ⓑ Ⓒ Ⓓ
3. Ⓐ Ⓑ Ⓒ Ⓓ
4. Ⓐ Ⓑ Ⓒ Ⓓ
5. Ⓐ Ⓑ Ⓒ Ⓓ

Selección 11

1. Ⓐ Ⓑ Ⓒ Ⓓ
2. Ⓐ Ⓑ Ⓒ Ⓓ
3. Ⓐ Ⓑ Ⓒ Ⓓ
4. Ⓐ Ⓑ Ⓒ Ⓓ
5. Ⓐ Ⓑ Ⓒ Ⓓ
6. Ⓐ Ⓑ Ⓒ Ⓓ
7. Ⓐ Ⓑ Ⓒ Ⓓ

Selección 12

1. Ⓐ Ⓑ Ⓒ Ⓓ
2. Ⓐ Ⓑ Ⓒ Ⓓ
3. Ⓐ Ⓑ Ⓒ Ⓓ
4. Ⓐ Ⓑ Ⓒ Ⓓ
5. Ⓐ Ⓑ Ⓒ Ⓓ

Selección 13

1. Ⓐ Ⓑ Ⓒ Ⓓ
2. Ⓐ Ⓑ Ⓒ Ⓓ
3. Ⓐ Ⓑ Ⓒ Ⓓ
4. Ⓐ Ⓑ Ⓒ Ⓓ
5. Ⓐ Ⓑ Ⓒ Ⓓ
6. Ⓐ Ⓑ Ⓒ Ⓓ
7. Ⓐ Ⓑ Ⓒ Ⓓ

Selección 14

1. Ⓐ Ⓑ Ⓒ Ⓓ
2. Ⓐ Ⓑ Ⓒ Ⓓ
3. Ⓐ Ⓑ Ⓒ Ⓓ
4. Ⓐ Ⓑ Ⓒ Ⓓ
5. Ⓐ Ⓑ Ⓒ Ⓓ
6. Ⓐ Ⓑ Ⓒ Ⓓ
7. Ⓐ Ⓑ Ⓒ Ⓓ

Listening Comprehension Practice Exercises

Selección 1

Tema curricular: La vida contemporánea
Primero tienes un minuto para leer la introducción y prever las preguntas.

> **Introducción:** El siguiente audio es una entrevista con Ana Nemesio, surfista que cuenta de su taller de yoga y cómo se aplica al surf. La entrevista fue publicada en RTVE en junio de 2015. La grabación dura dos minutos treinta segundos.

Track 11

1. ¿Cuál es el propósito de la entrevista?

   (A) Revelar lo difícil que es hacer el surf y el yoga
   (B) Exponer la cantidad de lesiones que el surf y el yoga pueden provocar
   (C) Informar sobre la utilidad del yoga al surf
   (D) Proponer que los surfistas hagan yoga para salir mejor en las competiciones de surf

2. Según Ana Nemesio, ¿qué aporta el surf?

   (A) Experiencias maravillosas pero con dolor corporal
   (B) Sensaciones de fatiga y cansancio
   (C) Emociones de alegría y de entusiasmo
   (D) Efectos poco placenteros pero con beneficios físicos

3. ¿Qué afirma Ana Nemesio en cuanto a las lesiones que experimentan los que hacen el surf?

   (A) Los hombres mayormente son los que encuentran lesiones haciendo el surf.
   (B) La mayoría de las lesiones se encuentran en la parte superior del cuerpo.
   (C) Muchas lesiones se producen en la parte inferior del cuerpo.
   (D) Las lesiones suelen ser más duras que las que se experimentan en otros deportes.

4. ¿A qué se refiere Ana Nemesio cuando dice que la práctica del yoga es "una cuestión de inversión del futuro"?

   (A) Al número de surfistas que van a dedicarse al yoga
   (B) Al incremento de la calidad del surf y de perduración de poder practicar el deporte
   (C) Al hecho de que el yoga puede prolongar las lesiones causadas por el surf
   (D) A que el yoga es un deporte menos costoso que el surf

5. Según la entrevista, ¿cuál de las siguientes opciones no es un beneficio mencionado que aporta el yoga al surf?

   (A) Hace que a uno le guste más el surf
   (B) Mejora la postura del surfista
   (C) Aumenta la fuerza física y flexibilidad
   (D) Incrementa el equilibrio y elasticidad

6. ¿Cuál de las siguientes afirmaciones mejor reflejan el éxito del taller de yoga?

(A) A los adultos les gusta, pero a los niños no tanto.

(B) A los niños les gusta, pero a los adultos no.

(C) A ambos adultos y niños les gusta, y los dos grupos participan activamente y con vigor.

(D) A ambos adultos y niños les gusta, pero los adultos son un poco más perezosos que los niños.

7. Si quisieras investigar el tema un poco más a fondo, ¿cuál de las siguientes publicaciones sería más útil?

(A) *Los mejores destinos del mundo para surfear*

(B) *La importancia de practicar el yoga desde niños*

(C) *Deportes en sintonía: cómo mejorar tu entrenamiento de surf*

(D) *Los beneficios de ser surfista*

Cultural Awareness

Cultural perspective: The audio presents the usefulness of yoga and how it can help one become a better surfer.

How are the perspectives presented in this audio similar to or different from what you have observed in your own community?

Selección 2

Tema curricular: Los desafíos mundiales

Primero tienes un minuto para leer la introducción y prever las preguntas.

> **Introducción:** El siguiente audio, titulado *Efectos de la soledad*, trata de la soledad en la tercera edad. Es una producción del programa *Cuaderno mayor* y fue emitido por Radio 5 en junio de 2015. La grabación dura aproximadamente tres minutos.

Track 12

1. ¿Cuál es el propósito del audio?

   (A) Exponer unas causas y los efectos de la vida solitaria
   (B) Llamar la atención a un problema anteriormente desconocido
   (C) Destacar las consecuencias de los que eligen vivir en soledad
   (D) Motivar a que el público tome medidas para afrontar problemas relacionados con la soledad

2. ¿Qué usa la locutora para poder apoyar su presentación?

   (A) Citas de personas que han sido afectadas por la soledad
   (B) Datos procedentes de varias investigaciones y citas proporcionadas por expertos
   (C) Sus propias opiniones del tema
   (D) Interpretaciones de comentarios hechos por unos expertos

3. Según la grabación, ¿cuál de las siguientes opciones no es un factor que provoca el aislamiento?

   (A) Problemas financieros
   (B) El no compartir la vivienda con otros
   (C) Problemas asociados con la salud
   (D) Conflictos entre miembros familiares

4. ¿Qué información provee la grabación en cuanto al número de mayores que viven en soledad?

   (A) Menos hombres mayores viven en soledad que mujeres mayores.
   (B) La minoría de los mayores vive en soledad.
   (C) La mayoría de la población mayor vive en soledad.
   (D) La mayoría de los mayores que viven en soledad tiene más de 85 años.

5. ¿Qué se sabe de la situación en cuanto al número de personas que vive en soledad?

   (A) La mayoría de ellas son de la tercera edad.
   (B) Ha incrementado en años recientes.
   (C) Ha provocado más problemas de salud.
   (D) Muchas de ellas no tienen familiares.

6. Según la grabación, ¿con qué frecuencia recibe una visita una persona que vive en soledad?

   (A) Una vez o menos cada siete días

   (B) Típicamente más de una vez cada siete días

   (C) Una vez o menos cada treinta días

   (D) La mayoría no recibe visitas

7. ¿Por qué dice la grabación que hay que afrontar la soledad como un "problema social"?

   (A) Porque se prevé que la población mayor va a aumentar, y por consiguiente los problemas asociados con la soledad.

   (B) Porque los que viven en soledad experimentan varios problemas con la salud, tanto físicos como sicológicos.

   (C) Porque todavía no se han encontrado soluciones para combatir los efectos que produce la vida solitaria.

   (D) Porque el público en general no sabe de las causas y efectos de la vida solitaria.

8. Si quisieras formar parte de un programa cuya meta es solucionar el problema mencionado en la grabación, ¿cuál de las siguientes sería el mejor?

   (A) *Adopta a un anciano*

   (B) *Ahorro para la jubilación*

   (C) *Jóvenes contra la injusticia social*

   (D) *Fundación del corazón: deporte y ejercicio para mayores*

Cultural Awareness

Cultural practice: The audio presents a practice that affects the elderly in Spain.

Cultural perspective: The audio also presents a perspective relating to the effects that loneliness has on the elderly.

How are the practices and perspectives presented in this audio similar to or different from what you have observed in your own community?

Selección 3

Tema curricular: Las familias y las comunidades

La siguiente grabación trata del sistema de votación en Chile. Fue publicado el 12 de julio de 2017 en la página web de la Biblioteca del Congreso Nacional de Chile / BCN. La grabación dura aproximadamente dos minutos, cuarenta y dos segundos.

Track 13

1. ¿Cuál es el propósito de esta grabación?

   (A) Animar a la gente a que vote
   (B) Describir algunos derechos que tienen los votantes
   (C) Informar sobre cambios en el sistema de votación
   (D) Promover cambios en el sistema de votación

2. Según la grabación, ¿quiénes pueden votar?

   (A) Los que tienen más de 18 años el día de la votación
   (B) Sólo los que cumplen 18 años el día de la votación
   (C) Los que tienen 18 años o más el día de la votación
   (D) Todos los que cumplen años el día de la votación

3. ¿A qué se refiere la grabación cuando dice que el documento de identidad o pasaporte tiene que estar "vigente"?

   (A) A que los documentos tienen que ser actuales
   (B) A que los documentos tienen que ser verdaderos
   (C) A que los documentos no pueden ser de otro país
   (D) A que los documentos deben pertenecer a la persona que los presenta

4. ¿Cuántas horas están abiertas las mesas para votar típicamente?

   (A) 18 horas
   (B) 2 horas
   (C) 4 horas
   (D) 12 horas

5. Si quisieras más información sobre el tema presentado en la grabación, ¿cuál sería la pregunta más apropiada para formular?

   (A) Mi abuelo quiere votar pero usa una silla de ruedas. ¿Hay un centro específico donde tiene que votar?
   (B) ¿Soy inmigrante a Chile? ¿También puedo votar?
   (C) ¿Hay un local específico en el que me corresponde votar o puedo ir a cualquier local?
   (D) Tengo que trabajar en Alemania durante seis meses. ¿Todavía puedo votar en las elecciones presidenciales de Chile?

Cultural Awareness

Cultural practice: The audio presents the practice of voting in Chile.

How is this practice similar to or different from what you have observed in your own community?

Selección 4

Tema curricular: La belleza y la estética

Primero tienes un minuto para leer la introducción y prever las preguntas

---

Introducción: El siguiente audio trata del Día Internacional de la Juventud. La grabación fue publicada en agosto de 2014 en la página ecuatoriana Radialistas Apasionadas y Apasionados (*www.radioalistas.net*). La grabación dura un minuto veintisiete segundos.

Track 14

1. ¿Qué tipo de grabación es esta?

   (A) Una canción al estilo hip hop
   (B) Un reportaje de la música rap
   (C) Un anuncio para un evento venidero
   (D) Un fragmento de una obra teatral

2. ¿Cómo se describiría la actitud de la mujer y del hombre al comienzo de la grabación?

   (A) De condena
   (B) De asombro
   (C) De apoyo
   (D) De apatía

3. ¿Qué aspecto del joven se critica?

   (A) Su afición por la patineta
   (B) Su forma de moda
   (C) La forma en que habla
   (D) Su gusto musical

4. ¿Qué quiere el joven que hagan los demás?

   (A) Que respeten sus decisiones de ocio
   (B) Que no rechacen los gustos de los demás
   (C) Que participen también en un deporte
   (D) Que actúen de la misma manera que él

5. ¿Con cuál de los siguientes refranes estaría más de acuerdo el rapero de la grabación?

    (A) Dime con quién andas y te diré quién eres.

    (B) La ociosidad es madre de todos los vicios.

    (C) Por la facha y el traje, se conoce al personaje.

    (D) No juzgues un libro por su portada.

Cultural Awareness

Cultural product: The audio presents an advertisement for an upcoming event that celebrates the youth.

Cultural perspective: The audio also inherently presents a perspective about how young people are seen and how they should be seen.

How are the products and perspectives presented in this audio similar to or different from what you have observed in your own community?

Selección 5

Tema curricular: Los desafíos mundiales

Primero tienes un minuto para leer la introducción y prever las preguntas.

> **Introducción:** El siguiente audio es un fragmento de una entrevista sobre emisoras de radio que sirven zonas rurales de América Latina. La grabación fue publicada en febrero de 2016 por Radio Naciones Unidas, Nueva York, y dura cuatro minutos quince segundos.

Track 15

1. ¿Cuál es el propósito de esta entrevista?

   (A) Promocionar las emisoras de radio que sirven las poblaciones rurales

   (B) Exponer el papel que tienen unas emisoras de radio en diferentes zonas rurales

   (C) Proponer que las emisoras más potentes transmitan en zonas rurales

   (D) Informar sobre la comercialización de radios locales

2. ¿Qué se sabe de la población a la que se dirigen las radios campesinas?

   (A) La mayoría son oyentes de las radios campesinas.

   (B) Es gente que vive en un territorio bastante extenso y diverso.

   (C) Es mayormente muy pobre.

   (D) Se preocupa mayormente por asuntos económicos.

3. ¿Cuál de los siguientes no es un papel un papel de las radios campesinas?

   (A) Informar a la gente de asuntos locales y globales

   (B) Promover y reforzar las identidades de la gente de la zona

   (C) Servir como una fuente de aprendizaje

   (D) Estimular el comercio de bienes en diferentes mercados

4. ¿Qué quiere comunicar el Profesor Rivadeneyra cuando dice que las comunidades rurales "tienen en la radio un aliado"?

   (A) Que la radio no los hace sentir tan aislados

   (B) Que mucha gente en estas comunidades escucha la radio para entretenerse

   (C) Que la radio les ofrece conocimientos para poder mejorarse

   (D) Que la radio les brinda oportunidades económicas a los oyentes

5. Según la entrevista, ¿qué comunidades son las mencionadas que se benefician de un sistema de alerta temprana?

   (A) Las comunidades cercanas al mar

   (B) Las poblaciones que se encuentran al pie de los Andes

   (C) Las comunidades andinas que viven en alturas superiores a unos 3.000 m s. n. m.

   (D) Todas las comunidades rurales, no importa su ubicación

6. En cuanto a temas económicos, ¿qué información proveen las radios campesinas a sus oyentes?

    (A) Consejos de cómo adaptarse ante un clima cambiante

    (B) Pronósticos de las tendencias económicas

    (C) Información sobre el cambio climático y su impacto global

    (D) Recomendaciones para el mejor tipo de animal que criar en estas zonas

7. ¿Cuál de las siguientes ideas destaca el Profesor Rivadeneyra en cuanto a la nutrición?

    (A) Una madre expectante bien nutrida favorece un buen parto y crianza.

    (B) Las madres y niños en zonas rurales tradicionalmente no se nutren bien.

    (C) Las madres deben nutrirse bien durante los primeros tres años de su vida.

    (D) Los niños y las madres carecen de oportunidades de nutrirse bien.

8. ¿Qué pregunta sería más apropiada hacerle al Profesor Rivadeneyra al fin de su entrevista?

    (A) ¿Conoce usted el nombre de un programa específico de las radios campesinas que haya tenido un impacto positivo en un asunto que ha mencionado?

    (B) ¿Sabe usted cómo reciben fondos estas emisoras?

    (C) ¿Nos podría informar de unos tipos de desastres climáticos que impulsarían el uso del sistema de alerta temprana?

    (D) ¿En qué países de América Latina se encuentran emisoras de este tipo?

Cultural Awareness

Cultural product: The audio presents the creation of radio stations specifically designed for farmers.

How is the product presented in this audio similar to or different from what you have observed in your own community?

Selección 6

Tema curricular: La vida contemporánea

Primero tienes un minuto para leer la introducción y prever las preguntas.

> **Introducción:** La siguiente grabación pertenece a una serie titulada *Pueblos con encanto*, que trata de varias localidades de La Rioja, una comunidad autónoma en el noreste de España. Esta grabación fue producida por Producciones Laboreo (España) en marzo de 2014 y dura aproximadamente dos minutos y medio.

Track 16

1. ¿Cuál es el propósito de esta grabación?

   (A) Animarle al oyente a tomarse unas vacaciones
   (B) Destacar las características más llamativas de unos pueblos riojanos
   (C) Hacer un viaje virtual de una localidad
   (D) Estimular el interés de visitar La Rioja

2. Según la grabación, ¿cuál de las siguientes opciones mejor describe Arnedo en la actualidad?

   (A) Ha logrado balancear el desarrollo con la preservación de su pasado histórico.
   (B) Su población está formada por un crisol de diversas razas.
   (C) Mantiene vivas varias costumbres culturales de su historia medieval.
   (D) Es un centro industrial y de fuerte carácter artístico.

3. ¿Cuál de las siguientes opciones tuvo el impacto más grande en el desarrollo de Arnedo?

   (A) La conversión de palacios en museos
   (B) La fabricación del calzado
   (C) El descubrimiento de minerales preciosos y fósiles en la zona
   (D) La llegada de importantes figuras religiosas

4. ¿Qué aspecto de la iglesia de Santo Tomás llama más la atención?

   (A) Su tamaño
   (B) Su arquitectura
   (C) Su localidad
   (D) Sus parroquianos

5. Basándose en la información provista en la grabación, ¿por qué son importantes las cuevas de los Cien Pilares?

   (A) Son usadas para ceremonias religiosas.
   (B) Todavía hay gente que vive en ellas.
   (C) Son valiosas para el estudio de poblaciones antiguas.
   (D) Es la atracción turística más popular de la zona.

6. Al final de la grabación, el locutor menciona los *fardelejos*. ¿Qué es un *fardelejo*?

   (A) Un tipo de comida

   (B) Una persona típica de la zona

   (C) Un tipo de calzado

   (D) El nombre que se les da a los visitantes

7. Si quisieras saber más información del tema presentado, ¿cuál de las siguientes sería la pregunta más apropiada hacerle al locutor de esta grabación?

   (A) ¿Hace cuánto tiempo que la industria del calzado ha existido en Arnedo?

   (B) ¿Me podría dar un ejemplo de algo que recuerde el pasado musulmán de Arnedo?

   (C) ¿Cuán lejos de Logroño, la capital de La Rioja, queda Arnedo?

   (D) ¿Ofrece Arnedo actividades de ocio en la naturaleza?

Cultural Awareness

Cultural product: The audio presents a town in the northern part of Spain.

Cultural perspective: The audio also explains why this area is special and worth visiting.

How does this town compare to those in your own community?

Selección 7

Tema curricular: Las identidades personales y públicas

Primero tienes un minuto para leer la introducción y prever las preguntas.

Introducción: En el siguiente audio, Fidel Revilla Castro, santero cubano, explica aspectos de la santería a los presentadores del programa de radio español *El canto del grillo*. La grabación fue publicada por RTVE en febrero de 2016 y dura aproximadamente cuatro minutos.

Track 17

1. ¿Cuál es el propósito de esta presentación?

   (A) Presentar la historia de una religión española
   (B) Informar sobre el origen y algunas características de una religión de las Américas
   (C) Presentar las particularidades de una religión africana
   (D) Dar una crítica de las influencias ajenas en la religión

2. ¿Cómo se puede mejor definir la *santería*?

   (A) Es el resultado de una mezcla de dos culturas.
   (B) Fue creado por los africanos que vinieron a trabajar en Cuba.
   (C) Es una religión con varios aspectos problemáticos.
   (D) Es una creación de los que colonizaron las Américas.

3. ¿Cómo define Fidel Revilla Castro las religiones africanas y la católica?

   (A) Los africanos eran idólatras, mientras los católicos veneraban las representaciones de figuras religiosas.
   (B) Los africanos veneraban las representaciones de figuras religiosas, mientras los católicos eran idólatras.
   (C) Las dos veneraban las representaciones religiosas.
   (D) Las dos eran idólatras.

4. ¿Qué aspecto de la *santería* se considera algo problemático?

   (A) El deseo de salvar a las personas
   (B) Unos de los métodos que se practican
   (C) Que no se pueden resolver todos los problemas
   (D) Su aplicación de la fe en sus tratamientos

5. ¿Qué ejemplo usa Fidel Revilla Castro para clarificar la idea de "la alquimia"?

   (A) Presenta varios trabajos que los santeros cumplen en sus procedimientos.
   (B) Explica la forma en que los santeros se limpian.
   (C) Explica el uso de plantas como parte de un tratamiento.
   (D) Presenta unas influencias negativas que pueden afectarle a alguien.

6. ¿Cómo se podría mejor definir el "baño de florecimiento" a alguien que no haya escuchado esta grabación?

    (A) Es un tipo de rito religioso.

    (B) Es como un tratamiento homeopático.

    (C) Es una pócima o bebida medicinal.

    (D) Es una influencia negativa.

7. Basándose en esta presentación, ¿con cuál de las siguientes declaraciones estaría de acuerdo Fidel Revilla Castro?

    (A) La santería es una religión pagana.

    (B) En la santería la fe desempeña un papel poco importante.

    (C) Para entender la santería, se necesitan conocimientos de los astros.

    (D) La mayoría de la gente cubana practica la santería.

8. ¿Cuál de las siguientes técnicas usa Fidel Revilla Castro para comunicar su mensaje?

    (A) Incorpora citas de distintos santeros.

    (B) Desarrolla sus ideas usando ejemplos.

    (C) Presenta las ideas más importantes en forma de lista.

    (D) Relata acontecimientos históricos y su influencia actual.

Cultural Awareness

Cultural product: The audio presents a religion that was created in Cuba.

Cultural perspective: The audio also presents certain rituals that are a part of this religion.

How does this religion and its practices compare with or differ from what you have observed in your own community?

Selección 8

Tema curricular: Las identidades personales y públicas

Primero tienes un minuto para leer la introducción y prever las preguntas.

Introducción: El siguiente audio, titulado Tecún Umán, trata de un capitán indígena k'iche', héroe nacional de Guatemala por su lucha contra los españoles. La grabación fue emitida por el grupo ArmadilloSound (Guatemala) en junio de 2015. La grabación dura aproximadamente dos minutos y medio.

Track 18

1. ¿Cuál de las siguiente opciones mejor describe el tipo de relato presentado en el audio?

    (A) Es una biografía.

    (B) Es un relato histórico.

    (C) Es un cuento de ficción.

    (D) Es una leyenda.

2. ¿En qué siglo se supone probablemente ocurrieron los eventos narrados en esta historia?

    (A) Durante el siglo XV

    (B) Durante la colonización de las Américas

    (C) Durante la independencia de Guatemala

    (D) Es imposible predecir basándose en la información del audio

3. ¿Qué le causó miedo a Tecún Umán?

    (A) La posibilidad de enfrentar al enemigo solo

    (B) El tamaño del ejército español

    (C) La alucinante figura que avanzaba hacia él

    (D) El poder mítico que tenía don Pedro

4. ¿Cuál es el "destino" al que don Pedro se refiere cuando le habla a Tecún Umán?

    (A) La victoria a manos de los invasores

    (B) La muerte de muchos indígenas en la batalla

    (C) La inevitable derrota de los españoles

    (D) La batalla que iba a ocurrir

5. ¿Qué le sorprendió a Tecún Umán durante la batalla?

    (A) Que hubiera subestimado la fuerza del caballo

    (B) Que los caballos no contuvieran el espíritu del jinete

    (C) Que hubiera matado al caballo

    (D) Que los españoles no tuvieran un dios

6. ¿Qué consecuencia tuvo el error cometido por Tecún Umán?

   (A) Supo cómo matarle a don Pedro
   (B) Perdió su única lanza
   (C) Don Pedro lo mató
   (D) Perdió su espíritu guardián

7. ¿Qué recuerda la historia de Tecún Umán hoy en día?

   (A) Cada lucha que enfrenta el pueblo indígena
   (B) El plumaje de un ave endémico de la zona
   (C) El color rojo que se le pone en el pecho a un recién nacido
   (D) Los homenajes que se hacen a los dioses

Cultural Awareness

Cultural product: The audio presents a legend from Guatemala about an indigenous leader.

How is this legend similar to or different from what you have observed in your own community?

Selección 9

Tema curricular: La ciencia y la tecnología

Primero tienes un minuto para leer la introducción y prever las preguntas

---

Introducción: En la siguiente entrevista, la subdirectora ejecutiva de la Agencia de Gestión de Emergencia de Desastres del Caribe habla de la experiencia del Caribe en el manejo de los desastres naturales. La entrevista fue transmitida el 23 de mayo de 2013 por Radio Naciones Unidas. La grabación dura aproximadamente tres minutos y treinta segundos.

Track 19

1. ¿Cuál es el propósito de la entrevista?

   (A) Revelar los desafíos que se encuentran en el Caribe para afrontar los desastres naturales

   (B) Exponer el número e impacto de desastres naturales en la región

   (C) Informar sobre el sistema que existe en el Caribe para hacer frente a los desastres naturales

   (D) Proponer unos cambios al manejo de ayuda que existe actualmente

2. Según la entrevista, ¿cómo ha cambiado la región del Caribe en los últimos 30 a 50 años?

   (A) Ha habido un incremento en el número de desastres naturales.

   (B) Los países se han modernizado para minimizar el número de víctimas.

   (C) Los desastres naturales han sido más devastadores que nunca.

   (D) En Haití se ha visto una disminución en la pérdida de vida.

3. ¿Cómo se destaca el modelo caribeño?

   (A) Ha tenido una gran cantidad de inversión de varias fuentes.

   (B) Cuenta con la colaboración de muchos de los países de la región.

   (C) Ha prevenido la muerte de millones de sus ciudadanos.

   (D) Ha minimizado los efectos de los desastres naturales a la infraestructura.

4. ¿Qué quiere comunicar la subdirectora ejecutiva cuando dice "El terremoto puso sobre el tapete la vulnerabilidad de ciudades caribeñas"?

   (A) Que el evento hizo descubrir un punto débil en el sistema

   (B) Que el sismo causó mucho daño a las zonas urbanas

   (C) Que no se revelaron de inmediato los efectos del terremoto

   (D) Que el terremoto hizo la localidad más vulnerable a otros desastres

5. Según la entrevista, ¿qué elemento es esencial para la gestión de emergencia?

   (A) Tener líderes capaces de afrontar diferentes situaciones
   (B) La coordinación entre diferentes entidades de ayuda y rescate
   (C) Restaurar los servicios de comunicación lo antes posible
   (D) Prestar atención inicialmente a las áreas que sufrieron más daño

6. Si quisieras investigar el tema un poco más a fondo, ¿cuál de las siguientes publicaciones sería más útil?

   (A) *Prepárate: 5 pasos preparatorios para sobrevivir cualquier desastre natural*
   (B) *Los desastres naturales más catastróficos del siglo XIX*
   (C) *Prevenir los riesgos y mitigar las consecuencias de desastres naturales*
   (D) *Enciclopedia de los riesgos naturales del Caribe*

Cultural Awareness

Cultural practice: The audio presents certain actions that are taking place in the Caribbean to become better prepared for natural disasters.

How are the practices mentioned in this audio similar to or different from what you have observed in your own community?

Selección 10

Tema curricular: La ciencia y tecnología

Primero tienes un minuto para leer la introducción y prever las preguntas.

> **Introducción:** El siguiente podcast trata de unas consideraciones que hay que tener en cuenta cuando se piensa viajar a un país exótico. El podcast original fue publicado por Radio 5 en 2011.

Track 20

1. ¿Cuál es el propósito del mensaje?

   (A) Informar sobre las enfermedades que se pueden contagiar en lugares exóticos
   (B) Promover unos medicamentos que ayudan a los viajeros a no enfermarse
   (C) Recomendar unos pasos para evitar enfermedades cuando se viaja
   (D) Dar un panorama de los diferentes medicamentos para varias enfermedades

2. Según la grabación, ¿qué es importante hacer cuando uno decide vacunarse?

   (A) Escoger una vacuna que sea efectiva contra los riesgos en la zona que desea visitar
   (B) Recordar que las vacunas son más eficaces durante el verano
   (C) Buscar un centro de vacunación que ofrece el servicio deseado
   (D) Pedir una vacuna unas semanas antes del viaje

3. Según la grabación, ¿cuándo hay que pedir consulta al médico?

   (A) Cuando sabes que has contagiado una enfermedad durante tu viaje
   (B) Antes de viajar a un lugar exótico
   (C) Antes, como medida de precaución y cuando experimentas síntomas durante el viaje
   (D) Cuando no experimentas un viaje placentero

4. Según la entrevista, ¿cuál de las siguientes afirmaciones es correcta?

(A) Con un poco de cautela, se puede mitigar la posibilidad de enfermarse al viajar a un lugar exótico.

(B) Las enfermedades que se pueden contagiar en lugares exóticos pueden ser muy dañinas si no se tratan a tiempo.

(C) Hay que investigar bien las vacunas de antemano para saber cuáles serán más efectivas contras las enfermedades de un lugar particular.

(D) Las enfermedades en lugares exóticos son peligrosas porque son más intensas durante el verano cuando a los españoles les gusta viajar.

5. ¿Qué pregunta sería más apropiada para el doctor Agustín Benito al final de su presentación?

(A) ¿Hay otras cosas que uno puede hacer para no exponerse a posibles enfermedades aparte de vacunas y medicamentos?

(B) ¿Puede darnos un ejemplo de cómo uno puede contagiarse?

(C) ¿Hay una vacuna que nos pueda proteger de todas las enfermedades o tenemos que buscar vacunas particulares?

(D) Si me enfermo, ¿dónde puedo conseguir información de los centros médicos en el área?

Cultural Awareness

Cultural perspective: The audio presents ideas about how best to prepare before visiting an exotic location.

How does the perspective presented in this audio compare with or differ from what you have observed in your own community?

Selección 11

Tema curricular: Las familias y las comunidades

Primero tienes un minuto para leer la introducción y prever las preguntas.

Introducción: La siguiente grabación trata de la Tomatina, una fiesta en Buñol, España. La grabación dura aproximadamente tres minutos.

Track 21

1. ¿A qué público se dirigiría esta grabación?

   (A) A estudiantes de español
   (B) A empresarios de una compañía turística
   (C) A visitantes al municipio
   (D) A aficionados de los deportes extremos

2. Según la grabación, ¿cuál de las siguientes afirmaciones mejor describe la fiesta?

   (A) Es relativamente nueva.
   (B) Es difícil de entender.
   (C) Incluye una mezcla de varias culturas.
   (D) Es bastante violenta.

3. ¿Por qué se celebra la Tomatina?

   (A) Para vender muchos tomates
   (B) Para protestar contra el gobierno
   (C) Para entretener a la población valenciana
   (D) Para honrar la tradición de su historia

4. ¿Cómo se originó la celebración?

   (A) Un joven se enfadó con un vendedor de tomates.
   (B) Un gigante de un desfile atacó a un espectador.
   (C) Algunas personas se vieron involucradas en un disturbio.
   (D) Una persona le quitó el disfraz a otra en una pelea.

5. ¿Qué reacción provocó el acontecimiento original?

   (A) El ayuntamiento no quiso permitir una repetición.
   (B) El gobierno distribuyó tomates para mejorar la fiesta.
   (C) Los vendedores trajeron más y más tomates para dárselos al público.
   (D) El público observó la prohibición del ayuntamiento contra la fiesta.

6. Hoy en día, ¿cómo se ha mejorado la fiesta?

   (A) Sólo se permiten tomates.

   (B) Se organizaron más juegos.

   (C) La gente lleva palos para defenderse.

   (D) Se usa jabón para limpiar los palos con jamón.

7. Imagina que tienes que dar una presentación oral a tu clase sobre el tema de la grabación y necesitas información adicional para ampliar tu presentación. ¿Cuál de las siguientes publicaciones te sería más útil?

   (A) *Cuando el tomate es un arma de destrucción masiva*

   (B) *Gastronomía y cultura en España—historia del tomate*

   (C) *Juegos tradicionales de la comunidad valenciana*

   (D) *Conozca todo sobre el tomate*

Cultural Awareness

Cultural product: The audio presents an annual festival in Spain.

Cultural practice: The audio also presents certain practices that are a part of this festival.

How does this festival and its practices compare with or differ from what you have observed in your own community?

Selección 12

Tema curricular: La belleza y la estética

Primero tienes un minuto para leer la introducción y prever las preguntas.

Introducción: El siguiente podcast trata sobre cómo convertirse en mejor escritor. El podcast original fue publicado por el podcast Aprendiendo a escribir en 2011. La grabación dura aproximadamente tres minutos, cuarenta segundos.

Track 22

1. ¿Cuál es el propósito del informe?

   (A) Dar consejos para hacerse escritor profesional
   (B) Presentar información útil para escribir mejor
   (C) Informar sobre los retos de convertirse en escritor
   (D) Presentar maneras en que unos escritores tuvieron éxito

2. Según el presentador, ¿por qué no les gustan a unas personas sus sugerencias?

   (A) Porque son unos pasos complicados.
   (B) Porque se tarda mucho tiempo en perfeccionarlas.
   (C) Porque no contienen la magia que ofrecen otras sugerencias.
   (D) Porque ya son escritores exitosos.

3. ¿Qué dice el presentador acerca de los escritores profesionales?

   (A) Que se tranquilizan en cuanto han alcanzado su objetivo.
   (B) Que les resulta más fácil ser publicados.
   (C) Que siguen desarrollando su capacidad.
   (D) Que les suele tomar una vida entera cumplir su meta.

4. ¿Con cuál de las siguientes afirmaciones estaría de acuerdo el presentador?

   (A) La culminación de cada escritor es de ser publicado.
   (B) Cuanto más escribes, más oportunidades tendrás para que el público conozca tu obra.
   (C) Hay que encontrar un tema que le agrade al público para que tu obra sea publicada.
   (D) Los mejores escritores son los que imitan las técnicas de los grandes escritores.

5. ¿Cuál de las siguientes técnicas utiliza el presentador para comunicar su mensaje?

    (A) Incluye citas de editores profesionales.

    (B) Utiliza varias anécdotas de escritores famosos.

    (C) Da ejemplos concretos de métodos que utilizan los grandes escritores.

    (D) Presenta su propia experiencia y opiniones.

Cultural Awareness

Cultural perspective: The audio presents the opinion of one man on what one must do in order to become a better writer.

How does this perspective compare with or differ from what you have observed in your own community?

Selección 13

Tema curricular: Las identidades personales

Primero tienes un minuto para leer la introducción y prever las preguntas.

> **Introducción:** La siguiente grabación se trata del veganismo. Fue publicada en La Nota, una página web de Tucumán, Argentina, en noviembre de 2022. La grabación dura aproximadamente dos minutos, cuarenta segundos.

Track 23

1. ¿Cuál es el propósito de la fuente auditiva?

   (A) Celebrar el Día del Veganismo
   (B) Compartir recetas veganas
   (C) Desmentir mitos sobre el veganismo
   (D) Promover una dieta basada en legumbres y verduras

2. ¿Qué opción mejor resume el argumento presentado sobre el veganismo?

   (A) Es una dieta costosa y limitada en opciones alimenticias.
   (B) Es una forma de vida que mejora la salud y evita la crueldad hacia los animales.
   (C) Requiere habilidades culinarias avanzadas y es adecuado para chefs experimentados.
   (D) Es una práctica alimentaria que puede adaptarse a cualquier presupuesto y ofrece una amplia variedad de ingredientes y sabores.

3. Según la grabación, ¿por qué algunas personas piensan que los veganos tienen una dieta poco abundante?

   (A) Porque los veganos no conocen recetas culinarias variadas y solo comen papas, lechuga y tomate.
   (B) Porque los veganos no usan suficientes condimentos en sus alimentos.
   (C) Porque las plantas se digieren más rápidamente, lo que puede llevar a sentir hambre nuevamente después de comer.
   (D) Porque la representación de los veganos en los medios de comunicación crea un estereotipo erróneo sobre su dieta.

4. Según la grabación, ¿qué significa la palabra "«sosa»"?

   (A) Abundante en condimentos y sabores
   (B) Sin sabor o insípida
   (C) Rica en nutrientes y vitaminas
   (D) Algo que se cocina rápidamente

5. ¿Qué beneficios personales menciona la chef desde que es vegana?

   (A) Mayor energía y aumento de peso
   (B) Menos problemas digestivos y mayor felicidad
   (C) Mejora en habilidades culinarias y creatividad
   (D) Aumento en el consumo de proteínas y carbohidratos

6. ¿Cuál es la opinión de la chef sobre el uso de condimentos en la comida vegana?

   (A) Son innecesarios ya que las verduras tienen sabor propio
   (B) Deben usarse moderadamente para no alterar los sabores naturales
   (C) Son esenciales para evitar que la comida sea insípida
   (D) Solo deben usarse condimentos veganos especiales

7. Si quisieras aprender más sobre el tema presentado en la grabación, ¿cuál de las siguientes publicaciones sería la mejor elección?

   (A) *Historia de la Gastronomía Mundial: Un recorrido por diversas culturas y sus prácticas alimenticias*
   (B) *Explorando Sabores Alternativos: Introducción a platos basados en plantas y sustitutos de alimentos tradicionales*
   (C) *El Impacto Ambiental de la Agricultura: Un estudio sobre sostenibilidad y recursos naturales*
   (D) *Psicología de la Alimentación: Entendiendo las elecciones dietéticas y sus efectos en el comportamiento humano*

Cultural Awareness

Cultural perspective: The audio presents the perspective about the value of being vegan.

How is this perspective in your community of being vegan?

Selección 14

Tema curricular: Las identidades personales y públicas

Primero tienes un minuto para leer la introducción y prever las preguntas.

> **Introducción:** El siguiente audio se trata del tomate. La grabación fue publicada por Radialistas Apasionadas y Apasionados y dura aproximadamente tres minutos, cuarenta y cinco segundos.

Track 24

1. ¿Cuál es la idea principal del audio?

   (A) La travesía del tomate desde su origen hasta su aceptación en diferentes partes del mundo
   (B) La variedad de platos que se pueden preparar con tomates
   (C) Las diferentes opiniones y creencias sobre el tomate en distintas culturas y épocas
   (D) La adaptación del tomate a diversas regiones y su importancia en la gastronomía global

2. ¿A quién está dirigida la grabación?

   (A) A los agricultores interesados en el cultivo de tomates
   (B) A los amantes de la cocina mediterránea y la gastronomía internacional
   (C) A los historiadores que investigan sobre la difusión de plantas en diferentes culturas
   (D) A cualquier persona interesada en conocer la historia e importancia del tomate en distintas partes del mundo

3. ¿Qué importancia tenía el tomate para los antiguos mexicanos?

   (A) Lo consideraban una planta sin importancia.
   (B) Lo apreciaban tanto como el pimiento en su cocina.
   (C) Lo utilizaban como planta ornamental.
   (D) No le atribuían ningún valor en su dieta o cultura.

4. ¿Qué se puede inferir del término «manzana de oro», utilizado al referirse al tomate?

   (A) Que el tomate era una fruta extremadamente cara en la antigüedad.
   (B) Que el color rojo del tomate simboliza la pasión y el deseo.
   (C) Que el tomate era muy valorado por sus propiedades nutritivas.
   (D) Que el tomate tenía un alto valor comercial similar al del oro.

5. ¿Qué papel jugaron los ingleses en la historia del tomate?

   (A) Contribuyeron a su aclimatación en regiones frías.
   (B) Lo consideraron venenoso y no confiaron en él.
   (C) Lo llamaron «manzana del paraíso» basándose en investigaciones.
   (D) Fueron los primeros en llevar semillas de tomate a Europa.

6. ¿Qué hicieron los italianos para domesticar el tomate?

   (A) Lo llamaron « "manzana de oro" ».
   (B) Lo convirtieron en salsa de tomate.
   (C) Seleccionaron las variedades más grandes y apetitosas.
   (D) Lo consideraron una planta venenosa y no quisieron saber de él.

7. Según el audio, ¿cuál de las siguientes afirmaciones de los tomates se puede comprobar?

   (A) Han disminuido en tamaño y sabor desde su introducción en Europa.
   (B) Son más sabrosos y grandes.
   (C) Han mantenido sus características desde su descubrimiento.
   (D) Han perdido su popularidad en la cocina mediterránea debido a su evolución genética.

Cultural Awareness

Cultural product & perspectives: The audio presents the history of the tomato (product) and its importance today (perspective). Even though it was not initially considered a food of value early on, it has become indispensable in today's society.

What is the importance of tomato in your community? Are there other fruits or vegetables in your community that are indispensable?

Answers Explained

Selección 1

1. **(C)** The interview is based entirely around the benefits of yoga for surfing, making this the clear choice. Option (A) is incorrect because there is no reference to the difficulty of yoga or surfing. Option (B) is incorrect because, although the interview does mention the number of injuries that surfing can cause, it never states that yoga also causes injuries. Option (D) is incorrect because, although one can deduce that because yoga can make one a better surfer that this can translate into better performances in surfing competitions, this is never explicitly stated nor is it the reason for this interview.

2. **(A)** Ana Nemesio states that surfing is a sport that combines the good ("sensaciones estupendas") with the bad ("lesiones"), making option (A) the only logical answer. Options (B) and (C) are incorrect because they focus solely on the negatives (option (B)) or only on the positive (option (C)). Option (D) is incorrect because it is the opposite of option (A).

3. **(B)** During the interview, the only two body parts mentioned are "hombros" (shoulders) and "lumbares" (lower back), both of which are in the upper part of the body. Be careful with option (A) because you don't want to confuse *hombros* with *hombres*. Option (C) is clearly incorrect because it refers to the wrong part of the body, and option (D) is incorrect because there is never any mention as to how the injuries experienced in surfing compare to those in other sports.

4. **(B)** Ana Nemesio states that in order to surf well and for a long time, one must take good care of his or her body. We therefore can infer that yoga can accomplish this goal, making option (B) the best answer. Option (A) is incorrect because there is no reference, direct or indirect, to the number of surfers who are going to take on yoga. Option (C) is incorrect because yoga does not prolong injuries, but rather helps prevent them, and option (D) is incorrect because there is never any reference to the cost of yoga *vs.* surfing.

5. **(A)** Be careful with this question, for it is asking which of the options is not mentioned. Options (B), (C), and (D) are all clearly stated in the audio, whereas option (A) is not.

6. **(D)** By listening to the entirety of Ana Nemesio's response to the success of the yoga workshop, the adverb most often repeated is *"bien,"* making options (A) and (B) incorrect because they assume that one group did not enjoy it. Ana Nemesio does say that the adults were more "vago" (lazy), making option (C) incorrect. Although the adults were not as energetic as the younger kids, this does not mean that they disliked the program (at least, not from Ana's point of view).

7. **(C)** This was a tough question, and it requires one to make some inferences in order to find the correct answer. Remember to focus first on what the question is asking. The theme of the interview is the benefits of yoga for surfing, two different sports in which the practice of one is advantageous for practicing the other. This makes option (C) the best answer because it refers to at least two sports by using the plural form of *deportes,* and refers to how the harmony (*sintonía*) between these sports can improve surf training. Options (A), (C), and (D) all ignore the relationship between surfing and another sport, making them incorrect answers.

Selección 2

1. **(A)** The audio provides an objective overview of loneliness, making option (A) the best answer. There is nothing in the audio to suggest that this issue was unknown beforehand; therefore, option (B) is incorrect. Option (C) is incorrect because it refers solely to those who choose to live a solitary life, whereas the audio speaks to all the elderly who live a solitary life, whether by choice or not. Option (D) is incorrect because, although a listener may feel inclined to help solve this issue, this is not the main purpose of the audio.

2. **(B)** The audio mentions "estudios," "encuestas," and "expertos," therefore indicating that the information provided is based on facts and

expert opinion. This makes option (B) the best answer. The speaker does not directly quote people who live alone, making (A) incorrect, nor does she inject her own opinion or interpret those of others, thus making options (C) and (D) also incorrect.

3. **(D)** Be careful when reading this question because it is asking which of the following does _not_ lead to loneliness and isolation. Options (A), (B), and (C) are all stated in the audio ("vivir solo," "no dotar de buena salud," and "insolvencia económica"). There is nothing that mentions family strife or conflict that leads to this isolation. Note that the audio mentions "situaciones de duelo," which is a good idiomatic expression to know. It means _grief_, as in the emotion that one feels following the death of a loved one.

4. **(A)** This answer is an example of testing to see if the listener is focusing on the idea being communicated over the words being used. The audio states that of all the elderly who live alone, "la mayoría son mujeres," which means that the minority are men. Read carefully what each answer is saying because options (B) and (C) cannot be substantiated by the audio text, and option (D) is clearly incorrect, as the audio states that 42% of the elderly who live alone are older than 85.

5. **(B)** The audio states the following: ". . . se ha producido un aumento en el número de hogares unipersonales . . . ," which is the same idea that option (B) communicates using different words. Although some or all the information presented in options (A), (C), and (D) could be true, there is nothing in the audio to substantiate these claims, therefore making them incorrect choices.

6. **(C)** The answer to this question largely rests on whether or not you understood the word "mensual," meaning _month_, which would automatically eliminate options (A) and (B) from contention. The audio continues to say, "una visita . . . y en algunos casos, estas visitas no existen," making option (D) incorrect because most get visitors, albeit infrequently.

7. **(A)** Toward the end of the recording, the speaker mentions that ". . . esta situación se puede incrementar a tenor [_in relation_] de las expectativas demográficas . . . ," which implies that in the future, social demographics will be comprised of more elderly people. There is nothing in the audio to substantiate options (C) and (D), and, although the statement made in option (B) is partially correct, there is nothing in the audio to say that all of those who live alone suffer from these problems, nor is it clear how this is a social problem.

8. **(A)** Option (A) is the clear answer to this question because it is the one that most directly addresses the issue that the audio presents. If one were to "adopt" an elderly person, that means that they would be establishing a relationship with that person, thus alleviating his/her feeling of loneliness. Option (B) is self-serving, for it will help someone who is not yet retired save money, but it does not address those who are currently in need. Option (C) is too general in nature because "injusticia social" can cover multiple areas, including political issues, problems with education, economic issues, etc. Option (D) is also incorrect because, although it promotes exercise and health benefits, it is unclear whether there is a social aspect of this program, for many exercises can be done alone at home.

Selección 3

1. **(B)** The audio throughout details who can vote, what identification is needed, and some information regarding access to voting. All these are best categorized as some of the citizen's rights to vote. There is nothing in the audio text to suggest that what is described is somehow different than in the past, making option (C) incorrect, and there is also nothing indicating that the audio is trying to persuade its audience, thus making options (A) and (D) incorrect.

2. **(C)** Most of the answer options for this question look similar, but they communicate different ideas. The audio clearly states that voters must have had their 18th birthday by the time they vote, making option (C) the correct choice. Options (A) and (D) are saying that only those who have birth-

days on the day of voting can vote, while option (B) is saying that one has to be older than 18 in order to vote.

3. **(A)** Remember that the adjective *actual* is a false cognate, and means *current* or *up to date*, which is what *vigente* also means. Even if you forgot this, option (A) is still the best option because the other ones don't make common sense. One would expect any document to be real and not fake, making option (B) incorrect, and common sense also says that, in order to vote, a person would need a valid identification document issued by the country in which he is voting and that the document pertains to that person and not to someone else, thus making options (C) and (D) also incorrect.

4. **(D)** The audio states that the voting tables must begin operating at 8:00a.m. and close at 18:00 hours, which is 6:00p.m. The audio also states that, as an exception, tables can open at 9:00a.m. or 10:00a.m., but those are outlier cases and not the norm.

5. **(C)** When answering these types of questions, remember to select the option that is both logical within the context and whose answer was not already given in the text. In this case, the audio already addresses how immigrants and expatriates can vote, as well as access to voting for those with disabilities, thus making options (A), (B), and (D) incorrect. The audio does not mention whether or not there is a designated voting location for voters, making option (C) a logical choice.

Selección 4

1. **(C)** You can tell at the very end of the recording that this is advertising the *Día internacional de la juventud*, which makes option (C) the best answer. Although there is some rapping in the recording, this is not a song, therefore eliminating option (A), and this is definitely not a news report, making option (B) also incorrect. Option (D) is incorrect because, although parts of this recording are like a play, it is not a theater production.

2. **(A)** Both the lady and the man at the beginning of the recording are quite critical of the clothing, piercings, and tattoos of the young man they are looking at. Options (B) and (C) are incorrect

because they both refer to positive emotions (*asombro* means surprise or admiration; *apoyo* means support), and they are definitely not apathetic, making option (D) also incorrect.

3. **(B)** The recurring critique from the man and the woman at the beginning and the defense from the rappers all relate to his clothing and style. The young man being critiqued is indeed a skater, but skating itself is never being targeted, therefore making option (A) incorrect. There is nothing in the audio to suggest that his way of speaking is being criticized, thus eliminating option (C), and, although you, the listener, may not like his rapping, there is nothing in the audio that suggests that his musical taste is being criticized, which takes option (D) off the table.

4. **(B)** Around the one minute mark, the youth says that others should *ser más abiertos, tratar de comprender mejor*—in other words, not reject what others enjoy to do or their style. Option (A) is incorrect because the critique is never about his choice of sport, and he mentions his sport as an example of something that he enjoys, but not that it is something that needs to be respected. Options (C) and (D) are incorrect because there is nothing in the audio to support them.

5. **(D)** This is a tough question if you have trouble understanding sayings or proverbs. However, you should be able to identify the meaning of option (D) because its literal translation is *Don't judge a book by its cover*. This saying communicates the same message of the recording because it asks others to not critique the youth simply because they have a different style, and it is what's inside that counts. If you are unfamiliar with the other sayings in the list, they mean *Show me who your friends are, and I'll tell you who you are* (option (A)), *Idleness is the mother of all vices* (option (B)), and *Clothes make the man* (option (C)). It is a good idea to learn a few proverbs and sayings in Spanish, because using them appropriately in your communicative tasks as part of your topic development can really help elevate your overall performance.

Selección 5

1. **(B)** The purpose of this interview is to show how *radios campesinas* (rural radio stations) are benefiting the audience they serve. Option (A) is incorrect because the interview is not trying to promote or advertise (*promocionar*), but is to rather inform about these radio stations. Option (C) is also incorrect because the word "proponer" implies that the interview has another agenda beyond informing, and (D) is incorrect because there is nothing in the audio to suggest that rural radio stations are becoming more commercial.

2. **(B)** Professor Rivadeneyra states that these stations serve a vast territory, and he also mentions that some of these communities live in the Andes mountains, therefore making (B) the best answer. Options (A), (C), and (D) are incorrect because there is never any reference to how many people in these communities listen to the radio nor of their social status or of their interests.

3. **(D)** Be careful when reading this question because there are three correct answers, and you are asked to identify the one that is *not* correct. The audio mentions the first three options as being roles that community radios play, but never mentions option (D).

4. **(C)** In this question, you have to use context to figure out the best meaning of the word *aliado* (ally). Option (C) is the best answer because, just like the question beforehand, community radio provides information and knowledge that can help these communities better manage their conditions and environments. Option (A) is not correct because there is no reference to whether or not listeners feel less isolated by listening to the radio, or whether they listen to it for entertainment purposes, making option (B) also incorrect. Option (D) is incorrect because there is never any mention that these radio stations don't provide economic opportunities to their listeners.

5. **(C)** The audio states that the communities that are most affected are those 3,500 meters above sea level (*m. s. n. m.* means *metros sobre nivel del mar*). Don't be distracted by words such as *mar*, which may lead you to select incorrect option (A).

6. **(A)** The speaker mentions this information at least twice in the audio, and the idea is that the radio programs help teach communities how to learn how to adapt (*adaptarse*) to a changing climate (*clima cambiante*). Note how the form of words is different in the answer than was used in the audio. This is done to see if you are listening for specific words or listening to the whole idea. If you were only listening for specific words, you may have selected one of the other options, which contain specific words from the audio (*económico, cambio climático*) but do not communicate ideas that are stated in the audio text.

7. **(A)** The speaker highlights the importance of nutrition for expectant mothers and how this will have a positive impact on the gestation, birth, and childrearing during the first few months. Options (B) and (D) are incorrect because, although the temptation exists to deduce that people who live in rural areas may likely have less access to medical care and/or resources, and this could result in poor nutrition, there is nothing in the audio that explicitly states this to be true. Remember that the argument could also be made that because they live in rural areas, their nutrition is actually healthier because they eat a lot of vegetables, grains, fruits, etc. Always validate your answers with the text. Finally, option (C) is a little tricky. It is incorrect because the printed answer says that the mother has to nourish herself during her first three years of life, but the audio says that the mother has to nourish herself during the first three years of her *baby's* life.

8. **(B)** When you see questions like these, you have to pick the response whose answer was not already given in the audio or print text. There is never any mention as to how these community radio stations are funded. Are they government funded? Do volunteers run these radio stations? Do they rely on revenue from advertising like the big stations? All other questions have already been answered in the audio text. Option (A) was answered at the end (*La radio saludable*), option (C) was answered when talking about the *sistema de alerta temprana* and several weather conditions were mentioned, and option (D) was answered throughout the interview where several

countries, including Bolivia, Perú, and Colombia, were mentioned.

Selección 6

1. **(C)** The purpose of this audio is to give a quick overview of Arnedo, a city in La Rioja. Since this overview is done via audio, it can also be considered a virtual tour. Some may be enticed to select option (B) because the introduction states that the series is dedicated to several towns in La Rioja. But note that the question asks about this particular audio, not the series, therefore making option (B) incorrect. Options (A) and (D) are very similar, and, although one who listens to this audio may want to take a vacation and possibly take it to La Rioja, that is a secondary benefit of the audio, and not its primary purpose.

2. **(A)** The audio mentions the "simbiosis perfecta entre modernidad y tradición" (fusion of modernity and tradition), making option (A) a clear choice. Option (B) is incorrect because, although different civilizations occupied the area at one time, there is nothing in the audio to suggest that the town's population today is comprised of many different races. There is nothing in the audio that refers to cultural customs, and, although it mentions the shoe industry (*industria de calzado*) several times, the shoe industry is not a custom, therefore making option (C) incorrect. Option (D) is incorrect because, although Arnedo has a strong shoe industry, there is no mention of its arts scene. Most museums mentioned showcase items extracted from the local mines (*fósiles y minerales*) and archeological sites, as well as the evolution of the shoe industry.

3. **(B)** This is the clear option not only because the audio directly states it (*una ciudad cuyo crecimiento ha ido paralelo al desarrollo de una notable industria del calzado*), but also because there are museums dedicated to this craft, and it is an important part of the industry today.

4. **(B)** The audio states that the church is admired for its beauty and structural originality ("belleza y originalidad constructiva"), thus making option (B) the clear choice. Don't forget that the word "tamaño" means size and "parroquiano" means

patron or *parishioner*, as in a member of a local church.

5. **(C)** When talking about the caves, the audio gives three bits of information: (1) their location (in the mountain behind the church), (2) their use today (as *bodegas*, or wine cellars), and (3) their archaeological importance (because people used to live in them). Based on the last bit of information, one can infer that those people were from ancient civilizations, therefore making option (C) the best answer.

6. **(A)** There are two important clues in the audio that this is the correct answer. They are "postre" (dessert) and "¡Buen provecho!" (enjoy your meal!). Don't be distracted by the word "típico" in both the recording and in option (B). Just because the same word is used, it does not mean that it is the correct answer.

7. **(D)** When answering hypothetical questions such as these, remember to select the most logical and appropriate response. The audio highlights some of the cultural, historical, and food attractions of this area, and, although options (A), (B), and (C) may seem like appropriate questions, they have already been answered in the audio (the audio states that the shoe industry has been around since the 11th century, the *fardelejo* is from Arab origin, and at the beginning of the audio it states that Arnedo is located 48 km from the capital of La Rioja). Option (D) is a logical question because a visitor to the town may also want to know if there are any outdoor activities that can be enjoyed.

Selección 7

1. **(B)** This is the best answer because it includes all aspects of the presentation. Although the speaker uses *santería* in Cuba as an example, this religion is also practiced in other areas of Central and South America, particularly in areas that border the Caribbean. Options (A) and (C) are incorrect because they ignore the combination of cultures that helped form *santería*. Option (D) is incorrect because the speaker never criticizes the religion, but rather gives an honest (and personal) description of it.

2. **(A)** *Santería* is a result of syncretism between African religions and Catholic beliefs when slaves from Africa were brought to the island of Cuba to work in the sugarcane fields. Option (B) is incorrect because it suggests that African slaves created this religion upon arriving in the New World, which is not entirely correct since the current religion is partially based on ideas and practices that originated in Africa. This is the same reason option (D) is incorrect. It ignores the African influence found in the religion. Finally, option (C) is incorrect because the idea that *santería* is problematic is a matter of opinion, not fact. The speaker only gives one example that is considered problematic, but then goes on to discount this notion.

3. **(A)** This answer may have been more difficult if you did not know the meaning of the word *idólatra* (idolatry, or the worshiping of idols). The speaker in the audio makes reference to how the religions from Africa worship rocks (*piedras*), tools (*herramientas*), and sea shells (*caracol*), which are types of idols. The Catholics, on the other hand, revere God through images, not the images themselves.

4. **(B)** The speaker makes direct reference to how the *santeros* resolve issues through faith and alchemy, which is his way of referring to specific procedures and actions that the *santeros* use. Options (A), (C), and (D) are incorrect because it is not the *santeros'* desire to heal or whether or not they can solve all problems or that they have faith that is problematic to others, but rather their actual actions.

5. **(C)** The speaker gives only one example of the use of "alchemy" in *santería*, and that is the *baño de florecimiento*, which we learn is a bath with many herbs, such as *salvia* (sage), *menta* (mint), and *lavanda* (lavender). Option (A) is incorrect because the speaker never mentions multiple jobs, but only gives one example, and it is not of a job, but of an actual treatment. Option (B) is not correct because the audio never makes reference to how the *santeros* cleanse themselves. You may have chosen this answer by focusing on *lavarse*, but remember that this is a reflexive verb and,

therefore, refers back to the subject. The example given in the audio is how *santeros* help others. Finally, option (D) is incorrect because, although the speaker does mention negative influences, they are an example of the symptom that the alchemy seeks to cure, not a definition of the alchemy itself.

6. **(B)** Remember that *baño* means bath and, as explained in the previous answer, a *baño de florecimiento* is a bath with many herbs, which is most like a homeopathic procedure as the speaker himself states (*"situaciones de homeopatía"*). Option (A) is incorrect because it is not a religious rite or ceremony, but rather a treatment (*tratamiento*). Option (C) is incorrect because it is not a drink, but rather a bath, and option (D) is incorrect because the bath itself is not a negative influence, but rather serves to rid one of negative influences.

7. **(A)** A pagan religion is a non-monotheistic religion, meaning that it involves belief in more than one deity. Since *santería* includes the devotion to idols, this makes option (A) the best answer. Option (B) is incorrect because faith is indeed important in *santería*. There is nothing in the audio to support option (C), and the word *astro* is only mentioned once at the end in another context. There is never any mention in the audio as to how many people in Cuba practice *santería*, therefore making option (D) incorrect.

8. **(B)** This question asks you to look at *how* the speaker delivers his message. He does give a brief explanation as to the origins of *santería*, but then gives specific examples of a practice that is done in *santería*. The speaker never quotes another santero, thus making option (A) incorrect, and he does not present the information in a list form, making option (C) also incorrect. Be careful with option (D), for, although the speaker does give some historical background as to the origins of *santería*, he never mentions any specific historical event (*acontecimiento*) nor how it continues to influence *santería* today.

Selección 8

1. **(D)** The story, although based in fact, is a legend because it (1) includes supernatural elements,

such as an "espíritu guardián" that comes to speak to Tecún Umán and (2) at the end uses the story to teach a lesson, which is why the Quetzal bird has a red chest. One might argue that option (C) is also a possibility, but the reason it is not the *best* answer is that "cuentos" tend to be a lot longer and don't have the purpose of teaching a lesson or explaining a natural phenomenon.

2. **(B)** It is clear from the words such as "conquistador" and "conquista" that this story takes place during the colonization of the Americas, therefore making option (B) the correct answer. Option (A) is incorrect because the 15th century comprises the years 1400–1499, and since the Americas were discovered in October of 1492, it is highly unlikely that a full-scale colonization effort was organized in less than seven years.

3. **(C)** The first part of the audio speaks to the imposing figure of don Pedro riding his horse. Since horses were foreign animals to this land, the sight of don Pedro approaching was what would have caused Tecún Umán to feel some fear, therefore making option (C) the best answer. One could argue that option (B) could also be a possibility, but the size of the Spanish army is not mentioned until quite a bit later in the audio, so it is not the best answer.

4. **(A)** Don Pedro asks Tecún Umán to surrender (*rendirse*) several times and asks him to accept his destiny. One can infer that this destiny is the inevitable victory that the Spanish army would have, therefore making option (A) the best answer. Option (B) is incorrect because the audio never mentions how many natives die in battle, and option (C) is incorrect because the Spanish eventually win, not lose. Option (D) is incorrect because don Pedro wants Tecún Umán to surrender, not engage in battle.

5. **(B)** Just as Tecún Umán had a guardian spirit in the form of the Quetzal bird that lands on his shoulder, he felt that the horse contained the spirit of its rider, or *jinete*. When Tecún Umán kills don Pedro's horse but don Pedro does not die, Tecún Umán is surprised to realize that the horse is simply an animal, not the guardian spirit, therefore making option (B) the correct answer. If

you did not know what the word *jinete* meant, you may have had some difficulty with this question. A good strategy when you find yourself in this situation is to eliminate the other options one by one. Option (A) is incorrect because it implies that the horse was stronger than it really was. Tecún Umán kills the horse pretty quickly, so this statement is untrue. Option (C) is incorrect because it would not surprise Tecún Umán that he killed the horse since it was the horse he was aiming for all along. Finally, option (D) is incorrect because there is really nothing in the audio to substantiate it. The Spaniards clearly state that God is on their side, so Tecún Umán clearly knew that they believed in at least a god.

6. **(C)** The mistake of Tecún Umán thinking that the horse and rider were spiritually connected cost him his life. It was at the moment of realization when ". . . la lanza de don Pedro le atravesó directamente en su corazón . . ." (don Pedro's spear went straight through Tecún Umán's heart).

7. **(B)** The phenomenon this legend teaches is why a certain bird, the Quetzal, has a red chest. Earlier in the audio you meet the Quetzal, for it is the ". . . espíritu guardián con la forma del ave de Quetzal . . . ," so when they mention the Quetzal at the end, you should already know that it is a bird (*ave*). Don't be scared of the word "endémico." It means *endemic* or *local to a particular region*. Even if you do not know what "endemic" means, you still have enough information to select it as the correct choice. Don't be tempted to choose answers simply because they contain many words that are mentioned in the audio text, as is the case with option (C). Focus on whether or not the idea being communicated is correct.

Expansión

Now that you have learned about a legendary hero from Guatemala, can you think of a legendary hero from your own community? You may also want to consider more fictional figures, such as Paul Bunyan, if you are a United States resident. Do you know of landmarks in the United States that were "built" by Paul Bunyan? If you don't, you may want to research this and other legends and internalize key words so that you can tell these stories in Spanish. This is the type of practice that will pay huge dividends on the oral presentation portion of the exam.

Selección 9

1. **(C)** The purpose of this audio is to inform, not persuade, so you can easily eliminate option (D) from contention. The only question is whether it is presenting problems or showing what the area is doing to combat these problems. Since the speakers talk about the development of infrastructure over the past fifty years and, although they certainly could use more, it is enough to prove that this audio is showing the system in place and how it works. Option (A) is not the best answer, for it suggests that there are only challenges, and the audio clearly provides examples of systems in place that, although not perfect, do address many of the challenges.

2. **(B)** Liz Riley says that there has been ". . . inversión significativa en infraestructura nueva . . ." and that the damages caused by natural phenomena have impacted ". . . la infraestructura, no tanto a la pérdida de vidas . . ." (with exception of Haiti).

3. **(B)** The speaker says that the Caribbean is one of the best-prepared regions because of their ". . . mecanismo intergubernamental de coordinación de respuesta . . ." where all countries that participate can take advantage of the resources of each country. This means that several countries work well with each other to minimize the effects that natural disasters can have.

4. **(A)** The speaker uses the earthquake in Haiti to point out the vulnerabilities in some cities in the region, where she says that many of the basic services are located. If a natural disaster takes out a city, then the services also will be destroyed, so they have to come up with plans to minimize this impact.

5. **(B)** Liz Riley provides this information at the very end of the interview, when she says, "En momentos de crisis el liderazgo y la cohesión de los dirigentes en un frente unido para dirigir al pueblo es fundamental." The word *gestionar* in the question means to manage, and one can see that the speaker believes that there has to be a coordi-

nated effort between multiple entities to help in a time of crisis.

6. **(C)** Since the audio deals with how to minimize the effects of loss of life during a natural disaster, option (C) is the only publication that suggests it is on the same topic. A good word to learn is *mitigar*, which means to minimize.

Selección 10

1. **(C)** The majority of the audio is spent giving recommendations about what travelers need to do in order to ensure that they stay healthy. Although a list of diseases and illnesses are mentioned at the beginning, the bulk of the audio is spent on how to avoid these.

2. **(D)** The word *vacuna* means vaccine, and the doctor says that the vaccine needs to be administered ". . . con suficiente antelación . . . entre uno o dos meses antes del viaje. . . ."

3. **(C)** In the second half of the audio, the doctor says that one needs to go to the doctor "previamente al viaje" and ". . . al mínimo momento en que puedas tener algún tipo de sintomatología . . ."—in other words, the moment one has any symptom.

4. **(A)** The purpose of the audio is not to scare the listener, but rather to give some tips that can be used to minimize one becoming sick while visiting an exotic location. Options (B) and (D) focus more on the illnesses, and not preventative measures, so they are not the best options. Option (C) is not the best choice either because the audio gives advice on how to avoid all illnesses in general, not specific ones.

5. **(C)** When answering these types of questions, always consider what is most appropriate. Options (A), (B), and (D) are incorrect because the doctor has already answered them.

Selección 11

1. **(C)** As you can tell from the audio, this event is not aimed at any particular age group or demographic. Even though young people will probably be more attracted to it, the purpose of the audio is to talk about the *Tomatina* and its history.

Therefore, it is most likely directed to anyone interested in visiting this part of Spain.

2. **(A)** The celebration as it is known today began in 1945, which is relatively recent considering Spain as a country that has been around for over 500 years (since its unification, of course).

3. **(C)** Although the celebration started as a protest, it is now a fun event, with no additional intent other than to provide entertainment for locals and tourists alike.

4. **(C)** In the middle of the audio, the speaker mentions how a fight broke out because a young man wanted to be a part of a parade, and he hit some of the people in the parade. This led to a bigger fight, and someone decided to use vegetables as ammunition, and the rest is history.

5. **(A)** The audio continues by saying how a group of people congregated the next year at the same spot with "cajones de tomates," but that the government did not approve and, year after year, "prohibía la batalla vegetal."

6. **(B)** Toward the end of the audio, the speaker mentions a number of additional activities that take place in today's festival. These include "carreras de sacos" (sack races) and "cucañas" (having to climb to the top of a greasy pole).

7. **(C)** When selecting a publication on the festival, try to find one that deals with the spirit of the festivity today. The third publication is on traditional games in the Valencia community, where the *Tomatina* takes place. This is the best option because it clearly deals with the topic. Don't be tempted to pick option (A) because, although tomatoes are used, they certainly should not be considered weapons of mass destruction. Options (B) and (D) seem to deal with tomatoes as a food item, not as part of a celebration.

Selección 12

1. **(B)** Both the introduction to the audio and the majority of the audio itself indicate that this piece is about becoming a better writer. The speaker in the audio does mention several times that one can become a professional, but also explicitly states that becoming a professional writer ". . . no debería ser su meta" (should not be your goal).

2. **(B)** At the beginning of the audio, the speaker says that many don't like his answers because they either look for ". . . una solución rápida . . ." or ". . . una fórmula mágica . . . ." Therefore, you can safely assume that the speaker believes that becoming a better writer is a long process.

3. **(C)** The speaker urges one to keep reading and writing, and at one point says that he has never met a professional writer who said that he or she has learned enough and could not get better (". . . aprendí suficiente. Más no puedo mejorar.").

4. **(B)** At the end of the audio, the speakers says, ". . . cuanto más fortalezca su escritura, más fácil será alcanzar la segunda meta . . . ," and *la segunda meta* is to find your market or readership. Although the speaker does mention that writers may not get published because of the theme they chose to write about, he does not suggest that writers adapt their themes to their public, but rather continue to try and find their own voice, and the readers will come.

5. **(D)** This presentation is solely based on the speaker's own experiences. The only time he gives some sort of quote (". . . aprendí suficiente. Más no puedo mejorar.") is one he invents because he said that he never heard anyone say that to him.

Selección 13

1. **(C)** The audio source's primary focus is on debunking myths about veganism, as indicated by the speaker's effort to address and correct three common misconceptions about veganism.

2. **(D)** The speaker emphasizes that veganism is adaptable to any budget and provides a wide variety of ingredients and flavors, challenging the myths of it being expensive and having limited food options.

3. **(D)** The speaker mentions that plant-based foods are digested more quickly, which can lead to feeling hungry again after eating, contributing to the misconception of a less abundant diet.

4. **(B)** The term "sosa" is used by the speaker to describe food that lacks flavor or is bland. She debunks this myth by arguing that if the food is bland, it is because the person preparing it is bland.

5. **(B)** The speaker shares her personal benefits since becoming vegan, which include fewer digestive problems and increased happiness.

6. **(C)** The chef emphasizes the importance of using condiments in vegan cooking to ensure that the food is flavorful. She also emphasizes that most condiments are also made of plants.

7. **(B)** This publication would be most relevant for someone interested in learning more about plant-based diets and alternative flavors, which aligns with the theme of the audio source discussing veganism.

Selección 14

1. **(A)** The audio chronicles the journey of tomatoes from their origins in the Americas, their introduction to Europe, and their eventual acceptance and adaptation into various cuisines worldwide. This theme encompasses their historical and cultural impact, making it the main idea of the audio.

2. **(D)** The audio provides a comprehensive history of the tomato, appealing to anyone interested in the story and significance of this plant in various cultures, rather than focusing on a specific group like farmers or gastronomy enthusiasts.

3. **(A)** The audio indicates that, unlike the pepper which was highly valued in Aztec cuisine, the tomato was initially a wild plant of little value to the ancient Mexicans.

4. **(D)** Calling the tomato "la manzana de oro" (golden apple) implies a high commercial value, akin to gold, especially considering the tomato's widespread use and importance in various cuisines.

5. **(B)** The English were initially distrustful of the tomato, considering it a poisonous fruit and part of the nightshade family, hence not embracing it like other European cultures.

6. **(C)** The Italian gardeners focused on selecting the larger, juicier, and more appealing varieties of tomatoes, leading to the domesticated versions we know today.

7. **(B)** The audio describes how the tomato was bred for better taste and size, particularly by the Italians, who selected the more appealing varieties, leading to an improvement in flavor and size from its original form.

PART 4
Writing Skills

6

General Considerations

Descriptions of the Writing Tasks of the Exam

The writing portion of the exam is divided into two tasks: Task 1: Email Reply and Task 2: Argumentative Essay. Both types of responses require that you showcase your ability to communicate effectively in Spanish on the assigned task. In Task 1: Email Reply, your main objective is to maintain a formal exchange. For Task 2: Argumentative Essay you will have to clearly present and defend your point of view about a question printed in your test book.

Scoring the Writing Tasks

The grading of the writing samples is holistic, meaning that they are analyzed as a whole. No specific item or aspect of language has any point value. Rankings proceed along a continuum from strong, good, fair, weak, and poor. The difference between each level largely hinges on your treatment of the topic within the context of the task and on language use. A common misconception is that if you can write well in Spanish, you will score well on this portion of the exam. However, that is only true if what you write is relevant within the context of the task. Therefore, before putting pen to paper, you need to clearly understand the task. Here are some strategies when approaching the writing portions of the exam:

- Read the introduction and understand the instructions.
- Address the task assigned as fully as you can.
- Use a formal tone throughout. This not only includes the choice of register, but also choice of ideas. *What* you say is as important as *how* you say it.
- Time yourself as you write. Your goal for Task 1: Email Reply is to write for 10 minutes. Your goal for Task 2: Argumentative Essay is to write for 35 minutes. This will give you enough time to proofread what you write.
- Always proofread your writings. Look for mistakes with language use but more importantly ensure that your ideas are clearly understood by an unsympathetic reader.

7

Section II, Part A—Task 1: Email Reply

The first part of Section II is the Interpersonal Writing task. For this task you are to write a formal response to an email. In your test book, you will be given an email and a brief description of the reason you received this email. You then have 15 minutes to read the email and respond. In your response, you have to do the following:

- Write a response that clearly maintains the exchange,
- Use a formal tone throughout,
- Answer all questions asked in the original email,
- Ask more information about something mentioned in the original message or is relevant to the topic of the message.

Scoring Your Email

Your score will be based on how well you are able to accomplish this task and can roughly be broken into the following categories:

1. **What you were able to do.**
   - Did you maintain the exchange?
   - Did you answer all questions and elaborate on your answers?
   - Did you ask a question relating to the topic?
   - Did you use a formal tone throughout?

2. **How you were able to do it.**
   - Is your response fully comprehensible?
   - Did your use of language show some sophistication?
   - Is your response well organized?

If you answered yes to all the above questions, your performance on this section likely will score in the high range. There are some criteria that are more important than others. For example, a response that includes sophisticated language but fails to maintain the exchange will earn a low score. This usually happens when the student misunderstands something in the original message, and this causes a response that is not entirely on task. Likewise, a response in which the student attempts to maintain the exchange but whose language ability makes the reply mostly incomprehensible will also earn a low score.

A great way to understand how you will be evaluated is to put yourself in the shoes of the recipient. Imagine that you are the person who sent the original printed in the test and you receive the response. Does it address all your questions and concerns? Is the tone appropriate? Did the student put heart and soul into the response? If the email does all this, then you are on the path to scoring a "5."

Strategies for Task 1: Email Reply

The following is a guideline about how you should budget your time.

Read the introduction and the email (2 to 3 minutes).
- Identify who sent this email and why.
- Identify the questions you need to answer. Underline them so that you can refer back to them quickly.
- Make note of any information that is mentioned that you could ask for more details about.
- Make note of any cultural references in the original message (origin of the author, and so on).

Writing your reply (8 to 10 minutes).
- Use the formal register throughout your response.
- Structure your response correctly (greeting, opening, body, closing, goodbye).
- Respond to all the questions being asked and elaborate briefly on your responses.
- Request more information about something that was mentioned or about something related to the theme.
- Vary your vocabulary.
- Keep your ideas simple and clear.
- Include a variety of tenses and/or moods, if appropriate. Do not try to force the use of different tenses or moods, as this will count against you if it makes your response confusing.
- If you make a mistake, draw a line through it and keep writing.

After you finish writing (2 to 5 minutes).
- Proofread your reply to make sure that . . .
  - . . . you have addressed all the elements in the email, including asking for more details;
  - . . . you have used a variety of vocabulary;
  - . . . your ideas are clear and concise; and
  - . . . you used correct orthography, punctuation, and paragraphing.

Writing Your Email

As you prepare to write your email, you need to consider how the message should be structured. A good email should be divided into the following 5 sections:

1. **GREETING.** Should be appropriate for a formal correspondence.
2. **OPENING.** These are one or two sentences in which you acknowledge receipt of the message and convey any feelings and emotions from having read this message and/or in which you make a general comment related to the topic.
3. **BODY.** This is the bulk of your response. Answer the questions asked in the original email and elaborate briefly on each answer. Be creative with your elaboration but make sure that the ideas you write are appropriate for a formal situation. Include a question that is relevant and appropriate within the context.
4. **CLOSING.** This is one or two sentences in which you again express your gratitude to the recipient of the email, reiterate some of the information mentioned in the body, and/or express that you look forward to hearing back from this person soon.
5. **GOODBYE.** Should be appropriate for a formal correspondence.

Here are a few examples of simple greetings, openings closings, and goodbyes appropriate for a formal situation.

Formal greetings	Opening comments
■ Estimado(a) Señor(a) ■ Buenos días, Señor(a)	■ Le agradezco mucho por su mensaje. ■ Espero que todo esté bien con usted.

Closing comments	Formal goodbyes
■ Muchas gracias por su amable atención. ■ Quedo a la espera de su respuesta. ■ Quedo a su disposición para facilitarle cualquier otra información.	■ Le saluda cordialmente ■ Atentamente ■ Respetuosamente

In addition to ensuring that your language use is appropriate for a formal correspondence, you also need to pay attention to organization of thought. This is where transitions can be useful and they should be incorporated in your response. Here are some useful transitions that you can use often in your email replies:

Uses of transitions	Examples	
To introduce an idea	*Para empezar . . .*	*En primer lugar . . .*
To add to ideas	*Además . . .*	*También . . .*
To contrast ideas	*En cambio . . .* *No obstante . . .*	*Por otro lado . . .* *Sin embargo . . .*
To change topic	*Con respecto a . . .*	*En cuanto a . . .*
To show effect	*Como resultado . . .* *Debido a lo anterior . . .* *Entonces . . .*	*Por consiguiente . . .* *Por eso . . .* *Por esa razón . . .*
To give examples	*Por ejemplo . . .*	*En particular . . .*
To finalize	*Finalmente*	*Para concluir*

You should practice incorporating transitions in all your speaking and writing activities. Often you will find that you can easily use 4–5 in a simple email response. They will help you organize your thoughts and make your response sound more sophisticated.

Sample Email Reply

| DIRECTIONS: You will write a reply to an email that you received. You have 15 minutes to read the message and write your reply. | Vas a escribir una respuesta a un mensaje de correo electrónico. Tienes 15 minutos para leer el mensaje y escribir tu respuesta. |

DIRECTIONS: You will write a reply to an email that you received. You have 15 minutes to read the message and write your reply.

Your reply should include an appropriate greeting and closing and should answer all the questions and requests in the original message. In addition, your reply should ask for more details about something that was mentioned in the message. You should use a formal tone in your response.

Vas a escribir una respuesta a un mensaje de correo electrónico. Tienes 15 minutos para leer el mensaje y escribir tu respuesta.

Tu respuesta debe incluir un saludo y despedida apropiada y contestar a todas las preguntas y peticiones del mensaje original. También tu respuesta debe pedir más información de algo mencionado en el mensaje original. Debes usar el tono formal en tu respuesta.

Tema curricular: Las identidades personales y públicas

Este mensaje electrónico es de María José Martínez Vargas, directora de un programa al que has solicitado. Te escribe para informarte que has sido seleccionado finalista.

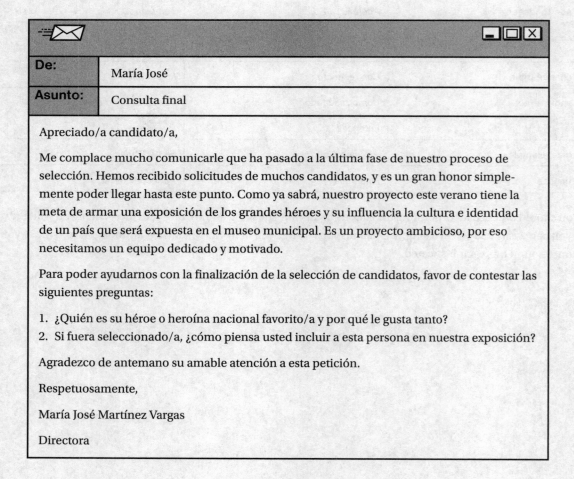

De: María José

Asunto: Consulta final

Apreciado/a candidato/a,

Me complace mucho comunicarle que ha pasado a la última fase de nuestro proceso de selección. Hemos recibido solicitudes de muchos candidatos, y es un gran honor simplemente poder llegar hasta este punto. Como ya sabrá, nuestro proyecto este verano tiene la meta de armar una exposición de los grandes héroes y su influencia la cultura e identidad de un país que será expuesta en el museo municipal. Es un proyecto ambicioso, por eso necesitamos un equipo dedicado y motivado.

Para poder ayudarnos con la finalización de la selección de candidatos, favor de contestar las siguientes preguntas:

1. ¿Quién es su héroe o heroína nacional favorito/a y por qué le gusta tanto?
2. Si fuera seleccionado/a, ¿cómo piensa usted incluir a esta persona en nuestra exposición?

Agradezco de antemano su amable atención a esta petición.

Respetuosamente,

María José Martínez Vargas

Directora

Response

By now you should know well the directions of this task, which are the following:

1. Reply to the email
2. Answer all questions asked
3. Ask an appropriate question related to the topic
4. Use a formal tone

The first step in your response is to read the introduction. This is a crucial step because it gives you the context of the correspondence. For this email, we learn the following important information:

1. You have applied for this position (so it is something of obvious interest to you).
2. You have _not_ received the position but are a finalist for it.
3. The person who is writing to you is the director of the program, and she is female.

You need to be aware of all this information because it will help you craft your response. Remember, you don't want to give the impression that you have already won the job, for this won't be maintaining the exchange. You also need to imagine that you _really_ want the job, so your response needs to show that you are a motivated candidate who wants this position.

As you begin to put pen to paper, you need to think quickly about how you will answer the questions she has asked. In her email, María José wants to know the following:

1. Who is your favorite national hero and why?
2. How do you plan on showcasing this person at the exposition?

Since the term "hero" can be vague, you have the freedom to pick anyone. It can be a sports hero, a historical figure, and so on. It really does not matter whether the person you select is indeed your favorite hero in real life; the most important part is that you convey that this person is your favorite hero in your response.

The next part is to figure out how you would include this figure in the exposition. You will have to be creative here, but anything that would be appropriate in a museum setting could work.

The last part is to identify something that you may need to know more about. In this email, there are several questions that you could ask. Here are a few:

1. How many candidates are finalists?
2. When will the exposition take place?
3. How long will the exposition last?
4. How many people will form the team?
5. What types of resources will be available to assemble the exposition?
6. Is this a paid position?
7. When will the selected candidates be announced?
8. When in the summer is the exposition?

Once you have identified the questions you need to answer and thought of a question that you could ask, it is time to write your response. The first step is to address the recipient appropriately, which can be tricky sometimes because, as in this case, the person to whom you are writing has four names. In Spanish cultures, people generally have two last names: the first is the paternal last name and the second is the mother's maiden name. It is customary to only use the paternal last name, which in this case would be Martínez. However, if you are unsure, you could simply write her whole name out or simply refer to her as _directora_, which is the title she uses at the end of her email.

Sample Response

Here is what a sample response could look like:

Estimada Directora,

En primer lugar quisiera agradecerle por haberme seleccionado como finalista. Estoy muy emocionado de saber que tengo la oportunidad de participar en esta fantástica exposición.

Para contestar a sus preguntas, de niño, siempre me han fascinado los grandes héroes nacionales, pero si fuera de solamente escoger uno, sería José Martí. Me fascina tanto porque a través de su literatura ayudó a crear una identidad cubana, que sirvió de fuerza unificadora para la gente de la isla. También, murió en batalla tratando de liberar su país de los españoles.

En la exposición, me gustaría incorporar ejemplos de su literatura para mostrar cómo sirvió para crear esta identidad nacional. Sería interesante incorporar partes de sus Versos Sencillos, y crear talleres donde los visitantes pueden mejor comprender su obra y formar versos originales que definan su propia identidad cultural.

Me emociona muchísimo saber que soy finalista. ¿Sabe usted cuándo van a seleccionar al solicitante ganador?

Muchísimas gracias otra vez por la correspondencia, y quedo a su disposición para facilitarle cualquier otra información.

Atentamente,

Javier Benavidez

As you look over this response, make note of the following:

1. The organization of the response into the five distinct portions (greeting, opening, body, closing, goodbye)
2. Use of transitions (*En primer lugar . . . , Para contestar a sus preguntas . . . , También . . .*)
3. Elaboration following the answer of each question
4. Use of formal tone throughout
5. Use of a variety of verb moods and tenses (present, preterit, conditional, imperfect subjunctive)

Also note what is *not* in the response, such as your email address or the date. These elements are not required for this task and are simply a waste of time.

Email Reply Practice Exercises

Email Reply 1

Tema curricular: Los desafíos mundiales

Este mensaje electrónico es del señor Javier Gaitán, el presidente del Club Planeta Verde. Él está planeando publicar un informe sobre la situación del medio ambiente. Has recibido este mensaje porque vives en la comunidad en que se ubica este club.

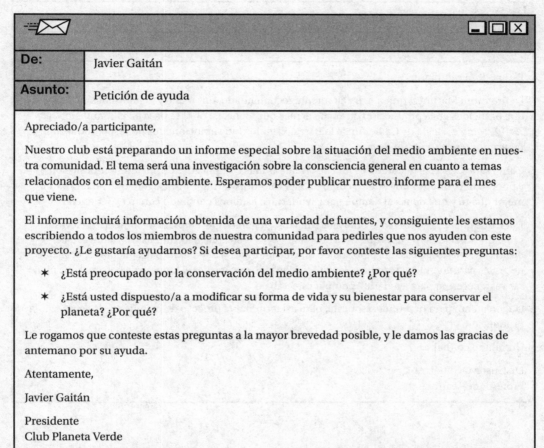

De:	Javier Gaitán
Asunto:	Petición de ayuda

Apreciado/a participante,

Nuestro club está preparando un informe especial sobre la situación del medio ambiente en nuestra comunidad. El tema será una investigación sobre la consciencia general en cuanto a temas relacionados con el medio ambiente. Esperamos poder publicar nuestro informe para el mes que viene.

El informe incluirá información obtenida de una variedad de fuentes, y consiguiente les estamos escribiendo a todos los miembros de nuestra comunidad para pedirles que nos ayuden con este proyecto. ¿Le gustaría ayudarnos? Si desea participar, por favor conteste las siguientes preguntas:

* ¿Está preocupado por la conservación del medio ambiente? ¿Por qué?

* ¿Está usted dispuesto/a a modificar su forma de vida y su bienestar para conservar el planeta? ¿Por qué?

Le rogamos que conteste estas preguntas a la mayor brevedad posible, y le damos las gracias de antemano por su ayuda.

Atentamente,

Javier Gaitán

Presidente
Club Planeta Verde

Email Reply 2

Tema curricular: La belleza y la estética

Este mensaje te lo envió el Profesor Gutiérrez, profesor de teatro de tu escuela. Te escribe porque quiere hacerte encargo del decorado para la obra de teatro *Sueño*, que va a estrenar el próximo mes.

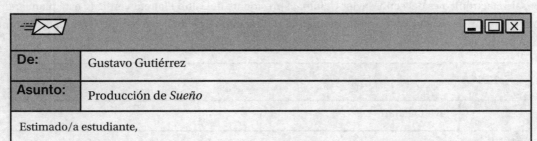

De:	Gustavo Gutiérrez
Asunto:	Producción de *Sueño*

Estimado/a estudiante,

La Profesora Martínez, quien te ha altamente recomendado, nos mandó tu información, y quiero que participes en la producción de *Sueño* el mes que viene. La obra se basa en el drama del siglo XVII *La vida es sueño* de Calderón de la Barca. Estamos muy emocionados por esta producción, y pensamos que va a ser un exitazo.

Como sabes, crear el decorado es una de las tareas más complicadas de cualquier producción, y por eso necesitamos un experto como tú. La Profesora Martínez me aseguró que no hay nadie mejor que tú y que tienes el tiempo para ayudarnos. Estamos contando con tu experiencia.

Dado que queremos estrenar la obra en treinta días, tenemos que empezar de inmediato. Necesito saber qué materiales piensas que vas a necesitar y el cálculo anticipado de gastos. Tienes el taller de la escuela a tu disposición, pero te pido que me informes si hay alguna herramienta especial que necesites para completar el trabajo. Finalmente, te pido que me des el número de personal que piensas vas a necesitar para ayudarte a cumplir este trabajo.

Quedo atento para tu pronta respuesta, para así terminar el proceso de planificación y empezar la producción.

Un saludo cordial,

Dr. Gustavo Gutiérrez
Profesor de Teatro

Email Reply 3

Tema curricular: La vida contemporánea

Este mensaje electrónico es de la señora Carmen Cienfuegos, la directora de *Voluntariado Universal*. Has recibido este mensaje porque has aceptado participar en uno de sus programas en Argentina.

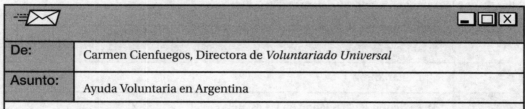

De:	Carmen Cienfuegos, Directora de *Voluntariado Universal*
Asunto:	Ayuda Voluntaria en Argentina

Estimado/a voluntario/a,

Muchas gracias por su respuesta y por haber aceptado participar en nuestro programa. Aunque somos una compañía bastante joven, debido a la generosidad de nuestros voluntarios hemos podido crecer rápidamente y aumentar nuestros programas. Trabajamos con niños y jóvenes socialmente marginados que viven bajo la línea de la pobreza, y creamos actividades con el fin de mejorar las condiciones de su vida. Como voluntario, su trabajo será de trabajar estrechamente con los chicos y ayudar a crear un ambiente saludable y feliz, compartiendo afecto y risas.

Tenemos dos programas distintos, uno en el suburbio de Buenos Aires, y el otro trabajando con la comunidad indígena en la jungla de Misiones. Las dos localidades presentan retos distintos, ya que en Misiones se presentan problemas con el alcance de elementos básicos, como agua potable y atención sanitaria, y en Buenos Aires hay todos los problemas y peligros típicos de un barrio pobre de una metrópolis. Ofrecemos programas de dos a cuatro semanas, y para poder finalizar nuestra lista, quisiera que nos proveyera la siguiente información:

- Primero, queremos aprovechar de los talentos e intereses de los voluntarios. Por lo tanto, ¿nos podría precisar en qué programa quiere participar y por qué?

- Segundo, para poder tener los mejores equipos, buscamos formar los grupos con voluntarios que tengan distintos talentos. ¿Nos podría proveer información de cualquier talento y/o habilidad que tenga y cómo esto puede beneficiar al grupo?

Le rogamos que nos provea esta información en cuanto pueda. Quedo atenta a su pronta respuesta y estoy pendiente para cualquier consulta que necesite.

Le saluda cordialmente,

Carmen Cienfuegos
Directora
Voluntariado Universal

Email Reply 4

Tema curricular: Las identidades personales y públicas

Eres estudiante en el colegio y tu escuela va a patrocinar una mesa redonda sobre la religión. Una profesora tuya, quien va a ser una de los panelistas, quiere incorporar las ideas de varios estudiantes. Te manda un mensaje electrónico pidiendo que la ayudes en prepararse para la discusión.

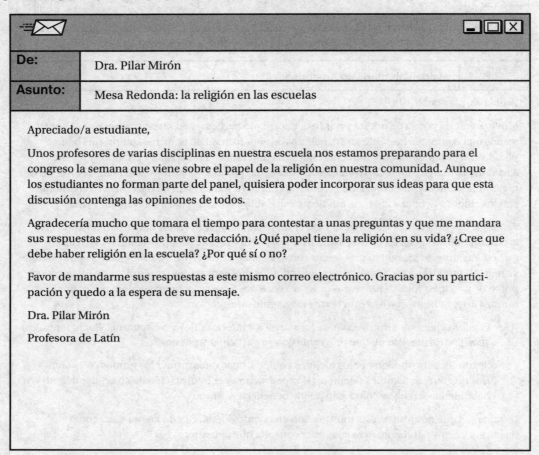

De:	Dra. Pilar Mirón
Asunto:	Mesa Redonda: la religión en las escuelas

Apreciado/a estudiante,

Unos profesores de varias disciplinas en nuestra escuela nos estamos preparando para el congreso la semana que viene sobre el papel de la religión en nuestra comunidad. Aunque los estudiantes no forman parte del panel, quisiera poder incorporar sus ideas para que esta discusión contenga las opiniones de todos.

Agradecería mucho que tomara el tiempo para contestar a unas preguntas y que me mandara sus respuestas en forma de breve redacción. ¿Qué papel tiene la religión en su vida? ¿Cree que debe haber religión en la escuela? ¿Por qué sí o no?

Favor de mandarme sus respuestas a este mismo correo electrónico. Gracias por su participación y quedo a la espera de su mensaje.

Dra. Pilar Mirón

Profesora de Latín

Email Reply 5

Tema curricular: Las familias y las comunidades

Un periodista de una revista popular está preparando un artículo sobre las diferentes tradiciones que se celebran en distintas comunidades. Te manda un mensaje electrónico pidiendo que respondas a unas preguntas para ayudarlo en terminar su trabajo.

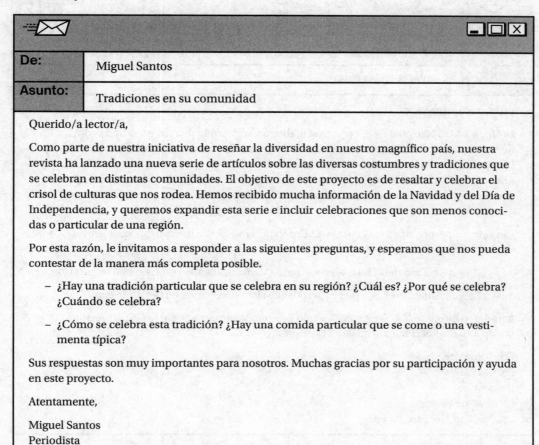

De: Miguel Santos

Asunto: Tradiciones en su comunidad

Querido/a lector/a,

Como parte de nuestra iniciativa de reseñar la diversidad en nuestro magnífico país, nuestra revista ha lanzado una nueva serie de artículos sobre las diversas costumbres y tradiciones que se celebran en distintas comunidades. El objetivo de este proyecto es de resaltar y celebrar el crisol de culturas que nos rodea. Hemos recibido mucha información de la Navidad y del Día de Independencia, y queremos expandir esta serie e incluir celebraciones que son menos conocidas o particular de una región.

Por esta razón, le invitamos a responder a las siguientes preguntas, y esperamos que nos pueda contestar de la manera más completa posible.

– ¿Hay una tradición particular que se celebra en su región? ¿Cuál es? ¿Por qué se celebra? ¿Cuándo se celebra?

– ¿Cómo se celebra esta tradición? ¿Hay una comida particular que se come o una vestimenta típica?

Sus respuestas son muy importantes para nosotros. Muchas gracias por su participación y ayuda en este proyecto.

Atentamente,

Miguel Santos
Periodista

Email Reply 6

Tema curricular: La ciencia y la tecnología

Eres estudiante a punto de empezar tu primer semestre en la universidad y un decano te escribe un mensaje electrónico. Quiere saber tus opiniones sobre si se debería permitir el uso de teléfonos celulares en las aulas.

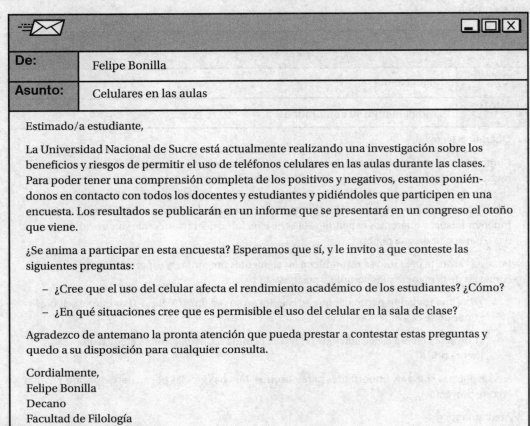

De:	Felipe Bonilla
Asunto:	Celulares en las aulas

Estimado/a estudiante,

La Universidad Nacional de Sucre está actualmente realizando una investigación sobre los beneficios y riesgos de permitir el uso de teléfonos celulares en las aulas durante las clases. Para poder tener una comprensión completa de los positivos y negativos, estamos poniéndonos en contacto con todos los docentes y estudiantes y pidiéndoles que participen en una encuesta. Los resultados se publicarán en un informe que se presentará en un congreso el otoño que viene.

¿Se anima a participar en esta encuesta? Esperamos que sí, y le invito a que conteste las siguientes preguntas:

– ¿Cree que el uso del celular afecta el rendimiento académico de los estudiantes? ¿Cómo?

– ¿En qué situaciones cree que es permisible el uso del celular en la sala de clase?

Agradezco de antemano la pronta atención que pueda prestar a contestar estas preguntas y quedo a su disposición para cualquier consulta.

Cordialmente,
Felipe Bonilla
Decano
Facultad de Filología
Universidad Nacional de Sucre

Email Reply 7

Tema curricular: Los desafíos mundiales

Recibes un mensaje electrónico de Annet Romero, asistente ejecutiva del alcalde en tu ciudad. Están pensando en implementar unas reformas a unos programas sociales y quiere saber tu opinión sobre el asunto.

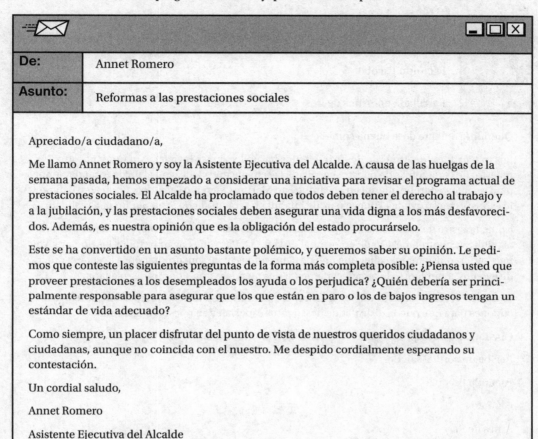

De: Annet Romero

Asunto: Reformas a las prestaciones sociales

Apreciado/a ciudadano/a,

Me llamo Annet Romero y soy la Asistente Ejecutiva del Alcalde. A causa de las huelgas de la semana pasada, hemos empezado a considerar una iniciativa para revisar el programa actual de prestaciones sociales. El Alcalde ha proclamado que todos deben tener el derecho al trabajo y a la jubilación, y las prestaciones sociales deben asegurar una vida digna a los más desfavorecidos. Además, es nuestra opinión que es la obligación del estado procurárselo.

Este se ha convertido en un asunto bastante polémico, y queremos saber su opinión. Le pedimos que conteste las siguientes preguntas de la forma más completa posible: ¿Piensa usted que proveer prestaciones a los desempleados los ayuda o los perjudica? ¿Quién debería ser principalmente responsable para asegurar que los que están en paro o los de bajos ingresos tengan un estándar de vida adecuado?

Como siempre, un placer disfrutar del punto de vista de nuestros queridos ciudadanos y ciudadanas, aunque no coincida con el nuestro. Me despido cordialmente esperando su contestación.

Un cordial saludo,

Annet Romero

Asistente Ejecutiva del Alcalde

Email Reply 8

Tema curricular: La vida contemporánea

Acabas de recibir un mensaje electrónico del gerente de tu restaurante favorito. Te escribe porque quiere que participes en un evento para recaudar fondos para un nuevo parque infantil.

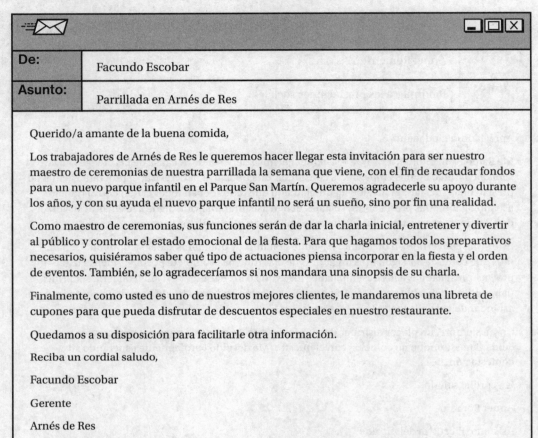

De: Facundo Escobar

Asunto: Parrillada en Arnés de Res

Querido/a amante de la buena comida,

Los trabajadores de Arnés de Res le queremos hacer llegar esta invitación para ser nuestro maestro de ceremonias de nuestra parrillada la semana que viene, con el fin de recaudar fondos para un nuevo parque infantil en el Parque San Martín. Queremos agradecerle su apoyo durante los años, y con su ayuda el nuevo parque infantil no será un sueño, sino por fin una realidad.

Como maestro de ceremonias, sus funciones serán de dar la charla inicial, entretener y divertir al público y controlar el estado emocional de la fiesta. Para que hagamos todos los preparativos necesarios, quisiéramos saber qué tipo de actuaciones piensa incorporar en la fiesta y el orden de eventos. También, se lo agradeceríamos si nos mandara una sinopsis de su charla.

Finalmente, como usted es uno de nuestros mejores clientes, le mandaremos una libreta de cupones para que pueda disfrutar de descuentos especiales en nuestro restaurante.

Quedamos a su disposición para facilitarle otra información.

Reciba un cordial saludo,

Facundo Escobar

Gerente

Arnés de Res

Email Reply 9

Tema curricular: Las familias y las comunidades

Eres estudiante y recibes un mensaje electrónico de tu profesor pidiendo información de tu proyecto final del curso.

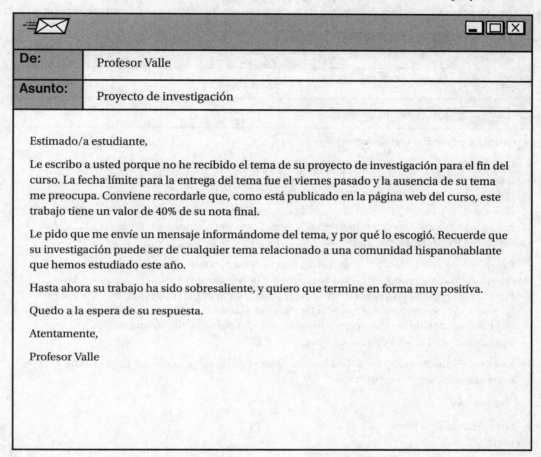

De: Profesor Valle

Asunto: Proyecto de investigación

Estimado/a estudiante,

Le escribo a usted porque no he recibido el tema de su proyecto de investigación para el fin del curso. La fecha límite para la entrega del tema fue el viernes pasado y la ausencia de su tema me preocupa. Conviene recordarle que, como está publicado en la página web del curso, este trabajo tiene un valor de 40% de su nota final.

Le pido que me envíe un mensaje informándome del tema, y por qué lo escogió. Recuerde que su investigación puede ser de cualquier tema relacionado a una comunidad hispanohablante que hemos estudiado este año.

Hasta ahora su trabajo ha sido sobresaliente, y quiero que termine en forma muy positiva.

Quedo a la espera de su respuesta.

Atentamente,

Profesor Valle

Email Reply 10

Tema curricular: La belleza y la estética

Eres un estudiante de diseño que acaba de calificarse a la siguiente ronda de un concurso de productos innovadores. Recibes un mensaje electrónico de la directora del concurso en que te felicita y te informa del próximo paso.

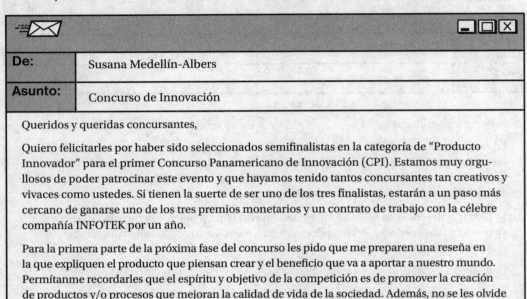

De:	Susana Medellín-Albers
Asunto:	Concurso de Innovación

Queridos y queridas concursantes,

Quiero felicitarles por haber sido seleccionados semifinalistas en la categoría de "Producto Innovador" para el primer Concurso Panamericano de Innovación (CPI). Estamos muy orgullosos de poder patrocinar este evento y que hayamos tenido tantos concursantes tan creativos y vivaces como ustedes. Si tienen la suerte de ser uno de los tres finalistas, estarán a un paso más cercano de ganarse uno de los tres premios monetarios y un contrato de trabajo con la célebre compañía INFOTEK por un año.

Para la primera parte de la próxima fase del concurso les pido que me preparen una reseña en la que expliquen el producto que piensan crear y el beneficio que va a aportar a nuestro mundo. Permítanme recordarles que el espíritu y objetivo de la competición es de promover la creación de productos y/o procesos que mejoran la calidad de vida de la sociedad. Además, no se les olvide que debe ser un producto a un precio asequible y hecho de materiales sostenibles, así les ruego que también me provean esta información.

Estoy pendiente de cualquier necesidad o pregunta que les surja. Les deseo buena suerte y espero su respuesta con gran interés.

Atentamente,

Susana Medellín-Albers
Directora
CPI

8

Section II, Part A—Task 2: Argumentative Essay

Task 2: Argumentative Essay showcases your ability to argue your point of view on a particular topic. You will be given a question to answer from three sources that present different points of view on the topic. Your task is to interpret the information presented on the topic in the sources, and then use it to support your argument. The first source is an article; the second is a chart, graph, or table; and the third is a listening source. You will be given 6 minutes to read the question and sources 1 and 2. You then will hear the audio played twice, with a 2 to 3 second pause in between. You then have 40 minutes to write your essay. Your Argumentative Essay must include the following:

- A clear answer to the question presented for this task
- Integration of all three sources in support of the overall argument
- Organization of thought
- Appropriate language for a presentational essay

Scoring Your Argumentative Essay

Your score will be based on how well you are able to accomplish this task and can roughly be broken into the following categories:

1. What you were able to do.
- Did you answer the question with a clear thesis?
- Did you incorporate information from all three sources in support of your argument?
- Does your argument drive the essay and is there frequent elaboration?

2. How you were able to do it.
- Is your response fully comprehensible?
- Did your use of language show some sophistication?
- Is your response well organized?

As with Task 1: Email Reply, it is important to remember that these two categories work together. If you answered yes to all the above questions, your essay will likely score in the high range. There are some criteria that are more important than others. For example, a response that does not clearly answer the question or in which the student starts the essay by defending one viewpoint but ends up defending another will not score well. Likewise a response in which the student clearly tries to answer the question but whose language ability makes the reply mostly incomprehensible will also earn a low score.

Another key element is to understand that your argument has to be the driving force of the essay, not the information in the sources. The information from the sources should serve as support for your ideas, not the other way around. Student essays whose argument relies heavily on summarizing information from the sources generally score in the "3" range. Also, you need to include at least one piece of information from each source. Failing to include information from one source in support of the essay will jeopardize your ability to earn a "5," even if all other parts of your response merit a score of a "5."

Strategies for Task 2: Argumentative Essay

The following is a guideline about how you should budget your time.

Read the question of the essay (30 seconds).
- Underline key words of the question so that it is absolutely clear what you need to answer.

Read source 1 (4 minutes).
- Read the introduction to the article.
- Read the title of the article.
- As you read, underline key words and phrases that will help you remember key ideas about the text.
- Focus on what it is you do know. Use context clues to infer the meaning of unfamiliar words, but do not spend too much time trying to decipher complicated information.
- When you finish reading, write down a few key words from the text that best summarize the point of view of the article.

Read source 2 (2 minutes).
- Read the introduction to the graph, chart, or table.
- Read the title of the graph, chart, or table.
- Analyze the information and come up with one or two ideas that clearly can be defended by the information in the graph, chart, or table. Remember that almost always this information presents objective data, and does not have a particular point of view. Don't force a point of view unless it is clearly presented in the graphic.

Listen to source 3 (5–7 minutes).
- Read the introduction to source 3 when directed to do so. Make a prediction of the point of view that this audio might take. Generally speaking, the audio will contain information that presents a different point of view than the article.
- Listen to the audio the first time to get a general idea of the overall argument. Visualize as you listen.
- When you listen the second time, take notes of key words that will help you remember one or two ideas from the audio source relating to the topic.
- Focus on what it is you understand and don't get hung up on what you don't understand. Use contextual clues to help you understand unfamiliar words or phrases.

Writing your essay (35 minutes)
- Begin by rereading the question you have to answer.
- Make a decision as to your answer to the question.
- Structure your essay correctly (introduction, body, and conclusion).
- Present your argument and use information from the sources to support your argument. Cite the sources as you use them.
- Vary your vocabulary. Make sure that you also use vocabulary from the sources correctly.
- Make sure that your ideas are clear and succinct.
- Include a variety of tenses and/or moods, if appropriate. Do not try to force the use of different tenses or moods, as this will count against you if it makes your response confusing.
- If you make a mistake, draw a line through it and keep writing.

After your finish writing (5 minutes)

- Proofread your essay and ensure that . . .
  - . . . you clearly answered the question;
  - . . . your overall argument is clear and supported by information from the sources;
  - . . . your ideas are clear to an unsympathetic reader; and
  - . . . you used correct orthography, punctuation, and paragraphing.

Writing Your Argumentative Essay

When writing your essay, you should imagine that you are writing to someone who probably is not familiar with the topic. Therefore, your essay should be organized in such a way that you help guide the reader through your train of thought. Here is a general outline of how your essay should be organized:

- **Introduction (1 paragraph).**
  - Present the topic of the essay,
  - Present the two points of view on the essay, and
  - Clearly state your thesis.

- **Body (2 paragraphs).**
  - **Paragraph 1**
    - Begin by introducing your first idea that defends your thesis.
    - Use evidence from one or two of the sources to support your idea. Cite the sources as you use them.
    - Finish by elaborating why your idea is valid.

  - **Paragraph 2**
    - Begin by presenting the opposite point of view.
    - Use evidence from one of the sources as evidence to support this opposite point of view. Cite the source as you use it.
    - Reject this point of view and reaffirm your own point of view. Use information from the sources to support this rejection and reaffirmation. Cite the sources as you use them.

  - **Conclusion (1 paragraph).**
    - Restate your thesis.
    - Summarize the evidence that you used to prove your thesis.
    - Make a final remark or call to action that gives your essay a sense of closure and ending.

Citing Sources

When you cite sources, be as brief as possible. You can write something as simple as "Según fuente # . . ." or write "F#" in parenthesis after you present the idea from the source.

Useful Vocabulary

One way to ensure that your essay flows well is to use transitional phrases. Here is a list that you can use. Practice using them regularly so that you will remember them easily on the exam.

To introduce an idea	*Como punto de partida . . .* *Para empezar . . .*
To add to an idea	*Además . . .* *En segundo lugar . . .*
To explain an idea	*Por ejemplo . . .* *Para ilustrar . . .*
To contrast	*Por otro lado . . .* *Sin embargo . . .* *No obstante . . .*
To compare	*De la misma manera . . .*
To show a result	*Por consiguiente . . .* *Como resultado . . .* *Debido a lo anterior . . .*
To conclude or summarize	*Por fin . . .* *En suma . . .* *Para concluir . . .*

Sample Argumentative Essay

DIRECTIONS: You will now write an argumentative essay. The essay topic is based on the following three print and audio sources. First, you will have 6 minutes to read the essay topic and the printed sources. Next, you will hear the audio material twice. Then, you will have 40 minutes to plan and write your essay.

In your essay, you should make reference to specific information from the three source materials. Do not simply summarize what is contained in the sources. Incorporate them into your essay and cite them in the proper manner. In addition, you should also clearly present your own viewpoints on the topic and defend them thoroughly. Your essay should be organized into clear paragraphs, and you should use appropriate vocabulary and grammar.

Ahora vas a escribir un ensayo argumentativo. El tema del ensayo se basa en las siguientes fuentes escritas y auditivas. Primero, tendrás 6 minutos para leer las fuentes impresas. Después, vas a escuchar la fuente auditiva dos veces. Finalmente, tendrás 40 minutos para planear y escribir tu ensayo.

En tu ensayo, debes hacer referencia a información específica de las tres fuentes. Debes evitar simplemente resumir la información de las fuentes. Incorpórala en tu ensayo e identifícalas apropiadamente. Además, debes presentar claramente tus propios puntos de vista y defenderlos bien. Tu ensayo debe ser organizado en distintos párrafos bien desarrollados y debes usar vocabulario y gramática apropiada.

Tema curricular: La ciencia y la tecnología

Primero tienes seis minutos para leer el tema del ensayo, la fuente número 1 y la fuente número 2.

Tema del ensayo: ¿Es verdaderamente necesario dormir ocho horas para tener una vida saludable?

Fuente 1

Introducción: El siguiente artículo, escrito por Pablo Bejerano, cuestiona la verdad de si dormir ocho horas es necesario. El artículo fue publicado en la página web *http://Blogthinkbig.com.*

El tiempo ideal de sueño varía de una persona a otra, pero las investigaciones demuestran que las ocho horas diarias no son necesarias.

Dormir es una de las partes más importantes de nuestro día a día. No en vano lo más probable es que sea la actividad en la que empleemos más tiempo a lo largo de nuestra vida. Por supuesto, el resto de tareas diarias se ven condicionadas por las necesidades de reposo que requiere el organismo. Pero,

Línea
(5)
¿cuántas horas necesitamos dormir realmente? No son ocho, como dicta la creencia popular, y no necesariamente resulta beneficioso alargar el tiempo de sueño.

Hoy en día, cuando los niveles de productividad se estudian al detalle y se trata de optimizar al máximo el rendimiento en el trabajo, cobra cada vez más importancia el descanso. Ya hace tiempo que se desmontó el mito de las ocho horas diarias de sueño y, aunque no hay una sola idea concluyente de cuántas horas necesitamos dormir, se puede tomar como referencia lo que han descubierto

(10)
algunos investigadores.

Uno de los especialistas en sueño más prestigiosos, Daniel Kriple, ha constatado en su último estudio que la gente que duerme entre 6,5 horas y 7,5 horas, además de vivir más tiempo, es más feliz y más productiva. Otra de las claves que apunta tiene que ver con dormir más de las ocho horas tradicionales. Según sus conclusiones, dormir 8,5 horas podría ser peor que dormir 5 horas.

(15)
Estas cifras pueden variar ligeramente de unas personas a otras, pues no todo el mundo tiene las mismas necesidades debido a su genética, complexión e incluso a su actividad diaria. ¿Pero qué ocurre si dormimos menos de lo necesario? Una de las creencias extendidas es que perdemos capacidad para enfrentarnos a nuestras tareas. No es del todo cierto. Una persona falta de sueño puede llevar a cabo las mismas funciones que otra que sí haya descansado bien.

(20)
La diferencia—nada desdeñable—está en que la persona que ha dormido poco tiene más dificultad para recuperar la concentración. Y es que todos nos distraemos constantemente, pero cuando el cerebro se encuentra en buenas condiciones tiene más facilidad para volver a centrarse, algo mucho más costoso cuando hay falta de sueño. Además, alguien con este impedimento para concentrarse no repara en su déficit, algo que contribuye a la infravaloración del sueño.

(25)
La siesta puede convertirse en otra de las claves para mejorar la calidad del sueño. De hecho, algunos historiadores han señalado que hasta hace pocos siglos era habitual la práctica de segmentar el sueño en dos etapas. El escritor Michael S. Hyatt afirma que diariamente duerme la siesta alrededor de las tres de la tarde, cuando nota que su productividad cae en picado. Tras el reposo cuenta con otra hora y media de alto rendimiento.

(30)
Eso sí, las recomendaciones siempre hablan de no excederse en el tiempo de siesta, que no supere los 25 minutos o media hora. Este hábito lógicamente lleva a estar menos cansado, de lo que se deriva que se tenga mejor ánimo, algo que constituye una base sólida para estar más contento.

Fuente 2

Introducción: La siguiente tabla presenta las horas recomendadas de sueño según la National Sleep Foundation.

Edad	Horas recomendadas
Recién nacidos	14–17
Bebés	12–15
Niños y preescolares	10–14
Escolares y adolescentes	8–11
Adultos jóvenes y adultos	7–9
Adultos mayores	7–8

Fuente 3

Introducción: El siguiente audio trata del tema de si se debe dormir ocho horas o no. Es un fragmento de la grabación titulada "Dormir o no dormir," y fue emitida por Radio Ciudad del Mar (Cuba) en octubre de 2012. La grabación dura aproximadamente tres minutos y medio.

Track 25

Response

By now you should know well the directions of this task, which are the following:

- You are to write an argumentative essay in which you answer the question with your own viewpoint.
- You must use information from all three sources in support of your argument.
- When you use information from the sources, cite them appropriately.
- Organize your essay.

The first step is to read the question and underline key words. In this case, the key words are "necesario dormir ocho horas" and "vida saludable." One could argue that there are three possible responses to this question.

1. Yes, it is important to sleep 8 hours as part of a healthy lifestyle.
2. No, it is not important to sleep 8 hours to maintain a healthy lifestyle.
3. Maybe . . . for some it is important while for others it is not important.

It is easiest to take a definitive position, such as defending one of the first two options. You only have 40 minutes to write, so you want to defend the idea that is easiest for you to defend. It does not matter whether or not you personally believe the idea that you defend; the strength of your argument in the essay is what will be evaluated.

The next step is to read the sources. Make sure that you do the following:

- Read the introduction and title.
- As you read, underline key words that will help you remember important ideas from the source.
- Try to find at least one good idea from each source.

Here are some ideas that you can extract from the sources in this example.

- Fuente 1—Sleeping 8 hours isn't necessary, and some studies show that sleeping more than 8 hours can have worse effects than sleeping less than 5 hours and that those who sleep 6.5 to 7.5 hours are more productive and happier.
- Fuente 2—The National Sleep Foundation recommends that young children sleep much more than 8 hours, while adults can sleep 7–8 hours.
- Fuente 3—The interviewees feel that sleeping 8 hours is vital to keep healthy and to perform adequately.

Now that you have an idea from each source, go back and re-read the question. Once you have done so, choose what side of the argument you plan to defend and begin writing your essay. Here is a sample essay:

Sample Essay

El sueño es una parte fundamental de nuestra salud y bienestar. Aunque todos concuerdan que es vital que la gente tenga la oportunidad de recuperarse de los esfuerzos físicos y mentales que nos enfrentan diariamente, no hay consenso del número de horas que hay que dormir. Unos dicen que hay que dormir un mínimo de ocho horas diariamente, mientras otros dicen que no son necesarias. Para mí, creo que es imprescindible que la gente duerma ocho horas como mínimo porque beneficia la calidad de nuestra productividad y ayuda a mantener una vida sana.

Como punto de partida, dormir ocho horas es beneficioso para la salud mental y física. Nosotros nos encontramos en un mundo lleno de estímulos, y muchas veces es difícil manejar todas las expectativas que nos rodean. Los estudiantes, por ejemplo, tienen un sinfín de obligaciones académicas, y es común que ellos trasnochen completando un proyecto o estudiando para un examen. Pero no dormir lo suficiente puede causar peor rendimiento (fuente 3). Además, puede llevar a problemas físicos. Según la fuente 3, no dormir lo suficiente aumenta el riesgo de contraer enfermedades, tal como la obesidad y cáncer. Los expertos concuerdan, y el prestigioso National Sleep Foundation recomienda un mínimo de 8 horas para todas las edades, y cuanto menos años uno tiene, más tiene que dormir. Por consiguiente, es lógico que la gente duerma ocho horas cada día.

Por otro lado, hay unos que argumentan que dormir ocho horas no es necesario. Ellos argumentan que alguien que duerme menos de ocho hora puede llevar a cabo las mismas funciones que alguien que haya dormido ocho horas, y hacen referencias a estudios que muestran que dormir más de ocho horas es peor que dormir menos de cinco horas (fuente 1). Sin embargo, también admiten que dormir menos de ocho horas afecta la capacidad de poder concentrarse (fuente 1), una consecuencia bastante grave particularmente si es un estudiante tomando un examen u operador de equipo pesado donde la falta de concentración puede causarle fracasar un examen o matar a alguien. Por lo tanto, no parece que valga la pena poner a sí mismo o a otros a riesgo por la falta de sueño.

Para concluir, a mi parecer es imprescindible que durmamos lo suficiente cada noche, y tanto los expertos como la muchedumbre están de acuerdo que lo suficiente equivale a ocho horas diarias (fuentes 2 y 3). Dormir ocho horas no sólo permite que uno pueda llevar a cabo bien sus responsabilidades, sino también ayuda a prevenir trastornos físicos. Con todos los beneficios que aporta, ¿quién no dormiría ocho horas?

As you look over this response, make note of the following:

1. The organization of the response into the three distinct portions (introduction, body, conclusion)
2. The organization of each of the portions:
   a. Introduction—Introduces the topic, presents the contrasting points of view, and then clearly presents a thesis.
   b. Body 1—Introduces an idea in support of the thesis. Uses evidence from sources 3 and 2 in support of the idea.
   c. Body 2—Presents the other point of view. Uses evidence from source 1 to support this point of view. Rejects the point of view, and goes back to defending original thesis.
   d. Conclusion—Reaffirms thesis, summarizes evidence to support thesis, and closes the essay with a final comment.
3. The information from the sources serves to support the argument
4. Use of transitional phrases (*Como punto de partida . . . , por ejemplo . . . , Además . . . , Por consiguiente . . . , Por otro lado . . . , Por lo tanto . . . , Para concluir . . .*)
5. Elaboration throughout
6. Use of a variety of verb moods and tenses (present, present subjunctive) and a wide range of vocabulary

Argumentative Essay Practice Exercises

Ensayo 1

Tema curricular: La vida contemporánea

Primero tienes seis minutos para leer el tema del ensayo, la fuente número 1 y la fuente número 2.

Tema del ensayo: ¿Se debería n eliminar los deberes de las escuelas?

Fuente 1: El siguiente artículo trata de los deberes escolares. Fue publicado en la página web Global Voices en Español (*es.globalvoices.org*) en 2016.

¿Para qué sirven los deberes escolares? Un debate en España

¿Tiene sentido que una niña o una niño tengan que permanecer largas horas después de clase haciendo deberes? ¿Tiene sentido que padres e hijos acaben peleando porque hacer los deberes significa decir "no" a jugar, ir al parque, ver la televisión o simplemente tumbarse a la bartola?

Línea
(5) España es uno de los países donde más deberes se mandan: 6,5 horas de media a la semana frente a las 4,9 de media en los 34 países miembros de la Organización para la Cooperación y el Desarrollo Económicos (OCDE). En Colombia los estudiantes dedican el mismo número de horas a la semana a hacer deberes en casa que los españoles; en Argentina y Chile sólo cuatro. Una encuesta de la Organización Mundial de la Salud publicada en marzo pasado, muestra a España como uno de los países con un mayor porcentaje de niños y niñas que se sienten "presionados" por las tareas para casa, una presión que

(10) aumenta a medida que los niños crecen.

Y no es que España como país sea precisamente "el primero de la clase." El sobre-esfuerzo no se traduce en un mejor rendimiento escolar. Así lo pone de manifiesto el informe del Programa para la Evaluación Internacional de Alumnos (PISA, por sus siglas en inglés). El rendimiento educativo de España en matemáticas, lectura y ciencias permanece por debajo de la media de los países de la

(15) OCDE. Además, la equidad en los resultados educativos ha empeorado. Los alumnos con un nivel socio-económico favorecido superan a los alumnos menos favorecidos en 34 puntos en matemáticas en 2012, una diferencia 6 puntos superior a la observada en 2003.

¿Sirven los deberes?

El debate no es reciente. Para unos, los deberes son una medida educativa necesaria, que hace

(20) que los escolares se esfuercen y les ayuda a asentar el conocimiento. Para otros son un abuso, producto de la falta de planificación, que acrecienta las desigualdades entre los escolares. La OCDE advierte que los deberes son una carga para los alumnos con desventajas socioeconómicas, algo que también señala un informe de la Fundación BBVA y el Instituto Valenciano de Investigaciones Económicas.

El informe PISA reconoce que los deberes sí pueden servir para mejorar los resultados, pero la

(25) tendencia actual es reducir su cantidad. En 2003 la media era de 5,9 horas a la semana, una hora más que en 2012. Países cuyos sistemas educativos destacan como los primeros del mundo, presentan una carga mucho menor: 2,8 horas a la semana en Finlandia o 2,9 en Corea del Sur. Numerosos expertos en educación coinciden en la necesidad de reducir las tareas escolares que realizan los niños españoles.

Los deberes a examen en España

(30) Eva Bailén es madre de tres hijos, y su propia experiencia familiar con los deberes la llevó a iniciar una petición en change.org por la racionalización de los deberes en el sistema educativo español, una petición que se ha convertido ya en todo un movimiento. Eva lanzó su petición hace poco más de un año, en marzo de 2015, y obtuvo un respaldo inmediato. En un mes consiguió 100.000 firmas, y hoy ya supera las 205.000.

Fuente 2: El siguiente gráfico presenta el tiempo medio (en minutos) por semana que dedican los estudiantes a la instrucción y tareas escolares. Se basa en datos publicados por la OCDE (Organización para la Cooperación y Desarrollo Económicos) en 2012.

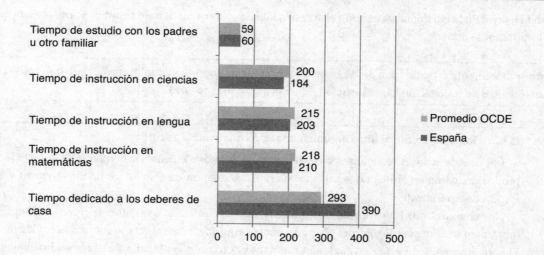

Fuente 3: El siguiente audio trata un debate sobre los deberes escolares. El audio forma parte de la serie titulada *Por la educación* en RTVE. Fue emitido en octubre de 2015 y dura aproximadamente tres minutos.

Track 26

Apuntes:

Ensayo 2

Tema curricular: La belleza y la estética

Primero tienes seis minutos para leer el tema del ensayo, la fuente número 1 y la fuente número 2.

Tema del ensayo: En la era digital y con todo el acceso a tabletas y otros medios de comunicación, ¿vale la pena seguir imprimiendo libros?

Fuente 1: El siguiente artículo trata de los beneficios que todavía aporta el libro impreso. Fue publicado por el Centro Nacional de Innovación e Investigación Educativa (España) en 2015.

El libro impreso frente al libro digital: hacia una convivencia pacífica

Los nuevos avances tecnológicos y la influencia que estos ejercen en la conducta de la sociedad han producido, como en tantos otros aspectos de nuestra vida, un cambio en los hábitos lectores y en las formas de aprendizaje.

Línea
(5) Nos encontramos rodeados de ordenadores, tabletas, móviles, televisiones, vídeos, videojuegos y herramientas afines como internet y las redes sociales que favorecen el acceso continuo a la información. El aprendizaje puede surgir en cualquier momento y en cualquier lugar, solo es necesario alguien con ganas de aprender y acceso tecnológico a la información que necesita.

En este contexto, la aparición del libro en formato digital como alternativa al libro impreso era, cuanto menos, predecible. Pero el debate entre uno y otro formato se perpetúa. Es indudable que la elección de
(10) uno u otro supone una serie de ventajas e inconvenientes. A favor del libro impreso estaría la relación física y emocional que establece el lector con las páginas. Por su parte, el libro digital, más "frío," ofrece un enorme ahorro de espacio, es más fácil de transportar, puede ajustar el tamaño de letra y, en muchos casos, es más económico. Además, continuamente surgen nuevas iniciativas para facilitar el acceso al formato digital, como la creación de bibliotecas públicas 100% digitales (como en San Antonio, Texas).
(15) A pesar de todas estas aparentes ventajas muchos lectores aún prefieren el libro de papel. ¿Por qué? ¿Cuáles son realmente las ventajas o desventajas del uso de cada uno de ellos? ¿Cómo afecta la lectura digital a la compresión lectora o al aprendizaje?

Numerosos estudios se han realizado ya sobre las virtudes e inconvenientes de la utilización de libros digitales frente a los libros impresos, pero los datos obtenidos, lejos de ser concluyentes, son
(20) contradictorios en muchos aspectos. Por ejemplo, los estudios realizados por Anne Mangen en el Reading Centre of the University of Stavanger o los llevados a cabo por Jean-Luc Velay de la Universidad de Aix-Marseille, indican que leer libros impresos favorece la comprensión lectora; por otro lado, un reciente estudio llevado a cabo por Jim Johnson de la Universidad Estatal de Indiana o el realizado por la psicóloga Sara Margolin de la Universidad Brockport, señalan justamente lo contrario, que el soporte no afecta a
(25) la comprensión lectora.

Otros estudios, como el llevado a cabo por Anne Campbell de la Open University of Scotland, concluyen que los dispositivos móviles promueven una lectura más profunda pero un menor aprendizaje activo. En España también se han desarrollado estudios sobre lectura digital. Entre ellos destaca el proyecto Territorio Ebook de la Fundación Germán Sánchez Ruipérez que recoge algunos indicios sobre los cambios
(30) que el soporte digital puede provocar en las generaciones futuras.

Fuente 2: El primer gráfico presenta el precio medio del libro en papel vs. digital entre 2011–2014. Fue publicado por el Observatorio de la Lectura y el Libro, un organismo perteneciente al Ministerio de Educación, Cultura y Deporte de España. El segundo gráfico presenta los resultados de una encuesta hecha por un estudio titulado *Estudio sobre el uso de los libros electrónicos en las bibliotecas universitarias de Castilla y León*, publicado en la página web de la Universitat de Barcelona en 2013.

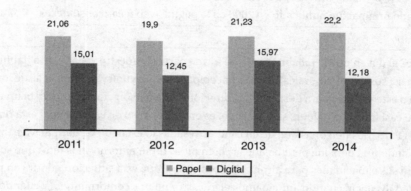

Uso de la versión electrónica frente a la impresa

Fuente 3: El siguiente audio titulado *Un libro digital puede ser cientos de veces más barato que uno impreso* trata de los beneficios económicos y sociales de los libros digitales. Fue emitido por Radio Naciones Unidas en abril de 2014 y dura aproximadamente tres minutos y medio.

Track 27

Apuntes:

Ensayo 3

Tema curricular: La ciencia y la tecnología

Primero tienes seis minutos para leer el tema del ensayo, la fuente número 1 y la fuente número 2.

Tema del ensayo: ¿Es beneficioso o perjudicial experimentar estrés en la vida?

Fuente 1: El siguiente artículo, titulado "El estrés nuestro de cada día," trata del impacto del estrés en la vida cotidiana. El artículo original fue publicado en 2008 en la página web *www.consumer.es*.

Raro es el día en que la palabra estrés no forme parte de nuestro vocabulario habitual. Algunos expresan así sus penas laborales, otros lo hacen para pedir ayuda y muchos más de los que pensamos recurren a este vocablo para despertar admiración: "qué persona más exitosa y ocupada," es su frase.

Línea En lo que casi todos coinciden, sin embargo, es en que el nivel de estrés actual está por encima del
(5) deseable. Pero, ¿las personas que dicen estar estresadas lo están de verdad? Se vive una situación de estrés cuando una persona percibe que las demandas de su entorno y los retos que se ha impuesto superarán sus capacidades para afrontarlos con éxito y que esta situación pondrá en peligro su estabilidad. Es decir, cuando anticipamos el fracaso y no nos conformamos (y cuando lo hacemos solemos deprimirnos), tendemos a estresarnos.

(10) **El estrés como aliado**

El estrés se ha convertido en un compañero de viaje habitual en nuestras vidas. No sólo no puede evitarse, sino que facilita la adaptación a cualquier cambio que irrumpa en nuestro entorno. Esta forma de reaccionar ante problemas, demandas y peligros, viene predeterminada por una actitud innata de lucha/huida heredada de nuestros antepasados: sobrevivieron aquellos que, ante situacio-
(15) nes amenazantes para su integridad física (ver un enemigo) o que informaban de la posibilidad de obtener un beneficio (cobrar una presa), mejor activaban su organismo. Dilatación de pupilas para aumentar la visión periférica y permitir una mayor entrada de luz en la oscuridad, músculos tensa-dos para reaccionar con más velocidad y fuerza, aumento de la frecuencia respiratoria y cardiaca para mejorar la oxigenación y aportar mayor flujo de sangre al cerebro y al resto de órganos vitales, son
(20) algunos de los cambios que les proporcionaba una clara ventaja sobre sus enemigos y sus presas.

Pero el inconveniente de este fabuloso mecanismo de adaptación es que genera un importante desgaste del organismo y un alto consumo de energía, por lo que es necesario desarrollar unos cuidados y un periodo de recuperación del que no siempre somos conscientes.

Fuente 2: El siguiente gráfico presenta los síntomas asociados con el estrés. Fue publicado originalmente en el blog *La Coctelera* en 2008.

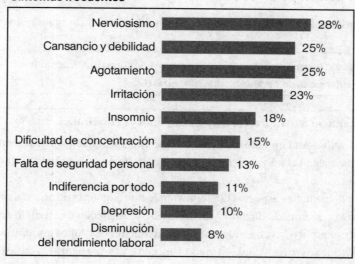

Síntomas frecuentes

Síntoma	Porcentaje
Nerviosismo	28%
Cansancio y debilidad	25%
Agotamiento	25%
Irritación	23%
Insomnio	18%
Dificultad de concentración	15%
Falta de seguridad personal	13%
Indiferencia por todo	11%
Depresión	10%
Disminución del rendimiento laboral	8%

Fuente 3: La siguiente entrevista es con José Buendía, profesor de psicopatología de la Universidad de Murcia. La grabación dura aproximadamente dos minutos y treinta segundos.

Track 28

Apuntes:

Ensayo 4

Tema curricular: Las familias y las comunidades

Primero tienes seis minutos para leer el tema del ensayo, la fuente número 1 y la fuente número 2.

Tema del ensayo: ¿Es la responsabilidad de los padres o de los docentes educar a los niños y jóvenes?

Fuente 1: El siguiente artículo provee unos consejos a los padres de cómo inculcar valores a sus hijos. Fue publicado en la página web *http://enfermedadesytratamientos.com* en 2013.

Consejos para educar a tu hijo en la responsabilidad y la disciplina

La sociedad actual está en continuo proceso de transformación, y estos cambios, también se dan en la enseñanza. Hasta los años sesenta no existían escuelas mixtas, los alumnos/as se dirigían a sus profesores/as de usted.

Línea
(5) Actualmente hay muchos aspectos diferentes en lo que a materia de enseñanza se refiere y podíamos llegar a hablar de un alumnado distinto. Muchos niños/as no tienen un ejemplo de modelo adulto en sus casas y, por ende, tampoco lo ven en los maestros. En muchas ocasiones los niños/as ven a sus profesores como colegas, ya que sus padres también lo son para ellos. Y lo que ocurre es que muchos padres y madres no quieren estropear los momentos que pasan con sus hijos/as con una serie de negativas, exigiéndoles responsabilidades . . . No quieren llevar a cabo la educación de antaño y dan paso a una educación permisiva.

(10) Ciertamente hay ventajas en la educación actual:

—Se tiene más en cuenta al niño/a, llegando a conocer mejor sus etapas y necesidades.

—Se le explican las cosas, se le escucha y todo este conjunto de cambios hace que los niños/as de hoy en día sean mucho más asertivos, aunque corremos el riesgo de no exigir el esfuerzo suficiente, limitando las responsabilidades y llegando a un consentimiento excesivo.

(15) Para no caer en esta trampa podemos seguir los siguientes consejos:

—Tenemos que ser estrictos con nuestros hijos/as. Cuando decimos que "no," tenemos que llevar ese "no" hasta el final, sin importarnos la insistencia que lleven a cabo.

En relación con esto mismo, es muy importante que tanto el padre como la madre estén dentro de la misma línea educativa y, entre otras cosas, esto implica no ceder cuando el otro progenitor exige . . .

(20) —Hay que exigir responsabilidades de acuerdo a la edad del niño/a.

—Controlar el tiempo que pasa viendo la tele o jugando a videojuegos. A medida que aumenta la edad, podemos ir aumentando el tiempo que pasa delante de la consola . . .

No podemos permitir que nuestros hijos sólo busquen la estimulación visual por medio de una pantalla, que no sean capaces de crearla en su mente. Vamos a facilitar que puedan emocionarse con el

(25) simple hecho de contarles una historia, un cuento . . .

—En relación con lo anterior, es muy importante que dediquemos un tiempo, todos los días para hablar y jugar con nuestros hijos/as . . .

—Debemos intentar comer en familia, al menos una vez al día, sin la tele encendida, fomentando el dialogo, los buenos hábitos y modales.

(30) —Es conveniente realizar actividades con nuestros hijos, por ejemplo, los fines de semana. Vamos a intentar que con alguna de estas actividades que hacemos juntos, en familia, se estimulen aspectos como la creatividad, el deporte, el respeto al medio ambiente, a los demás, el trabajo en equipo, . . .

Fuente 2: El siguiente gráfico muestra los resultados de un estudio patrocinado por la Fundación Hogar del Empleado (FUHEM) y publicado en noviembre de 2007.

Porcentaje de profesores, familias y alumnos que considera que los siguientes factores tienen bastante o mucha influencia en la educación.

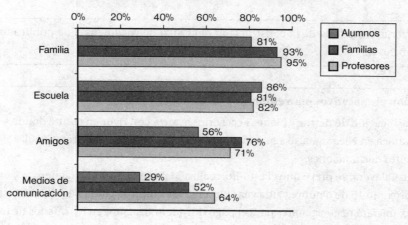

Fuente 3: El siguiente audio es un fragmento de un documental titulado *Redes—La revolución educativa*. En el fragmento, el psicólogo Robert Roesner ayuda a redefinir el papel de profesores y maestros en la educación de los jóvenes. Fue emitido por RTVE en 2010, y dura aproximadamente cuatro minutos.

Track 29

Apuntes:

Ensayo 5

Tema curricular: Los desafíos mundiales

Primero tienes seis minutos para leer el tema del ensayo, la fuente número 1 y la fuente número 2.

Tema del ensayo: ¿Se debería permitir que se construyera el canal de Nicaragua?

Fuente 1: El siguiente texto trata de la construcción del Canal de Nicaragua. Fue publicado en la página web *Nuestromar.org* en 2013.

Continúan preparativos para emprender el Canal de Nicaragua

La clasificación de tierras y bienes accesorios avanza con rigor en la ruta donde se construirá la vía interoceánica en Nicaragua, aseguró el miembro de la Comisión del Gran Canal, Telémaco Talavera, en recientes declaraciones.

Línea
(5)   Según Talavera, se prevé que el estudio, realizado por expertos nicaragüenses y extranjeros, esté listo el próximo 15 de octubre y una vez culminado la empresa china HKND, concesionaria del proyecto, iniciará negociaciones para el pago de indemnizaciones a los dueños de territorios afectados.

La longitud del canal, cuya ruta fue anunciada en julio último, será de aproximadamente 278 kilómetros, de los cuales un tramo de 105 estará en el lago de Nicaragua.

(10)   Pasará por la desembocadura del río Brito, en el sureño departamento de Rivas, a unos 100 kilómetros de esta capital, cruzará el lago y recorrerá las cercanías del río Tule hasta la desembocadura en Punta Gorda.

En referencia a una marcha organizada por algunos habitantes de Rivas para manifestar su inconformidad con las labores relacionadas con el canal, Talavera afirmó que su construcción favorecerá a

(15)   todos y respetará los derechos de los pobladores.

En algunos casos existe desinformación, en otros la influencia de manipuladores, pero tenemos la certeza de que todas las personas en la ruta y fuera de ella van a respaldar este proyecto porque es en su beneficio y para el desarrollo económico, social y humano de Nicaragua, señaló.

Reportes oficiales indican que la construcción de la obra, a iniciarse en diciembre próximo y cuya

(20)   duración se estima en cinco años, generará alrededor de 50 000 empleos y otros 200 000 en una etapa posterior.

Además del canal, se trabajará en subproyectos como un aeropuerto, varias carreteras, una zona de libre comercio, complejos turísticos y dos puertos, uno del lado del océano Pacífico y otro en el Atlántico.

Fuente 2: La siguiente tabla presenta la comparación entre el Canal de Nicaragua y el Canal de Panamá. Se basa en datos recopilados por el Gobierno de Nicaragua.

Detalles del proyecto		
	Canal de Nicaragua	Canal de Panamá
Profundidad	22 m	13,8 m
Longitud	286 km	80 km

El canal de Nicaragua tendrá la capacidad de recibir barcos de hasta 250.000 toneladas métricas, y hasta 285 m de largo.

Fuente 3: En el siguiente audio, la abogada ambientalista nicaragüense Mónica López Baldotano, presenta las razones por las que quiere detener la construcción del Canal Interoceánico de Nicaragua. La grabación fue publicada en noviembre de 2015 por RTVE y dura aproximadamente cuatro minutos.

Track 30

Apuntes:

Ensayo 6

Tema curricular: La ciencia y la tecnología

Primero tienes seis minutos para leer el tema del ensayo, la fuente número 1 y la fuente número 2.

Tema del ensayo: Descargas ilegales: ¿afectan o no afectan negativamente a las industrias de entretenimiento?

Fuente 1: El siguiente texto presenta un argumento que las descargas ilegales de música no afectan negativamente a esta industria. Fue publicado en la página web Asociación de Internautas (*www.internautas.org*) el 20 de marzo de 2013.

La UE es clara: la "piratería" de música no perjudica a los propietarios de los derechos de autor

Un estudio publicado esta misma mañana por el *Joint Research Centre* de la Unión Europea afirma algo que ya ha sido comentado en otras ocasiones: que la piratería de música en internet no afecta negativamente a las ventas en los canales de pago o legales.

El estudio de la Unión Europea llega a estas conclusiones después de analizar el comportamiento de 16 mil internautas de UK, Francia, Alemania, Italia y España. Este análisis se concentra en conocer los hábitos de los europeos, midiendo la relación entre las visitas a páginas web de descarga de música

Línea frente a opciones legales y de pago o streaming.

(5) Además de destacar el hecho de que un alto número de visitas a páginas de descargas se corresponden con un número también elevado de visitas a canales legales, el estudio que fue realizado con la ayuda de Nielsen destaca también las siguientes conclusiones:

- Parece que la mayoría de la música que es consumida ilegalmente por los individuos de nuestra muestra no habría sido comprada si las páginas de descargas ilegales no estuviesen disponibles
(10) - Los servicios de streaming de música tienen un efecto todavía mayor, al creerse que tienen un efecto de estímulo hacia el pago de contenidos
- Nuestras conclusiones sugieren que la piratería de música digital no debería ser vista como una preocupación para los propietarios de los derechos de autor. Además, nuestros resultados indican que nuevos métodos de consumo como el *streaming* de música afectan positivamente a los
(15) propietarios de dichos derechos

Aunque el estudio fue realizado analizando Internautas de los cinco países mencionados anteriormente, es importante destacar que existen diferencias significativas entre los países. En España e Italia, por ejemplo, el número de clicks en páginas de descarga gratuita de música fueron mucho mayores que en el resto de países. Y en clicks a páginas legales de contenidos, España fue segunda por
(20) la cola, sólo superada por Italia.

Con este informe se vuelve a destacar que no existe una relación tan estrecha entre piratería y pérdida de ventas, y que la primera no tiene un efecto significativo y negativo sobre la segunda. Eso sí, el informe vuelve a poner de relieve otro detalle que se ha apuntado en previas ocasiones, y es que en la Europa del sur (principalmente España e Italia), una mayor proporción de usuarios se decantan por
(25) la descarga gratuita de música, en vez de optar por los canales de pago y *legales*.

Fuente 2: El primer gráfico muestra los tipos de multimedia obtenidos por los encuestados que hicieron descargas ilegales durante los últimos 12 meses. El segundo muestra cuánto pagarían los encuestados por descargarla legalmente.

Tipos de descargas ilegales

Música, 75%   Películas, 82%   Televisión, 88%

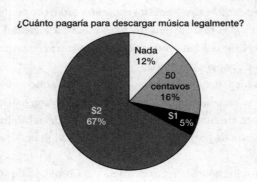

¿Cuánto pagaría para descargar música legalmente?

Nada 12%
50 centavos 16%
$1 5%
$2 67%

Fuente 3: El siguiente audio presenta los resultados de la lucha contra descargas ilegales. Fue publicado por el programa *Entre paréntesis* en Radio 5 (España) en marzo de 2015. La grabación dura aproximadamente tres minutos, cuarenta y cinco segundos.

Track 31

Apuntes:

Ensayo 7

Tema curricular: Las familias y las comunidades

Primero tienes seis minutos para leer el tema del ensayo, la fuente número 1 y la fuente número 2.

Tema del ensayo: ¿Es una buena idea tener servicio militar obligatorio para los jóvenes?

Fuente 1: El siguiente texto critica el servicio militar obligatorio. Fue publicado en la página web *http://suramericapress.com* en octubre de 2011.

¿El Servicio Militar Obligatorio instruye a los jóvenes?

Pese a que algunos sectores conservadores e individualidades califican a los objetores de: "antipatriotas, desviados sociales, cobardes" y muchos otros adjetivos que no vale repetir en este artículo, lo

Línea
(5)
cierto es que los/as jóvenes que impulsan esta campaña están proponiendo algo nuevo para la sociedad, tienen el valor y el coraje de pensar y proponer una sociedad más pluralista, con mayores libertades y elevar la responsabilidad y autonomía juvenil en la construcción de una patria para todos y todas, llena de colores de esperanza y vida.

Los que defienden la idea de que el Servicio Militar Obligatorio es una escuela de aprendizaje para los jóvenes, donde se enseñan valores patrióticos, que ayuda a disminuir la delincuencia juve-
(10)
nil, deberían tener muy en cuenta los siguientes datos, que dicen totalmente lo contrario y muestran a varios militares en situación de prepotencia, alcoholismo y violencia, lejos de ser un "ejemplo" para la sociedad:

- El sub oficial Víctor Ramón Guerrero Brizuela del Comando de Ingeniería en estado de ebriedad atropella y mata a un motociclista, el hecho ocurrió sobre la ruta I, km 21 Posta Ybycuá, de
(15)
la ciudad de Capiatá. (fecha: 21-03-2010)
- El Sargento ayudante de la Fuerza Militar Fernando Carracela Cristaldo disparó contra un motociclista en la ciudad de Asunción, 2 impactos de balas dieron en la moticicleta de la víctima, el militar fue detenido y se comprobó que estaba en estado de ebriedad, tenía en su poder una pistola 9mm, escopeta calibre 12 y arma blanca. (fecha: 27-09-2010)
(20)
- El Teniente de Infantería Rubén Gustavo Pratt Moreira, fue denunciado por los vecinos de Luque por escuchar música a todo volumen, en estado de ebriedad, haciendo alarde de su arma 9mm en la cintura, al llegar la policía, el militar reaccionó prepotentemente y no quiso some-
terse a la prueba de alcotest. (fecha: 30-10-2010).
- Sub oficial Teniente de infantería, Joel Alejandro Velázquez Meza, a bordo de su motocicleta
(25)
realizaba disparos en la vía pública en estado de ebriedad en la ciudad de Fernando de la Mora, uno de los periódicos nacionales titulaba el hecho: "Motocicleta, alcohol y arma de fuego deri-
van en detención de Militar." (fecha: 30-07-2011)

A estos hechos de particular irresponsabilidad, de homicidios incluso, protagonizados por militares le podríamos agregar muchos otros casos similares, además de mencionar los últimos casos de
(30)
tortura ocurridos recientemente en la Academia Militar (Academil), varias irregularidades y violacio-
nes de derechos humanos de los cuarteles donde según algunos "se hace patria."

Fuente 2: La siguiente tabla presenta la política de alistamiento en diferentes países del mundo. Se basa en datos recopilados por el autor.

País	Política de alistamiento
Bolivia	Obligatorio
Chile	Obligatorio
Costa Rica	No hay fuerzas armadas
España	No obligatorio
Paraguay	Obligatorio

Fuente 3: El siguiente audio, titulado *Ley fácil—Servicio militar*, es una dramatización creada por la Biblioteca del Congreso Nacional de Chile (BCN). Trata de las responsabilidades de los ciudadanos chilenos en cuanto al servicio militar. La grabación dura aproximadamente dos minutos y medio.

Track 32

Apuntes:

Ensayo 8

Tema curricular: Los desafíos mundiales

Primero tienes seis minutos para leer el tema del ensayo y las fuentes número 1 y 2.

Tema del ensayo: ¿Ayuda o perjudica el ecoturismo a una comunidad?

Fuente 1: El siguiente artículo trata de los desafíos asociados con el ecoturismo. Fue publicado por Global Voices en septiembre de 2022.

¿Pueden coexistir armónicamente el turismo y la conservación ambiental?

Mucha gente ve el ecoturismo de forma positiva, lo asocia con la conservación ambiental y la preservación de la naturaleza amenazada. Al buscar ecoturismo, abundan las imágenes envidiables: playas aisladas y prístinas, fascinantes arrecifes de coral para bucear, montañas y tierras salvajes que recorrer, turistas inmersos en las culturas locales.

Línea
(5) Pero este tipo de viajes suelen tener potenciales aspectos negativos: pueden resultar en contaminación y otros daños ambientales, con frecuencia causan grandes huellas de carbono por el transporte aéreo, marítimo y de otras clases, y pueden crear alteraciones sociales y culturales a las comunidades locales. Estos son algunos lugares que están experimentando con el ecoturismo.

Islas Galápagos: El proyecto Discovering Galapagos produce material de estudio sobre estas islas,
(10) en el que examina el impacto del turismo: "Entre los efectos positivos, el turismo trae dinero a las islas, y es una fuente de ingresos para muchos galapagueños. No obstante, también hay efectos negativos. Según aumentan los turistas que visitan las islas, hacen falta más alojamientos, lo que significa que podrían construirse grandes hoteles que pondrían en peligro la vida salvaje cercana."

La revista Annals of Tourism Research Empirical Insights publicó recientemente el estudio
(15) «Repensar y reiniciar el turismo en islas Galápagos: La opinión de las partes interesadas sobre la sostenibilidad del desarrollo turístico», que plantea numerosas cuestiones preocupantes: "Un descubrimiento clave del estudio es que los interesados comparten la opinión de que un crecimiento sin restricciones del turismo es contraproducente, por su impacto social y ambiental. El tratamiento de los efectos del exceso de turismo en las Galápagos, así como en otras islas tropicales, puede impli-
(20) car estrategias de decrecimiento, o una transición con vistas a desacelerar el turismo que brinde un mecanismo para incrementar los ingresos y el empleo provenientes del turismo, y a la vez reduzcan el impacto per cápita en los recursos isleños."

Machu Picchu: La ciudad inca de Machu Picchu en Perú atrae enormes multitudes cada año. Mucha gente recorre el legendario Camino Inca para llegar hasta allí. La comunidad en línea CATA-
(25) LYST es «una fuente de contenido sobre viajes y acciones sociales para activistas y viajeros con conciencia global». En mayo de 2022, ya advirtieron: "La falta de infraestructura que soporte estos números conduce a un impacto aún mayor. Solo hay un retrete en la entrada, y los desechos humanos son un enorme problema. El pueblo más cercano, Aguas Calientes, ha recurrido a bombear excrementos al río Urubamba. El incremento en basura en el Camino Inca, sobre todo botellas de plástico, también contribuye al descontrol de los desechos."

Fuente 2: El siguiente gráfico presenta los datos de un estudio de las actividades que más ecoturistas realizan durante sus viajes, publicado en 2022 por el Ministerio de Industria, Comercio y Turismo de España.

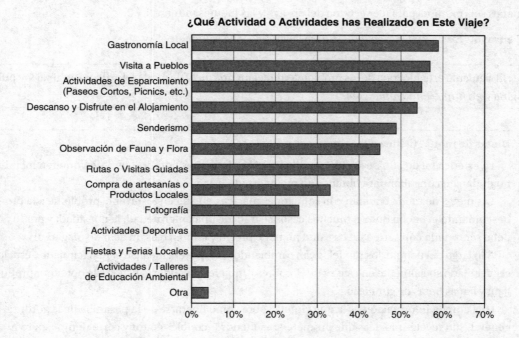

¿Qué Actividad o Actividades has Realizado en Este Viaje?

Fuente 3: El siguiente audio promociona el ecoturismo en el corredor ecoturístico Darién-Atrato de Colombia. La grabación fue publicada por la Organización de las Naciones Unidas para la Alimentación y la Agricultura (FAO) en 2021 y dura aproximadamente tres minutos, treinta segundos.

Track 33

Apuntes:

Ensayo 9

Tema curricular: La vida contemporánea

Primero tienes seis minutos para leer el tema del ensayo y las fuentes número 1 y 2.

Tema del ensayo: ¿Existe una perfecta dieta para llevar una vida saludable?

Fuente 1: El siguiente artículo trata de los problemas de seguir una dieta de moda. El artículo original fue publicado en la página web *http://Enplenitud.com*.

Dietas de moda. Crítica a las promesas milagrosas

La estética ha dejado de ser monopolio de las mujeres. Los hombres también quieren lucir bien y no dudan en consultar para obtener un mejor estado físico.

Línea (5)

Las <u>dietas</u> de moda circulan con soluciones mágicas que dicen resolver el problema a la brevedad, descuidando el hecho que en muchos casos se trata de una enfermedad, la obesidad, y por lo tanto debe ser tratada con seriedad. La salud no tiene precio y tampoco es un acto de magia.

A lo largo del tiempo, los modelos van cambiando y, lo que era ideal en el Renacimiento, está lejos de ser aceptado socialmente en este siglo. Hombres y mujeres no dudan a la hora de optar por <u>productos light</u> y largas horas de gimnasio.

(10)

Una amplia información es la que circula sobre cómo liberarse de la pesadilla de la gordura. En general, son recetas mágicas que prometen resultados increíbles en muy corto tiempo; pero luego de varios intentos y sin conseguir el tan ansiado logro, los "dietantes" pierden las esperanzas, hasta que aparece una nueva alternativa milagrosa.

El charlatanerismo prolifera cada vez más, basándose en dietas absurdas y promesas de curación definitiva.

(15)

Es un negocio, y se basa en la falta de lectura crítica y en la credulidad popular, pero lo que ofrece es tentador y ¿quién no intentó alguna vez las famosas dietas de la Luna, la Sopa, la Fuerza Aérea, la Disociada, etcétera?

El remedio es sencillo: intentar comer de forma más ordenada, tratando de evitar aquellos alimentos de alto valor calórico, pero sin sufrir grandes privaciones.

(20)

Realizar actividad física y si es posible consultar a un nutricionista con el fin de obtener la información adecuada para lograr una alimentación balanceada.

El objetivo: sentirse bien, y alcanzar el peso ideal, que no es aquel que marcan las tablas o las fórmulas, sino el que nos permitirá llegar a una mayor longevidad con una mejor calidad de vida.

Mucho es lo que se podría hablar de este tema pero, resumiendo: una dieta prefabricada, general y adaptable a cualquier persona no es más que un producto para vender. Está en cada uno analizar la situación para evitar frustraciones futuras.

(25)

No debemos olvidar que se trata de la salud y así como no se busca en revistas el remedio para la presión, tampoco debería hacerse en este caso.

Fuente 2: El siguiente gráfico presenta el consumo ideal de la dieta mediterránea. El gráfico original fue publicado en la página web *www.enterbio.es* el tres de marzo de 2013.

Fuente 3: La siguiente grabación, titulada "El vegetarianismo y la dieta vegetariana," trata de las recomendaciones de los teóricos de seguir una dieta vegetariana. Se basa en un artículo publicado en *http://Terra.com*.

Track 34

Apuntes:

Ensayo 10

Tema curricular: La belleza y la estética

Primero tienes seis minutos para leer el tema del ensayo y las fuentes número 1 y 2.

Tema del ensayo: En un mundo globalizado en que muchas comunidades se están mezclando, ¿todavía se puede decir que la gastronomía refleja la cultura de un país?

Fuente 1: El siguiente texto trata de un nuevo restaurante en Venezuela. El artículo original fue publicado por *http://nebraskamagazine.blogspot.com* en enero 2016.

"Cow," restaurante y carnicería gourmet, llega a Maracaibo con un concepto único

Con una concepción completamente diferente, en donde se mezcla un restaurante de carnes y hamburguesas al estilo americano y una carnicería con los cortes más finos del mercado, Cow abre sus puertas en Maracaibo para ofrecer calidad, buen servicio y un excelente concepto gastronómico.

Línea
(5)   "Uno de nuestros claros objetivos es brindar una buena atención y destacar como innovadores. Me di la tarea de recorrer las carnicerías más prestigiosas de Venezuela y ninguna es tan completa como Cow, porque aquí podrás almorzar, desayunar, cenar, tomar un café, un jugo o simplemente hacer compras de carnes, pan o embutidos," destacó Gamaliel López, creador del concepto.

Asimismo, explicó que el slogan "simple, caliente y sabroso" fue pensado porque en el área del restaurante no sólo probarán la mejor comida, sino que además siempre estará recién hecha y a la
(10)   temperatura ideal para degustarla.

En el área de carnicería, Cow ofrece cortes Premium, piezas completas y asesoría personalizada; es decir, un chef siempre estará recomendándole cortes, recetas y estilos de preparación, con el propósito de ofrecer una atención VIP y única en Maracaibo. Pero si de desayunos se trata, Cow tienta a sus clientes a hacerlo como todo un rey, con desayunos cinco estrellas.

(15)   "Quisimos hacer un sitio gourmet muy completo. Desayunos al estilo hotel, hamburguesas americanas, estación de cafés hechos por expertos, set de jugos y frutas, además de la carnicería," resaltó López.

Hamburguesas de otro mundo

Para quien ande en busca de la auténtica hamburguesa americana, Cow es el lugar indicado.
(20)   "En esta onda de hamburguesas gourmet, hacía falta una que representara el verdadero sabor de la hamburguesa. Por eso, en nosotros decidimos hacer las mejores", dijo Gamaliel López, gerente general del lugar.

Absolutamente todos los ingredientes son hechos por el restaurante, en donde además podrán comprar su combo "crudo" para preparar dichas hamburguesas en su propia casa. El pan, otra de las
(25)   grandes sensaciones de Cow, siempre está fresco y los expertos ya los pronostican como el mejor de la ciudad; pero bastará con visiten el lugar para que se den cuenta de todo por ustedes mismos.

Fuente 2: El siguiente gráfico presenta los resultados de una encuesta por la Universidad San Ignacio de Loyola en Perú. Los encuestados eran de diferentes edades y todos respondieron a la pregunta "¿A qué se debe la diversidad de nuestros platos?"

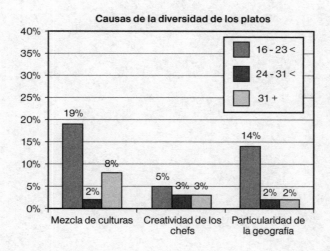

Fuente 3: La siguiente grabación es una entrevista entre un turista de la ruta gastronómica española y Ramón Inique, natural de Barcelona. La grabación dura aproximadamente dos minutos, quince segundos.

Track 35

Apuntes:

PART 5
Speaking Skills

General Considerations

Descriptions of the Speaking Tasks of the Exam

The speaking portion of the exam is divided into two tasks: Task 3: Conversation and Task 4: Cultural Comparison. Both tasks require that you showcase your ability to communicate effectively in Spanish in formal and informal situations. In Task 3: Conversation, you will engage in a simulated conversation. The context of this conversation could be formal or informal, and in your test book you will be given an outline indicating the flow of the conversation. For Task 4: Cultural Comparison, your task is to give a formal oral presentation on a specific topic. In your presentation, you need to compare a community from the Spanish-speaking world with your own community. The question you need to answer will be printed in your test book.

Scoring the Speaking Tasks

The grading of the speaking samples is holistic, meaning that they are analyzed as a whole. No specific item or aspect of language has any point value. Rankings proceed along a continuum from strong, good, fair, weak, and poor. The difference between each level largely hinges on your how well you complete the task. Here are some strategies when approaching the speaking portions of the exam:

- Read the introduction and understand the task you have been assigned to complete.
- For Task 3: Conversation, identify if the context is formal or informal. For Task 4: Cultural Comparison, remember to use a formal tone throughout.
- Address the task as fully as you can and make sure what you say is appropriate within the context of the task.
- Speak for the entire allotted time.
- Do not use English unless there is absolutely no Spanish equivalent.

10

Section II, Part B—Task 3: Conversation

The third task of Section II is the Conversation. For this task you are to participate in a simulated conversation. As you begin this task, you will be given a set of directions, an introduction to the conversation, and an outline showing you the flow of the conversation. You will have one minute to read the directions and one additional minute to read the introduction and outline of the conversation. In the outline, the shaded parts indicate the part of the conversation that has already been recorded, and your part is the unshaded part. Following the two minutes, the conversation will begin. Each speaking prompt will be given only once. After each time the other person speaks, you will have 20 seconds to record your response. You can expect to have to respond a total of 5 different times throughout the entire conversation. Typically you won't be expected to initiate the conversation.

Scoring Your Conversation

Your score will be based on how well you are able to accomplish this task and can roughly be broken into the following categories:

1. **What you were able to do.**
   - Did you maintain the exchange?
   - Was it clearly appropriate within the context of the task?
   - Did you provide all information with frequent elaboration?
   - Did you use an appropriate tone throughout?

2. **How you were able to do it.**
   - Were your responses fully comprehensible?
   - Did your use of language show some sophistication?

Remember that these two categories work together, and if you answered yes to all the above questions, your reply will score in the high range. One way to know if you are on the path to success is to put yourself in the shoes of the other person in this conversation. Was this a successful conversation? Did you receive all the information you needed? Was it fully comprehensible? If you answered yes to all of these questions, then you are on your way to earning a "5" on this task.

Strategies for Task 3: Conversation

Because of its design, this task is inherently the most artificial of the communicative tasks. It requires you to be able to think on your feet and be able to improvise quickly. One great way to prepare for this is to really immerse yourself in the role you have been asked to play. This will help you be more engaged in this conversation and could lead to a better score.

The following is a guideline about how you should budget your time.

Read the introduction and flow of the conversation (2 minutes).
- Identify with whom you will be conversing and any information about this person.
- Identify immediately the tone that you should use (formal or informal).

- Identify the context of this conversation and where it is taking place (home, school, a sporting event, and so on).
- Make note of any specific type of reactions you are expected to make. Jot down key words that may help you with this reaction. For example, if you are asked to respond negatively, you could jot down *No creo que* (then use the subjunctive). If you are asked to thank someone you could jot down *muchas gracias por* (then use the infinitive form of a verb).

As you speak (20 seconds per response).
- Follow the printed outline. Make a check mark after each prompt so you don't lose your place as you are speaking.
- Try to visualize the person with whom you are speaking. Speak with energy and emotion. If this person is supposed to be your friend, act like he or she is your friend. If this person is a teacher, act more formally and with more respect.
- Answer any questions directly. Do not repeat the question before you answer it.
- Speak for the entire 20 seconds. Do not leave long pauses.
- Speak calmly. Do not try to rush the information. If you sound nervous, the conversation will feel awkward.
- Elaborate often. Be creative with your responses and give lots of information.
- Correct yourself if you make a mistake.

What happens if during the conversation you fail to understand a question?
Because the speaking prompts are only spoken once, at times students may have difficulty understanding a question that was asked. If this happens, the best thing to do is to respond by telling the person that you did not understand the question and then use the rest of the response time to elaborate on something mentioned earlier. The worst thing you can do if you don't understand a question is to say "uhhh" or "ummm" or not say anything at all. This task is evaluating your speaking ability, and therefore you need to provide something that can be evaluated.

Useful Vocabulary

Here is a list of useful phrases and vocabulary that may come in handy during Task 3: Conversation.

To greet someone	*Buenos días* (formal) *Hola, ¿qué tal?* (informal)
To show positive emotion	*¡Qué bien!* *¡Cuánto me alegra!*
To suggest an idea	*Yo recomiendo que . . .* (+ present subjunctive) *Sería mejor que . . .* (+ imperfect subjunctive)
To respond negatively	*No creo que . . .* (+ present subjunctive) *Desafortunadamente no . . .* (+ present indicative)
To thank someone	*Muchas gracias por . . .* (+ infinitive verb) *Agradezco su (tu) . . .* (+ noun)
To end a conversation	*Tengo que irme. Nos vemos.* (Informal) *Adiós.* (Formal and informal) *Hasta luego.* (Formal and informal)

Sample Conversation

Below is a sample of a script similar to the sort you will see on the informal speaking part. Following the script are the steps you will follow to fulfill this part of the exam.

DIRECTIONS: You will now take part in a simulated conversation. First, you will have 1 minute to read a preview of the conversation, including the script for both parts. Then, the conversation will begin and follow the script. Each time it is your turn to speak, you will have 20 seconds to respond.

You should engage in the conversation as much and as appropriately as possible.

Ahora vas a participar en una conversación simulada. Primero, tendrás un minuto para leer la introducción y el esquema de la conversación. Después, empezará la conversación, siguiendo el esquema. Cada vez que te toque hablar, tendrás 20 segundos para responder.

Debes participar en la conversación de la forma más completa y apropiada posible.

1. **Tema curricular:** *La belleza y la estética*

    Tienes un minuto para leer la introducción y el esquema de la conversación.

> **Introducción:** Esta es una conversación con Paco, un amigo tuyo que te ha llamado pidiendo que lo llamaras. Quiere invitarte a un evento en tu escuela.

Track 36

Paco:	Contesta el teléfono.
Tú:	Salúdalo y explica la razón por tu llamada.
Paco:	Continúa la conversación.
Tú:	Reacciona apropiadamente.
Paco:	Continúa la conversación.
Tú:	Reacciona apropiadamente dando detalles.
Paco:	Continúa la conversación.
Tú:	Responde afirmativamente con detalles.
Paco:	Continúa la conversación.
Tú:	Finaliza los planes. Despídete.
Paco:	Concluye la conversación.

2. Note that in the exam, every time it is your turn to speak, you will have 20 seconds to do so. When the speaker finishes, you will hear a tone and then have 20 seconds to respond. The tone will sound at the end of 20 seconds indicating that you should stop speaking and listen to the next part. You should engage in the conversation as much as possible.

> **NOTE**
>
> For the purpose of this sample only, we are providing the following dialogue script with a sample conversation for your reference. You can practice speaking the sample responses, so that you can become more comfortable with the flow and pace of the conversation.

Paco:	Hola
Tú:	Hola Paco, ¿cómo estás? Hace much tiempo que no hablamos. ¿Cómo van las cosas? Acabo de salir de mi clase de ciencias. ¡Qué aburrido! El profesor no dejó de hablar y no contestó ninguna pregunta. Pero, no quiero molestarte con estas cosas. Te llamo porque recibí tu mensaje. Cuéntame, ¿qué novedad tienes?
Paco:	Ah, sí, gracias por llamarme. Querría invitarte a acompañarme a la escuela este fin de semana. Hay un drama buenísimo que se da, se llama *Sueño*.
Tú:	¿De veras? ¡Qué divertido! Ya sabes cuánto me fascinan las obras de teatro. No recuerdo la última vez que fui a una obra. He oído muy buenas cosas de esta obra, y no veo la hora de poder acompañarte. Muchas gracias por pensar en mí.
Paco:	Me dijeron que nuestro compañero de clase es fantástico en el drama. Interpreta el papel del rey. Como recuerdas, leímos una parte de este drama en la obra *La vida es sueño* en la clase de español hace un mes. Me gustaron esos versos de "¿Qué es la vida? Una ilusión,". . . etcétera.
Tú:	Miguel es un actor muy talentoso, y seguro que un día ganará el premio Oscar por una actuación suya. La verdad es que aunque recuerdo haber leído este drama, no puedo recordar muy bien la trama. Desafortunadamente no tengo tan buena memoria como tú.
Paco:	Sí, los otros de la clase ya han ido y dicen que les gustó. ¿Te gustaría ir conmigo? Te invito.
Tú:	Obviamente que me gustaría ir. Tengo unas tareas que completar antes pero seguro que voy a poder asistir contigo. Si la obra es tan buena como dicen los demás, va a ser una noche para no olvidar.
Paco:	¡Estupendo! Te encontraré enfrente del teatro a las siete.
Tú:	Perfecto. Entonces, por qué no planeamos tomar algo después. Ya sabes que no me gusta comer tan pronto, y creo que tendremos suficiente tiempo para tomarnos un cafecito. Mira, tengo que irme porque tengo un montón de tarea. Pero muchas gracias otra vez. Te veré el sábado.
Paco:	De acuerdo amigo. Nos vemos.

3. The recording is finished. You will check to see that your voice was recorded.

Now study the model above and complete the practice exercises that follow. This will give you enough practice, so that when you get to the exam, the task will be familiar to you. You can easily imagine your own sample conversations with a little practice. The more you practice, the more comfortable and relaxed you will be and the better your speech sample will be.

Conversation Practice Exercises

DIRECTIONS: You will now take part in a simulated conversation. First, you will have 1 minute to read a preview of the conversation, including the script for both parts. Then, the conversation will begin and follow the script. Each time it is your turn to speak, you will have 20 seconds to respond.

You should engage in the conversation as much and as appropriately as possible.

Ahora vas a participar en una conversación simulada. Primero, tendrás un minuto para leer la introducción y el esquema de la conversación. Después, empezará la conversación, siguiendo el esquema. Cada vez que te toque hablar, tendrás 20 segundos para responder.

Debes participar en la conversación de la forma más completa y apropiada posible.

Conversación 1

Tema curricular: *La vida contemporánea*

Tienes un minuto para leer la introducción y el esquema de la conversación.

Introducción: Tú estás de viaje. Te encuentras en una ciudad desconocida y te has perdido en el centro, no muy lejos del hotel. Tienes que preguntar a alguien cómo se llega al hotel. Entras en una tienda para preguntar a un dependiente cómo llegar allá.

Track 37

Dependiente:	Te salúda.
Tú:	Responde apropiadamente. Hazle una pregunta.
Dependiente:	Contesta a la pregunta. Te hace una pregunta.
Tú:	Responde que no tienes la dirección.
Dependiente:	Te pide otros nombres.
Tú:	Nómbrale otro lugar.
Dependiente:	Responde con otra pregunta.
Tú:	Dale otro descriptivo. Pídele la dirección.
Dependiente:	Te dice que la reconoce. Te instruye cómo llegar.
Tú:	Reacciona. Despídete del dependiente.

Conversación 2

Tema curricular: *Los desafíos mundiales*

Tienes un minuto para leer la introducción y el esquema de la conversación

> **Introducción:** Imagina que estás en una entrevista con un profesor tuyo para recibir una beca este verano para estudiar más a fondo un asunto relacionado con el medio ambiente.

Track 38

Profesor Sánchez:	Te saluda y empieza la conversación.
Tú:	Saluda y responde apropiadamente.
Profesor Sánchez:	Continúa la conversación y te hace otra pregunta.
Tú:	Contesta la pregunta ofreciendo detalles.
Profesor Sánchez:	Continúa la conversación y te hace otra pregunta.
Tú:	Contesta la pregunta con detalles.
Profesor Sánchez:	Continúa la conversación.
Tú:	Contesta negativamente, y ofrece una alternativa.
Profesor Sánchez:	Termina la conversación y se despide.
Tú:	Termina la conversación y despídete.

Conversación 3

Tema curricular: *Las identidades personales y públicas*

Tienes un minuto para leer la introducción y el esquema de la conversación.

Introducción: Tú eres un estudiante nuevo en una escuela. Tu familia acaba de mudarse a esta nueva ciudad y tú tienes que cultivar un nuevo grupo de amigos en la escuela.

Track 39

Cristina:	Saluda y te hace una pregunta.
Tú:	Saluda y responde apropiadamente.
Cristina:	Continúa la conversación y te hace otra pregunta.
Tú:	Reacciona apropiadamente con detalles.
Cristina:	Continúa la conversación y te hace otra pregunta.
Tú:	Contesta la pregunta con detalles.
Cristina:	Continúa la conversación y te invita a un evento.
Tú:	Contesta negativamente, y ofrece una alternativa.
Cristina:	Termina la conversación y se despide.
Tú:	Termina la conversación y despídete.

Conversación 4

Tema curricular: *La vida contemporánea*

Tienes un minuto para leer la introducción y el esquema de la conversación.

> **Introducción:** Este verano necesitas encontrar empleo para ahorrar dinero para la universidad. Tienes una entrevista con la gerenta de una compañía donde quieres obtener empleo. Imagina la conversación entre tú y la gerenta.

Track 40

Gerenta:	Te saluda.
Tú:	Responde apropiadamente.
Gerenta:	Te hace una pregunta.
Tú:	Explícale tus razones.
Gerenta:	Reacciona de buena manera. Te hace otra pregunta.
Tú:	Responde. Cuéntale algo que has hecho. Expresa tus esperanzas. Pregúntale cuánta experiencia hace falta para el trabajo.
Gerenta:	Te contesta. Te ofrece un puesto.
Tú:	Reacciona favorablemente. Acepta.
Gerenta:	Te responde
Tú:	Dale las gracias. Despídete de ella.

Conversación 5

Tema curricular: *La ciencia y la tecnología*

Tienes un minuto para leer la introducción y el esquema de la conversación.

> **Introducción:** Para la próxima edición del periódico de tu revista estudiantil necesitas entrevistar al director de la cafetería de su escuela porque los alumnos acaban de hacer una encuesta sobre la comida en la cafetería y la falta de comida nutritiva en el menú.

Track 41

Director:	Te saluda.
Tú:	Respóndele apropiadamente.
Director:	Comentario sobre sus relaciones con los estudiantes. Te hace una pregunta.
Tú:	Explícale el propósito de la visita. Hazle una pregunta.
Director:	Contesta a la pregunta.
Tú:	Cuéntale los resultados de la encuesta. Hazle otra pregunta.
Director:	Te hace una pregunta de respuesta.
Tú:	Comunica los deseos de los estudiantes.
Director:	Propone una idea.
Tú:	Reacciona favorablemente.
Director:	Responde con sus deseos.
Tú:	Despídete de él.

Conversación 6

Tema curricular: *Las familias y las comunidades*

Tienes un minuto para leer la introducción y el esquema de la conversación.

> **Introducción:** Imagina que ves a Luis durante el almuerzo un día. Está un poco molesto y tú quieres saber por qué.

Track 42

Tú:	Salúdale y pregunta por su estado de ánimo.
Luis:	Te informa de lo que lo está molestando.
Tú:	Reacciona y trata de consolarlo.
Luis:	Continúa la conversación y te hace otra pregunta.
Tú:	Contesta la pregunta con detalles.
Luis:	Continúa la conversación y te invita a un evento.
Tú:	Contesta la pregunta con detalles.
Luis:	Continúa la conversación y te invita a un evento.
Tú:	Contesta negativamente y ofrece una alternativa. Despídete.
Luis:	Termina la converación.

Conversación 7

Tema curricular: La belleza y la estética

Tienes un minuto para leer la introducción y el esquema de la conversación.

Introducción: Imagina que eres una estudiante y que estás en el norte, en febrero, y necesitas una blusa de cierto estilo para un papel en un drama en la escuela. Vas a comprarla. Entras en una tienda y hablas con una dependienta sobre lo que necesitas.

Track 43

Dependienta:	Se dirige a ti.
Tú:	Responde apropiadamente. Explícale lo que necesitas.
Dependienta:	Comenta sobre tu pedido. Comenta sobre la mercancía. Ofrece mostrártela.
Tú:	Agradécele. Dile lo que buscas en particular.
Dependienta:	Te sugiere algo. Te hace una pregunta.
Tú:	Contesta la pregunta. Expresa una preferencia. Hazle otra pregunta.
Dependienta:	Contesta. Expresa una opinión.
Tú:	Responde.
Dependienta:	Concluye el trato.
Tú:	Expresa gratitud.
Dependienta:	Te responde. Te invita a volver.

Conversación 8

Tema curricular: *La vida contemporánea*

Tienes un minuto para leer la introducción y el esquema de la conversación.

> **Introducción:** Imagina que trabajas en un restaurante. Un día un cliente entra para almorzar. Parece que es la primera vez que esta persona ha venido al restaurante.

Track 44

Tú:	Dirígete apropiadamente al cliente. Hazle una pregunta.
Cliente:	Responde. Pide más información.
Tú:	Responde. Hazle otra pregunta.
Cliente:	Te pide información.
Tú:	Nombra unos platos.
Cliente:	Te pide una sugerencia.
Tú:	Sugiere uno de los platos que acabas de nombrar. Descríbelo con más detalle.
Cliente:	Acepta tu sugerencia. Te hace una pregunta.
Tú:	Nombra la selección.
Cliente:	Completa tu selección.
Tú:	Termina la conversación.

Conversación 9

Tema curricular: *La ciencia y la tecnología*

Tienes un minuto para leer la introducción y el esquema de la conversación.

Introducción: Un día te despiertas con síntomas tan malos que no puedes asistir a tus clases. Tienes que llamar a la enfermera del consultorio de tu doctor para pedir una cita.

Track 45

Tú:	Suena el teléfono.
Enfermera:	Saluda.
Tú:	Responde apropiadamente. Explica el motivo de tu llamada.
Enfermera:	Te hace una pregunta.
Tú:	Explica tus síntomas.
Enfermera:	Te hace otras preguntas.
Tú:	Contesta. Haz una pregunta.
Enfermera:	Comenta sobre tu estado. Hace una pregunta.
Tú:	Explica que sí, pero con una condición.
Enfermera:	Responde.
Tú:	Responde apropiadamente. Despídete.
Enfermera:	Se despide.

Conversación 10

Tema curricular: *Las identidades personales y públicas*

Tienes un minuto para leer la introducción y el esquema de la conversación.

> **Introducción:** Imagina que estás en un café con tu amiga Carlota. Ella te pidió que la encontraras porque quiere hablarte de un problema que tiene.

Track 46

Tú:	Saluda y empieza la conversación.
Carlota:	Te explica su dilema.
Tú:	Reacciona y pídele más información.
Carlota:	Continúa la conversación y te hace una pregunta.
Tú:	Contesta la pregunta con detalles.
Carlota:	Continúa la conversación y te hace otra pregunta.
Tú:	Contesta la pregunta con detalles.
Carlota:	Continúa la conversación y te hace otra pregunta.
Tú:	Contesta negativamente explicando por qué. Termina la conversación y despídete.
Carlota:	Termina la conversación y se despide.

11

Section II, Part B—Task 4: Cultural Comparison

The final task of Section II is the Cultural Comparison. For this task you are to answer a question printed in your test book. In your response, you need to use an example from a community in the Spanish-speaking world and one from your own community as evidence to support your answer. You will have one minute to read the directions and four minutes to read the question and prepare your presentation. You then will have two minutes to present.

Scoring Your Cultural Comparison Presentation

Your score will be based on how well you answer the question and your knowledge of the target cultures. Your overall grade can be broken into the following categories:

1. **What you were able to do.**
   - Is your treatment of the topic clearly effective?
   - Do you clearly compare your own community with the target culture?
   - Do you demonstrate good understanding of the target culture?

2. **How you were able to do it.**
   - Was your response fully comprehensible?
   - Was your response well organized and cohesive?
   - Did your use of language show some sophistication?

As with all other tasks in Section II, these two categories work together. If you answered yes to all the above questions, your reply will score in the high range.

Strategies for Task 4: Cultural Comparison

Cultural knowledge is vital in your ability to answer this question. You can use information that you have learned from any source, including materials that you may have read; conversations with native speakers; programs on television, radio, and the internet; and any experiences that you may have had first-hand. The best way to be prepared to talk about the possible topics is by familiarizing yourself with as much culture from the Spanish-speaking world as possible.

The following is a guideline about how you should budget your time.

Read the introduction question (4 minutes).
   - Underline key words from the question.
   - Identify a key example from <u>one</u> Spanish-speaking community and one from your own community.
   - Create a flow chart like the following to help organize your ideas.

Palabras clave de la pregunta			
Evidencia			
	¿Dónde?	Descripción del ejemplo	¿Cómo responde a la pregunta?
Comunidad hispanohablante			
Mi comunidad			

As you speak (2 minutes).

- Relax! Your presentation does not have to be exhaustive. It simply is a sample that demonstrates that you have good knowledge of Spanish-speaking communities and your own community, and that you can present your ideas clearly and concisely.
- Organize your presentation with a brief introduction (10 seconds max.) in which you inform your audience of your topic.
- Begin your body with an example from the Spanish-speaking world. Use the flow chart as you present your ideas.
- Present your second example from your own community. Explain how it is similar to or different than the one used for the Spanish-speaking community.
- If you have time, give a conclusion. However, a conclusion is not necessary.
- Speak for the entire 2 minutes. Do not end too early and make sure you get in both examples before the 2 minutes expire.
- Correct yourself if you make a mistake.

It is quite difficult to give a detailed oral presentation in two minutes, and most students will not be able to finish within the allotted time. This does not mean, however, that your goal should be not to finish, but rather it should be to give the strongest presentation you can, regardless of whether or not you finish it in two minutes.

Useful Vocabulary

Just like with Task 2: Argumentative Essay, any formal presentation is enhanced by the use of transitional phrases. Here are some that will be helpful.

To introduce an idea	*Como punto de partida . . .* *Para empezar . . .*
To add to an idea	*Además . . .* *En segundo lugar . . .*
To explain an idea	*Por ejemplo . . .* *Para ilustrar . . .*
To contrast	*Por otro lado . . .* *Sin embargo . . .* *No obstante . . .*
To compare	*De la misma manera . . .*
To show a result	*Por consiguiente . . .* *Como resultado . . .* *Debido a lo anterior . . .*
To conclude or summarize	*Por fin . . .* *En suma . . .* *Para concluir . . .*

Sample Cultural Comparison Presentation

DIRECTIONS: You will now prepare an oral presentation for your class on a specific topic. You will have 4 minutes to read the topic and prepare your presentation. Then, you will have 2 minutes to record your presentation.

In your presentation, compare your own community to one of the Spanish-speaking world with which you are familiar. You should demonstrate your understanding of cultural features of the Spanish-speaking world. Your presentation should also be well organized.

Ahora vas a preparar una presentación oral para tu clase de español sobre un tema cultural. Primero, tendrás 4 minutos para leer el tema y preparar tu presentación. Después, tendrás 2 minutos para grabarla.

En tu presentación, compara tu comunidad con una del mundo hispanohablante con el que estés familiarizado. Debes demostrar tu comprensión de los aspectos culturales en el mundo hispanohablante. También, tu presentación debe ser bien organizada.

Tema curricular: Las familias y las comunidades

Tema de la presentación: ¿Qué papel tienen las compañías e instituciones privadas para mejorar el bienestar de una comunidad?

Compara tus observaciones de las comunidades en que has vivido con tus observaciones de una región del mundo hispanohablante que te sea familiar. Puedes referirte a lo que has estudiado, vivido, observado, etc.

Response

The first step is to read the directions to the task and the question. It is a good idea to underline key words so that you know exactly what you need to talk about. The questions will be very general by design, and therefore there are many ways to answer them. Your job is to come up with one good example from your own community and one from a Spanish-speaking country that answers the question. You need to move quickly and jot down a quick outline or flow chart. Here is an example of one way to answer the question above.

Palabras clave de la pregunta	*Compañías e instituciones privadas; mejorar el bienestar; comunidad*		
Evidencia			
	¿Dónde?	**Descripción del ejemplo**	**¿Cómo responde a la pregunta?**
Comunidad hispanohablante	*Colombia*	*Crépes y Waffles—restaurante que contrata a mujeres cabeza de familia*	*Beneficios: vivienda, seguro médico Oportunidad a las mujeres de superarse Confianza, mejora autoestima*
Mi comunidad	*Estados Unidos*	*Tom's Shoes—Compañía de zapatos Donación: sistema de agua sana; fundaciones ayudan a los sin techo*	*Ayuda a los clientes sentir que están contribuyendo a mejorar la comunidad*

Sample Speaking Response

The following is an example of an oral presentation. Note how it follows the flow chart above.

Buenos días. Estoy aquí para presentarles cómo las compañías e instituciones privadas mejoran el bienestar de una comunidad.

Como punto de partida, en Colombia hay una compañía que se llama Crépes y Waffles. Es una cadena de restaurantes cuyos empleados son mayormente mujeres cabeza de familia. Esta compañía no solo les ofrece a las mujeres una forma de mantener a su familia, sino también les ofrece muchos beneficios como el seguro médico y ayuda financiera adicional para poder comprarse una vivienda. Por consiguiente, estas mujeres tienen la oportunidad de superarse y esto ayuda a mejorar su confianza y autoestima. De la misma manera, en los Estados Unidos hay una compañía que se llama Tom's Shoes. Es una compañía que produce zapatos pero que también hace una donación por cada producto que alguien compra. Estas donaciones han ayudado a varias comunidades. Por ejemplo Tom's Shoes ha donado dinero para financiar un sistema de agua sana en barrios pobres y ha donado dinero a fundaciones que ayudan a los sin techo. Además de ayudar a las comunidades que reciben las donaciones, también ayuda a los clientes sentir que están contribuyendo a mejorar la comunidad mundial.

Para concluir, Tom's Shoes y Crépes y Waffles son ejemplos de compañías que actualmente tienen un impacto positivo en mejorar el bienestar de sus comunidades. Si más compañías tuvieran la misma consciencia social, el mundo sería un mejor lugar para todos. Muchas gracias por su amable atención.

Cultural Comparison Practice Exercises

Número 1

Tema curricular: Los desafíos mundiales

Tema de la presentación: ¿Qué impacto tienen los inmigrantes en la economía de un país?

> Compara tus observaciones acerca de las comunidades en las que has vivido con tus observaciones de una región del mundo hispanohablante que te sea familiar. En tu presentación, puedes referirte a lo que has estudiado, vivido, observado, etc.

Número 2

Tema curricular: Los desafíos mundiales

Tema de la presentación: ¿Cuál es la importancia de crear espacios naturales protegidos?

> Compara tus observaciones acerca de las comunidades en las que has vivido con tus observaciones de una región del mundo hispanohablante que te sea familiar. En tu presentación, puedes referirte a lo que has estudiado, vivido, observado, etc.

Número 3

Tema curricular: Los desafíos mundiales

Tema de la presentación: ¿Qué desafíos tienen que enfrentar las comunidades con respecto al tráfico?

> Compara tus observaciones acerca de las comunidades en las que has vivido con tus observaciones de una región del mundo hispanohablante que te sea familiar. En tu presentación, puedes referirte a lo que has estudiado, vivido, observado, etc.

Número 4

Tema curricular: Los desafíos mundiales

Tema de la presentación: ¿Quién es responsable por el bienestar social de una sociedad?

> Compara tus observaciones acerca de las comunidades en las que has vivido con tus observaciones de una región del mundo hispanohablante que te sea familiar. En tu presentación, puedes referirte a lo que has estudiado, vivido, observado, etc.

Número 5

Tema curricular: La ciencia y la tecnología

Tema de la presentación: ¿Cuál es el impacto del uso de teléfonos inteligentes en una comunidad?

> Compara tus observaciones acerca de las comunidades en las que has vivido con tus observaciones de una región del mundo hispanohablante que te sea familiar. En tu presentación, puedes referirte a lo que has estudiado, vivido, observado, etc.

Número 6

Tema curricular: La ciencia y la tecnología

Tema de la presentación: ¿Cuál es la actitud de la gente con respecto a mantener un equilibrio entre el avance y el bienestar de nuestro planeta?

> Compara tus observaciones acerca de las comunidades en las que has vivido con tus observaciones de una región del mundo hispanohablante que te sea familiar. En tu presentación, puedes referirte a lo que has estudiado, vivido, observado, etc.

Número 7

Tema curricular: La ciencia y la tecnología

Tema de la presentación: ¿Cuál es la actitud de la gente con respecto al impacto del ser humano en los fenómenos naturales?

> Compara tus observaciones acerca de las comunidades en las que has vivido con tus observaciones de una región del mundo hispanohablante que te sea familiar. En tu presentación, puedes referirte a lo que has estudiado, vivido, observado, etc.

Número 8

Tema curricular: La ciencia y la tecnología

Tema de la presentación: ¿Cuál es la actitud de la gente con respecto a los avances en la ciencia y la tecnología?

> Compara tus observaciones acerca de las comunidades en las que has vivido con tus observaciones de una región del mundo hispanohablante que te sea familiar. En tu presentación, puedes referirte a lo que has estudiado, vivido, observado, etc.

Número 9

Tema curricular: La vida contemporánea

Tema de la presentación: ¿Cuál es la actitud de la gente con respecto a tener un título universitario?

> Compara tus observaciones acerca de las comunidades en las que has vivido con tus observaciones de una región del mundo hispanohablante que te sea familiar. En tu presentación, puedes referirte a lo que has estudiado, vivido, observado, etc.

Número 10

Tema curricular: La vida contemporánea

Tema de la presentación: ¿Qué aspectos del tiempo libre y del ocio valoran más los jóvenes?

> Compara tus observaciones acerca de las comunidades en las que has vivido con tus observaciones de una región del mundo hispanohablante que te sea familiar. En tu presentación, puedes referirte a lo que has estudiado, vivido, observado, etc.

Número 11

Tema curricular: La vida contemporánea

Tema de la presentación: Al viajar a otro país para conocer mejor su cultura, ¿qué consideraciones son importantes tener en cuenta?

Compara tus observaciones acerca de las comunidades en las que has vivido con tus observaciones de una región del mundo hispanohablante que te sea familiar. En tu presentación, puedes referirte a lo que has estudiado, vivido, observado, etc.

Número 12

Tema curricular: La vida contemporánea

Tema de la presentación: ¿Qué importancia tienen las tradiciones en una comunidad?

Compara tus observaciones acerca de las comunidades en las que has vivido con tus observaciones de una región del mundo hispanohablante que te sea familiar. En tu presentación, puedes referirte a lo que has estudiado, vivido, observado, etc.

Número 13

Tema curricular: Las identidades personales y públicas

Tema de la presentación: ¿Qué importancia tienen las figuras históricas en el orgullo nacional de un país?

Compara tus observaciones acerca de las comunidades en las que has vivido con tus observaciones de una región del mundo hispanohablante que te sea familiar. En tu presentación, puedes referirte a lo que has estudiado, vivido, observado, etc.

Número 14

Tema curricular: Las identidades personales y públicas

Tema de la presentación: ¿Qué elementos de una cultura mejor definen su identidad?

Compara tus observaciones acerca de las comunidades en las que has vivido con tus observaciones de una región del mundo hispanohablante que te sea familiar. En tu presentación, puedes referirte a lo que has estudiado, vivido, observado, etc.

Número 15

Tema curricular: Las identidades personales y públicas

Tema de la presentación: ¿Qué aspectos de la vida cotidiana influencian la autoestima de una persona?

Compara tus observaciones acerca de las comunidades en las que has vivido con tus observaciones de una región del mundo hispanohablante que te sea familiar. En tu presentación, puedes referirte a lo que has estudiado, vivido, observado, etc.

Número 16

Tema curricular: Las identidades personales y públicas

Tema de la presentación: ¿Cuál es la actitud de la gente con respecto a aprender una lengua extranjera?

Compara tus observaciones acerca de las comunidades en las que has vivido con tus observaciones de una región del mundo hispanohablante que te sea familiar. En tu presentación, puedes referirte a lo que has estudiado, vivido, observado, etc.

Número 17

Tema curricular: Las familias y las comunidades

Tema de la presentación: ¿De qué forma han cambiado las estructuras de la familia?

Compara tus observaciones acerca de las comunidades en las que has vivido con tus observaciones de una región del mundo hispanohablante que te sea familiar. En tu presentación, puedes referirte a lo que has estudiado, vivido, observado, etc.

Número 18

Tema curricular: Las familias y las comunidades

Tema de la presentación: ¿Cuál ha sido la influencia de redes sociales en las relaciones interpersonales?

Compara tus observaciones acerca de las comunidades en las que has vivido con tus observaciones de una región del mundo hispanohablante que te sea familiar. En tu presentación, puedes referirte a lo que has estudiado, vivido, observado, etc.

Número 19

Tema curricular: Las familias y las comunidades

Tema de la presentación: ¿Qué beneficios aportan la vida urbana y la campestre?

Compara tus observaciones acerca de las comunidades en las que has vivido con tus observaciones de una región del mundo hispanohablante que te sea familiar. En tu presentación, puedes referirte a lo que has estudiado, vivido, observado, etc.

Número 20

Tema curricular: Las familias y las comunidades

Tema de la presentación: ¿Cuál es la actitud de la gente con respecto a comer juntos?

Compara tus observaciones acerca de las comunidades en las que has vivido con tus observaciones de una región del mundo hispanohablante que te sea familiar. En tu presentación, puedes referirte a lo que has estudiado, vivido, observado, etc.

Número 21

Tema curricular: La belleza y la estética

Tema de la presentación: ¿Qué influencia tienen las películas y programas de televisión a la cultura de la gente?

> Compara tus observaciones acerca de las comunidades en las que has vivido con tus observaciones de una región del mundo hispanohablante que te sea familiar. En tu presentación, puedes referirte a lo que has estudiado, vivido, observado, etc.

Número 22

Tema curricular: La belleza y la estética

Tema de la presentación: ¿Qué importancia tiene la música en la vida de los jóvenes?

> Compara tus observaciones acerca de las comunidades en las que has vivido con tus observaciones de una región del mundo hispanohablante que te sea familiar. En tu presentación, puedes referirte a lo que has estudiado, vivido, observado, etc.

Número 23

Tema curricular: La belleza y la estética

Tema de la presentación: ¿De dónde viene la inspiración para la creación artística?

> Compara tus observaciones acerca de las comunidades en las que has vivido con tus observaciones de una región del mundo hispanohablante que te sea familiar. En tu presentación, puedes referirte a lo que has estudiado, vivido, observado, etc.

Número 24

Tema curricular: La belleza y la estética

Tema de la presentación: ¿Qué función tiene el arte en reflejar la vida y los valores de una sociedad?

> Compara tus observaciones acerca de las comunidades en las que has vivido con tus observaciones de una región del mundo hispanohablante que te sea familiar. En tu presentación, puedes referirte a lo que has estudiado, vivido, observado, etc.

PART 6
Practice Tests

ANSWER SHEET
Practice Test 1

Section 1: Part A

1. Ⓐ Ⓑ Ⓒ Ⓓ
2. Ⓐ Ⓑ Ⓒ Ⓓ
3. Ⓐ Ⓑ Ⓒ Ⓓ
4. Ⓐ Ⓑ Ⓒ Ⓓ
5. Ⓐ Ⓑ Ⓒ Ⓓ
6. Ⓐ Ⓑ Ⓒ Ⓓ
7. Ⓐ Ⓑ Ⓒ Ⓓ
8. Ⓐ Ⓑ Ⓒ Ⓓ

9. Ⓐ Ⓑ Ⓒ Ⓓ
10. Ⓐ Ⓑ Ⓒ Ⓓ
11. Ⓐ Ⓑ Ⓒ Ⓓ
12. Ⓐ Ⓑ Ⓒ Ⓓ
13. Ⓐ Ⓑ Ⓒ Ⓓ
14. Ⓐ Ⓑ Ⓒ Ⓓ
15. Ⓐ Ⓑ Ⓒ Ⓓ
16. Ⓐ Ⓑ Ⓒ Ⓓ

17. Ⓐ Ⓑ Ⓒ Ⓓ
18. Ⓐ Ⓑ Ⓒ Ⓓ
19. Ⓐ Ⓑ Ⓒ Ⓓ
20. Ⓐ Ⓑ Ⓒ Ⓓ
21. Ⓐ Ⓑ Ⓒ Ⓓ
22. Ⓐ Ⓑ Ⓒ Ⓓ
23. Ⓐ Ⓑ Ⓒ Ⓓ
24. Ⓐ Ⓑ Ⓒ Ⓓ

25. Ⓐ Ⓑ Ⓒ Ⓓ
26. Ⓐ Ⓑ Ⓒ Ⓓ
27. Ⓐ Ⓑ Ⓒ Ⓓ
28. Ⓐ Ⓑ Ⓒ Ⓓ
29. Ⓐ Ⓑ Ⓒ Ⓓ
30. Ⓐ Ⓑ Ⓒ Ⓓ

Section 1: Part B

31. Ⓐ Ⓑ Ⓒ Ⓓ
32. Ⓐ Ⓑ Ⓒ Ⓓ
33. Ⓐ Ⓑ Ⓒ Ⓓ
34. Ⓐ Ⓑ Ⓒ Ⓓ
35. Ⓐ Ⓑ Ⓒ Ⓓ
36. Ⓐ Ⓑ Ⓒ Ⓓ
37. Ⓐ Ⓑ Ⓒ Ⓓ
38. Ⓐ Ⓑ Ⓒ Ⓓ
39. Ⓐ Ⓑ Ⓒ Ⓓ

40. Ⓐ Ⓑ Ⓒ Ⓓ
41. Ⓐ Ⓑ Ⓒ Ⓓ
42. Ⓐ Ⓑ Ⓒ Ⓓ
43. Ⓐ Ⓑ Ⓒ Ⓓ
44. Ⓐ Ⓑ Ⓒ Ⓓ
45. Ⓐ Ⓑ Ⓒ Ⓓ
46. Ⓐ Ⓑ Ⓒ Ⓓ
47. Ⓐ Ⓑ Ⓒ Ⓓ
48. Ⓐ Ⓑ Ⓒ Ⓓ

49. Ⓐ Ⓑ Ⓒ Ⓓ
50. Ⓐ Ⓑ Ⓒ Ⓓ
51. Ⓐ Ⓑ Ⓒ Ⓓ
52. Ⓐ Ⓑ Ⓒ Ⓓ
53. Ⓐ Ⓑ Ⓒ Ⓓ
54. Ⓐ Ⓑ Ⓒ Ⓓ
55. Ⓐ Ⓑ Ⓒ Ⓓ
56. Ⓐ Ⓑ Ⓒ Ⓓ
57. Ⓐ Ⓑ Ⓒ Ⓓ

58. Ⓐ Ⓑ Ⓒ Ⓓ
59. Ⓐ Ⓑ Ⓒ Ⓓ
60. Ⓐ Ⓑ Ⓒ Ⓓ
61. Ⓐ Ⓑ Ⓒ Ⓓ
62. Ⓐ Ⓑ Ⓒ Ⓓ
63. Ⓐ Ⓑ Ⓒ Ⓓ
64. Ⓐ Ⓑ Ⓒ Ⓓ
65. Ⓐ Ⓑ Ⓒ Ⓓ

Practice Test 1

Section I: Part A—Interpretive Communication: Print Texts

TIME: APPROXIMATELY 40 MINUTES

DIRECTIONS: Read the following passages. After each passage there are a number of questions for you to answer, based on the information provided in the reading selection. For each question, choose the response that is best according to the selection and mark your answer on the answer sheet.

Lee los siguientes textos. Cada texto va acompañado de varias preguntas que debes contestar, según la información en el texto. Para cada pregunta, elige la mejor respuesta según el contexto y escríbela en la hoja de respuestas.

Selección 1

Tema curricular: Las familias y las comunidades

Introducción: El siguiente fragmento, que trata de un rito de pasaje, proviene del cuento Pequeñeces por P. Luis Coloma.

La orquesta dio principio al acto, tocando magistralmente la obertura de *Semíramis*. El rector, anciano religioso, honra y gloria de la *Línea* Orden a que pertenecía, pronunció después un
(5) breve discurso, que no pudo terminar. Al fijarse sus apagados ojos en aquel montón de cabecitas rubias y negras, que atentamente le miraban, apiñadas y expresivas como los angelitos de una gloria de Murillo, comenzó a balbucear, y las lágri-
(10) mas le cortaron la palabra.

—¡No lloro porque os vais!—pudo decir, al cabo—. ¡Lloro porque muchos no volverán nunca! . . .

La nube de cabecitas comenzó a agitarse nega-
(15) tivamente y un aplauso espontáneo y bullicioso brotó de aquellas doscientas manitas, como una protesta cariñosa que hizo sonreír al anciano en medio de sus lágrimas.

El secretario del colegio comenzó a leer enton
(20) ces los nombres de los alumnos premiados: levantábanse estos ruborosos y aturdidos por el miedo a la exhibición y la embriaguez del triunfo; iban a recibir la medalla y el diploma de manos del arzobispo, entre los aplausos de los compañeros,
(25) los sones de la música y los bravos del público, y volvían presurosos a sus sitios, buscando con la vista en los ojos de sus padres y de sus madres la mirada de inmenso cariño y orgullo legítimo, que era para ellos complemento del triunfo.

1. ¿Qué evento narra este fragmento?

   (A) Una fiesta religiosa
   (B) Un concierto de música clásica
   (C) La otorgación de premios después de un concurso
   (D) Una celebración escolar

2. ¿Por qué no pudo terminar el rector su discurso?

   (A) Se conmovió.
   (B) Vio una aparición.
   (C) Alguien lo interrumpió.
   (D) Se le olvidó lo que iba a decir.

3. ¿A qué se refieren las "cabecitas" (líneas 6 y 14)?

   (A) A unos ángeles
   (B) A una obra de arte
   (C) A los jóvenes
   (D) A los padres

4. ¿Qué adjetivo mejor describe la relación entre el rector y el público al que habla?

   (A) Odiosa
   (B) Indiferente
   (C) Hostil
   (D) Afectuosa

5. ¿Quiénes son los "premiados" (línea 20)?

   (A) Jóvenes universitarios
   (B) Niños pequeños
   (C) Miembros de la iglesia
   (D) Ex miembros de una escuela

6. ¿Qué emoción predomina en este fragmento?

   (A) Tristeza
   (B) Alegría
   (C) Nostalgia
   (D) Molestia

7. ¿Cuál de lo siguiente sería o más probable que ocurriera inmediatamente después de esta escena?

   (A) El comienzo de las clases
   (B) Un sermón de regaño
   (C) Un festejo entre familiares
   (D) Un recorrido musical por diferentes estilos

Selección 2

Tema curricular: La vida contemporánea

Introducción: La siguiente fuente es un anuncio de una compañía en el sector de viajes que les pueda interesar a sus clientes.

Ahora, visitar a familiares y amigos le cuesta hasta un 35 por ciento menos de nuestras tarifas ya rebajadas. Aeronaves quiere celebrar con
Línea usted su nuevo y cómodo servicio a Mérida,
(5) México, y a Tegucigalpa, Honduras, vía Houston, ¡con tarifas superespeciales! Y para celebrar en grande, se han rebajado las tarifas a todas las ciudades que sirve en Latinoamérica. Pero apúrese, porque debe comprar sus boletos de
(10) ida y vuelta, mínimo 7 días antes de viajar, y sólo tiene hasta el 8 de febrero para comprarlos. La nueva y comodísima terminal internacional de Aeronaves en el aeropuerto hace más fácil que nunca viajar a Latinoamérica, incluyendo los
(15) trámites de aduana e inmigración. Además, cada vez que viaja con Aeronaves, gana millaje con nuestro programa Número Uno, una de las maneras más rápidas de ganar viajes gratis. ¡Inscríbase y comience a ganar!
(20) Estas tarifas están basadas en la compra de boletos de ida y vuelta, los que deben adquirirse no más tarde del 8 de febrero, o sea una semana en adelante. Los boletos deben comprarse un mínimo de 7 días antes de viajar. La máxima
(25) estadía es de 60 días y todos los viajes deben terminar el 23 de marzo del año actual, o antes. El importe de los boletos no es reembolsable. Hay un cargo de US$75 si se hacen determinados cambios en las reservaciones. Solicite los detalles.
(30) Estas tarifas son para viajes que se originan en Tejas. El servicio a Guayaquil comenzará el 6 de febrero. Estas tarifas están sujetas a la aprobación del gobierno y pueden cambiar sin previo aviso.

8. ¿Qué anuncia esta selección?

(A) Maneras de conseguir viajes gratuitos con el programa Número Uno
(B) Una nueva manera de facilitar los trámites de aduana e inmigración
(C) Consejos para saber cuándo es mejor comprar boletos aéreos
(D) Una venta de vuelos con destino a unos países al sur de EE.UU.

9. ¿Con qué motivo se promueve esta oferta?

(A) Celebra el Año de la Familia.
(B) Celebra el establecimiento del programa Número Uno.
(C) Celebra su nuevo servicio del nuevo aeropuerto.
(D) Celebra iniciar vuelos con destinos distintos para la línea.

10. Una persona puede aprovechar esta oferta con tal de que . . .

(A) compre el boleto sin hacer ningunos cambios en el itinerario.
(B) se salga rumbo al sur de Tejas en el viaje.
(C) se inscriba en el programa Número Uno.
(D) permanezca más de dos meses en su destino.

11. Si por alguna razón una persona no puede usar el boleto, ¿qué recurso tiene?

(A) Se puede recibir un reembolso por el precio del boleto.

(B) Se puede cambiarlo con un pago adicional.

(C) Se puede usarlo para recibir un descuento en otro boleto.

(D) No se ofrecen reembolsos ni modificaciones.

12. ¿En qué mes habría aparecido este texto?

(A) En el mes de enero

(B) En el mes de febrero

(C) En el mes de marzo

(D) En el mes de abril

Selección 3

Tema curricular: Los desafíos mundiales

Fuente 1

Introducción: El siguiente artículo trata del envejecimiento de la población en España. El artículo original fue publicado en Eroski Consumer en 2005.

Abuelos en adopción

El envejecimiento de España se ha convertido en una realidad creciente. La población mayor de 65 años en nuestro país es siete veces mayor
Línea que la registrada a comienzos del siglo XX. En
(5) concreto, más de siete millones de españoles se hallan dentro de la denominada tercera edad y más de un millón, el 20%, vive solo todo el año, una cifra que se multiplica durante los meses de verano. Para ellos, la soledad se ha convertido
(10) en uno de los problemas más graves al que se enfrentan, tanto es así que según las estadísticas les preocupa más que otras cuestiones como la salud y las pensiones tan ajustadas que reciben muchos de ellos.

(15) El papel que en la actualidad ocupan nuestros mayores poco tiene que ver con el de generaciones anteriores. Diluido el concepto de 'barrio,' sobre todo en las grandes ciudades, donde incluso se les trataba de 'Don,' las rela-
(20) ciones humanas en los núcleos urbanos se han modificado y ha dejado de ser habitual que, por ejemplo, los vecinos se dirijan a ellos para preguntarles si necesitan algo.

La ONG Solidarios, consciente de esta nece-
(25) sidad de compañía tan demandada por los mayores, trabaja desde el año 1995 con más de 600 voluntarios en el programa 'Acompaña-miento de ancianos,' del que se benefician cerca de 1.000 ancianos en todo el país. Su iniciativa
(30) consiste en poner en contacto a la persona que ofrece la compañía y al anciano que demanda un acompañante.

A esta preparación se suman los 'cursos de cuidados,' centrados en las tareas prácticas
(35) que deben llevar a cabo en su compañía; cómo promover actividades de ocio, conocimientos

básicos para los más enfermos, minusválidos o personas con discapacidad física y mental.

Una vez seleccionada la pareja, el programa
(40) fija en dos horas el tiempo que deben pasar juntos. En ese tiempo el voluntario se adapta a los deseos o necesidades de la persona mayor: puede acompañarle al médico, realizar trámites administrativos, llevarle a una cafetería con sus
(45) amigos o quedarse en casa charlando con él. La ONG advierte de que no se puede superar este tiempo de compañía. No obstante, el voluntario suele hacer un seguimiento de su pareja por telé-fono, le pregunta sobre su salud, si ha tomado la
(50) medicación, etc.

Respecto a la financiación del proyecto, éste cuenta con la colaboración de Iberdrola para promocionar la campaña de ayuda a los mayores 2005 y cubrir los gastos mínimos de transporte
(55) de los voluntarios y las necesidades más urgentes de los ancianos: taxis adaptados, sus traslados en metros y autobuses, etc.

Fuente 2

Introducción: La siguiente tabla presenta la tasa de dependencia en España en 2012 y la predicción para el año 2052. Se basa en datos del Instituto Nacional de Estadísticas de 2012.

Años	Mayores de 64 años	Menores de 16 años	Total (menores de 16 y mayores de 64 años)
2012	26,14	24,25	50,39
2022	33,30	24,81	58,11
2032	45,24	22,49	67,73
2042	62,23	24,27	88,50
2052	73,09	26,41	99,50

La tasa de dependencia se expresa en porcentaje. Las cifras representan la relación entre la población de menores de 16 años y mayores de 64 años por cada 100 miembros de la población entre 16 años y 64 años.

13. ¿Cuál es el propósito del artículo impreso?

(A) Presentar la situación demográfica en España en este momento
(B) Analizar cómo se puede afrontar el envejecimiento en España
(C) Informar sobre una iniciativa para ayudar a los de tercera edad
(D) Resumir las causas y efectos del envejecimiento en general

14. ¿Qué usa el autor para apoyar sus afirmaciones iniciales?

(A) Datos específicos
(B) Testimonios de los de tercera edad
(C) Opiniones de varios expertos
(D) Sólo usa su propia convicción

15. ¿A qué se refiere el número 20% (línea 7)?

(A) Al porcentaje de población mayor en relación a la población española
(B) Al incremento de la población de tercera edad desde el siglo XX
(C) Al porcentaje de la población mayor de 65 años que vive sola durante el verano
(D) Al porcentaje de gente de tercera edad que tiene que cuidarse sola

16. Según el artículo, ¿qué cambios se han notado en la sociedad en general?

(A) Los de tercera edad tienden a ser más independientes.
(B) El vínculo entre los residentes de una comunidad no es tan estrecha como antes.
(C) Hay menos recursos para la gente mayor de 65 años.
(D) La población mayor de 65 años se enferma más que anteriormente.

17. ¿Qué ofrece la ONG Solidarios a los de tercera edad?

(A) Apoyo emocional y financiero
(B) Cursos de capacidades básicas
(C) Compañerismo afectuoso
(D) Oportunidades de servir como voluntarios en la comunidad

18. ¿Qué se puede deducir es la función primaria de los acompañantes?

(A) Desarrollar una relación personal
(B) Proveer ayuda médica
(C) Comunicarse con su pareja diariamente
(D) Darles apoyo emocional

19. ¿Cómo financia la ONG Solidarios los gastos de su programa?

    (A) Recibe dinero de los mayores.
    (B) Recauda fondos con la ayuda de otra compañía.
    (C) Los voluntarios pagan sus propios gastos.
    (D) Depende de la caridad de otras organizaciones.

20. ¿Cuál de las siguientes afirmaciones mejor resume el artículo?

    (A) Hay un crecimiento de programas en España para darles apoyo a los que más lo necesitan.
    (B) Se necesitarán más jóvenes voluntarios en los próximos años para ayudar con los problemas sociales.
    (C) Hay que entrenar bien a los voluntarios para que cumplan debidamente con las tareas asignadas.
    (D) Continuará habiendo un aumento en el número de gente de tercera edad que necesitará ayuda personal.

21. ¿Qué información presenta la tabla?

    (A) Los aumentos constantes en tasa de dependencia de cada población estudiada
    (B) El incremento de porcentaje de población total española que dependerá de los demás
    (C) El crecimiento de la población total en España
    (D) El aumento de los sectores demográficos de España en relación a la Unión Europea

22. Según la tabla, ¿qué pasará en 2022?

    (A) La mayoría de la población se encontrará en edad de trabajar.
    (B) 58,11% de la población total será inactiva.
    (C) Por cada 10 personas en edad de trabajar, habrá casi 6 que dependerán de ellos.
    (D) Habrá más mayores para cuidar a los menores de 16 años.

23. ¿Cuál de las siguientes afirmaciones es correcta según el artículo y la tabla?

    (A) Se necesitarán ampliar programas de cuidado para los mayores de 64 años durante las próximas décadas.
    (B) Con el aumento de la población joven, habrá más voluntarios para cuidar a los de tercera edad.
    (C) El incremento de jubilados significa que habrá más trabajo para los que están en edad de trabajar.
    (D) Los menores de 16 años formarán parte del grupo de voluntarios para cuidar a los de tercera edad.

Selección 4

Tema curricular: Las familias y las comunidades

Introducción: Este texto es una carta de Julio a sus padres.

Queridos y amados padres:

Estoy en la azotea de mi casa y contemplo un hermoso atardecer de noviembre, los campos ya se están secando y el color dorado aparece por
Línea doquier, los recuerdos se agolpan en mi mente,
(5) ahora que soy joven, voy madurando poco a poco como esos campos que ahora contemplo, que con tanto ahínco cuida el labrador; así pienso en ustedes amados padres, cuanto amor, cuanto cariño, cuanto esmero han puesto en mí para ser
(10) el joven que soy ahora con una vida por delante, con un campo lleno de ilusiones.

A papá por enseñarme a amar a mi prójimo, gracias por enseñarme a ser fuerte y no doblegarme ante una derrota, gracias también por
(15) hacer de mi un hombre que desea triunfar y forjar la templanza en todo mi ser.

A ti mamá, por inculcarme la ternura, el amor y el deseo inmenso de verme un triunfador que sepa dar afecto, amor, regalar caricias, abrazos,
(20) y sobre todo saber apreciar las cosas que nos da la vida.

Quiero que sepan que los amo, los aprecio, los adoro y este amor que les tengo, no se podría pagar ni con todo el oro del mundo, por que es
(25) amor único.

Termino estas líneas viendo el horizonte y hermoso atardecer, donde muere el día y empieza la oscura noche, solo que en mi vida nace la esperanza y el deseo inmenso de vivir para agradecer
(30) a Dios el tenerlos y disfrutar de su presencia.

Padre, madre, benditos sean ahora y siempre.

Con cariño su hijo:

Julio

24. ¿Para qué les escribe esta carta el autor a sus padres?

   (A) Para informarles de unos planes que tiene previstos
   (B) Para gratificarles por todo lo que le han hecho
   (C) Para despedirse de ellos antes de irse
   (D) Para compartir su creencia y fe

25. ¿Con qué relaciona el cuidado que sus padres le dieron?

   (A) Con la casa en que vive actualmente
   (B) Con la fe que tiene
   (C) Con la persistencia de los campesinos
   (D) Con los triunfos que experimentó en la vida

26. ¿A qué se refiere el autor de la carta cuando escribe ". . . un campo lleno de ilusiones" (líneas 11–12)?

   (A) Al entusiasmo que tiene por la vida futura
   (B) A la vista casi irreal de su casa
   (C) Al tamaño del campo que tiene delante
   (D) A la cantidad de trabajo que tiene que hacer

27. ¿Qué características suyas les atribuye a sus padres?

   (A) A su padre, el cariño; a su madre, el amor
   (B) A su padre, la fortaleza; a su madre, su compasión
   (C) A su padre, el respeto por los héroes; a su madre, el deseo de triunfar
   (D) A su padre, la prudencia; a su madre, la tenacidad

28. ¿Qué perspectiva cultural predomina en la carta?

   (A) La creencia religiosa
   (B) El amor a los demás
   (C) El valor del trabajo duro
   (D) La solidaridad en la familia

29. ¿Qué figura retórica incluye el autor en su carta para comunicar sus ideas?

   (A) Metáfora
   (B) Símil
   (C) Cacofonía
   (D) Repetición

30. Según la carta, ¿cuál de las siguientes afirmaciones mejor describe la personalidad del autor?

   (A) Es solitario.
   (B) Es cauteloso.
   (C) Es optimista.
   (D) Es valiente.

Section I: Part B—Interpretive Communication: Print and Audio Texts (Combined)

TIME: APPROXIMATELY 55 MINUTES

DIRECTIONS: You will listen to several audio selections. The first two also include print texts. When there is a print text, you will have an additional amount of time to read it.

For each audio selection, you will have a designated amount of time to read the introduction of the selection and to preview the questions and answers that follow. Each audio selection will be played twice.

Following the first listening, you will have one minute to begin answering the questions. After the second listening, you will be given 15 seconds per question to finish answering. For each question, select the best answer according to the selection and mark your answer on your answer sheet.

Vas a escuchar a varias grabaciones. Las primeras dos van acompañadas de textos escritos. Cuando hay un texto escrito, tendrás tiempo adicional para leerlo.

Para cada selección auditiva, vas a tener un tiempo determinado para leer la introducción de la selección y prever las preguntas que siguen. Vas a escuchar cada fuente auditiva dos veces.

Después de escuchar cada selección la primera vez, vas a tener un minuto para empezar a contestar las preguntas. Después de escucharla la segunda vez, vas a tener 15 segundos por pregunta para terminarlas. Para cada pregunta, elige la mejor respuesta según el contexto y escríbela en la hoja de respuestas.

Selección 1

Tema curricular: La familia y las comunidades

Fuente 1: Primero tienes un minuto para leer la fuente número 1.

Introducción: El siguiente gráfico presenta los pasos recomendados para poder elegir una universidad. Se basa en información publicada en *Guiat.net*

Track 47

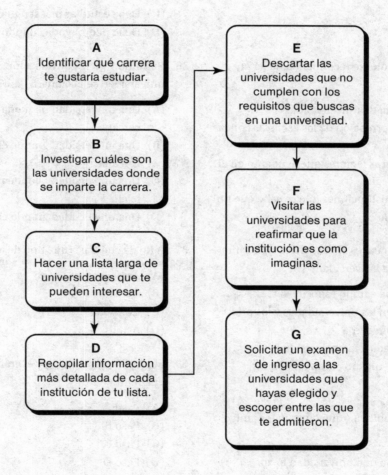

A
Identificar qué carrera te gustaría estudiar.

B
Investigar cuáles son las universidades donde se imparte la carrera.

C
Hacer una lista larga de universidades que te pueden interesar.

D
Recopilar información más detallada de cada institución de tu lista.

E
Descartar las universidades que no cumplen con los requisitos que buscas en una universidad.

F
Visitar las universidades para reafirmar que la institución es como imaginas.

G
Solicitar un examen de ingreso a las universidades que hayas elegido y escoger entre las que te admitieron.

Fuente 2: Ahora tienes un minuto para leer la introducción y prever las preguntas.

Introducción: La siguiente fuente auditiva trata de una conversación entre Raúl, un estudiante, y el Sr. Gómez, su consejero. Hablan del futuro estudiantil de Raúl. La grabación dura aproximadamente tres minutos.

31. Según el gráfico, ¿cuándo se debe profundizar la investigación de la universidad a la que uno piensa asistir?

    (A) En el paso B
    (B) En el paso C
    (C) En el paso D
    (D) En el paso F

32. Según el gráfico, ¿qué se recomienda hacer en el paso E?

    (A) Reducir la lista de universidades
    (B) Pedir más información de las escuelas con las que hay duda
    (C) Considerar otros factores que ayudarán en el proceso de elegir
    (D) Eliminar las instituciones que se sabe que no van a admitirle

33. Según el gráfico, ¿cuál es el paso más importante en seleccionar una universidad?

    (A) Decidir en qué campo especializarse
    (B) Investigar bien las universidades y los programas que ofrecen
    (C) Solicitar entrada a las universidades
    (D) Identificar las que no cumplen con tus requisitos

34. Según la fuente auditiva, ¿qué querían los amigos de Raúl?

    (A) Que asistiera a una universidad local
    (B) Que los acompañara a una universidad pequeña
    (C) Que consultara con el Sr. Gómez acerca de la situación
    (D) Que escogiera una universidad preferida por ellos

35. Según la conversación, ¿qué problema debe remediar Raúl este año?

    (A) Debe entregar su tarea a tiempo.
    (B) Debe tratarles a sus profesores con más respeto.
    (C) Debe estudiar más lenguas.
    (D) Debe pedir ayuda cuando la necesita.

36. Basándote en la conversación, ¿qué tipo de universidad seleccionará Raúl?

    (A) Una universidad pequeña en una ciudad cercana
    (B) Una universidad grande en una ciudad cercana
    (C) Una universidad pequeña en una ciudad lejana
    (D) Una universidad grande en una ciudad lejana

37. A fin de cuentas, ¿qué tipo de alumno es Raúl?

    (A) Arrogante
    (B) Considerado
    (C) Consciente
    (D) Astuto

38. Según la conversación y el gráfico, ¿en qué paso se encuentra Raúl?

    (A) Paso A
    (B) Paso B
    (C) Paso C
    (D) Paso D

PRACTICE TEST 1

Selección 2

Tema curricular: Los desafíos mundiales

Fuente 1: Primero tienes cuatro minutos para leer la fuente número 1.

Introducción: El siguiente fragmento trata de la agricultura de la civilización incaica. Fue publicada en la página web *www.holistica2000.com*.

Track 48

La destrucción de la agricultura incaica—Fragmento.

Por Antonio Elio Brailovsky y Dina Foguelman
(*www.holistica2000.com.ar/ecocolumna226.htm*)

El imperio incaico fue un espectacular ejemplo de eficiencia en el manejo de la tierra y en el respeto al equilibrio ecológico de la región.
Línea Ningún sistema posterior consiguió alimen-
(5) tar a tanta población sin degradar los recursos naturales. Los incas basaron su civilización en una relación armónica con su ambiente natural, integrado por los frágiles ecosistemas andinos, y desarrollaron complejos y delicados mecanis-
(10) mos tecnológicos y sociales que les permitieron lograr una sólida base económica sin deterioros ecológicos.

Se pueden ver aún las terrazas de cultivo, construidas como largos y angostos peldaños
(15) en los faldeos de las montañas, sostenidos por piedras que retenían la tierra fértil. Las terrazas cumplían la función de distribuir regularmente la humedad. Allí el agua de lluvia iba filtrándose lentamente desde los niveles superiores a los
(20) inferiores, utilizándose plenamente la escasa cantidad de líquido disponible. En las áreas más lluviosas y en las de mayor pendiente, las terrazas permitían evitar la erosión, al impedir que el escurrimiento superficial del agua de lluvia
(25) arrastrara las partículas del suelo. También facilitaron el aprovechamiento de los diversos pisos ecológicos.

El suelo de las terrazas se mezclaba con guano, el excremento de aves marinas acumulado en las
(30) islas y costas. Este recurso era cuidadosamente administrado, porque de él dependía en buena medida la alimentación de la población: para extraerlo, cada aldea tenía asignada una parte de isla o costa, marcada con mojones de piedra
(35) que no era permitido alterar.

Había muy poco suelo que fuera naturalmente apto para el cultivo y había que construirlo metro a metro. Había que ir a buscar el agua a las nacientes de los arroyos y encauzarla mediante una red
(40) de canales. A veces, al cruzar un valle, era necesario sostener el canal sobre columnas para que el nivel del agua no perdiese altura, construyéndose acueductos similares a los romanos.

Fuente 2: Tienes dos minutos para leer la introducción y prever las preguntas.

Introducción: Esta grabación titulada *El uso del suelo en América Latina* trata de las tendencias en la agricultura latinoamericana. Se basa en un artículo publicado en la página web *www.eurosur.org*. La grabación dura aproximadamente tres minutos, veinte segundos.

39. ¿Cuál es el propósito del artículo impreso?

   (A) Narrar la ruina de un antiguo sistema de agricultura
   (B) Presentar las características del cultivo de la tierra de los incas
   (C) Elogiar las innovaciones de la civilización incaica
   (D) Promover el uso sostenible de tierras como hicieron nuestros antepasados

40. ¿Qué impacto tuvo la agricultura de los incas a su alrededor?

   (A) Cambió la frecuencia de lluvias en distintas zonas.
   (B) Disminuyó los recursos naturales del área.
   (C) Perjudicó al medioambiente.
   (D) Se mantuvo en equilibrio con el entorno.

41. Según el artículo, ¿cuál era un beneficio del uso de las terrazas?

   (A) Suministraban el flujo de agua.
   (B) Aseguraban que el guano se escurriera.
   (C) Facilitaban el acceso a la cosecha.
   (D) Debilitaba las laderas de las montañas.

42. En el artículo, ¿a qué se refiere la frase "de él dependía en buena medida la alimentación de la población" (líneas 31–33)?

   (A) Al guano, que servía de alimento para la gente incaica.
   (B) Al ambiente en que vivían las aves, que les proveían comida a las aldeas.
   (C) Al administro del excremento, para asegurar que hubiera suficiente para el cultivo.
   (D) Al suelo que se mezclaba con guano, que sin él no era suficientemente fértil.

43. ¿Cuál de los siguientes adjetivos mejor describiría a los Incas en cuanto a su agricultura?

   (A) Innovadores
   (B) Trabajadores
   (C) Inconscientes
   (D) Explotadores

44. Según la fuente auditiva, ¿qué cambio se ha notado en la agricultura de América Latina?

   (A) Se han encontrado más áreas de cultivo.
   (B) Particularmente en Brasil y en México, se ha reducido la cantidad de tierra cultivable.
   (C) Se cultivan diferentes plantas ahora que anteriormente.
   (D) Más tierras están siendo designadas para la agricultura.

45. Según la fuente auditiva ¿qué impacto tiene la ganadería?

   (A) Ha impulsado la creación de ranchos.
   (B) Es en parte responsable por la reducción de los bosques.
   (C) Ha ayudado a incrementar las tierras destinadas al cultivo.
   (D) Ha llegado a ocupar más de 50% de las tierras de cultivo de América Latina.

46. ¿A qué se refiere la fuente auditiva cuando dice que las actividades agropecuarias ". . . tienen mayor incidencia sobre el medio ambiente . . ."?

   (A) A que las actividades que ocurren en zonas no urbanas son más dañinas
   (B) A que muchas actividades en este sector se encuentran en zonas peligrosas
   (C) A que las actividades en este sector mayormente tienen lugar encima de la tierra
   (D) A que son las que más impactan el entorno

47. ¿Qué predicción hace la fuente auditiva en cuanto al futuro de la agricultura?

    (A) Que no habrá suficiente tierra cultivable para sostener el cultivo
    (B) Que habrá modificaciones del suelo por el uso de productos químicos
    (C) Que será cada vez más caro poder expandir las tierras cultivables
    (D) Que el uso de la genética mejorará el rendimiento de producción agrícola

48. Imagina que quieres escribir un informe que contiene las ideas presentadas en las dos fuentes, ¿cuál de las siguientes publicaciones sería más apropiada?

    (A) *El impacto del cultivo de frijoles y maíz en América Latina*
    (B) *Implementando prácticas agrarias del pasado para superar retos del presente*
    (C) *Teorías sobre la destrucción de nuestras tierras cultivables*
    (D) *El cultivo de la soja y la ganadería: el futuro de comestibles para una población creciente*

Selección 3

Tema curricular: La belleza y la estética

Primero tienes un minuto para leer la introducción y prever las preguntas.

Introducción: La siguiente entrevista, titulada *Concurso de hip hop en Colombia,* trata de un evento de música en Colombia. La entrevista original fue publicada por Radio Naciones Unidas el 31 de mayo de 2012 en Estados Unidos. La grabación dura aproximadamente tres minutos.

Track 49

49. ¿Cuál es el propósito del concurso?

   (A) Mostrar cómo el hip hop les ha cambiado la vida a unos jóvenes colombianos
   (B) Difundir mensajes positivos por el hip hop
   (C) Promover la seguridad y convivencia
   (D) Presentar los diversos estilos musicales de varias regiones de Colombia

50. ¿Quiénes pueden participar en este evento?

   (A) Artistas musicales y visuales de varias ciudades
   (B) Músicos hip hop de distintos países
   (C) Jóvenes a quienes les gusta la música hip hop
   (D) Todos los interesados en el género del hip hop

51. ¿En qué se va a enfocar el festival?

   (A) En exponer los diferentes temas asignados
   (B) En presentar a los ganadores del concurso
   (C) En grabar la música de los artistas
   (D) En convertirse en un nuevo evento nacional

52. Según la entrevistada, ¿qué representa el hip hop para los jóvenes?

   (A) Es una forma en que pueden expresarse.
   (B) Es una manera en que aprenden de temas que no conocen.
   (C) Es una oportunidad para sobresalir en la sociedad.
   (D) Es una herramienta que les trae mucha belleza en su vida.

53. ¿Qué más se espera de este evento?

   (A) Que se reduzca el consumo de drogas durante el concurso
   (B) Que la gente cambie su opinión de los jóvenes
   (C) Que los jóvenes entiendan que el hip hop trae beneficios
   (D) Que se repita este evento en años sucesivos

Selección 4

Tema curricular: Las identidades personales y públicas

Primero tienes un minuto para leer la introducción y prever las preguntas.

Introducción: Esta grabación titulada El *Popol Vuh* dura aproximadamente tres minutos.

Track 50

54. ¿Qué narra el *Popol Vuh*?

   (A) La historia de una tribu mexicana

   (B) La procedencia de los maya quiché

   (C) La conversión de los indígenas al cristianismo

   (D) La conquista de los indígenas por los españoles

55. ¿De qué materia se crearon los hombres?

   (A) De materia vegetal

   (B) De la tierra del altiplano

   (C) De los dioses gemelos de la muerte

   (D) Del aliento de Hunahpú y Xbalanqué

56. ¿Cómo era el primer texto impreso después de la conquista española?

   (A) Apareció en lengua quiché.

   (B) Fue una traducción al español.

   (C) Tomó la antigua forma pictórica.

   (D) Incluyó ambas lenguas a la vez.

57. ¿Dónde se conserva una copia del primer libro impreso en español y quiché?

   (A) En la universidad de Guatemala

   (B) En una ciudad estadounidense

   (C) En Francia, donde un abad francés lo dejó

   (D) En España, donde un padre dominicano lo depositó

58. ¿Por qué se tradujo el título del *Popol Vuh* a "Libro del Consejo"?

   (A) Hace referencia a los reyes indígenas.

   (B) Hace referencia a los orígenes de los linajes indígenas.

   (C) Hace referencia a la autoridad de los gobernantes de las tribus.

   (D) Hace referencia a la narrativa de la creación del mundo.

Selección 5

Tema Curricular: La vida contemporánea

Primero tienes un minuto para leer la introducción y prever las preguntas.

> **Introducción:** La siguiente grabación es una entrevista con José Antonio de Urbina, diplomático y autor del libro *El arte de invitar*. La grabación dura aproximadamente tres minutos, cuarenta segundos.

Track 51

59. ¿A quién se dirige este experto del protocolo internacional?

(A) A los presidentes de naciones
(B) A cualquier deseosa de asegurar que los huéspedes se sientan cómodos
(C) A los directores de protocolo contratados para organizar cenas
(D) A los anfitriones de huéspedes ilustres en funciones formales

60. ¿Cuál es el propósito de tener un protocolo?

(A) Para que el hombre sea tratado como si fuera rey en su casa
(B) Para que todos los invitados al Palacio Real se comporten cortésmente
(C) Para facilitar la comunicación y respetar la dignidad de cada persona
(D) Para que una persona se sienta cómoda al aceptar una invitación

61. ¿Dónde debe sentarse a una pareja o a un matrimonio?

(A) Siempre se coloca al hombre cerca de una señora o señorita guapa.
(B) Hay que colocar a la señora al lado de otra para que puedan conversar.
(C) Hay que alternar los géneros para promocionar conversación.
(D) Es buena idea separarlos para evitar disputas durante la cena.

62. ¿Por qué no se debe sentar a una mujer en las puntas de la mesa?

(A) Es poco cortés.
(B) Es reservado para los hombres.
(C) Es para parejas.
(D) Es mala suerte.

63. ¿Qué se puede hacer cuando un invitado no puede venir, y el número de invitados queda en trece?

(A) Se puede matar a uno de los invitados.
(B) Se puede invitar a dos personas más y contar con la ausencia de una.
(C) Se puede invitar a otro amigo íntimo al último momento.
(D) Se puede retractar la invitación de otro invitado.

64. ¿Con qué autoridad habla esa persona en la narrativa?

   (A) Ha estudiado el protocolo del Palacio Real Español.
   (B) Es un embajador español.
   (C) Ha vivido y trabajado en el Palacio Real.
   (D) Ha organizado eventos para el Palacio Real.

65. Imagina que tienes que dar una presentación oral sobre el mismo tema y quieres investigarlo más. ¿Cuál de los siguientes libros sería más apropiado citar?

   (A) *Organización de reuniones y eventos*
   (B) *El manual de buenos modales*
   (C) *Como evitar incomodidades en una amistad*
   (D) *Pasos para elevar la autoestima de los demás*

Section II—Interpersonal Writing: Email Reply

TIME: 15 MINUTES

DIRECTIONS: You will write a reply to an email that you received. You have 15 minutes to read the message and write your reply.

Your reply should include an appropriate greeting and closing and should answer all the questions and requests in the original message. In addition, your reply should ask for more details about something that was mentioned in the message. You should use a formal tone in your response.

Vas a escribir una respuesta a un mensaje de correo electrónico. Tienes 15 minutos para leer el mensaje y escribir tu respuesta.

Tu respuesta debe incluir un saludo y despedida apropiados y contestar a todas las preguntas y peticiones del mensaje original. También tu respuesta debe pedir más información de algo mencionado en el mensaje original. Debes usar el tono formal en tu respuesta.

Tema curricular: Las identidades personales y públicas

Introducción: El siguiente mensaje electrónico es de tu profesor a quien le has pedido que te escribiera una carta de recomendación para enviarla con tu solicitud de ingreso a una universidad.

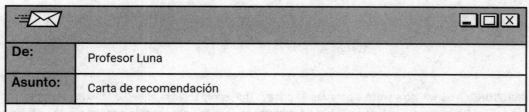

De: Profesor Luna

Asunto: Carta de recomendación

Apreciados/as estudiantes,

Primero quiero tomar la oportunidad de agradecerles por haberme pedido que les escriba su carta de recomendación para la universidad. Es una parte integral de su solicitud a la universidad y entre todos los profesores que podían haber escogido, me siento muy orgulloso de que me hayan seleccionado a mí. Es un trabajo en que pongo mucho esfuerzo y ánimo y dedico a cada carta la atención que merece.

Como parte de este proceso, siempre me gusta conocer un poco mejor a mis estudiantes. Tengo bien claro lo que pueden hacer académicamente, pero no tanto el aspecto personal, por ejemplo sus creencias e intereses. Por eso me gustaría que tomaran el tiempo para considerar las siguientes preguntas y que me contesten individualmente con sus respuestas con ejemplos si pueden:

- ¿A qué tipo de persona admiran ustedes? ¿Qué cualidades creen son importantes en una persona? ¿Por qué?

- ¿Creen que ustedes encarnan estas mismas cualidades? ¿Por qué sí o no?

Debo salir para una conferencia en dos días así que me harían un gran favor si me pudieran mandar sus respuestas lo más antes posible para que tenga la oportunidad de contemplarlas durante mi viaje.

Saludos cordiales,

Profesor Eduardo Luna

Section II—Presentational Writing: Argumentative Essay

TIME: APPROXIMATELY 55 MINUTES

Track 52

DIRECTIONS: You will now write a persuasive essay. The essay topic is based on the following three print and audio sources. First, you will have 6 minutes to read the essay topic and the printed sources. Next, you will hear the audio material twice. Then, you will have 40 minutes to plan and write your essay.

In your essay you should make reference to specific information from the three source materials. Do not simply summarize what is contained in the sources. Incorporate them into your essay and cite them in the proper manner. In addition, you should also clearly present your own viewpoints on the topic and defend them thoroughly. Your essay should be organized into clear paragraphs and you should use appropriate vocabulary and grammar.

Ahora vas a escribir un ensayo persuasivo. El tema del ensayo se basa en las siguientes fuentes escritas y auditivas. Primero, tendrás 6 minutos para leer el tema del ensayo y las fuentes impresas. Después, vas a escuchar la fuente auditiva dos veces. Finalmente, tendrás 40 minutos para planear y escribir tu ensayo.

En tu ensayo, debes hacer referencia a información específica de las tres fuentes. Debes evitar simplemente resumir la información de las fuentes. Incorpóralas en tu ensayo e identifícalas apropiadamente. Además, debes presentar claramente tus propios puntos de vista y defenderlos bien. Tu ensayo debe ser organizado en distintos párrafos bien desarrollados y debes usar vocabulario y gramática apropiados.

Tema curricular: La vida contemporánea

Primero tienes 6 minutos para leer el tema del ensayo, la fuente número 1 y la fuente número 2.

Tema del ensayo: ¿Se debería permitir el uso de inteligencia artificial (IA) en las escuelas?

Fuente 1

Introducción: El siguiente artículo se trata de la preocupación del uso de inteligencia artificial por los estudiantes. Fue publicado en la página web de la Biblioteca Nacional del Congreso de Chile en septiembre de 2023.

Inteligencia Artificial Generativa impacta la Educación

Una de las principales preocupaciones es que los estudiantes puedan utilizar herramientas de inteligencia artificial generativa para hacer
Línea trampa o plagiar sus tareas escritas y exámenes.
(5) De hecho, una encuesta reciente entre estudiantes universitarios encontró que casi uno de cada tres estudiantes había utilizado alguna forma de IA, como un software de generación de ensayos, para completar sus estudios.
(10) Aproximadamente un tercio de los estudiantes universitarios encuestados (tamaño de muestra 1000) en los EE. UU. han utilizado el chatbot de IA como ChatGPT para completar tareas escritas, y el 60 % utiliza el programa en más de la mitad
(15) de sus tareas.

El tipo ChatGPT de herramientas de inteligencia artificial generativa es capaz de imitar la escritura humana, y algunos estudiantes la usan para hacer trampa. El estudio encontró que el 75% de
(20) los estudiantes cree que usar el programa para hacer trampa está mal, pero aun así lo hace, y casi el 30% cree que sus profesores desconocen el uso de la herramienta. El estudio también señaló que algunos profesores están considerando incluir
(25) ChatGPT en sus lecciones o unirse a llamadas para prohibir, y el 46% de los estudiantes dicen que sus profesores o instituciones han prohibido la herramienta para las tareas. Esto ha llevado a solicitar regulaciones y sanciones más estric-
(30) tas por mala conducta académica que involucre a la IA.

Otra preocupación es que el uso de la IA generativa pueda provocar una disminución de las habilidades de escritura y pensamiento crítico
(35) de los estudiantes, a medida que se vuelven más dependientes de herramientas automatizadas para completar su trabajo. Algunos académicos sostienen que esto podría tener un impacto negativo en la calidad de la educación y, en última
(40) instancia, perjudicar los resultados de aprendizaje de los estudiantes.

Estas preocupaciones han llevado a algunas universidades a prohibir el uso de IA generativa en sus programas académicos. Ocho de las 24
(45) universidades del prestigioso Russell Group del Reino Unido han declarado el uso del robot de IA para tareas como mala conducta académica, incluidas Oxford y Cambridge. Mientras tanto, muchas otras universidades de todo el mundo se
(50) apresuran a revisar sus políticas contra el plagio citando preocupaciones sobre la integridad académica. Algunas universidades australianas han tenido que modificar sus procedimientos de examen y evaluación para volver a utilizar lápiz
(55) y papel.

Sin embargo, también hay quienes sostienen que la IA generativa tiene el potencial de revolucionar la educación y mejorar la experiencia de aprendizaje de los estudiantes. Por ejemplo, algunos
(60) expertos sugieren que la IA generativa podría usarse para brindar retroalimentación y apoyo personalizados a los estudiantes, ayudándolos a identificar áreas de debilidad y mejorar sus habilidades de manera adaptativa.

Fuente 2

Introducción: El siguiente gráfico presenta los resultados de una encuesta global de si se debería prohibir el uso de inteligencia artificial en las escuelas. Se basa en los resultados de una encuesta realizada por Ipsos en 2023.

¿Debería ser Prohibido el uso de IA, Incluso Chat GPT, en las Escuelas?

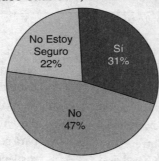

8.071 encuestados en 29 países entre junio 23 y julio 7 de 2023 por Ipsos.

Track 53

Fuente 3

Introducción: El siguiente audio, titulado "Inteligencia artificial en la educación", fue publicado por Innovación Educativa, una iniciativa de la Universidad Peruana de Ciencias Aplicadas. Fue publicado en septiembre de 2023 y dura aproximadamente tres minutos.

Section II—Interpersonal Speaking: Conversation

TIME: APPROXIMATELY 10 MINUTES

Track 54

DIRECTIONS: You will now take part in a simulated conversation. First, you will have 1 minute to read a preview of the conversation, including the script for both parts. Then, the conversation will begin and follow the script. Each time it is your turn to speak, you will have 20 seconds to respond.

You should engage in the conversation as much and as appropriately as possible.

Ahora vas a participar en una conversación simulada. Primero, tendrás un minuto para leer la introducción y el esquema de la conversación. Después, empezará la conversación, siguiendo el esquema. Cada vez que te toque hablar, tendrás 20 segundos para responder.

Debes participar en la conversación de la forma más completa y apropiada posible.

Tema curricular: La vida contemporánea

Tienes un minuto para leer la introducción y el esquema de la conversación.

Introducción: Esta es una conversación con Eva, una amiga tuya que te llama y te dice que sus padres acaban de darle permiso para invitarte a Florida durante las vacaciones escolares de primavera.

Eva:	Te saluda y te da las noticias.
Tú:	Salúdala y reacciona a sus noticias. Pide detalles.
Eva:	Continúa la conversación.
Tú:	Reacciona apropiadamente. Hazle una pregunta.
Eva:	Continúa la conversación.
Tú:	Ponte de acuerdo con ella. Agrega un deseo propio.
Eva:	Continúa la conversación.
Tú:	Reacciona apropiadamente.
Eva:	Continúa la conversación y te ofrece una alternativa.
Tú:	Acepta apropiadamente. Despídete.
Eva:	Concluye la conversación.

Section II—Presentational Speaking: Cultural Comparison

TIME: APPROXIMATELY 6 MINUTES

DIRECTIONS: You will now prepare an oral presentation for your class on a specific topic. You will have 4 minutes to read the topic and prepare your presentation. Then, you will have 2 minutes to record your presentation.

In your presentation, compare your own community to one of the Spanish-speaking world with which you are familiar. You should demonstrate your understanding of cultural features of the Spanish-speaking world. Your presentation should also be well organized.

Ahora vas a preparar una presentación oral para tu clase de español sobre un tema cultural. Primero, tendrás 4 minutos para leer el tema y preparar tu presentación. Después, tendrás 2 minutos para grabarla.

En tu presentación, compara tu comunidad con una del mundo hispanohablante con la que estés familiarizado. Debes demostrar tu comprensión de los aspectos culturales en el mundo hispanohablante. También, tu presentación debe estar bien organizada.

Tema curricular: Las identidades personales y públicas

Tema de la presentación: ¿Qué importancia tienen los deportes en una comunidad?

Compara tus observaciones de las comunidades en que has vivido con tus observaciones de una región del mundo hispanohablante que te sea familiar. Puedes referirte a lo que has estudiado, vivido, observado, etc.

Answers Explained

1. **(D)** The text clearly makes reference to a school in lines 19, 20, and 23 "colegio," "alumnos," and "diploma." The text also indicates that this is a celebratory event in line 23 with the words "diploma" and "medalla" (medal). Don't be fooled by option (A). It is not a religious event, even though the celebration does take place at a religious school.

2. **(A)** The verb "conmoverse" means *to become emotional*, which is clearly seen in line 10 when "las lágrimas le cortaron la palabra" (tears stopped his speech) and the word "lloro" (I cry) in line 11. Options (B) and (C) are incorrect because there is nothing to suggest that he saw an apparition or a ghost of some sort or that he was interrupted by someone else. Option (D) is incorrect because he didn't forget what he wanted to say.

3. **(C)** The word "cabecitas" is the diminutive form of the word "cabeza" and means *little head*s. This is in clear reference to the heads of the young students who are about to receive their diplomas. Option (A) is incorrect because they are human, not angels. Option (B) is incorrect because, although the narrator compares the students to little angels in a Murillo painting, they are still real humans and not images. Option (D) is clearly incorrect because the parents are tertiary figures in this fragment and are not little, as the word "cabecitas" suggests.

4. **(D)** The whole tone is one of affection, making option (D) the best answer. Options (A) and (C) are incorrect because they convey an emotion that is completely contrary to that in this text, and option (B) is incorrect because the rector, or headmaster, clearly loves these children who are about to graduate.

5. **(B)** The word "premiado" is the adjective of "premio," which means *prize*. Therefore, those who receive the prize, in this case the diploma and medals, are the students. Option (B) is the best answer also because in question 3 we saw that the narrator, when referencing the students, uses the words "cabecitas" and "angelitos," which clearly suggest that they are younger students and there-fore cannot be "Jóvenes universitarios," or option (A).

6. **(B)** Don't be fooled by the emotions at the beginning of the fragment, but rather look at the text as a whole, which is what this question is asking you to do. Although the "rector" (headmaster) becomes emotional, the students react in applause (lines 14–16), which makes him smile ("sonreír," line 17). There is more applause in line 24, as well as references to proud parents (lines 27–28) and being triumphant (line 23). All this clearly makes this a joyous occasion, which makes option (B) the best answer.

7. **(C)** After a graduation, most families gather to celebrate, thus making option (C) the most logical answer. Option (A) is clearly incorrect because this event celebrates the end of the school year, not the beginning. Option (B) is incorrect because, although a sermon could happen, it certainly would not be one of *scolding* ("regaño"). Option (D) is not the best answer because, although the ensuing celebrations could include a showcase of different musical styles, there is nothing in the text to suggest that this would be the case.

8. **(D)** The text is announcing an extra special sale to all cities in Latin America (lines 6–8), making option (D) the best answer. Option (A) is incorrect because, even though there is a program called "Número Uno," it is an ongoing program and not something new, whereas the sale is. Option (B) is incorrect because the new airport is what provides this service, not the air company. Option (C) is incorrect because all information about dates is in reference to the conditions of the sale, not general advice about when to travel.

9. **(D)** Lines 3 through 6 make reference to the new service to several cities in Central America via Houston, making D the best answer. Don't be fooled by option (C), which seems similar, but it states that the airport is new, and there is nothing in the text that explicitly says this. There is a new terminal in the airport (line 12), but the airport itself is not new.

10. **(B)** The advertisement is promoting sales to all cities in Latin America that the airline serves, therefore making option (B) the best answer because they are all located south of Texas. Although these are roundtrip tickets, the ad suggests that the departure is from Houston. Option (A) is incorrect because changes can be made, for a charge. Option (C) is incorrect because passengers can receive an additional benefit by signing up with "Número Uno," but their signing up is not a condition of this offer. Option (D) is clearly incorrect because the text says that the maximum stay ("máxima estadía," lines 24–25) has to be 60 days, or no more than two months.

11. **(B)** This information is provided in lines 28 and 29 ("Hay un cargo de US$75 si se hacen determinados cambios . . .").

12. **(A)** The advertisement mentions that the route will begin in February (line 32) and that the trip has to end by the 23rd of March (line 26). Therefore, it makes sense that the announcement would be made before this time, which leaves January as the only logical option out of the four.

13. **(C)** The majority of the text presents the work of the nonprofit organization *Solidarios* (line 24) and their program *Acompañamiento de ancianos*, making option (C) the best answer. Option (A) is incorrect because the focus is on the elderly persons and not demographics in general in Spain. Option (B) is incorrect because the article does not argue how one can tackle the problem of taking care of the elderly, but rather describes a program that exists. Option (D) is incorrect because the article does not provide any cause or effects of aging in general.

14. **(A)** In addition to providing some statistics of the number of volunteers involved (lines 26–27) and the number of elderly who have benefited from this program (lines 28–29), the text also provides examples of the types of activities the nonprofit organization offers. This clearly makes option (A) the best answer.

15. **(D)** The key here is the information that follows the percentage ("vive solo todo el año," lines 7 and 8). Option (C) is incorrect because it implies

that this only happens part of the year (during the summer), and the other two options relate to information presented before these statements.

16. **(B)** This information can be found in lines 15 to 23, where the text informs how the role of the elderly in today's society is very different than in the past. Option (A) is incorrect because, although many elderly persons may live alone, this is not by choice and the reader can infer that many cannot be independent and need assistance from the outside world. Option (C) is incorrect because the rest of the article clearly talks about a program aimed toward helping the elderly, and option (D) is incorrect as there is nothing in the article suggesting that today's elderly are more prone to becoming sick than elderly people in the past.

17. **(C)** The key word here is "compañerismo" (camaraderie, or one who shares in activities with another), which is what the nonprofit offers. This information can be found in lines 29 through 50. Option (A) is incorrect because the nonprofit does not offer monetary support to the elderly. Option (B) is incorrect because, although this option is offered by the nonprofit, it is only for the most sick and disabled, thus limited to a subgroup of the elderly. Option (D) is incorrect because the elderly are not the volunteers.

18. **(A)** This is another example of thinking about what is the *best* answer. The volunteers help the elderly with a number of tasks and check in on them. This makes the relationship more personal in that the volunteers must know the needs and schedule of the person they are caring for. Option (B) is not the best answer because volunteers themselves do not provide medical assistance, but they accompany the elderly person to a medical appointment. Option (C) is not the best answer because there is nothing in the text that says they have to communicate daily. Option (D) is not the best answer because, although emotional support may be given to the elderly, this is not the primary function of the volunteer.

19. **(B)** This information can be found in lines 51–56 where the text refers to the collaboration with Iberdrola to cover the costs. Even if you don't

know what Iberdrola is, the fact that the first letter is capitalized tells you that this is a proper noun, which likely is the name of a company.

20. **(D)** Although this question comes toward the end, the answer can be found at the beginning of the text. In lines 1–2 the text states that the aging of Spain is a growing reality, and therefore you can comfortably assume that this will be a problem that will continue to grow and, given the change in the role of society and its relationship with the elderly, more and more elderly people will need personal help.

21. **(B)** This information can be found in the introduction and the description of the table. The percentages are the people who will need to rely financially on others (working people). Option (A) is incorrect because the increase is not consistent among all age groups ("Menores de 16 años" will experience a decrease within 20 years). Option (C) is incorrect because it refers to the entire population of Spain, and not those who will need to rely on others. Option (D) is incorrect because the table makes no reference to other European countries.

22. **(C)** This question will evaluate if you really understand the information in the table. The table presents the expected percentage of the population that will depend on those who are working. Therefore, those over 64 and under 16 won't be working, and, in 2022, 58% of those who will not be working (or 6 out of 10) will rely financially on those who do. Option (A) is incorrect because the majority of people will be outside of the working age population. Option (B) is incorrect because there is nothing to suggest that they will be inactive simply because they will not be working. Option (D) is incorrect because there is nothing to suggest that the elderly will take care of those under 16.

23. **(A)** Both the article and the table show how the percentage of elderly will continue to increase in Spain and, therefore, there will be a bigger need for assistance in the upcoming years. Options (B) and (D) are incorrect because they suggest a willingness on the part of the youth that cannot be supported by the text (we don't know if they will

want to or if they can serve as volunteers). Option (C) is incorrect because there is no evidence that the higher number of retirements will lead to more job openings.

24. **(B)** This answer should be pretty clear after reading lines 13 through 22, where Julio thanks his parents for all they have done.

25. **(C)** This information can be found in lines 4 through 12, where Julio relates his own growth to that of the fields, comparing the care his parents showed him to the workers who care for the fields.

26. **(A)** Remember that the word "ilusión" means *hope* or *dreams*, thus making option (A) the most logical answer. Further evidence can be found in lines 27 through 32, where Julio talks about his hope ("esperanza") and desire to live a righteous life ("deseo inmenso de vivir para agradecer a Dios . . .").

27. **(B)** Once again, this information can be found in lines 13 through 22. When speaking about his father, Julio uses the word "fuerte," "no doblegarme ante una derrota" (to not beat oneself up following a defeat), and for his mother he uses words such as "ternura," "amor," and "afecto," which are qualities of compassion.

28. **(D)** This is the best answer because throughout the letter, Julio speaks to the importance of family and what they taught him about life. All other options are values and qualities of those mentioned in the letter, but they are not predominant in the letter, and therefore do not answer the question.

29. **(A)** The answer can be found in lines 8 through 12, and again in lines 27 through 32. Julio uses the field to represent his future, and the dusk to represent birth of hope and desire. These are images that he uses to create a new meaning, which makes option (A) the best answer.

30. **(C)** This quality is evident throughout the letter, where he talks about "campo de ilusiones" (field of dreams, lines 11–12), "desea triunfar" (wants to triumph, line 16), etc.

31. **(C)** This is evident by the information in the box, where it says to compile "información más

detallada de cada institución de tu lista" (more specific information from each institution on your list).

32. **(A)** The key word here is "descartar" (discard, to get rid of), and that the applicant needs to discard those schools that no longer fit his or her requirements. The only other option to consider is option (D), but it is not the correct answer because it implies that the school is the one who makes the decision, not the applicant.

33. **(A)** This is the most important step because it determines all the subsequent steps. None of the other steps in the image would be useless if the applicant does not know what course to study.

34. **(D)** In the audio, Raúl says, "me han recomendado que los acompañe a las escuelas que ya han elegido . . ." and says that he does not want to go because they are "lejos y son muy enormes." Be careful with option (B), for as it uses the same verb used in the audio; the schools his friends are going to are not small, but enormous.

35. **(D)** Raúl spends a considerable part of the audio talking about his struggles with languages, and in particular with English. He also admits that he did not go to see the teacher for extra help, which is a problem that he says he needs to work on.

36. **(A)** Raúl says directly that he likes the idea of a smaller university so that he can get personalized help with his work, and he indirectly says that he does not want to go to a university far away when he talks about what his friends suggest he do. He says that the universities
". . . están muy lejos . . . ," and we can therefore assume that he prefers a school that is closer.

37. **(C)** This is the best option because Raúl recognizes his faults and areas in which he needs to improve. This makes him self-aware.

38. **(A)** At one point the counselor, Sr. Gómez, tells Raúl that the best thing to do is to think about what course of study he wants to pursue, which is the first step in the process. This makes option (A) the clear answer.

39. **(B)** The text presents how efficient the Incas were in terms of agriculture, which makes option (B)

the best answer. One could consider option (C), but the text solely talks about agriculture, not innovations in general, which does not make this the best option. Option (A) is incorrect because, although the title refers to the destruction of Incan agriculture, this particular fragment from the text does not address this topic.

40. **(D)** There is ample evidence throughout the text to support this, such as in lines 3 ("equilibrio ecológico"), 5 ("sin degradar los recursos"), etc. Options (B) and (C) are incorrect because they suggest a negative relationship, and option (A) is incorrect because the Incans did not affect the frequency of rain.

41. **(A)** This information can be found in lines 16 through 21, where it talks about how the terraces would distribute the water regularly and slowly, which was a way of maximizing the small amount of liquid that was available in the area.

42. **(C)** The idea here can be found in lines 28 to 30, where it states how the excrement from bats (guano) and birds was mixed by the Incans into the soil in order to make it more fertile. This makes option (C) the best answer because it refers to how this excrement was used.

43. **(A)** This is the clear answer because throughout the text we see examples of how innovative the Incan practices were when it came to agriculture.

44. **(C)** One could infer that this option is the correct answer simply by reading the title of the audio in the introduction, and the beginning of the audio confirms this when it talks about the new plants being cultivated (soy and sorghum) instead of traditional ones (beans and corn).

45. **(B)** During the first half of the audio, it talks about the relationship between "deforestación y aumento de pastizales para ganadería," making option (B) the best answer. Options (A) and (C) are incorrect because the ideas they suggest are not supported by the audio. Option (D) is incorrect because, even though the audio mentions the number "54%," it does so in reference to new lands and only in Colombia, whereas option (D) suggests all lands in all of Latin America.

46. **(D)** The word "incidencia" in the question means *impact*, and "medio ambiente" is a synonym, in this context, of "entorno." This makes option (D) the only choice.

47. **(B)** During the last third of the audio, it talks about "modificaciones del suelo por intervención humana" and "fertilizantes sintéticos," which are chemicals used to modify the soil. Don't be fooled by option (D), for the audio text does not talk about genetic modification.

48. **(B)** The key here is to find something that connects the Incan agricultural practices with those currently happening in Latin America. Option (B) is the only one that makes this connection.

49. **(C)** The audio says that the contest serves to "utilizar rap . . . en la difusión de mensajes propositivos sobre la convivencia, la legalidad, sobre una vida libre de drogas . . . ," making option (C) the best answer. Don't be fooled by option (B), because the contest does not want to simply show the role of hip-hop and rap in culture, but rather wants people to use this music to achieve a specific set of goals.

50. **(A)** Remember that this is a contest, and the audio informs the listener that they have invited young artists and musicians from different parts of Colombia (Barranquilla, Calí, etc.). The audio mentions hip-hop, breakdance, and graffiti, thus clearly showing that this contest is not simply musical, but also visual.

51. **(D)** Halfway through the audio, the interviewee says, ". . . es la intención de este festival que sea un gran evento nacional . . . ," making option (D) the best answer. Don't be fooled by option (C) because, even though the audio also says that they will make recordings after the event, it is not the focus of the contest.

52. **(A)** This is a theme throughout the recording, but specifically at the end the interviewee states how young people have so much to say and are more than simply the clothes that they wear. Although options (B), (C), and (D) could be true, the audio does not say this information, and for this reason they are not the correct answer.

53. **(B)** Just like in the previous answer, the interviewee hopes that this contest will help young people express themselves positively and that others will realize that the youth ". . . tienen mucho más que decir . . . ." One can safely infer then that this event may change how people view young hip hop and graffiti artists, making option (B) the correct choice.

54. **(B)** This is evident throughout the audio, which talks about the "creación del mundo", "creación del hombre," "orígenes de los linajes gobernantes . . . ," etc., and that it was written in "quiché."

55. **(A)** At the beginning of the audio, it talks about the "creación del hombre a partir del maiz" (corn). This makes option (A) the logical answer.

56. **(D)** At the beginning of the second half of the audio, the speaker says that Ximénez "presentó en doble columna el texto quiché junto a la versión española . . . ," which is what option (D) says: both languages were used at the same time.

57. **(B)** This information can be found in the second half of the audio, when the speaker says that the manuscript "se encuentra en la colección . . . de la Biblioteca Newberry de la ciudad de Chicago." Options (A) and (C) refer to previous locations of the text, not the most current one. Option (D) is incorrect because it was a Dominican monk who made the first translation, but there is nothing in the audio saying where he put it.

58. **(C)** This is the best option because the original title means "libro de la estera" (literally *book of the sleeping mat*). The mats were used as a symbol of authority of kings, governors, and members of the court. Option (C) addresses all these figures, making it the best answer.

59. **(B)** The author, Antonio de Urbina, clearly states this in his first response when he says that the book is ". . . para todos, para todos" and a few seconds later when he says that he dedicated the second half to the common reader.

60. **(C)** This is the best answer because the audio talks about the importance of everyone feeling comfortable when attending an event, which facil-

itates communication and makes them feel equal to others in the room. Don't be fooled by option (A), for it suggests that one feel superior to others in the room. Option (B) is incorrect because the protocols are not limited to visitors to the Royal Palace, and option (D) is incorrect because the protocols are to ensure comfort at the event itself, not simply when they accept the invitation.

61. **(C)** This information is stated specifically when the first speaker says, ". . . chico, chica, chico, chica . . . ." option (A) is incorrect because there is nothing in the audio to suggest that physical characteristics are a consideration, and option (D) is incorrect because, although the audio does say that married couples should be separated, it does not say that this is to avoid arguments.

62. **(A)** The speakers say that the "puntas" are the last spots at the table, and that it is a basic courtesy to not seat them there. Option (B) is not the best answer because, although women should not be seated at this spot, the audio does not say this is because it is reserved for men, but rather because it would be a lack of courtesy to sit a woman there.

63. **(C)** This information is given at the end of the recording, when the speaker says that the trick is to call "un íntimo amigo," so that they don't end up with thirteen.

64. **(A)** The only evidence we have is given at the beginning of the audio when it states that José Antonio de Urbina is "experto en protocolo de la Corte Española," which suggests that he has studied it. Option (B) is incorrect because, even though he is a diplomat, this does not explain why he is an expert on the art of inviting others. There is no evidence that he lived and worked in the Royal Palace, nor that he organized events for the Royal Palace, which makes options (C) and (D) also incorrect.

65. **(B)** The whole audio talks about good manners when hosting a party, which is what option (B) addresses, making it the best option. Don't be fooled by option (A). It relates somewhat to the topic, but the title suggests that its focus is more on the planning of an event and not on helping guests feel comfortable at the event.

ANSWER SHEET
Practice Test 2

Section 1: Part A

1. Ⓐ Ⓑ Ⓒ Ⓓ
2. Ⓐ Ⓑ Ⓒ Ⓓ
3. Ⓐ Ⓑ Ⓒ Ⓓ
4. Ⓐ Ⓑ Ⓒ Ⓓ
5. Ⓐ Ⓑ Ⓒ Ⓓ
6. Ⓐ Ⓑ Ⓒ Ⓓ
7. Ⓐ Ⓑ Ⓒ Ⓓ
8. Ⓐ Ⓑ Ⓒ Ⓓ

9. Ⓐ Ⓑ Ⓒ Ⓓ
10. Ⓐ Ⓑ Ⓒ Ⓓ
11. Ⓐ Ⓑ Ⓒ Ⓓ
12. Ⓐ Ⓑ Ⓒ Ⓓ
13. Ⓐ Ⓑ Ⓒ Ⓓ
14. Ⓐ Ⓑ Ⓒ Ⓓ
15. Ⓐ Ⓑ Ⓒ Ⓓ
16. Ⓐ Ⓑ Ⓒ Ⓓ

17. Ⓐ Ⓑ Ⓒ Ⓓ
18. Ⓐ Ⓑ Ⓒ Ⓓ
19. Ⓐ Ⓑ Ⓒ Ⓓ
20. Ⓐ Ⓑ Ⓒ Ⓓ
21. Ⓐ Ⓑ Ⓒ Ⓓ
22. Ⓐ Ⓑ Ⓒ Ⓓ
23. Ⓐ Ⓑ Ⓒ Ⓓ
24. Ⓐ Ⓑ Ⓒ Ⓓ

25. Ⓐ Ⓑ Ⓒ Ⓓ
26. Ⓐ Ⓑ Ⓒ Ⓓ
27. Ⓐ Ⓑ Ⓒ Ⓓ
28. Ⓐ Ⓑ Ⓒ Ⓓ
29. Ⓐ Ⓑ Ⓒ Ⓓ
30. Ⓐ Ⓑ Ⓒ Ⓓ

Section 1: Part B

31. Ⓐ Ⓑ Ⓒ Ⓓ
32. Ⓐ Ⓑ Ⓒ Ⓓ
33. Ⓐ Ⓑ Ⓒ Ⓓ
34. Ⓐ Ⓑ Ⓒ Ⓓ
35. Ⓐ Ⓑ Ⓒ Ⓓ
36. Ⓐ Ⓑ Ⓒ Ⓓ
37. Ⓐ Ⓑ Ⓒ Ⓓ
38. Ⓐ Ⓑ Ⓒ Ⓓ
39. Ⓐ Ⓑ Ⓒ Ⓓ

40. Ⓐ Ⓑ Ⓒ Ⓓ
41. Ⓐ Ⓑ Ⓒ Ⓓ
42. Ⓐ Ⓑ Ⓒ Ⓓ
43. Ⓐ Ⓑ Ⓒ Ⓓ
44. Ⓐ Ⓑ Ⓒ Ⓓ
45. Ⓐ Ⓑ Ⓒ Ⓓ
46. Ⓐ Ⓑ Ⓒ Ⓓ
47. Ⓐ Ⓑ Ⓒ Ⓓ
48. Ⓐ Ⓑ Ⓒ Ⓓ

49. Ⓐ Ⓑ Ⓒ Ⓓ
50. Ⓐ Ⓑ Ⓒ Ⓓ
51. Ⓐ Ⓑ Ⓒ Ⓓ
52. Ⓐ Ⓑ Ⓒ Ⓓ
53. Ⓐ Ⓑ Ⓒ Ⓓ
54. Ⓐ Ⓑ Ⓒ Ⓓ
55. Ⓐ Ⓑ Ⓒ Ⓓ
56. Ⓐ Ⓑ Ⓒ Ⓓ
57. Ⓐ Ⓑ Ⓒ Ⓓ

58. Ⓐ Ⓑ Ⓒ Ⓓ
59. Ⓐ Ⓑ Ⓒ Ⓓ
60. Ⓐ Ⓑ Ⓒ Ⓓ
61. Ⓐ Ⓑ Ⓒ Ⓓ
62. Ⓐ Ⓑ Ⓒ Ⓓ
63. Ⓐ Ⓑ Ⓒ Ⓓ
64. Ⓐ Ⓑ Ⓒ Ⓓ
65. Ⓐ Ⓑ Ⓒ Ⓓ

Practice Test 2

Section I: Part A—Interpretive Communication: Print Texts

TIME: APPROXIMATELY 40 MINUTES

DIRECTIONS: Read the following passages. After each passage there are a number of questions for you to answer, based on the information provided in the reading selection. For each question, choose the response that is best according to the selection and mark your answer on the answer sheet.

Lee los siguientes textos. Cada texto va acompañado de varias preguntas que debes contestar, según la información en el texto. Para cada pregunta, elige la mejor respuesta según el contexto y escríbela en la hoja de respuestas.

Selección 1

Tema curricular: La vida contemporánea

Introducción: El siguiente fragmento se trata de cuando dos amigos se enteran de la muerte de un conocido. Proviene del cuento "El tesoro misterioso" de Guillermo Le Queux, publicado en 1909.

—¡Muerto! ¡Y se ha llevado su secreto a la tumba!

—¡Jamás!

Línea   —Pero se lo ha llevado. ¡Mira! Tiene la quijada
(5)   caída. ¡No ves el cambio, hombre!

—¡Entonces, ha cumplido su amenaza, después de todo!

—¡La ha cumplido! Hemos sido unos tontos, Reginaldo . . . ¡verdaderamente
(10)   tontos!—murmuré.

—Así parece. Confieso que yo esperaba confiadamente que nos diría la verdad cuando comprendiese que le había llegado el fin.

—¡Ah! tú no lo conocías como yo—observé
(15)   con amargura.—Tenía una voluntad de hierro y un nervio de acero.

—Combinados con una constitución de caballo, porque, si no, haría mucho tiempo que se hubiera muerto. Pero hemos sido engañados .
(20)   . . completamente engañados por un moribundo.

(25)   Nos ha desafiado, y hasta el último momento se ha burlado de nosotros.

—Blair no era un tonto. Sabía lo que el conocimiento de esa verdad significaba para nosotros: una enorme fortuna. Lo que ha hecho, sencilla-
(30)   mente, es guardar su secreto.

—Y dejarnos sin un centavo. Aunque hemos perdido miles, Gilberto, no puedo menos de admirar su tenaz determinación. Recuerdo que ha tenido que atravesar por momentos acia-
(35)   gos, y ha sido un buen amigo, pero muy bueno, con nosotros; por lo tanto, creo que no debemos abusar de él, aun cuando nos cause mucho sentimiento el hecho de que no nos haya dejado su secreto.

(40)   —¡Ah, si esos labios blancos pudiesen hablar! Una sola palabra, y los dos seríamos hombres ricos—exclamé con pena, contemplando la cara pálida del muerto, con sus ojos cerrados y su barba afeitada, que yacía sobre la almohada.

1. ¿Qué efecto produce el hecho de que el autor comienza la narración *in medias res* (en medio de la acción)?

    (A) Ayuda a proveer detalles significativos a la trama.
    (B) Facilita que el lector conozca mejor a los personajes principales.
    (C) Ayuda a presentar diferentes puntos de vista acerca del evento.
    (D) Produce un aire dramático y alienta al lector a que siga leyendo.

2. ¿Quién ha muerto?

    (A) Reginaldo
    (B) Gilberto
    (C) Blair
    (D) No es posible saber por este fragmento

3. ¿Qué se puede inferir de la muerte del hombre?

    (A) Murió de repente.
    (B) Fue asesinado.
    (C) Se sabía que iba a morir.
    (D) Murió al aire libre.

4. ¿Qué se sabe del fallecido?

    (A) Era de carácter tierno.
    (B) Confiaba en los demás.
    (C) Compartía información íntima.
    (D) Era una persona adinerada.

5. ¿Qué quiere comunicar uno de los protagonistas cuando dice que el muerto "ha tenido que atravesar por momentos aciagos" (línea 30)?

    (A) Ha experimentado mucho éxito.
    (B) Mantuvo buenas relaciones con todos.
    (C) Tuvo unas situaciones de mala suerte.
    (D) Supo manejar bien todo tipo de negocios.

6. ¿Por qué quieren los protagonistas saber el secreto del fallecido?

    (A) Porque conocían bien al hombre muerto
    (B) Porque no quieren que el hombre siga burlándose de ellos
    (C) Porque les traería mucha riqueza
    (D) Porque eran muy buenos amigos de él

7. ¿Qué actitud demuestran los protagonistas?

    (A) Tristeza
    (B) Decepción
    (C) Frustración
    (D) Alivio

Selección 2

Tema curricular: La vida contemporánea

Fuente 1

Introducción: El siguiente artículo se trata de la ciclovía en Lima, Perú. Fue publicado por Chiqaq News, una página de noticias locales de la Facultad de Letras y Ciencias Humanas de la Universidad Nacional Mayor de San Marcos en Lima, Perú. Fue publicado en junio de 2021.

EDUARDO QUISPE HUARINGA

El pasado 3 de junio de 2020, Jorge Muñoz, alcalde de Lima, entregó la nueva ciclovía Carlos Izaguirre que recorre la avenida del mismo nombre. Esta vía une los distritos de Los Olivos, San Martín de Porres e Independencia. Abarca alrededor de 1,8 kilómetros en el tramo comprendido entre las avenidas Alfredo Mendiola y Universitaria.

La construcción del nuevo carril comenzó a mediados de febrero. Según el municipio metropolitano, la obra consistió en la remodelación de rampas, veredas y del pavimento. Además, se colocó nueva señalización reglamentaria y preventiva de accidentes. Estas modificaciones se realizaron, principalmente, con el fin de conectarse de forma segura con la ciclovía de la avenida Universitaria.

El proyecto también contempló la instalación de un estacionamiento de bicicletas, equipos de gimnasia y módulos de reciclaje. Asimismo, para la restauración de sus áreas verdes se necesitó del sembrado de 7,045 m2 de pasto, 165 árboles y 145 m2 de ornamentación de flores. Se realizó una inversión aproximada de 1,7 millones de soles para la ejecución de esta obra municipal.

La renovada ciclovía beneficiará a más de 32 mil ciudadanos y vecinos de los 3 distritos antes mencionados. Pues, la bicicleta es un medio de transporte ecológico que se popularizó durante la pandemia de la covid-19. Y como medio individual evita el contacto con otras personas. Además, no consume combustible y supone un ahorro para su propietario.

"Hoy es un día muy especial porque entregamos a los ciudadanos una nueva ciclovía que permitirá la interconexión con más distritos. Encontramos menos de 200 km de ciclovías en Lima y hoy tenemos el objetivo de pasar los 300 km, pues la bicicleta ha cobrado un valor especial. Es un medio de transporte saludable, ecoamigable y nos permite evitar las aglomeraciones y por eso continuaremos trabajando", indicó el alcalde Muñoz.

La Municipalidad de Lima inauguró esta importante obra en el marco del día mundial de la bicicleta. La actividad también contó con la presencia de Felipe Castillo, alcalde de Los Olivos, otras autoridades locales y vecinos de la zona. Al término de la ceremonia, los asistentes realizaron un recorrido en bicicleta a lo largo de la ciclovía.

El medio de transporte más popular del 2020

Según Jason Huertas, director comercial de Linio Perú, en 2020 se registró un incremento de 300% en las ventas de bicicletas y productos relacionados. El perfil de sus consumidores son jóvenes entre 18 y 34 años que desean salir de casa, distraerse y realizar ejercicio, pero sin exponerse al contagio del coronavirus. El mismo caso ocurre en otras tiendas virtuales.

La «nueva normalidad» incentiva que los gobiernos locales -con respaldo de la Municipalidad de Lima- realicen obras de construcción y rediseño de sus ciclovías. A largo plazo, estos proyectos beneficiarán a los habitantes de su jurisdicción y distritos aledaños.

Fuente 2

Introducción: La siguiente tabla presenta el kilometraje de las ciclovías en distintas ciudades latinas entre 2015 y 2023.

Ciudad	2015	2023
Bogotá	392	564
Santiago	236	430
Buenos Aires	130	300
Monterrey	0,4	12,76
La Paz	14	78

8. ¿Cuál es el propósito general del artículo?

   (A) Describir los beneficios del uso de la bicicleta
   (B) Informar sobre la inauguración de una nueva ruta para bicicletas
   (C) Narrar la historia de la bicicleta en Lima
   (D) Comparar diferentes tipos de transporte en la capital peruana

9. ¿Quién entregó la nueva ciclovía?

   (A) Felipe Castillo
   (B) Jorge Muñoz
   (C) Carlos Izaguirre
   (D) San Martin de Porres

10. ¿Por qué se construyó el tramo de la ciclovía mencionado?

   (A) Por la alta demanda de transporte público en esa área
   (B) Para conectar varios distritos importantes de Lima
   (C) Es parte de un proyecto de renovación urbana.
   (D) Para promover un estilo de vida más saludable

11. ¿Cuál de los siguientes NO es un beneficio mencionado de la bicicleta?

   (A) Es un medio de transporte ecológico.
   (B) Ayuda a evitar aglomeraciones.
   (C) Consume combustible.
   (D) Es saludable y ecoamigable.

12. ¿Qué incluyó el proyecto de la ciclovía además de la vía?

   (A) Únicamente un estacionamiento de bicicletas
   (B) Una red de transporte público integrado
   (C) Nuevas rutas de autobuses
   (D) Equipos de gimnasia y módulos de reciclaje

13. ¿Qué se puede inferir sobre el uso de bicicletas durante la pandemia de la covid-19?

   (A) Aumentó por ser un medio de transporte individual.
   (B) Disminuyó debido a las restricciones de movilidad.
   (C) Se mantuvo igual que antes de la pandemia.
   (D) No tuvo impacto en el transporte de Lima.

14. Basándose en la información del artículo, ¿cuál es una predicción válida sobre el impacto de la nueva ciclovía en la movilidad urbana de Lima?

   (A) Reducirá significativamente el uso de automóviles en la ciudad.
   (B) Incrementará la congestión vehicular en las áreas aledañas.
   (C) Generará un cambio notable en los hábitos de transporte de los ciudadanos.
   (D) No tendrá un impacto significativo en la movilidad urbana de Lima.

15. ¿Cuál es el propósito de la tabla presentada en el artículo?

    (A) Comparar el costo de construcción de ciclovías
    (B) Listar las ciudades con las mejores ciclovías
    (C) Mostrar el cambio en distancia de ciclovías
    (D) Indicar el número de ciclovías en cada ciudad

16. Según la tabla, ¿qué ciudad tuvo el mayor aumento en el kilometraje de ciclovías entre 2015 y 2023?

    (A) Bogotá
    (B) Santiago
    (C) Buenos Aires
    (D) Monterrey

17. De acuerdo con la información del artículo y la tabla, ¿qué tendencia se observa en Latinoamérica respecto a las ciclovías?

    (A) Disminución en su construcción
    (B) Mantenimiento sin cambios significativos
    (C) Incremento constante en su longitud
    (D) Variación dependiendo de la ciudad

18. Basado en el artículo y la tabla, ¿cuál sería una predicción válida para el futuro de las ciclovías?

    (A) Permanecerán sin cambios en los próximos años.
    (B) Se ampliarán considerablemente.
    (C) Experimentarán un declive en su uso y extensión.
    (D) Serán reemplazadas por otros medios de transporte más modernos.

Selección 3

Tema curricular: La belleza y la estética

Introducción: El siguiente anuncio trata de un aviso para un evento de literatura. Fue publicado en la página web *www.escritores.org* en 2013.

Premio Nacional De Literatura Juvenil

El Ministerio de Culturas y Turismo, Entel y Santillana convocan a la primera versión del Premio Nacional de Literatura Juvenil, de

Línea acuerdo con las siguientes bases:

(5)   **Participantes**: Podrán optar al Premio todas las personas mayores de edad de nacionalidad boliviana que residan en Bolivia.

Presentación de la obra: El concursante deberá enviar en un sobre cerrado bajo el rótulo

(10) 1er. Premio Nacional de Literatura Juvenil una obra literaria para lectores juveniles de entre 13 y 18 años, escrita en lengua castellana, que sea original, rigurosamente inédita y que no haya sido premiada anteriormente en ningún otro

(15) concurso, ni corresponda a autores fallecidos con anterioridad al anuncio de esta convocatoria. La obra juvenil tendrá una extensión mínima de 60 páginas y un máximo de 80 páginas tamaño carta, numeradas, mecanografiadas a doble espa-

(20) cio por una sola cara, con letra de 12 puntos. Deberán enviarse dos ejemplares impresos, anillados, encuadernados o cosidos, y un CD con el texto completo en formato Word. Es obligatorio adjuntar un sobre cerrado con el título de la obra

(25) y el pseudónimo del autor que contendrá: Una

(30) hoja con los datos del autor —nombre y apellidos, dirección, correo electrónico y teléfono(s) de contacto—; una declaración firmada aceptando expresamente las bases y condiciones de este Premio, garantizando que la obra no se halla

(35) pendiente del fallo en ningún otro concurso y que el autor tiene la libre disposición de todos los derechos sobre la obra; y una fotocopia de la cédula de identidad. De faltar algunos de estos requisitos, la novela juvenil no será considerada

(40) en el concurso.

Recepción de obras: El plazo de admisión de los originales vence el día viernes 12 de julio de 2013. En caso de envíos por correo, se aceptará la fecha de recepción con el sello de origen.

(45)   **Premio**: El premio para el ganador será de Bs. 15.000 (quince mil bolivianos), de los que se detraerán los impuestos que fueran aplicables según la legislación boliviana. El monto es único e indivisible y cubre los derechos de autor de la

(50) primera edición de mil ejemplares.

Otras consideraciones: La editorial Santillana se reserva el derecho de opción preferente para la publicación de cualquier otra narración juvenil presentada al Premio que, no habiendo

(55) alcanzado el galardón, sea considerada de su interés.

19. ¿Cuál es el propósito del anuncio?

    (A) Promover el conocimiento de la literatura entre los jóvenes

    (B) Reclutar a jóvenes a que entreguen su obra favorita

    (C) Promocionar un evento para la creación literaria original

    (D) Proporcionar información sobre las diferentes formas de crear una obra

20. ¿A quién se dirige el anuncio?

    (A) A todos los amantes de la literatura

    (B) A los jóvenes bolivianos

    (C) A los residentes de Bolivia que sean mayores de cierta edad

    (D) A los bolivianos de tercera edad

21. ¿Qué se puede inferir de las obras literarias mencionadas en este anuncio?

    (A) Son de la literatura boliviana.

    (B) Son cuentos típicos de la literatura latinoamericana.

    (C) Son novelas bastante cortas.

    (D) Son ejemplares de literatura popular.

22. ¿Qué recibe el autor de la novela ganadora?

    (A) Un premio monetario equivalente a quince mil bolivianos

    (B) Un poco menos de Bs. 15.000 y la publicación de su obra

    (C) 15.000 bolivianos y un contrato con una empresa editorial

    (D) Un premio monetario, publicación de su obra, y estar exento de pagar impuestos

23. ¿Qué ocurre a las obras que no ganaron el premio?

    (A) No reciben un premio pero todavía pueden ser publicadas.

    (B) Son publicadas para que todos las disfruten.

    (C) Son regaladas a la editorial para ser publicadas en el futuro.

    (D) El anuncio no menciona esta información.

24. Necesitas más información que no está publicada en el anuncio y le llamas al organizador para clarificar tus dudas. ¿Cuál de las siguientes preguntas sería más apropiada?

    (A) "Perdona, ¿qué ocurre si mi entrega no contiene toda la información pedida?"

    (B) "Vivo lejos de la sede y tengo que enviar mi entrega. Aunque sé que la puedo mandar a tiempo, ¿qué pasa si llega después de la fecha límite publicada?"

    (C) "Mi entrega fue escrita por mi abuela, que murió hace dos años. ¿Todavía puedo enviarla?"

    (D) "Si mi entrega gana, ¿cuánto suele ser quitado por los impuestos?"

Selección 4

Tema curricular: Los desafíos mundiales

Introducción: Lo siguiente es una carta abierta al Presidente de la República de Uruguay sobre un asunto del medio ambiente. La carta original fue publicada en *El Observador* en 2010.

Sr. Presidente,

Me dirijo a Usted por este medio para conocer su opinión, sus respuestas a la infinidad de interro

Línea gantes que hoy nos formulamos los productores

(5) rurales de cuatro departamentos ante la presencia de la Minera Aratirí que avanza en sus trabajos de prospección y exploración en la búsqueda de hierro en una zona ganadera, donde los directamente afectados, los superficiarios, no hemos

(10) tenido una sola respuesta oficial al respecto, aún habiéndola solicitado en más de una oportunidad.

La Minera cavaría inmensos huecos en el corazón del país ocasionando una alteración permanente y definitiva del paisaje, de la red de

(15) drenaje, dada la imposibilidad de devolver a la zona su estructuración inicial. Esta alteración trae consecuencias ecológicas, sociales, económicas dramáticas ya que rompe una cadena productiva que será imposible reconstruir.

(20) Sabemos que "las aguas ácidas representan un grave riesgo ambiental ya que alteran las características químicas de las aguas receptoras contaminándolas y causando impactos en los ecosistemas," así lo dicen informes técnicos de

(25) profesionales expertos en la materia. Sabemos que con la crisis mundial de alimentos se vienen tiempos de valorización de los productos agrícolas (materias primas agropecuarias). Sabemos de la necesidad de control de sectores estratégicos

(30) como el rural y el agronegocio. Sabemos que un país como Brasil está legislando para impedir la extranjerización de la tierra previendo la crisis de alimentos y la escasez del agua.

Y si sabemos todo esto . . .

(35) ¿Es posible que estemos hipotecando nuestras fértiles praderas naturales en proyectos mineros que producen alteraciones irreversibles en ecosistemas naturales y que estemos hipotecando la salud y el futuro de nuestro país,

(40) el de nuestros hijos y nietos y que además no estemos informados?

No Señor Presidente, no es posible.

Por lo tanto queremos conocer su opinión y queremos ejercer nuestros derechos como

(45) ciudadanos, queremos ser escuchados, que nuestra opinión sea también válida, queremos ser atendidos porque todos ansiamos lo mejor para el País Natural que codician los extranjeros.

Atentamente,

(50) Rosina Mascheroni

18 de diciembre de 2010

25. ¿Cuál es el propósito de esta carta?

    (A) Informarle al presidente de unos problemas medioambientales
    (B) Solicitar trabajo en una compañía minera que se ubica en su zona
    (C) Llamarle la atención al gobierno sobre las preocupaciones de unos ciudadanos
    (D) Saber exactamente qué planes tiene el gobierno para el futuro del país

26. ¿A qué se refiere la autora cuando dice ". . . la infinidad de interrogantes . . ." (líneas 2–3)?

    (A) A las inquietudes del pueblo
    (B) A las demandas del gobierno
    (C) A las preguntas de la compañía minera
    (D) A la alta demanda de minerales de su zona

27. ¿Cuál es la preocupación más grande con Minería Aratirí?

    (A) Que no permita que los lugareños puedan solicitar trabajo
    (B) Que les quite todo el hierro de su zona
    (C) Que haga un daño permanente a la tierra
    (D) Que no les permita seguir trabajando con la ganadería

28. ¿Qué se puede inferir acerca de la compañía minera?

    (A) Es una filial de una compañía extranjera.
    (B) Ha tenido éxito previo en Brasil.
    (C) Es una de las compañías más prósperas de Uruguay.
    (D) Ha tomado medidas para el sostenimiento ecológico.

29. ¿De qué manera comunica la carta su mensaje sobre el impacto de la compañía minera?

    (A) Cuenta una historia previa de la compañía.
    (B) Incluye opiniones de la población afectada.
    (C) Relata unas experiencias de su propia situación.
    (D) Se refiere a datos y hechos específicos.

30. ¿Qué perspectiva cultural representa la carta?

    (A) Devoción a la tradición ganadera y de agricultura
    (B) Cautela ante el progreso
    (C) Valor de la democracia
    (D) Importancia del respaldo gubernamental

Section I: Part B—Interpretive Communication: Print and Audio Texts (Combined)

TIME: APPROXIMATELY 55 MINUTES

DIRECTIONS: You will listen to several audio selections. The first two also include print texts. When there is a print text, you will have an additional amount of time to read it.

For each audio selection, you will have a designated amount of time to read the introduction of the selection and to preview the questions and answers that follow. Each audio selection will be played twice.

Following the first listening, you will have one minute to begin answering the questions. After the second listening, you will be given 15 seconds per question to finish answering. For each question, select the best answer according to the selection and mark your answer on your answer sheet.

Vas a escuchar varias grabaciones. Las primeras dos van acompañadas de textos escritos. Cuando hay un texto escrito, tendrás tiempo adicional para leerlo.

Para cada selección auditiva, vas a tener un tiempo determinado para leer la introducción de la selección y prever las preguntas que siguen. Vas a escuchar cada fuente auditiva dos veces.

Después de escuchar cada selección la primera vez, vas a tener un minuto para empezar a contestar las preguntas. Después de escucharla la segunda vez, vas a tener 15 segundos por pregunta para terminarlas. Para cada pregunta, elige la mejor respuesta según el contexto y escríbela en la hoja de respuestas.

Selección 1

Tema curricular: Los desafíos mundiales

Fuente 1: Primero tienes un minuto para la leer fuente número 1.

Introducción: El siguiente gráfico presenta la cantidad de remesas, en millones de dólares, que se ha mandado a El Salvador. Se basa en información publicada por el Banco Nacional de Reserva de El Salvador.

Track 55

Remesas registradas por año en millones de dólares

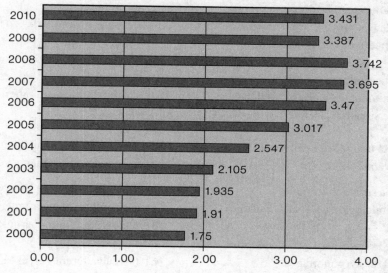

Año	Millones de dólares
2010	3.431
2009	3.387
2008	3.742
2007	3.695
2006	3.47
2005	3.017
2004	2.547
2003	2.105
2002	1.935
2001	1.91
2000	1.75

Fuente 2: Ahora tienes un minuto para leer la introducción y prever las preguntas.

Introducción: La siguiente fuente auditiva es una entrevista con el embajador de El Salvador en Radio Naciones Unidas. El tema es la migración y desarrollo en El Salvador. La entrevista original fue publicada en Nueva York por Radio Naciones Unidas el 23 de octubre de 2012. La grabación dura aproximadamente tres minutos, treinta segundos.

31. Según la tabla, ¿cuánto dinero fue enviado a El Salvador en 2003?

    (A) Dos mil ciento cinco dólares
    (B) Dos dólares, ciento cinco centavos
    (C) Dos millones, ciento cinco mil dólares
    (D) Dos mil millones, ciento cinco mil dólares

32. Según la tabla, ¿qué se puede afirmar de las remesas a El Salvador durante el período estudiado?

    (A) Ha habido un incremento constante.
    (B) Ha disminuido cada año.
    (C) En los últimos años hubo un descenso en relación a años anteriores.
    (D) En los últimos años hubo un ascenso en relación a años anteriores.

33. ¿Qué se puede deducir de la tabla que ocurrió entre el año 2000 y 2006?

    (A) Casi se duplicó la cantidad de dinero enviada a El Salvador.
    (B) Más salvadoreños emigraron a países con economías más prósperas.
    (C) Los emigrantes ganaron más dinero durante esta época.
    (D) La economía salvadoreña experimentó una crisis económica.

34. Según la entrevista, ¿cuál es la preocupación fundamental del gobierno salvadoreño?

    (A) Preservar la historia de su país
    (B) Crear condiciones para favorecer la permanencia en El Salvador
    (C) Facilitar el proceso de emigración a otros países
    (D) Fallen out of use, instead suministrar more common documentación a la población inmigrante de su país

35. ¿Qué iniciativa está tratando de emplear el gobierno salvadoreño?

    (A) Documentar a sus connacionales
    (B) Abrir vías de migración a Canadá, España y Australia
    (C) Asegurar que las remesas sigan siendo una parte integral de su economía
    (D) Obligar a los indocumentados a que regresen a su país

36. En la entrevista, ¿a qué se refiere el embajador cuando dice que "el inmigrante se vaya olvidando de su terruño"?

    (A) A una razón por la cual no van a volver a El Salvador
    (B) A una posible causa de la reducción de las remesas
    (C) Al deseo de los inmigrantes de invertir en su país sede
    (D) A que los inmigrantes van a perder las tierras de su familia

37. ¿Qué opina el embajador en cuanto a las remesas?

    (A) Aportan muchos beneficios a la economía salvadoreña.
    (B) Hay que encaminarlas en inversiones para mejorar el país.
    (C) No son tan productivas como eran anteriormente.
    (D) Muchas familias no saben qué hacer con ellas.

38. De acuerdo al gráfico y la fuente auditiva, ¿qué se puede deducir de la situación en El Salvador?

    (A) Muchos carecen de las oportunidades económicas para sostener a una familia.
    (B) A los salvadoreños les gusta compartir sus riquezas.
    (C) Los salvadoreños en el extranjero han ganado más durante los años.
    (D) Las familias en El Salvador tienen una mejor vida por la migración a otros países.

Selección 2

Tema curricular: La ciencia y la tecnología

> **Fuente 1:** Primero tienes cuatro minutos para leer la fuente número 1.
>
> **Introducción:** El siguiente artículo trata de la importancia de dormir bien. Fue publicado en la página web *www.consumer.es* el 22 de octubre de 2012.

Track 56

Para estudiar más no es beneficioso sacrificar el descanso nocturno y, menos, hacerlo antes de un examen. Al contrario, suele ser contrapro-
Línea ducente, ya que el rendimiento óptimo se logra
(5) cuando hay un equilibrio entre las horas dedicadas al estudio y al dormir, según los resultados de un trabajo reciente llevado a cabo en la Universidad de California en Los Ángeles (EE.UU.). Aunque no significa que no haya que estudiar,
(10) sino que hay que tener en cuenta que las horas de sueño pueden ser determinantes para el éxito académico.

Dormir para retener lo aprendido

Investigaciones anteriores ya habían constat-
(15) ado que lo aprendido se retiene mejor si se duerme justo después de hacerlo. Un trabajo de la Universidad estadounidense de Notre Dame señalaba que la memoria de lo aprendido era superior en los que habían dormido justo
(20) después de estudiar, respecto de los que habían dormido tras un día de vigilia.

Otro estudio presentado durante la reunión anual de la Asociación Americana para el Avance de la Ciencia, en 2010, llevado a cabo por
(25) investigadores de la Universidad de California en Berkeley, confirma que una de las principales funciones del sueño es la de "limpiar" la memoria a corto plazo para dejar sitio libre para más información. Los autores concluían que una
(30) noche sin dormir puede reducir la capacidad de asimilar conocimientos en casi un 40%, ya que las regiones cerebrales implicadas en el almacenaje no funcionan de forma correcta durante la falta de sueño.

(35) Las mejores horas para estudiar y dormir

Muchas de las personas que estudian por la noche dicen hacerlo porque se concentran mejor, rinden más y tienen menos interrupciones y distracciones. Un trabajo de 2008 del Hospi-
(40) tal Quirón de Valencia desbancó esta arraigada costumbre en muchos alumnos. Muchos especialistas aseguran que el periodo de máximo aprovechamiento coincide con la mañana, decrece a lo largo de la tarde y, sobre todo, de
(45) la noche, por lo que conviene trabajar la mayor parte de la materia al comienzo del día y dejar el repaso o la tarea más fácil para la última hora de la jornada.

Fuente 2: Ahora tienes dos minutos para leer la introducción y prever las preguntas.

Introducción: La siguiente fuente auditiva es un podcast de Mertxe Pasamontes, Psicóloga y Coach, que trata de la importancia de equilibrar el trabajo con el descanso. El podcast original fue transmitido el 25 de noviembre de 2011 en la página web *www.merxtepasamontes.com*. El podcast tiene una duración de aproximadamente dos minutos, cincuenta segundos.

39. ¿Qué técnica usa el autor en los primeros párrafos del artículo para comunicar su idea?

    (A) Presenta su opinión con ejemplos cotidianos.
    (B) Incluye anécdotas de diferentes expertos.
    (C) Provee ideas contrarias de varios grupos.
    (D) Incluye datos para apoyar el tema.

40. En el artículo, ¿qué comprobaron los investigadores en cuanto a retener la información estudiada?

    (A) Que se retiene más fácilmente si se duerme lo suficiente
    (B) Que se retiene mejor si se trasnocha estudiando
    (C) Que se retiene mejor si se duerme inmediatamente después
    (D) Que se retiene mejor el día después de estudiar

41. Según el artículo, ¿a qué se refiere el autor cuando dice "las regiones cerebrales implicadas en el almacenaje no funcionan" (líneas 32–33)?

    (A) A que el cerebro pierde la capacidad de memorizar
    (B) A la reducción de la capacidad de guardar información
    (C) A la incapacidad de entender información nueva
    (D) A la falta de capacidad de distinguir una cosa de otra

42. Según el artículo, ¿cuándo es el mejor tiempo para estudiar?

    (A) Durante la noche cuando hay menos distracciones
    (B) Por la tarde, después del almuerzo
    (C) Después del desayuno y antes del mediodía
    (D) Cuando quiera uno, siempre que tome un estimulante

43. Según el Podcast, ¿qué se menciona que es un valor en la sociedad?

    (A) El equilibrio de trabajo y descanso
    (B) La capacidad de saber cuándo ser productivo
    (C) El alto rendimiento en el ámbito laboral
    (D) Descansar lo suficiente para poder ser más productivo

44. ¿Con qué propósito incluye la fuente auditiva una cita de Sócrates?

    (A) Para presentar que el valor del descanso no es novedoso
    (B) Para subrayar la importancia de la productividad
    (C) Para añadir más ejemplos a los beneficios del descanso
    (D) Para exponer otra hipótesis del valor del ocio

45. Según la psicóloga de la fuente auditiva, ¿cuándo hay que aprovecharse del descanso?

    (A) En el ámbito laboral
    (B) Fuera del trabajo y de los deberes domésticos
    (C) Tanto en el trabajo como fuera
    (D) En las actividades de ocio y de tiempo libre

46. ¿Cómo diferencia la psicóloga del Podcast el tiempo libre del ocio?

(A) El tiempo libre es el tiempo que uno tiene para divertirse.
(B) El ocio es el tiempo que se pasa con la familia.
(C) El ocio es el tiempo para realizar actividades domésticas.
(D) El tiempo libre es el tiempo para alimentarse y echarse una siesta.

47. ¿En qué coinciden la fuente escrita y la auditiva?

(A) Presentan la importancia del descanso en la productividad.
(B) Citan personajes históricos para apoyar sus ideas.
(C) Mencionan los beneficios de tomar tiempo libre.
(D) Critican el énfasis de la sociedad en ser productivos.

Selección 3

Tema curricular: Las identidades personales y públicas

Primero tienes un minuto para leer la introducción y prever las preguntas.

> **Introducción:** La siguiente grabación, titulada "¿Dónde está la felicidad?", se trata sobre el tema de la felicidad de los hombres. Fue publicada en *http://mariacristinasalas.blogspot.com* en 2011. La grabación dura aproximadamente tres minutos, cuarenta segundos.

Track 57

48. ¿Cuál de las siguientes opciones mejor resume cómo terminó la búsqueda del hombre?

    (A) Encontró lo que buscaba al encontrarse con un sabio.

    (B) Al desenvolver el paquete, descubrió la respuesta a su pregunta.

    (C) Todavía se quedó perplejo de lo que había encontrado.

    (D) Al verse en el espejo, encontró lo que buscaba.

49. ¿A qué se refiere la frase "se postró ante él y habló entre sollozos"?

    (A) A la humildad con que el hombre se presentó ante el sabio

    (B) Al apuro que tenía el hombre para encontrar la respuesta a su pregunta

    (C) A la compasión que tuvo el sabio para el hombre

    (D) A la confusión que tenía el hombre al ver al sabio

50. ¿Cuál de las siguientes frases mejor describe al sabio?

    (A) Es un hombre insensato.

    (B) Es un hombre mayor.

    (C) Es un hombre inquieto.

    (D) Es un hombre ocupado.

51. ¿Cuál es la actitud del hombre hacia el paquete regalado?

    (A) Confuso

    (B) Ansioso

    (C) Resignado

    (D) Tímido

52. Según el cuento, ¿cómo se describe el templo?

    (A) Lujoso

    (B) Descuidado

    (C) Arreglado

    (D) Protegido

53. ¿Qué ocurrió cuando el hombre colocó el pedazo que tenía en el espejo?

    (A) Se vio a si mismo por primera vez.

    (B) Se dio cuenta que estaba en el lugar incorrecto.

    (C) Pudo comprender la función de la palabra inscrita.

    (D) Sintió más delirio y confusión.

54. ¿Cuál es la moraleja del cuento?

    (A) Hay que meditar para encontrar la felicidad.

    (B) La felicidad se obtiene al viajar.

    (C) La verdadera felicidad se encuentra en un pedazo, que al colocarlo bien, hace uno lleno.

    (D) Sólo nosotros podemos darnos la felicidad.

Selección 4

Tema curricular: La belleza y la estética

Primero tienes un minuto para leer la introducción y prever las preguntas.

> **Introducción:** La siguiente grabación, titulada Día Internacional del Libro y del Derecho de Autor, fue publicada en Radio Naciones Unidas en 2012. La grabación dura aproximadamente tres minutos, cuarenta segundos.

Track 58

55. ¿Cuál es el propósito de esta selección?

    (A) Mostrar el impacto que ha tenido el festival en unos autores

    (B) Revelar lo que les inspiró a unos autores a la lectura

    (C) Resaltar la importancia de empezar a leer cuando eres joven

    (D) Informar sobre unos autores y sus recuerdos infantiles

56. ¿Qué tipo de cuentos se le leían a Carmen Boullosa?

    (A) Cuentos para jóvenes

    (B) Trozos de cuentos para niños

    (C) Partes de novelas famosas

    (D) Cuentos cómicos de diversos géneros

57. Según Carmen Boullosa, ¿qué le fascinaba de los libros para niños aparte del cuento?

    (A) Que eran cuentos marginalizados

    (B) Que había una gran variedad

    (C) Que eran historias de grandes autores

    (D) Que eran agradables a la vista

58. ¿Para qué empezó Sergio Ramírez a escribir cuentos?

    (A) Para que el género que tanto le gustaba no desapareciera

    (B) Para continuar a revivir las historias de su niñez

    (C) Para poder exponer los misterios que le fascinaban tanto

    (D) Para explorar más el universo y mundos extraños

59. ¿Por qué escogió Santiago Roncagliolo su primera novela?

    (A) Porque su padre se la había recomendado

    (B) Porque le fascinaba el tema

    (C) Porque le interesaba la portada

    (D) Porque no podía escoger cómics

60. ¿Qué se puede deducir de los tres autores?

    (A) Son todos aficionados de la gran literatura

    (B) Su amor por la literatura se fomentó a través de diversas experiencias

    (C) Llegaron a ser autores por la influencia de sus padres

    (D) Sienten mucho orgullo de formar parte del Día Internacional del Libro

Selección 5

Tema curricular: La ciencia y la tecnología

Primero tienes un minuto para leer la introducción y prever las preguntas.

> **Introducción:** La siguiente grabación trata de la dieta mediterránea. La grabación proviene del programa titulado Alimento y Salud emitido por Radio 5 en España. Fue publicada en abril de 2013 y dura aproximadamente dos minutos, treinta segundos.

Track 59

61. ¿Cuál es el propósito de la grabación?

   (A) Informar sobre un estudio hecho de la dieta mediterránea
   (B) Presentar las características de la dieta mediterránea
   (C) Dar consejos con base en estudios para cómo mantener una dieta saludable
   (D) Contar por qué la dieta mediterránea es mejor que otras dietas

62. ¿Qué sugiere el presentador acerca de la dieta mediterránea?

   (A) Todavía hacen falta más pruebas para averiguar sus beneficios
   (B) Se ha sabido por mucho tiempo que es la dieta más saludable
   (C) Hay diversos motivos por la cual la dieta es tan saludable
   (D) Las investigaciones comprobaron un conocimiento previo

63. ¿Qué se puede inferir del estudio hecho?

   (A) Fue completado en Estados Unidos.
   (B) Varios países participaron en él.
   (C) Fue realizado en un solo país.
   (D) Los participantes padecían de mala salud.

64. ¿Por qué se paró la investigación prematuramente?

   (A) Para ofrecerle a un grupo los beneficios que experimentaban los demás
   (B) Porque a los investigadores se les acabaron las finanzas para continuar el estudio
   (C) Porque unos participantes sufrieron unos problemas médicos
   (D) Para poder analizar los resultados de su investigación

65. ¿Con cuál de las siguientes afirmaciones estaría más de acuerdo el Dr. Ramón Estuch, el coordinador del estudio?

   (A) La dieta mediterránea es más saludable por ser baja en grasa.
   (B) Otros países deberían considerar promocionar las virtudes de la dieta mediterránea.
   (C) Las personas con sobrepeso deben limitar el consumo de grasas vegetales.
   (D) Es una obligación de los políticos cambiar los hábitos de consumo de la gente.

Section II—Interpersonal Writing: Email Reply

TIME: 15 MINUTES

> **DIRECTIONS:** You will write a reply to an email that you received. You have 15 minutes to read the message and write your reply.
>
> Your reply should include an appropriate greeting and closing and should answer all the questions and requests in the original message. In addition, your reply should ask for more details about something that was mentioned in the message. You should use a formal tone in your response.
>
> Vas a escribir una respuesta a un mensaje de correo electrónico. Tienes 15 minutos para leer el mensaje y escribir tu respuesta.
>
> Tu respuesta debe incluir un saludo y despedida apropiados y contestar a todas las preguntas y peticiones del mensaje original. También tu respuesta debe pedir más información de algo mencionado en el mensaje original. Debes usar el tono formal en tu respuesta.

Tema curricular: Las identidades personales y públicas

Introducción: El siguiente mensaje electrónico es de la editora de *Apreciarte* una revista dedicada al mundo artístico. La revista esta lanzando un nuevo blog relacionado al arte, y quiere que sus suscritores contribuyan sus ideas.

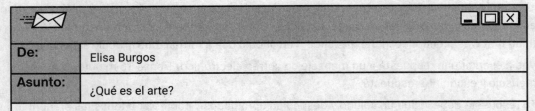

De: Elisa Burgos

Asunto: ¿Qué es el arte?

Querido suscritor,

Es mi placer informarle que la revista *Apreciarte* está a punto de lanzar un nuevo blog completamente dedicado al arte. Estamos muy orgullosos de este nuevo proyecto para que nuestros estimados y muy valorados lectores contribuyan y compartan sus ideas de la belleza del arte. La idea es de proponer un tema diferente cada mes y dejar que la gente lo discuta y que presente su opinión.

Antes del lanzamiento del blog, quisiéramos darles el honor a nuestros queridos suscritores a que ellos sean los primeros contribuyentes. Por esa razón, queremos invitarle a usted a que responda a las siguientes preguntas:

– ¿Cómo define usted el arte?

– Para usted, ¿qué hace que una obra de arte sea superior a otra?

No ponemos límite a su respuesta, así tome la oportunidad de expresarse tanto como quiera. Cuanto más pueda contribuir, mejor para el blog.

Le agradezco de antemano por su valioso tiempo y por considerar su participación en este proyecto tan emocionante.

Atentamente,

Elisa Burgos
Editora General *Apreciarte*

Section II—Presentational Writing: Argumentative Essay

TIME: APPROXIMATELY 55 MINUTES

Track 60

> **DIRECTIONS:** You will now write a persuasive essay. The essay topic is based on the following three print and audio sources. First, you will have 6 minutes to read the essay topic and the printed sources. Next, you will hear the audio material twice. Then, you will have 40 minutes to plan and write your essay.
>
> In your essay you should make reference to specific information from the three source materials. Do not simply summarize what is contained in the sources. Incorporate them into your essay and cite them in the proper manner. In addition, you should also clearly present your own viewpoints on the topic and defend them thoroughly. Your essay should be organized into clear paragraphs and you should use appropriate vocabulary and grammar.
>
> Ahora vas a escribir un ensayo persuasivo. El tema del ensayo se basa en las siguientes fuentes escritas y auditivas. Primero, tendrás 6 minutos para leer el tema del ensayo las fuentes impresas. Después, vas a escuchar la fuente auditiva dos veces. Finalmente, tendrás 40 minutos para planear y escribir tu ensayo.
>
> En tu ensayo, debes hacer referencia a información específica de las tres fuentes. Debes evitar simplemente resumir la información de las fuentes. Incorpóralas en tu ensayo e identifícalas apropiadamente. Además, debes presentar claramente tus propios puntos de vista y defenderlos bien. Tu ensayo debe estar organizado en distintos párrafos bien desarrollados y debes usar vocabulario y gramática apropiados.

Tema curricular: La vida contemporánea

Primero tienes seis minutos para leer el tema del ensayo, la fuente número 1 y la fuente número 2.

Tema del ensayo: ¿Es importante seguir los estudios después de la escuela secundaria?

Fuente 1

Introducción: El siguiente texto trata de la formación universitaria y su relevancia en el mercado laboral. El artículo fue publicado por *Eroski Consumer* en agosto de 2013.

¿Estudiar en la universidad me garantiza un empleo?

La formación universitaria está muy valorada en el mercado laboral, pero desde 2005, la tasa de paro ha aumentado un 7,4% entre universitarios y un 1,2% entre doctorados

Por Azucena García

No es un secreto. La tasa de paro ha aumentado desde 2007, ¿pero cómo ha afectado a los estudiantes que cada año salen de la universidad
Línea con un título bajo el brazo? El anuario "Datos y
(5) cifras del sistema universitario español," relativo al curso 2012–2013, del Ministerio de Educación, revela que la tasa de desempleo se ha incrementado entre ellos, aunque en menor medida que entre la población total. Mientras la tasa general
(10) pasó del 8,3% en 2007 al 21,6% en 2011, entre la población con educación superior no doctor ascendió del 5,4% al 12,8% y entre los doctorados, del 2,7% al 3,9%. "Estos datos ponen de manifiesto que la educación universitaria disminuye
(15) el riesgo de paro," asegura el informe.

La conclusión es halagüeña, pero conviene profundizar. Estar empleado no siempre implica desempeñar la tarea para la que se ha recibido formación. "Muchos trabajadores solamente

(20) consiguen empleos inferiores a la cualificación que poseen (subocupación)," detalla el informe "Panorama de la educación. Indicadores de la OCDE 2013." ¿Cuántos son muchos? "Un 36% de los titulados universitarios," de acuerdo a otro
(25) informe de la Fundación Conocimiento y Desarrollo (Fundación CYD).

La tasa de ocupación entre los graduados superiores ha descendido desde 2007 en nuestro país, pero también la media de la UE-27 ha regis-
(30) trado una caída. En concreto, en 2012, el informe de la Fundación CYD revela una tasa de ocupación española siete puntos inferior a la media europea. Por franja de edad, la mayor tasa de ocupación fue para los graduados superiores de
(35) 45 a 49 años (82,5%), mientras que la más baja— aparte de los mayores de 60 años (49,4%)—fue para el grupo de 25 a 29 años (66,6%) y de 30 a 34 años (77,2%).

El estudio de la OCDE concluye que "existe
(40) un posible exceso de oferta de titulados universitarios." Si bien reconoce que un mayor nivel de estudios aumenta las posibilidades de contratación, de tener un empleo estable y de adquirir mayores salarios, revela que no garan-
(45) tiza el futuro en el terreno laboral.

Fuente 2

Introducción: Los siguientes gráficos muestran las tasas de paro por nivel de formación académica en España. Se basan en estadísticas de la INE de 2022.

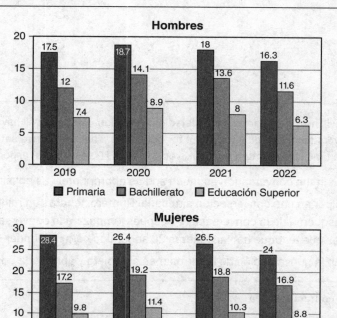

Fuente 3

Introducción: El siguiente reportaje trata de la vida moderna en Hispanoamérica. La conversación dura aproximadamente dos minutos.

Section II—Interpersonal Speaking: Conversation

TIME: APPROXIMATELY 10 MINUTES

Track 61

> **DIRECTIONS:** You will now take part in a simulated conversation. First, you will have 1 minute to read a preview of the conversation, including the script for both parts. Then, the conversation will begin and follow the script. Each time it is your turn to speak, you will have 20 seconds to respond.
>
> You should engage in the conversation as much and as appropriately as possible.
>
> Ahora vas a participar en una conversación simulada. Primero, tendrás un minuto para leer la introducción y el esquema de la conversación. Después, empezará la conversación, siguiendo el esquema. Cada vez que te toque hablar, tendrás 20 segundos para responder.
>
> Debes participar en la conversación de la forma más completa y apropiada posible.

Tema curricular: La vida contemporánea

Tienes un minuto para leer la introducción y el esquema de la conversación.

> **Introducción:** Imagina que has oído un anuncio clasificado de un puesto vacante este verano para un salvavidas en la piscina municipal. El ayuntamiento prefiere contratar a una persona que sea responsable y que tenga prueba de habilidad para el trabajo.

Empleada:	Te saluda y te da las noticias.
Tú:	Salúdala y explícale la razón por qué llamas.
Empleada:	Continúa la conversación. Te hace una pregunta.
Tú:	Contesta la pregunta con detalles.
Empleada:	Continúa la conversación. Te hace otra pregunta.
Tú:	Responde con detalles.
Empleada:	Continúa la conversación.
Tú:	Reacciona positivamente. Explícale una condición.
Empleada:	Continúa la conversación. Te hace otra pregunta.
Tú:	Responde apropiadamente. Despídete.
Empleada:	Concluye la conversación.

Section II—Presentational Speaking: Cultural Comparison

TIME: APPROXIMATELY 6 MINUTES

> **DIRECTIONS:** You will now prepare an oral presentation for your class on a specific topic. You will have 4 minutes to read the topic and prepare your presentation. Then, you will have 2 minutes to record your presentation.
>
> In your presentation, compare your own community to one of the Spanish-speaking world with which you are familiar. You should demonstrate your understanding of cultural features of the Spanish-speaking world. Your presentation should also be well organized.
>
> Ahora vas a preparar una presentación oral para tu clase de español sobre un tema cultural. Primero, tendrás 4 minutos para leer el tema y preparar tu presentación. Después, tendrás 2 minutos para grabarla.
>
> En tu presentación, compara tu comunidad con una del mundo hispanohablante con la que estés familiarizado. Debes demostrar tu comprensión de los aspectos culturales en el mundo hispanohablante. También, tu presentación debe estar bien organizada.

Tema curricular: La ciencia y la tecnología

Tema de la presentación: ¿Cómo ha cambiado la tecnología la manera en que uno se relaciona con los demás hoy en día?

> Compara tus observaciones de las comunidades en que has vivido con tus observaciones de una región del mundo hispanohablante que te sea familiar. Puedes referirte a lo que has estudiado, vivido, observado, etc.

Answers Explained

1. **(D)** *In medias res* is a good literary term to know, both in English and Spanish (it comes from Latin). This fragment starts in the middle of the action, which adds to the drama, making option (D) the obvious choice.

2. **(C)** This can be confirmed in lines 23 through 26 when one of the characters mentions that Blair kept his secret ("guardar su secreto"). Options (A) and (B) can safely be eliminated because these names all follow commas, which in this context means that they are being spoken to, not about.

3. **(C)** This information is found in lines 20–21, where one of the characters says that both men were "engañados por un moribundo" (tricked by someone at death's door), thus confirming that Blair knew he was close to dying, but did not tell anyone. We can also safely eliminate option (D) because at the end one of the characters talks about Blair's head resting on a pillow, thus safely inferring that he is somewhere indoors on a bed, and not outdoors.

4. **(D)** There are several hints that Blair had possession of a treasure. This can be found in lines 25 and 27–28 ("una enorme fortuna," "dejarnos sin un centavo...hemos perdido miles") and lines 37–38 ("los dos seríamos hombres ricos"). Remember that the adjective "adinerado" comes from the word "dinero" (*money*) and means *wealth*.

5. **(C)** The key word here is "aciagos," and there is sufficient context here to infer what this word means if one reads lines 27 to 33. We know by now that Blair has died without divulging the location of his wealth to Reginaldo and Gilberto, and therefore one could safely assume that they would be upset with him. However, in lines 27–32, Reginaldo says that even though they have lost thousands, he cannot help but admire his determination and that Blair had to go through "momentos aciagos." If he had to show determination to go through those moments, then they were not good moments, which gives us sufficient evidence to infer that "aciago" means *tragic, difficult,* or *of bad luck*.

6. **(C)** As with question number 4, there are numerous references to the wealth that both Reginaldo and Gilberto could have had, which makes option (C) the logical answer.

7. **(C)** This answer is pretty evident throughout the text. Examples are found in lines 11–12 when Reginaldo says, "esperaba...que nos diría la verdad" (I hoped that he would tell us the truth), and in lines 19–20 when he says, "engañados...completamente..." (tricked, completely). Option (C) is not the best answer because the two still admire Blair, as indicated in lines 27–32. However, they are disappointed that they cannot get their hands on his wealth, thus making option (B) the best answer.

8. **(B)** The general purpose of the article is to inform about the inauguration of a new bicycle lane and the infrastructure around it. This makes Option (B) the clear answer.

9. **(B)** Line 1 tells that the mayor of Lima is who inaugurated this addition to the "ciclovía (bicycle lane)." Careful with the other options, as Options (C) and (D) refer to street names, and Option (A) is referring to the mayor of a district of Lima.

10. **(B)** The reason for constructing the mentioned section of the "ciclovía" was to connect various important districts in Lima. The text discusses how this will benefit more than 32,000 citizens and neighbors in three districts, emphasizing its role in interconnecting these areas.

11. **(C)** Careful with this question because it asks for the option that is NOT a mentioned benefit of the bicycle. The obvious answer is Option (C) because the bicycle does not consume fuel.

12. **(D)** The "ciclovía" project included, in addition to the path, the installation of bicycle parking, gym equipment, and recycling modules (lines 10-11).

13. **(A)** It can be inferred in lines 15-16 that the use of bicycles increased during the COVID-19 pandemic as a means of individual transportation.

14. **(C)** A valid prediction about the impact of the new 'ciclovía' on urban mobility in Lima is that

it will generate a significant change in citizens' transportation habits. The article discusses the role of the "ciclovía" in the larger goal of expanding Lima's bike path network, indicating a shift in transportation preferences. There is nothing in the text to suggest that car use will decline significantly (albeit it may decline), making Option (A) not the best answer in this case.

15. **(C)** The purpose of the table presented in the article is to show the change in the distance of bike paths in different Latin American cities between 2015 and 2023. The word "kilometraje" means the distance in kilometers.

16. **(B)** This is a math problem, and the correct answer is reached by subtracting the current bike path mileage from the mileage in 2015. When one does this calculation, Santiago, Option (B), is the correct answer because it saw an increase of 194 km, which is greater than in Bogota's and Buenos Aires (172 km and 170 km) and far more than in Monterrey.

17. **(C)** The trend in both Lima and other major cities in Latin America regarding bike paths is a constant increase in their length. This makes Option (C) the clear answer. Careful with Option (D), because the word "variación" could also imply that some cities saw a reduction in length, which is not true in any of the cities mentioned in the sources.

18. *(B)* A valid prediction for the future of bike paths based on the article and the table is that they will expand considerably. This aligns with the trend of increasing bike path lengths in the cities mentioned in the sources.

19. **(C)** This information can be found in lines 8 through 12, where the text says that the contestants have to send "…una obra literaria…que sea original…." This is a contest, which is a type of event, making option (C) the clear answer.

20. **(C)** This information can be found in line 6, where the text says, "…las personas mayores de edad …." Lines 6–7 also say that they have to have Bolivian nationality and have to live in the country, further confirming that option (C) is the correct one. Don't be fooled by the age range in

Lines 11–12, for this is the target age of the reader of the original literary work, not those who write it. Option (A) is not the best answer because this group could include very young readers, and the text explicitly says that the contestants have to be older than a certain age, even though it does not say what age that is. The same is true for options (B) and (D), because they reference a particular demographic, and the text never gives this information.

21. **(C)** The text says in lines 17 and 18 that the work has to be between 60 and 80 pages. This is actually pretty short considering that most literary works aimed for readers between 13 and 18 years of age generally are longer than 100 pages at least.

22. **(B)** The prize information is found in lines 42 through 47. Here the text says that the winner will receive 15,000 bolivianos minus taxes ("impuestos"), and that the amount covers the copyright/royalties ("derechos de autor") for the first thousand copies. Option (A) is incorrect because the winner gets less than the money promised and could possibly earn more (depending on the royalties). Option (C) is incorrect because there is no mention of a contract for further writings, and option (D) is incorrect because the text clearly says that the winner has to pay taxes.

23. **(A)** The key word in the answer is "pueden," and the text says in lines 48–51 that the publishing company reserves the right to have the priority to publish any other text that it deems worthy. Therefore, they *could* be published, even if they don't win a monetary prize.

24. **(D)** This is the only information not mentioned somewhere in the text. For option (A), this information is found in lines 34–36, where it states that the work will not be considered. For option (B), the text provides this information in lines 39–41, and for option (C), the text says in line 15 that the work cannot be that of "autores fallecidos" (deceased authors).

25. **(C)** This open letter is from an individual representing a group of landowners who are concerned about mining that is advancing on their lands. In lines 10 through 12 we see that the landown-

ers have not received "...una sola respuesta oficial...habiéndola solicitado en más de una oportunidad" (not a single official answer, even though they have requested it on more than one occasion). Therefore, the letter is asking the government to pay attention to the concerns that the landowners have...concerns that so far have gone largely ignored.

26. **(A)** The word "interrogantes" means *unanswered questions*, and because these questions continue to be unanswered, this is causing great concern, or "inquietud," among the people.

27. **(C)** There is ample evidence in lines 13–20, where the author details the issues with the mining company. These include altering the drainage that will cause irreparable damage, as well as ecological, social, and economic consequences.

28. **(A)** This is admittedly a tricky question, one that requires careful reading. The information can be inferred in line 50 when the author references the "País Natural que codician los extranjeros" (the natural country that foreigners covet). In this case, the foreigner that covets the land is the mining company, and therefore we can assume that the company itself is foreign, or is a subsidiary of a foreign company. Option (B) is incorrect because in lines 32–35 the author says that Brazil actually introduced legislation to avoid foreign influence on its lands. Option (C) is incorrect because there is nothing in the text that talks about the success of the company, and option (D) is incorrect because the author references all the damage the mining company is doing to the land, and never once mentions their sustainable practices.

29. **(D)** The author gives several specifics in the second and third paragraphs, including quotes from a source regarding environmental damages that can occur. Since these are presented as facts and not opinions, this makes option (D) the clear answer.

30. **(A)** When you think of perspective, think of what people value to be important. In this case, the main issue is protection of lands for the ranching industry. If you are not already familiar with Uruguayan history, the people of this country,

along with the people of Argentina, are very proud of their *gaucho* culture, which are akin to the cowboys of the plains in the United States.

31. **(C)** At the top of the table and in the introduction, the text informs us that the amounts are in millions of dollars. Therefore, the total amount in 2003 is two million, one hundred five thousand dollars, which is what option (D) conveys.

32. **(C)** The amount of money sent back to El Salvador had a steady increase with the exception of the last two years of the period. This makes option (C) the best answer.

33. **(A)** Option (A) is the best answer because it is the only one that we can prove with data from the table. All other options point to factors that might be possible, but cannot be confirmed simply by looking at the text.

34. **(B)** This information is given in the introduction to the interview and in the first part of the interview itself, where the speakers say that the "preocupación principal" of the government is to generate "las condiciones de desarrollo nacional óptimas para evitar que la migración sea ... la mejor opción...." In other words, they want to improve their social infrastructure so that citizens don't find that they have to migrate in search of a better life.

35. **(A)** This information is given in the second response of the ambassador when he states that the government is collaborating with their "connacionales" or fellow citizens to get them documented so that they are not undocumented immigrants in their new country of residence.

36. **(B)** In the last third of the audio, the ambassador says that the money being sent back starts to decrease the longer emigrants become more entrenched in their new country. He says that the uprooting ("desarraigo") causes the emigrant to forget about his "terruño," or *homeland*.

37. **(B)** This information is found in the final response of the ambassador, when he says, "...hay que saberlas encauzar...y hay algunos programas ya para encauzar inversiones... en El Salvador...." The idea here is that there are

programs that aim to use this money to better the infrastructure of the country, making option (B) the clear answer.

38. **(A)** The key word is "carecer," which means *to lack*. We understand from the audio that many who leave El Salvador do so because of poor economic conditions, and this information is supported by the amount of money that is sent back to El Salvador from those who have left to help support their families.

39. **(D)** Once the author makes reference to studies ("...los resultados de un trabajo...," lines 6–7; "Investigaciones anteriores...," line 14), we can confirm that this information is based on data, making option (D) the clear answer.

40. **(C)** This information is found in lines 14 to 16, where studies show that information can be retained better if one sleeps right after having learned it.

41. **(B)** The key here is the term "el almacenaje," which means *storage*. The idea is that the brain's ability to store information doesn't work as well with lack of sleep, which is the idea that option (B) communicates. Remember the verb "guardar" means *to maintain* or *to keep*, which is a synonym of *to store*.

42. **(C)** Make sure to distinguish between what people say is the best time to study and what the studies show is the best time to study. The correct answer is option (C) because in lines 42 through 48 the studies show that the best time is in the morning.

43. **(C)** This information is found at the beginning of the podcast, where the psychologist says that we live in a society "...obsesionada con ser productivos, con hacer cosas..." and that this is valued "...en muchas empresas." This makes option (C) the correct answer as it speaks to the value of "rendimiento" (*performance*) in the work environment.

44. **(A)** This is the best answer because the psychologist is using a historical figure to talk about the importance of rest, and therefore that this is not a new concept, but something that we may have

lost along the way. This is a better option than option (C) because it does not talk about the *benefits* of rest, but rather that the concept of resting is important and that this idea has been around a long time.

45. **(C)** This information is mentioned halfway through the audio, when the speaker says, "...esa recuperación debe darse tanto dentro como fuera del ámbito laboral" (both in and outside the workplace).

46. **(D)** In the last part of the audio the psychologist says that time away from work is used to "...dormir, comer, higiene personal, eso no es tiempo de ocio." This is the same idea that option (D) communicates. Note that the word "ocio" means *leisure time*, and it refers to time that people use to do fun activities, such as exercise and social events.

47. **(A)** With these questions remember to identify what both sources have in common. Although the text does not explicitly mention the word "productividad," this is easily inferred as a clear benefit when it talks about the ability to concentrate better and perform better ("rinden más," line 38).

48. **(D)** This information is found at the end of the story, where the man sees himself in the mirror and reads: *Here you will see he who harbors happiness.* It is at this point when he realizes that he is the only one who can determine his ability to be happy.

49. **(A)** The noun "sollozos" means *sobs,* and this sentence illustrates how the man asked his question while sobbing. To cry when asking for help is a sign of humility, making option (A) the clear answer. Be careful not to confuse this with option (C), for although the wise man shows compassion, it is not he who is crying.

50. **(B)** We can infer that the "sabio" is an older person because he is "...muy famoso por sus buenos consejos..." (very famous for his good advice, implying that he has been around for a while), and that he has a "...barba y pelo canoso..." (beard and is grey-haired).

51. **(B)** Be careful with this answer because, although the man was confused once he opened the packet and saw the mirror shard, the question asks what his attitude was with the package itself, not with the contents of it. We know that the man could not resist the temptation not to open it, which shows that he was quite anxious to know what was inside. This makes option (B) the best answer.

52. **(B)** We hear in the last third of the audio that the temple "...estaba abandonado," and thus an unkempt place, which is what "descuidado" means.

53. **(C)** The word inscribed on the shard was the first part of the sentence "Aquí verás a quien alberga la felicidad," and therefore the man was able to understand that it was part of a larger message. This makes option (C) the clear choice.

54. **(D)** The message of this fable is that only we can make ourselves happy, and that is illustrated through the man seeing himself in the mirror and recognizing this reality.

55. **(B)** This information is clearly found in the introduction of the presenter and before each author speaks. The presenter says at the beginning that the three authors share "...los libros que los aficionaron a la lectura de niños" (the books that turned them on to reading when they were kids).

56. **(C)** This might be a tricky answer if you are not familiar with some of the great works of Spanish literature, such as *Don Quijote*. However, you can still get to the correct answer because Carmen Boullosa says that her parents did not read books for kids ("no leían libros para niños"), but that they read "...fragmentos de obras..." and "...clásicos mexicanos...," which should be enough to deduce that option (C) is the correct answer.

57. **(D)** Unlike the previous question that asks what books were read to her, this question asks what books Carmen Boullosa enjoyed reading. Here she mentions that they were "...libros... atractivos, bellos, clavado de imágenes... y de tipografía muy hermosa...." These are all physical attributes that are attractive to the eye, which makes option (D) the correct answer.

58. **(A)** Sergio Ramírez says that he felt the "...necesidad de transmitir a los demás lo que yo veía como singular en el universo..." and that what he was experiencing was something that someone else was missing, and therefore felt a need to tell them about it. This is the basic idea that option (A) communicates.

59. **(C)** Even though he says that his father is who brought him to the bookstore to pick his first book, his father did not pick the book for him, nor did he choose the book he did because he was unable to pick a comic. Santiago Roncagliolo says that he chose the book because he was attracted to its cover ("portada") of a shark chasing a woman. The book in question is *Jaws*, which inspired the movie of the same name.

60. **(B)** This is another example of being careful with what the options say. Option (B) is the correct choice because all three authors spoke about how their love for literature came through their experiences as a child, and all three were unique. Option (A) is not correct because there is no indication that they all currently love great literature. Option (C) is incorrect because, even though in most cases their parents were instrumental in their love of reading, there is no indication that the parents played a direct role in their wanting to become authors. Option (D) is also incorrect because none of the authors mention the Día Internacional del Libro or their affinity for it.

61. **(A)** This information is clear from the very beginning when the audio references "investigaciones" and "macroestudio publicado." It continues to give data from the study, making option (A) the clear answer.

62. **(D)** The audio presents the results of a recent investigation on the Mediterranean diet, and its entire focus is on the study and how it was conducted. At the beginning, the speaker says that there have been countless studies ("incontables") and that, for the most part, they don't do more than reinforce the prestige of the diet ("...en su mayor parte no hacen más que reforzar su prestigio..."). This makes option (D) the best answer. Be careful with option (C), for although it may be true that many have known for a long time that it

is the best diet, the audio's focus is on the current investigation, which option (C) does not mention.

63. **(C)** This is a tricky question if one does not read the answers carefully. Option (C) is the correct answer because at the beginning of the audio the speaker states that this latest investigation "…viene de nuestro país." This, combined with the fact that in the introduction it states that this is a program from Spain, is enough to confirm that the country is almost certainly Spain. Don't be fooled by option (A), for the study was published in an American journal, not conducted in the United States. Option (D) is not the correct answer because the audio states that the people studied did not have cardiovascular problems at the time of the study (which is what the answer suggests), even though they could develop them down the road.

64. **(A)** In the last third of the audio, the speaker states, "…la incidencia de problemas graves…era significativamente menor en los dos primeros grupos… que decidieron parar el estudio… para que el tercer grupo pudiera beneficiarse también…." This makes option (A) the clear answer.

65. **(B)** This is another question that asks you to make a prediction based on the information you just heard. Option (B) is the best answer because the audio presents an investigation that shows the benefits of this diet, and logically other countries should consider promoting these benefits to their own citizens. Options (A) and (C) are incorrect because the researcher says at the end that people have lost their fear of vegetable fat, and the group studied that was given less fat actually fared the worst of the three. Option (D) is not the best answer because there is no evidence that the researcher would advocate for a government mandate to change eating habits.